D1624673

WHITE HOUSE POLITICS AND THE ENVIRONMENT

Joseph V. Hughes Jr. and Holly O. Hughes
Series on the Presidency and Leadership

James P. Pfiffner, GENERAL EDITOR

A list of all titles in this series is available at the end of the book.

TEXAS A&M UNIVERSITY PRESS • COLLEGE STATION

White House Politics and the Environment

FRANKLIN D. ROOSEVELT TO GEORGE W. BUSH

Byron W. Daynes and Glen Sussman

Copyright © 2010 by Byron W. Daynes and Glen Sussman

Manufactured in the United States of America
All rights reserved

First edition

This paper meets the requirements of
ANSI/NISO Z39.48-1992 (Permanence of Paper).
Binding materials have been chosen for durability.

Library of Congress Cataloging-in-Publication Data

Daynes, Byron W.
    White House politics and the environment : Franklin D. Roosevelt to George W. Bush / Byron W. Daynes and Glen Sussman. — 1st ed.
        p.   cm. — (Joseph V. Hughes, Jr., and Holly O. Hughes series in the presidency and leadership)
    Includes bibliographical references and index.
    ISBN-13: 978-1-60344-202-2 (cloth : alk. paper)
    ISBN-10: 1-60344-202-2 (cloth : alk. paper)
    ISBN-13: 978-1-60344-203-9 (pbk. : alk. paper)
    ISBN-10: 1-60344-203-0 (pbk. : alk. paper)   1. Presidents—United States—Case studies.
2. Environmental management—Political aspects—United States—Case studies.   3. Environmental policy—United States—Decision making—Case studies.   4. Political leadership—United States—Case studies.   5. Political culture—United States—Case studies.   6. United States—Politics and government—Case studies.   I. Sussman, Glen.   II. Title.   III. Series: Joseph V. Hughes, Jr. and Holly O. Hughes series on the presidency and leadership.
    JK511.D39   2010
    333.7092'273—dc22

                                                                                    2010002425

Table of Contents

Table and Figure

Several years ago in our book *American Politics and the Environment*, we stated that "environmental policy is largely a composite of contributions and input from elected and appointed officials operating in political institutions at every level of government."[1] The first question any reader might ask us, then, is why we took several years to focus on presidential politics and the environment. Our response is that we recognized the ever-increasing importance of the environment to all Americans and the unquestioned significance of the president in our political system. Certainly since the 1960s and Rachel Carson's award-winning book *Silent Spring*, many of us have been made aware that with industrial development in the United States came many environmental challenges. It was President John Kennedy, in fact, who called America's attention to the billions of dollars lost to air pollution, including the five hundred million dollars in damage to agricultural products alone.[2] This made us wonder whether other modern presidents had been as sensitive to the environmental damage and health risk we all confront through air inversions, polluted water, toxic waste, and climate change, or were other presidents more concerned with economic development?

We also were interested in knowing what impact any one president could have in responding to such environmental problems. Both of us were well aware that Theodore Roosevelt understood the need to conserve resources and to have public accountability—concerns that stayed with him throughout his presidency. Moreover, we were aware that the conservation interests of TR in his day had grown in scope and complexity in our day to encompass the entire environmental movement, including such issues as ocean pollution, toxic and hazardous waste, wilderness preservation, biodiversity, climate change, and recycling. Inevitably, we asked whether the issues were far too complex and involved for a single president to begin to resolve. That question was our focus in this study.

We next addressed how we would go about examining presidential responses to environmental challenges. Our feeling was to limit our focus to the modern presidents—the twelve presidents since Franklin Roosevelt, ending with George W. Bush. We felt that what we discovered regarding these individual presidents would help us understand how all presidents responded to similar challenges.

But what would our method of assessment be? We were convinced that our examination needed to be as comprehensive as possible in order to compare the actions of the twelve presidents. We decided, therefore, to have a common framework and focus on four factors of analysis, namely, to look at the president's political communication, to assess the president's legislative leadership, to record the president's administrative actions, and to examine how active the president was in environmental diplomacy. We felt certain that in so examining these presidents, we would gain a more extensive understanding of each president's environmental legacy. We would also assess these presidents' interactions with other policy makers during the years these presidents served, since none of these presidents acted in isolation during their tenure in office. Often, in fact, it was presidential advisors, congressional leaders, court decisions, or agency findings that may have been as important, or more so, than the president's own actions in initiating policy.

Our next concern was how to organize the book as we analyzed the twelve presidents. Although chronological order would certainly be one way to approach the study of the presidency and the environment, we were convinced that there might be a better way of looking at presidents interacting with the environment. In consultation with Professor James Pfiffner, editor of the Hughes Series on the Presidency and Leadership Studies published by Texas A&M University Press, we determined it would make sense to divide the presidents into three separate categories. We looked first at those presidents who consistently had a more positive influence on the environment. Here we considered Franklin Roosevelt, Harry Truman, John Kennedy, Lyndon Johnson, Richard Nixon, Jimmy Carter, and Bill Clinton. The second category included those presidents who were somewhat inconsistent or had a mixed legacy in the way they looked upon the environment. In this category, we considered Dwight Eisenhower, Gerald Ford, and George H. W. Bush. In our final category, we considered those presidents who opposed using their influence to advance environmental concerns, thus having a negative impact on the environment. The two presidents in this category were Ronald Reagan and George W. Bush.

On the basis of our assessment of the presidents organized into these three categories, we developed in our concluding chapter a "continuum of greenness" in which the legacy of each president is depicted. To make this comparison, we relied on primary data including presidential speeches, executive orders, proclamations, bill signings, administrative appointments, treaties, and executive agreements. In addition, we took account of the research efforts of leading political scientists and historians who have examined individual presidents' interests in conservation and the environment. After our rather exhaustive study of the twelve modern presidents, we concluded that presidents, whether supportive of environmental protection or opposed to it, make a difference. Moreover, we also discovered a party difference among these presidents, Democratic presidents being more supportive of the environment than Republican presidents, with Richard Nixon the primary exception. Finally, we observed that the economy, foreign policy, and national security tended to be more important than the environment on a president's agenda in most every case, with few exceptions.

Certainly there is no way that we could have managed this massive comparative study on our own. We want to sincerely thank a number of people who contributed invaluable assistance to us over the years. To begin with, we want to give special thanks to Mary Lenn Dixon, editor-in-chief of Texas A&M University Press, who had confidence in our initial manuscript and offered enthusiastic support along the way. In addition, we give thanks to Professor James Pfiffner of George Mason University, who, as a faculty adviser to Texas A&M University Press, offered consistent support for our project.

We extend our sincere appreciation to the unnamed reviewers who read our manuscript and offered very helpful suggestions as to how we might improve our research, as well as pointing out new directions we might consider. Their careful reading of our manuscript ensured a much-improved final project.

We also give thanks to Thom Lemmons, managing editor of Texas A&M University Press, who worked with us on the project, and to the thorough effort of our copyeditor, Lona Dearmont, who worked to refine our manuscript chapter by chapter, endnote by endnote. We also extend our appreciation to Elizabeth Marie Burt for organizing and compiling a comprehensive index for this book.

Special thanks go to those who worked most closely with us, namely, our research assistants who diligently took our suggestions searching out materials and offering input on every aspect of our research over the years. Those representing Brigham Young University: Katie Barker, Kristin Baughman, Kristen Brown, David Buchner, Ashley Burton, Nicole Ferguson, Hilary Izatt, Jacqueline Kennedy, Brooke Ollerton, Mitch Park, Brook Roper, Hyrum Salmond, Erik Skoy, and Christy Watkins. Those representing Old Dominion University: Hilde Kramer, Anna Rulska, and Jaya Tiwari.

Certainly last but not least are our supportive wives—Kathryn M. Daynes and Buffy Masten—for their love and support, for the helpful suggestions they have made on our work, and for their patience with us in meeting deadlines. Thanks to all.

Introduction

The Modern Presidency and the Environment

During the first half of the twentieth century, the United States underwent periods of sudden growth and industrial development, as well as foreign involvement in two world wars. Accompanying this growth and development was a serious exploitation of natural resources both at home and abroad to meet the wartime defense needs and the demands of the postwar period. In addition, there was a decided increase in air and water pollution in both rural and urban America during this period. Those who lived in large cities did not have to be told about the health risks that came from the discomfort that smoggy, murky air brought to their lungs, nor did they have to be reminded about the causes for blackened downtown buildings, or why their drinking water tasted so unnaturally tart, or how it was that nearby forests appeared damaged and ravaged by insects.

Theodore Roosevelt and Gifford Pinchot, along with preservationist John Muir, first expressed the greatest concern about this waste of resources and damage to the environment in the United States, demanding some sort of public accountability and pointing to the need for more adequate management of public lands, and protection from further resource depletion. In addition to these individuals voicing their concerns, important environmental interest groups such as the National Wildlife Federation, the Audubon Society, and the Sierra Club saw a need for action to preserve the environment.

The importance of conservation and environmental protection to the American psyche was perhaps best expressed by Franklin D. Roosevelt when he suggested that it was *national parks* that most typified what America was all about. In his words, "There is nothing so American as our national parks. The scenery and wildlife are native. The fundamental idea behind the parks is native. It is, in brief, that the country belongs to the people, that it is in the process of making for the enrichment of the lives of all of us. The parks stand as the outward symbol of this great human principle."[1] For Franklin Roosevelt, preserving the national parks was intrinsically tied to preserving America and Americans. Not only did the national parks represent the best that America could offer the world, it also symbolized for Roosevelt that all-important tie Americans could have to their "motherland" or "fatherland." As a result of his unending interest and perspective on the environment, Franklin Roosevelt was rewarded by being recognized as the president who introduced the "golden age of conservation."[2]

By the early 1960s, the environmental problems associated with industrial development were quite evident. It was Rachel Carson's book *Silent Spring* in 1962 that informed the public about what the environmental costs for this development had been over time.[3] Carson documented the public health and environmental costs resulting from the use of pesticides. The following year, President John Kennedy in a message to Congress addressed yet another problem associated with industrial development: "Economic damage from air pollution amounts to as much as $11 billion every year in the United States. Agricultural losses alone total $500 million a year. Crops are stunted or destroyed, livestock become ill, meat and milk production are reduced. . . . In the light of the known damage caused by polluted air, both to our health and to our economy, it is imperative that great emphasis be given to the control of air pollution by communities, States and the Federal Government."[4]

Whenever presidents have dealt with environmental policy, or, for that matter, any social policy, they have frequently done so in a highly intense atmosphere, one where conflict is often present, and evidence of political and social consequences can also be seen.[5] This became quite clear in 1996 when President Bill Clinton created the Grand Staircase–Escalante National Monument, setting aside some 1.7 million acres of public land in southern Utah. His actions immediately infuriated southern Utah residents and the Utah congressional delegation as they saw this act of presidential "monument making" as a blatant political maneuver on the part of a removed and unfeeling Democratic President invading Republican Utah to take possession of public land that previously had been used by Utah residents for coal production, cattle grazing, and oil drilling.[6]

Social issues, including environmental policy, have become increasingly important in the last several years in presidential politics.[7] By at least one estimate, social issues have become as significant as economic issues.[8] The resulting consequences and challenges posed by the environment and other social issues should have surprised no one familiar with Ronald Inglehart's analytical argument that our culture has changed from a materialistic to a postmaterialist one, and this transition has been accompanied by new social cleavages that have replaced economic divisions.[9] As a result, instead of always concerning ourselves with wealth and poverty and social class divisions, we now focus our attention on such divisive environmental issues as biodiversity, acid rain, air inversions, polluted water, and global warming. Social cleavages caused by these issue conflicts always have the potential to alter lifestyles, disrupt social status and norms, and elicit strong responses from those directly affected.

The Uniqueness of Environmental Policy

The diversity and varieties of environmental policy have often been a concern to policy makers. Robert V. Percival argues, for example, that court judges, because of their background and training, do not always feel comfortable dealing with environmental issues; that in fact when it comes to the need to render decisions on the environment, they will often "shy away from or defer to the views of specialists in the area."[10] Similarly, presidents, because of their lack of professional expertise, often find themselves ill-equipped to make decisions on the technical aspects of environmental policy, often deferring to the views of specialists in the issue area.[11]

Another characteristic that makes environmental policy unique and difficult for presidents to deal with is the sheer number of issues that now fall under the category *environment*. They can be limitless and difficult to control. Presidents from the 1930s through the 1970s were able to focus their attention on a limited number of issues such as forestry, national parks, water conservation, land management, and the preservation of natural resources. Recent presidents, however, found that they did not have the luxury of such a focus, but because of the more expansive meaning of the concept *environment*, they had to be concerned not only with those environmental issues that FDR dealt with but also with the need to secure safe drinking water, the importance of overpopulation, the preservation of biodiversity, the significance of chemical pollution of agricultural lands, the challenges posed by trade that might affect the environment, the need for recycling, as well as being aware of the international environmental implications of global warming and stratospheric ozone loss. In addition, modern presidents have needed to generate governmental structures and coalitions to handle these issues. To further complicate this scenario, environmental pollution in the form of acid rain respects no borders, and thus can be a local concern to persons in one part of the country, while at the same time being a regional concern to a broader segment of the country and a multinational concern to persons in bordering countries. Thus, of all the social issues, the environment has perhaps the broadest and most diversified reach.

Environmental Policy and the American Presidency

The purpose of our research is to examine how American presidents have handled environmental challenges confronting them during their time in office.[12] Of course, this does not mean we will ignore other decision makers who have also faced these same challenges. In initiating policy leadership over environmental issues, individual presidents have frequently found themselves competing for policy dominance with members of Congress, with cabinet secretaries and staff persons in the Interior Department, the Environmental Protection Agency (EPA), the State Department (in those sections where the global environment is a concern), and with their own presidential advisors who might share a different perspective on the president's policy. Moreover, the president has also received support and confronted opposition from administrators in independent agencies, members of environmental interest groups, state elected officials, and from the courts, as well as attracting the expected opposition from anti-environmental interests, and from the opposition party.[13]

Both Richard Nixon and Bill Clinton found themselves in a position of constantly fighting for policy dominance on environmental concerns among these competing interests. We will make every effort to reflect the politics of this policy complexity in each administration we examine.

Presidents' policy leadership is also influenced by (1) their own *personal beliefs* and *values* regarding the environment; (2) their *party's stated position* on the environment; (3) their own social agenda; (4) the makeup of their *constituency base*; and (5) the *public's reaction* to environmental issues and to the president's stance on the environment. Lyndon Johnson and Richard Nixon, for example, both responded positively to environmental concerns of their day, due not only to their own interests and priorities but also because of the public's interest and congressional support for environmental policy change.[14] Overall, in fact, presidents and their administrations since the 1960s have become increasingly more active in environmental politics despite their lack of expertise and discomfort with the issue, because, as Lyn Ragsdale maintained, this discomfort may be due to their recognizing "the fallout they may experience because the policies, by definition, redistribute benefits from one group to another."[15] This has certainly been the case in the past with regard to environmental issues. Social policies have become an important part of the public agenda, and it is difficult for presidents to ignore them because it is difficult for the polity to ignore them. Although the environment has yet to become a so-called wedge issue in a presidential election, a president's involvement with the environment can mobilize segments of the electorate, creating issue-oriented politics that can be important in a close election. In the 2000 presidential campaign, for example, Democratic candidate Al Gore's reluctance to capitalize on his own environmental expertise allowed the Republican Party to control the environment as their own election issue, turning George W. Bush into a much "greener" candidate than he actually was, given his past record as governor of Texas.

The Presidents and the Time Frame

Barbara Hinckley has stated that "work comparing presidents and the repetition of events over time should have the highest priority."[16] We certainly agree with Hinckley's guideline for critical presidential research; nevertheless, some lines need to be drawn in our comparison of presidents. When we do this we understand that we run the risk of ignoring some events. In this book, for example, we limit our assessment to contemporary presidents beginning with Franklin Roosevelt. The one important exception that no researcher can ignore when approaching the American presidency and the environment, however, is the consideration of Theodore Roosevelt, the first president to take seriously the importance of conservation policy.

In limiting our observations to the modern time period, we are aware of those arguments advanced by such scholars as Fred Greenstein, who contends that the modern presidency should begin with an analysis of Dwight Eisenhower rather than Franklin Roosevelt, and Sidney Milkis and Michael Nelson, who advocate that we can only understand the actions of a particular president if we first take account of the complete history of the presidency beginning with 1776.[17] In response to the Greenstein argument, we can say that we pay attention to the presidency of Dwight Eisenhower but feel that to ignore both Franklin Roosevelt and Harry Truman, in office prior to Eisenhower, would be to ignore two very important presidents who uniquely contributed much to our understanding of how modern presidents dealt with environmental policy. As to the Milkis and Nelson contention, we acknowledge that some understanding of the presidency and public policy will certainly be lost in ignoring the pre-Roosevelt period, but we contend that in a limited study such as ours, choices must be made. One of those choices, with the exception of the Theodore Roosevelt presidency, was to disregard the pre-FDR period. Prior to FDR's presidency, little attention was paid to conservation and preservation of the environment by federal policymakers since social issues were then not a prominent part of a president's agenda. Thus, we are comfortable in directing our attention to the modern period beginning with Franklin Roosevelt and extending our analysis through the first-term presidency of George W. Bush.

Presidential Leadership and Environmental Policy Making

Presidents have a multitude of resources they can use in their attempts to set the public agenda. They normally will present to the Congress and to the people their concerns about issues they think deserve attention and give reasons why these should be high-priority issues.

On occasion, however, the modern president, as Samuel Kernell reminds us, will "go public" in an effort to make their case to the American people without the Congress interfering as an institutional filter.[18] Presidents can enhance the importance of issues they feel strongest about, as Jeff Cohen argues, when they cloak the issue with a sense of urgency.[19] Yet presidents may still find it difficult to control the public agenda because of certain built-in "constraints" in their efforts to reach out to policy makers and the public, as Richard Neustadt pointed out.[20] Under such constraints the president must make the most out of available resources, the relationship with Congress, and the goodwill of the American people.

At times, the president might circumvent the will of the Congress and the scrutiny of the American public, using his own authority to enforce his administration's agenda. In this way, as Kenneth Mayer argues, "presidents have used executive orders to make momentous policy choices, creating and abolishing executive branch agencies, reorganizing administrative and regulatory processes, determining how legislation is implemented, and taking whatever action is permitted within the boundaries of their constitutional or statutory authority."[21]

A president has the use of other powers as well, including the appointment power and budgeting process, and, as Robert Stanley has suggested, the "multilayered central clearance system of agency initiatives and operations through the Office of Management and Budget," to enforce administrative strategies.[22]

In the international arena the president has more flexibility and is less constrained in taking action. In this regard, the president can demonstrate leadership (or fail to do so) when deciding whether to attend an international conference or support or oppose international agreements. This is a crucial consideration, suggests Elizabeth DeSombre, since the "United States is important in the international arena, owing both to its economic size and influence and to its general leadership on environmental issues."[23]

Presidential leadership and policy making can look quite different depending on who the president happens to be. William Lammers and Michael Genovese in their discussion of leadership styles, indicated that during the 1950s, Dwight Eisenhower presided over the federal government using a "hidden hand" approach, where he preferred to avoid public conflict, and instead managed politics "behind the scenes."[24] Jimmy Carter, on the other hand, practiced "trusteeship" leadership where he took a long-term view of the public interest in his actions as president.[25] Still other leadership studies have emphasized "psychological factors," as advocated by James David Barber; "administrative factors," as suggested by Richard Nathan; and the "postmodern" presidency, as emphasized by Richard Rose.[26]

Several years ago, political scientists interested in presidential leadership and environmental policy contributed a number of articles to Dennis Soden's *The Environmental Presidency*, providing the first substantive look at presidents over time and their involvement in the environmental policy domain.[27] The approach taken in that book examined presidential roles and their impact on presidential behavior. Although it was a seminal study in first calling our attention to the association of presidents with the environment, it did not provide sufficient attention to the actions of individual presidents.

In discussing presidential powers and constraints involved in environmental policy making, it was Norman Vig who first argued that an insightful analysis can be conducted through the use of the policy cycle perspective. As Vig describes it, presidents "have a major role in *agenda setting;* can take the lead in *policy formulation;* can *legitimate policy;* influence *policy implementation;* and constantly *assess and evaluate*" public policies.[28]

Taken together, these studies provide the foundation upon which we will assess the American presidency and the environment using a longitudinal approach. In examining presidents from Franklin Roosevelt to George W. Bush, we employ four factors of analysis in order to compare the legacy of the twelve presidents who have occupied the White House over the last seven decades: (1) political communication, (2) legislative leadership, (3) administrative actions, and (4) environmental diplomacy.

Political Communication

Political communication involves the president's remarks and formal speeches to the American public regarding the environment, as well as positions on the environment that the president has taken as party leader. What message, in other words, has the president conveyed to the public and to competing decision makers regarding the environment? As Mary Stuckey has suggested, "The presidency has become the primary focus of national political attention, and the president's talk has become the primary focus of the presidency."[29]

In attempting to generate support for the administration's program, a president has the opportunity to use his skill in reaching out to the public to draw attention to issues that he considers most important and that are part his national agenda. Franklin Roosevelt, John Kennedy, and Ronald Reagan all had the skill and charisma to reach out to the people and persuade them to support their views on the environment.

For some presidential researchers, political communication is of primary importance in assessing a president's involvement with the environment. One recent book reflecting these views is *Green Talk in the White House*, a collection of essays by some of the leading communication scholars.[30] Of particular importance is Michael Vickery's thoughtful study of Richard Nixon's efforts to create the Environmental Protection Agency. Here Vickery suggests that not only was Nixon's "rhetorical style" of consequence, but his "political identity" and "administrative agenda" were equally important in the creation of the EPA.[31] His analysis seems closer to our own in recognizing that to fully assess presidents' environmental efforts, it is critical to move beyond a focus exclusively on political communication, and, as our research suggests, it is necessary to also examine other areas of their presidency.

Legislative Leadership

A president's legislative leadership is considered one of the most important aspects of his presidency since his overall accomplishments in office are often determined by his relationship with the Congress and his ability to develop a successful legislative agenda.

While some presidents have had the benefit of having their party in control of both houses of the Congress, other presidents have presided over divided government. In promoting legislative leadership, presidents have indicated their policy preferences by issuing special messages to Congress and by signing or vetoing important legislation to encourage environmental initiatives. Where some presidents have had difficulty exerting legislative leadership, others including Franklin Roosevelt and Lyndon Johnson were very effective in their relations with Congress.

No president who considers himself an "environmental president" can succeed without a supportive Congress. A president must find ways to persuade important policy leaders within the Congress to support his environmental agenda. To determine how successful individual presidents have been, we look at bills and other legislative outputs that may have been encouraged by the president and signed, or rejected through presidential veto.

Administrative Actions

While few presidents have been able to master the "institutionalized presidency," presidents have been able to shape environmental policy in several ways, including the establishment of new offices, staffing, appointments they have made, and in the issuing of executive orders and proclamations. Richard Nixon, for example, used his administrative powers to establish the Environmental Protection Agency, while Ronald Reagan initiated an "administrative" presidency in pursuit of his policy goals. But presidents risk becoming frustrated in implementing their agendas as well, since the Constitution fragments control over the bureaucracy, making it difficult for any one president to concentrate meaningful control over the executive branch and all of those agencies and individuals involved with public policy.

Environmental Diplomacy

It is not surprising that American presidents are intrinsically involved in foreign affairs given the preeminent role of the United States in international and global concerns. Modern presidents are increasingly drawn into global politics as a multitude of issues have become transnational in character. As the country's spokesperson in the international arena, the U.S. president is expected to offer diplomatic leadership on issues important to the global community, ranging from war and trade to environmental concerns. In doing so, the president represents American citizens at regional and international environmental conferences and is involved in multilateral environmental agreements. Some global issues bring countries together in an effort to resolve common problem, while others divide the international communities. Any international agreements made by the president and administration with another country or with multiple countries are a focus of attention, as is any other effort that affects the international arena.

Presidential Success

We consider a president environmentally successful if the president extends the reach of conservation to new areas, or enforces the laws of conservation currently available to him during his term in office. Presidents elected to office after 1970 have further options available to them. They can exhibit leadership in the environmental movement by taking action in such areas as global warming and biodiversity and by joining other nations to preserve precious resources in the global environment. As Marc Landy and Sidney Milkis argue in their book *Presidential Greatness*, "The great presidents were great because they not only brought about change but also left a legacy—principles, institutional arrangements and policies that defined an era."[32]

Drawing from this premise, our empirical investigation into individual presidents' rhetoric, legislative leadership, administration actions, and environmental diplomacy provides a broad perspective from which to assess the occupants of the White House and their environmental legacy. For instance, even though Franklin Roosevelt's time commitment was directed largely to the Great Depression and World War II, the president devoted enough resources and effort to conservation to be recognized as the president who ushered in the "golden age of conservation." The Johnson-Nixon period reflected an era of environmental legislation, highlighted by Richard Nixon declaring the 1970s to be the "decade of the environment" and supporting this through the establishment of such executive agencies as the Environmental Protection Agency (EPA) and the Council on Environmental Quality (CEQ).

We also see through presidential appointments how presidents can influence environmental policy. For example, Dwight Eisenhower's secretary of the interior, Douglas McKay, became known as "giveaway McKay" because of his anti-environmental governmental restrictions over natural resources, while Ronald Reagan's interior secretary, James Watt, became an anti-environmental lightning rod for the Reagan administration.

These appointments stand in stark contrast to the interior secretaries appointed by John Kennedy, Jimmy Carter and Bill Clinton. These secretaries—namely, Stewart Udall, Cecil Andrus, and Bruce Babbitt—all promoted an aggressive pro-environmental agenda for the administration during their time at the Interior Department. Although Jimmy Carter and Bill Clinton each had their respective problems with the Congress, both appointed pro-environmental individuals to administer the EPA, namely, Douglas M. Costle appointed by Carter and Carol Browner appointed by Clinton, and both Carter and Clinton established a public lands legacy to rival that of Theodore Roosevelt.

Contrasting agencies and policies can also tell us how important environmental concerns were to the president. Where Richard Nixon created the Environmental Protection Agency, for example, it was George H. W. Bush who established the anti-environmental Council on Competitiveness headed by Vice President Dan Quayle. Ronald Reagan's use of "cost-benefit analysis" to assess each environmental project slowed the advancement of environmental activity and instead benefited development and business interests. Bill Clinton's emphasis on "sustainable development" had just the opposite effect. Where Presidents Franklin Roosevelt, John Kennedy, Lyndon Johnson, Richard Nixon, Jimmy Carter, and Bill Clinton looked beyond their domestic environmental agenda toward the global arena (e.g., Nixon's support of the 1972 Stockholm Conference, Carter's initiation of the *Global 2000 Report to the President* (1980), and Clinton's signing of the 1992 Earth Summit's Biodiversity Treaty and the 1997 Kyoto Protocol), Ronald Reagan refused to find a successful resolution for the acid rain crisis with Canada. Moreover, George W. Bush pursued a unilateral approach to the global environment, and, as a consequence, renounced the Kyoto Protocol, a document supported by more than 170 countries and signed by President Bill Clinton.

We contend that our method of examining each president gives us a more extensive understanding of each president's importance in advancing environmental interests. As Norman Vig argues in his assessment of presidents and the environment, the success of a president "should be gauged in terms of [his] effects on the environment."[33] In short, while there are important empirical referents to employ in analyzing the presidents, merely counting the number of speeches and/or the number of bills passed, without more information and without political context, does not add a great deal to our understanding of how different presidents have addressed environmental policy. Our appraisal of presidential success in this area assesses the presidents' use of the power resources (political communication, legislative leadership, administrative actions, and environmental diplomacy) of the White House to help explain their environmental legacy.

Ordering and Organization

Now a word about the ordering and organization of our chapters. The reader
will note that we do not order our chapters strictly chronologically. We felt
the reader would get a clearer picture of the president's contribution to the
conservation of resources and to the environment in general if we ordered
the chapters beginning with those presidents who most advanced environmental policy, those who seemed to be innovators and leaders in the conservation and environmental movement, and ending with those presidents
who most frequently put constraints on these advances. This ordering we
refer to as a "continuum of greenness," a framework that we both begin with
and return to in our concluding chapter.

As we progressed in our research we saw useful similarities among those
presidents we considered together. This sort of comparison is not unlike
other examinations that political scientists have made when comparing
presidents. We begin our continuum with a look at those presidents who
seemed to be innovators and leaders in the conservation and environmental
movement.

Presidents who have had the most positive influence on the environment
are FDR, Truman, Kennedy, Johnson, Nixon, Carter, and Clinton. Through
their use of the powers of the presidency, these leaders left a conservation and
environmental legacy that was stronger than when they entered the White
House. For instance, where Franklin Roosevelt ushered in the "golden age of
conservation," and Harry Truman[34] advocated the value of conservation as
a foundation for a healthy economy for national security, Lyndon Johnson
spoke about the need to beautify America and to create a "new conservation"
for the Johnson period. Whereas John Kennedy reflected on the need to protect ocean resources, and called for a White House conference on conservation in 1962, Richard Nixon declared the 1970s to be the decade of the environment, and Jimmy Carter and Bill Clinton used their powers as president
to create a public land legacy equal to few other modern presidents. In short,
each of these presidents, in his own way, offered some leadership from the
Oval Office that advanced an environmental agenda.

Presidents Dwight Eisenhower, Gerald Ford, and George H.W. Bush did
not generally view the environment as an important policy issue. In the
few cases where they used their presidential power resources in support of
the environment (e.g., Eisenhower in devising the Mission 66 Program, and
Bush 41's efforts regarding the Clean Air Act of 1990), they did not use their

resources as president in a consistent manner to ensure long-term improvement in environmental quality.

At the far end of the continuum, we considered Ronald Reagan and George W. Bush as presidents who were opposed to presidential leadership in the environmental arena. These two presidents emphasized development and deregulation over preservation and conservation. Reagan and Bush 43 used the power resources of their office to promote production growth with little regard for the environment. They left an environmental legacy that was much weaker than when they entered the White House.

Similarities and differences among these presidents are harder to see immediately in a strict chronological arrangement. We feel that our ordering of chapters facilitates the sort of insights we wished to convey regarding presidential leadership and the environment.

Chapter Summary and Conclusion
To assist the reader in gaining a clearer picture of the efforts made by each of the twelve presidents in responding to environmental concerns, we added a comprehensive and analytical summary and conclusion at the end of each chapter that will capture and further assess the importance of each president's time in office, and his contributions to resolving the conservation and environmental concerns in each of the four areas focused on in the chapters, namely, political communications, legislative leadership, administrative actions, and the international arena. In this summary statement we note the forces that both supported presidential actions as well as constrained them.

Conservation and the Environment

One other difference that persisted over time among these presidents has been their orientation toward the environment. Presidents Franklin Roosevelt and Harry Truman, for example, were clearly conservationist in their orientation. It is easy to see this in both their rhetoric and actions that point to some of the same concerns exhibited by Theodore Roosevelt at the turn of the century. It was Gifford Pinchot, Theodore Roosevelt's chief of the U.S. Forest Service, who first defined "conservation" as "the foresighted utilization, preservation and/or renewal of forests, waters, lands and minerals, for the greatest good of the greatest number for the longest time."[35] Presidents from FDR through Lyndon Johnson, if they had an interest in the American outdoors, tended to focus their attention on the need for preserving natural resources, protecting and extending that protection of public land and forests, supporting laws for cleaner air and water, and ensuring the preservation of wildlife on land and in the water. These were their primary concerns.

With the publication of Rachel Carson's *Silent Spring* (1962), however, Americans became aware for the first time of the dangers of pesticides being used on crops. In addition, Americans were confronted during this period with a series of natural disasters that caught their attention, including excessive smog in both Los Angeles and London in the late 1960s, the Santa Barbara oil spill in 1969, and in that same year, the burning of the Ohio River due to industrial waste being poured into the river. These events became the visible signs of the critical environmental needs that had been left unfulfilled by the single-issue focus of conservation interests. Lee M. Talbot captured this need well when he argued, "Many came to recognize that the narrow approaches to conservation that had marked earlier efforts were no longer appropriate and that a more comprehensive environmental approach was needed. Conservationists began to become environmentalists."[36]

Whereas the concerns for presidents in the post-1970 period often focused on many of the same issues that presidents valued in pre-1970 period, there were just many more issues and demands with which to be concerned. John Kennedy, for example, had had a glimpse of the wider view of preservation when he reflected on the potential resource wealth contained in the oceans of the world. But this was only a glimpse. It wasn't until the administration of Richard Nixon that environmentalism began to take hold. This was an unusual time in that Congress, the public, and the executive were all unitedly focused on the necessity to resolve some of the most critical environmental concerns. Stacy J. Silveira makes the comparison between the conservation years and the environmental concerns this way:

> Modern environmentalism differs from the conservation and preservation era in two salient respects.... The first era emphasized the protection or efficient management of the natural environment, [whereas] the primary policy of modern environmentalism is based on the cleanup and control of pollution. Second, modern environmentalism displayed "social roots" decidedly absent from the first era. Charted by numerous citizen groups and studies of public attitudes, this change parallels the infusion of particular social values into the public arena and the widespread expression of those values in the environmental arena.[37]

If there was any president who comes near to being an environmental president it was Bill Clinton, who by the completion of his second term showed both a domestic as well as a global orientation in looking broadly at what could be done worldwide. Where Franklin Roosevelt could focus his attention on forestry, national parks, water conservation, land management, and wildlife and natural resource conservation, Bill Clinton had not only to respond to these issues of the Roosevelt period but also concern himself with polluted air and water cleanup, wilderness preservation, toxic wastes, and recycling.[38] In addition, there were the global concerns of warming and greenhouse gases, as well as assisting other nations in protecting forests, protecting endangered species, and establishing American national parks and monuments. It is this explosion of issue areas, and the expansion of what presidents must be concerned with, that best separates the *conservationists* from the *environmentalists*.

Foundation for an Environmental Presidency: Theodore Roosevelt and the Other Premoderns

In the chapters that follow, we examine the three categories of presidents in some detail, and in the concluding chapter we offer a comparative assessment of the "environmental" presidency and share some implications of our study. But we first turn our attention to the original environmental president, namely, Theodore Roosevelt, and also offer a brief treatment to those "premodern" presidents who followed him.

In looking at the first "environmental president," we note how dramatic the change was from previous administrations, and how his approach to conservation of resources was contrasted with that of William Howard Taft, his successor.

Theodore Roosevelt

Theodore Roosevelt set the pattern for other environmental presidents who would follow. As William McKinley's vice president, TR became president after McKinley's untimely assassination in 1901. He later ran successfully on his own, winning the presidency in 1904 and serving through 1908. He was a committed conservationist throughout his tenure in office. For him the environment had a direct connection to democratic ideals. As he expressed in 1903 concerning our national parks, their most important characteristic was their "essential democracy" in that the parks preserved wilderness and scenery "for all the people."[39] He repeatedly made it clear during his seven-and-one-half years in office that it was crucial for America to preserve natural resources for the generations that would follow. As he stated, "If there is any one duty which more than another we owe it to our children and our children's children to perform at once, it is to save the forests of this country, for they constitute the first and most important element in the conservation of the natural resources of this country."[40]

In assessing the central position of conservation to his presidency, Theodore Roosevelt indicated that "the underlying principle of conservation has been described as the application of common sense to common problems for the common good. If the description is correct, then conservation is the great fundamental basis for national efficiency."[41] Roosevelt also pointed out in his Seventh Annual Message to Congress on December 3, 1907, how central environmental concerns were to him. As he stated, "The conservation of our natural resources and their proper use constitute the fundamental problem which underlies almost every other problem of our nation."[42]

Roosevelt's flexible reading of the Constitution and his feeling regarding the expansiveness of presidential power was expressed in his "Stewardship Theory," whereby he contended that it was not only a president's "right but his duty to do anything that the needs of the nation demanded, unless such action was forbidden by the Constitution or by the laws." As he later stated, "I did not usurp power, but I did greatly broaden the use of executive power."[43] Convinced as TR was of the legitimacy for expanding presidential power, it is no surprise that the conservation movement was strengthened during his years in office. For example, he established the first federal bird preserve on March 14, 1903. But more important than its establishment was Roosevelt's attitude in making this decision. Ornithologists had long been concerned with protecting the birds from those who would use bird feathers and other parts of the bird in articles of apparel. When Roosevelt protected the birds on Pelican Island in Florida, he asked those near him, "Is there any law that will prevent me from declaring Pelican Island a Federal Bird Reservation?" When he was told that there was none, Roosevelt stated without hesitation, "Very well, then I so declare it."[44] In explanation of his decision, he said, "I acted on the theory that the President could at any time in his discretion withdraw from entry any of the public lands of the United States and reserve the same for forestry, for water-power sites, for irrigation, and other public purposes. Without such action it would have been impossible to stop the activity of the land thieves. No one ventured to test its legality by lawsuit."[45]

Political Communication

Roosevelt used his political oratory to good effect in both educating and selling conservation to the public. Teddy Roosevelt, along with others in the executive branch, not only used the "bully pulpit" to *sell* the message of conservation, but he also took opportunities at conventions and other public gatherings to *preach* conservation, placing it second only to the need to encourage public morality. As Roosevelt stated, "As a people we have the right and the duty, second to none other but the right and duty of obeying the moral law, of requiring and doing justice, to protect ourselves and our children against the wasteful development of our natural resources."[46]

In all cases TR used his vast energy to focus on conservation issues. As a result he garnered both support in and out of Congress and opposition to his cause. To some people his assertive style was offensive, while others viewed his conservation messages as extreme. Still others like William Howard Taft were most bothered by Roosevelt's free use of executive power to force home his message.

Yet even though TR offended some people in his environmental crusade, there is evidence from his speeches to suggest that he persuaded others to support him. In his "On Conservation" address given in 1904 he specifically mentioned that public opinion had changed in support of the president.[47] He also emphasized to the public the seriousness of the need to conserve wildlife: "When I hear of the destruction of a species, I feel just as if all the works of some great writer have perished."[48]

Roosevelt saw conservation as a moral crusade for Americans. As he pointed out in Kansas during the last of days of his presidency, "Of all the questions which can come before this nation . . . there is none which compares in importance with the great central task of leaving this land even a better land for our descendants than it is for us, and training them into a better race to inhabit the land and pass it on. Conservation is a great moral issue, for it involves the patriotic duty of insuring the safety and continuance of the nation."[49]

The Republican Party's rejection of Teddy Roosevelt in 1912 was not enough to undercut the emphasis he placed on conservation. To the contrary, as the Progressive Party candidate, Teddy Roosevelt shared the environmental objectives emphasized in the party platform, which called for the following provisions: "We heartily favor the policy of conservation, and we pledge our party to protect the national forests without hindering their legitimate use for the benefit of all the people." The platform also stated that "the remaining forests, coal and oil lands, water-powers, and other natural resources still in State or national control . . . are more likely to be wisely conserved and utilized for the general welfare if held in the public hands." One plank of the platform that did raise questions for environmentalists, however, was that which advocated opening up "the coal and other natural resources of Alaska . . . to development at once.[50] Roosevelt's support of this plank was less overt than his support for the platform's other aspects.

Legislative Leadership

Roosevelt pursued an aggressive legislative agenda in order to protect the environment. The president was particularly assertive in preserving national forests and establishing national monuments during his last two years in office, from 1907 to 1909. As legislative leader, his flexible reading of the Antiquities Act, a law passed by Congress in 1906, was very useful to him. This act allowed the president to "declare by public proclamation historic landmarks, historic and prehistoric structures, and other objects of historic or scientific interest that are situated upon the lands owned or controlled by the Government of the United States to be national monuments, and may reserve as a part thereof parcels of land."[51] Roosevelt used the Antiquities Act to set aside some eighteen national monuments—a record no other president has been able to match.[52]

As one might expect, Theodore Roosevelt's interpretation of the Antiquities Act to achieve his conservation goals eventually became a source of conflict between Congress and the executive branch. At first, Congress was supportive of granting this unchecked authority to the president, but with its more frequent use by Roosevelt, opposition to his efforts within Congress became stronger.

While Roosevelt was able to put together coalitions of support to sustain his environmental efforts, his strongest opposition came from western senators who were most upset with Roosevelt's extension of executive power through the Antiquities Act and his broadening of the meaning of the word *conservation* to include coal, gas, oil, timber, iron, and water, as well as grazing lands.[53] Congressional resistance to Roosevelt's efforts became particularly strong in the Sixtieth Congress when Senator Charles Fulton of Oregon immediately proposed an amendment to the 1907 Appropriations Bill for the

Department of Agriculture stating that the department responsible for the Forest Service would provide that "[h]ereafter no forest reserve shall be created within the limits of the states of Oregon, Washington, Idaho, Montana, Colorado, and Wyoming except by an act of Congress."[54] Roosevelt was not slowed in any way by the amendment but instead ignored it and went ahead to set aside an additional twenty-one forest reserves by executive order, totaling some 17 million acres. For his efforts, TR was almost censured by House speaker Joseph Cannon and Republican Senate majority leader Nelson Aldrich.[55]

Theodore Roosevelt also freely used his veto to turn back legislation that undercut environmental concerns that he had. As early as 1903, for example, Roosevelt vetoed a bill that would have given over the Muscle Shoals area—an area that would later become the center of the Tennessee Valley Authority (TVA) projects—to private development. TR ranks seventh in terms of the number of presidential vetoes, thirteen of his eighty-two vetoes were used to protect the environment.[56] The president made sure that he did all in his power to protect public resources from private interests. To protect forest lands from the ax of the timber industry, he used the proclamation. While an executive proclamation does not carry the impact that an executive order does, it is nevertheless an important formalized statement by the president that may or may not "carry legal effect."[57] As he stated when signing one of these proclamations, "Failure on my part to sign these proclamations would mean that immense tracts of valuable timber would fall into the hands of the lumber syndicates."[58]

Roosevelt never gave up trying to educate Congress about the need to protect the environment. In his 1908 annual message to Congress, he even brought photographs of China to illustrate his message about the havoc that had been caused in China when the mountains were deforested and when hillsides were stripped bare of vegetation. It was a warning to the United States as a whole. The Midwest would soon know the problems caused from a lack of grass and forest, as the south-central states suffered through the Dust Bowl period.[59]

Administrative Actions

Because of congressional opposition, Theodore Roosevelt sought other ways to advance environmentalism. He appointed persons to the administration who were sympathetic to Roosevelt's conservation goals.

Gifford Pinchot was perhaps Teddy Roosevelt's most important environmental appointment. He was a long-time acquaintance of the president's and one who advocated what Char Miller called "utilitarian conservation," an approach to conservation that supports the belief that "natural resources . . . [s]hould be sustainably used and that the federal government should regulate use."[60] Pinchot was appointed to the Forestry Commission, but more importantly, he became one of Roosevelt's closest advisers on the environment, which enhanced the president's influence over environmental policy.

James R. Garfield, Roosevelt's second secretary of the interior, is an example of the type of appointee that Teddy Roosevelt sought to fill positions in his cabinet. Of this appointment, TR would say that it "led to a new era in the interpretation and enforcement of the laws governing the public lands."[61] Garfield was a firm supporter of TR's efforts to expand executive power to conserve resources.

Roosevelt also set up a very important Conference of Governors as he attempted to unify state laws on environmental issues. To the conference, Roosevelt invited not only state governors but also Supreme Court justices, members of Congress, and representatives from conservation interests and industry.[62] Roosevelt had great hopes that this conference would bring about a sort of consensus on how to resolve some of the pressing environmental problems.[63]

TR also organized several other conferences and commissions to study and gather information about public lands and waterways. These included, among others, the Public Lands Commission, set up in 1903 to study public land policy; the Inland Waterways commission, established in 1907 to look at the river systems and water power; and the National Conservation Commission, established in 1908 to inventory national resources.[64]

Environmental Diplomacy

While President Roosevelt's rhetoric included concerns about international conservation, there were few examples where he used his foreign affairs authority in conjunction with his interest in conservation and the environment. Hilary Izatt noted one exception to TR's reluctance to stress the importance of conservation on a worldwide scale. She found that in six of his eight messages on Latin America, Roosevelt's rhetoric was "most often followed by a large tribute to the cause of conservation."[65]

A final exception to this reluctance to expand conservation worldwide took place in 1909, just two weeks before Roosevelt's term was to end. It involved the establishment of the North American Conservation Conference that met for five days, and resulted in a declaration of principles along with a request for a future international conservation conference to examine the conservation of world resources. Some forty-five nations were to be invited to send delegates.[66] Roosevelt hoped a future conference could meet in The Hague to give it more visibility.[67] But William Howard Taft, TR's successor, failed to follow up on preparations that had been made, and the international gathering never took place.[68]

Environmental Legacy

Theodore Roosevelt considered his conservation efforts to be some of the outstanding landmarks of his presidency.[69] As William H. Harbaugh summed it up, "From the winter of 1905 on scarcely a detail eluded his creative attention as he vigorously promoted the cause in public speeches, messages to Congress and executive actions. There followed such an era of enlightenment as the nation had never before experienced and would not again see until Franklin Roosevelt, himself nurtured on Theodore's conservation theories, came to power."[70]

By the end of his presidency, Teddy Roosevelt's legacy was unmatched. As Harbaugh contends, "Had Theodore Roosevelt's service to conservation ended with the proclamation of the sixteen million acres of Forest Reserves in 1907 or with his vigorous exposition of the findings of the Inland Waterways Commission, his conservation record would still have been distinguished beyond that of all of his predecessors."[71] But as Harbaugh suggested, it did not. TR had set aside some 230 million acres, according to a *National Geographic* estimate.[72] The areas that were set aside included some 150 national forests, four national game preserves, fifty-one federal bird reservations, five national parks, eighteen national monuments, and twenty-four reclamation projects. In addition, he convened seven conservation conferences and commissions while in office.[73]

While the tangible aspects of TR's conservation program involved reclaiming arid lands, preserving the forests, and saving wildlife,[74] Gifford Pinchot indicated that he felt that Roosevelt's greatest contribution was that he forever changed the way people thought about conservation. In Pinchot's words, "The greatest work that Theodore Roosevelt did for the United States, the great fact which will give his influence vitality and power long after we shall all have gone to our reward, is . . . that he changed the attitude of the American people toward conserving the natural resources."[75] This was TR's greatest legacy for the conservation movement, namely, in persuading Americans to look upon conservation with a different mind-set, recognizing its importance.

The Inter-Roosevelt Years: 1909–1932

While Theodore Roosevelt is considered the first "conservation" president, Franklin Roosevelt introduced the "golden age of conservation" to the modern era.[76] But what of those presidents who served between 1909 and 1933? What role did William Howard Taft, Woodrow Wilson, Warren G. Harding, Calvin Coolidge, or Herbert Hoover play related to the conservation movement?

William Howard Taft

Certainly more was expected of William Howard Taft as far as conservation was concerned, given that his presidency immediately followed Theodore Roosevelt's. Yet he failed to make a lasting imprint of his own on the conservation movement. While Taft felt that conservation was important, he did not feel that TR's methods of achieving success were necessarily legitimate, and so he made it a focus of his years in office to validate many of those same programs with what he considered to be a more legalistic approach.[77]

A specific example of how Taft approached what Roosevelt had done occurred on June 25, 1905, when Taft encouraged the Republican-controlled Congress to withdraw much of the same public land that Roosevelt had withdrawn by executive order, thus validating it by legislative rule. Certainly Taft's new approach to conservation was apparent when he told a gathering of some eleven thousand at a 1911 Public Lands Convention that the "'fetish' stage of the conservation movement had passed," and that the nation must now "settle down to a calm consideration of what ought to be done in the preservation of our natural and our national resources and that steps ought to be taken which the mistakes of the past show to be wise."[78] Taft was not specific in what he meant by "wise reforms." Progressives were particularly concerned, protesting that they could not understand Taft's line of reasoning.[79]

Taft made few independent advances on his own beyond refashioning many of TR's programs by basing them on a firmer legal ground, and the creation of Glacier National Park and several national monuments in Oregon, Utah, and Wyoming.[80]

Woodrow Wilson

Woodrow Wilson issued several proclamations creating a number of national monuments, but otherwise was limited in what he did for conservation. He did manage to sign a migratory bird act in 1913, as well as the federal tariff act that included one section prohibiting the importation of wild bird feathers. In 1914 he used a proclamation to create Papago Saguaro National Monument in Arizona, and in 1915 he established Dinosaur National Monument in Utah by proclamation. In the same year, Wilson signed a bill that Congress had passed creating the Rocky Mountain National Park in Colorado. But conservationists had to wait until 1916 to see Wilson support the congressional initiative to establish the National Park Service, that became a part of the Department of Interior.[81] That same year the president proclaimed one more national monument in Maine, the Sieur de Monts National Monument on Mount Desert Island. His final act for conservation came in 1918 when he issued two proclamations creating Zion National Monument in Utah—now Zion National Park—and Katmai National Monument in Alaska.

Warren G. Harding

Much of what Warren G. Harding might have done as president for the conservation movement was consumed in scandal involving the Interior Department and its secretary, Albert Fall. Fall was instrumental in transferring oil reserve land from the Department of the Navy's jurisdiction to the Department of the Interior. The Teapot Dome Reserve lands in Wyoming and the Elk Hills Reserve in California were then leased to oilmen Harry F. Sinclair and Edward L. Doheny. In exchange for these leases, Sinclair and Doheny paid Albert Fall more than $400,000.[82] As a result, Fall was forced to resign and was eventually convicted of accepting bribes, becoming in 1931 the only cabinet figure to be imprisoned for a felony committed while in office.[83] Either because of this scandal or in spite of it, Harding suggested that the United States probably needed a change of direction regarding conservation. He was particularly concerned with wasting natural resources through both "reckless exploitation" and "statutory nonuse." He also advocated more focus on water conservation and more cooperation between state and federal authorities in reclaiming public lands.[84]

Calvin Coolidge

Coolidge expressed some concern about the state of natural resources but took little substantive action. He asserted that natural resources had become endangered because of society's overproduction. On April 23, 1931, in one of his dispatches syndicated to the newspapers, he stated, "The old question of conservation of natural resources has become acute again in the inverted form of overproduction.... The reaction is sure to be bad."[85] Coolidge's major contribution was setting aside 1.4 million acres of land in Glacier Bay in Alaska.[86]

Herbert Hoover

Herbert Hoover was the "greenest" of the presidents elected during the years between TR and FDR, and he continued to focus on conservation throughout his presidency. In 1929 he supported the Norbeck-Anderson Act that provided funding to purchase wetlands protected by the federal government. In addition, Carlsbad Caverns National Park was created during his presidency.[87] That same year, in his State of the Union address, Hoover indicated that "conservation of national resources is a fixed policy of the government." He suggested that the most important concerns were oil, gas, overgrazing on public lands, and reclamation.[88] By 1931 his concern was to devise a policy that would both balance the preservation of the national forests while at the same time allowing limited logging in the forest areas to bolster the economy.[89] Kendrick Clements summed up Hoover's contributions in these words:

> Hoover the conservationist enjoyed many successes.... As president he increased the National Park Service's budget by 46 percent during the first three years of his term, and he supported the enlargement of existing parks, monuments, and national forests as well as the creation of such important new parks and monuments as Great Smoky, Shenandoah, Isle Royale, Canyon de Chelly, Death Valley, and Virginia's Colonial National Monument at Williamsburg. In the darkest days of the Depression at the end of his administration, Hoover provided more money for the Forest Service than any previous administration had ever appropriated.[90]

Conclusion

The U.S. presidents who served from 1909 through 1932 did not take the sort of initiatives to become effective environmental presidents that Theodore Roosevelt had taken. TR was a president willing to use his political authority and enterprise to advance the conservation movement and protect the environment. Environmentalists can certainly applaud the pioneering efforts of Theodore Roosevelt to use presidential power to strengthen the conservation movement. His name has become ever associated with *conservation*, a policy issue and movement that served as his highest priority. Modern-day presidents sympathetic to the environment look to the TR model as a way to help them to incorporate environmentalism into their own social agendas.

How have modern presidents responded to environmental concerns since the Teddy Roosevelt years? Certainly, the need for protection and conservation of resources today is as critical if not more so than during the early twentieth century, and today each policy issue has taken on global importance and specialization so that now the category "environment" has to accommodate an ever-expanding number of policy issues far beyond the limited number addressed by TR.

Have modern presidents learned the importance of environmental concerns since the Roosevelt years? Do any share TR's vision of what is needed for the United States in terms of conserving of natural resources? Or have some believed that ensuring the soundness of the environment is of less importance to society than economic development or foreign policy involvement? Has the environment grown in scope and complexity to the point it exceeds the capacity of any one president to make a difference? It is the modern presidents who have been confronted by and currently face a vast number of environmental challenges posed by the twentieth and twenty-first centuries, and it is the modern presidency on which we have chosen to focus our investigation beyond this chapter, beginning with the presidency of Franklin Roosevelt.

PART ONE

Presidents Having a Positive Impact on the Environment

CHAPTER I

Franklin D. Roosevelt and Harry S. Truman

Conservation and the environment once again became a primary focus of attention in the White House with the election of Franklin D. Roosevelt—our thirty-second president and fifth cousin of Theodore Roosevelt, our twenty-sixth president. As the nation's first modern environmental president, Franklin Roosevelt expressed an interest in conservation well before he became president. Anna Lou Riesch Owen pointed out that "in public office as senator, as Assistant Secretary of the Navy, and as governor he was active in promoting conservation. His conservation record as Governor of New York is merely repeated on a larger scale as President of the nation."[1]

Franklin Roosevelt

Conservationists saw in this president a person who would fully support their goals and objectives. He was a president who was willing—even in times of crisis—to set aside budget allotments to facilitate improvements to the environment. Franklin Roosevelt also saw himself as a conservationist wanting to educate others, much as had Theodore Roosevelt before him. Protecting nature and the management of resources was important to FDR. He urged Congress in 1935 to "start to shape our lives in a more harmonious relationship with nature." And he cautioned, "The future of every American family everywhere will be affected by the action we take."[2] Among other things, FDR explained the critical need for conservation, and why federal regulations were necessary to establish long-term planning and secure conservation as a working concept in the minds of Americans. This approach exposed private citizens to their overall responsibilities to preserve the land and resources.[3] As a citizen himself, Roosevelt wanted to be considered a "gentleman farmer," one who thought of "forestry"—or the sort of "forestry" he practiced on his Hyde Park estate—not just as the acquiring of land with trees and the maintaining of that land, but as the cultivating of trees as a "crop" that could be used much like a "crop of corn or wheat." Such thinking was consistent with how he saw each segment of conservation as interconnected with every aspect of American life. As he indicated in 1935, "We think of our land and water and human resources not as static and sterile possessions but as life giving assets to be directed by wise provision for future days. We seek to use our natural resources not as a thing apart but as something that is interwoven with industry, labor, finance, taxation, agriculture, homes, recreation, good citizenship."[4] And for this reason it was President Franklin D. Roosevelt who, despite Theodore Roosevelt's pioneering efforts in first focusing our attention on conservation, was recognized as having ushered in the "golden age of conservation."[5]

Political Communication

Franklin Roosevelt was a particularly effective and persuasive spokesperson for causes he believed in. Through speeches, press conferences, and radio addresses, he attempted to both convey his message as well as educate citizens and policy makers alike regarding the need to conserve resources. One way he reached a large audience of Americans with his high priority message was through his very popular and effective "fireside chats" on the radio.[6] He also visited the Civilian Conservation Corps (CCC) camps—the camps that had been recently established to employ some two million persons to build roads, construct trails, and engage in other activities to protect the environment—as forums to preach the need for conservation of resources to those who would listen.[7] Additionally, he made an effort to frequently talk to reporters both in formal press conferences as well as in informal settings. He averaged about 6.9 press conferences a month, a sizeable number when one compares the numbers of press conferences held by our last two presidents—Bill Clinton held around 3.4 press conferences a month and George W. Bush limited press conferences to a very few during his entire term in office.[8]

In his major public addresses Roosevelt, surprisingly, did not always make reference to the environment. In his 1937 State of the Union address, the president did not even mention conservation. Rather, the entire address discussed the economic problems facing the nation in his first term in office, the extension of democratic government to respond to these needs, and the impending war in Europe.[9] His 1936 State of the Union message, however, was an exception to the general rule with fully 6 percent of the address being devoted to conservation needs.

Unlike his formal speeches, conservation became a frequent topic of discussion with reporters. Roosevelt was quick to point out some of his own accomplishments when it came to forestry. At his estate at Hyde Park, New York, Roosevelt by 1938 had planted 29,500 trees. Such massive planting was often done in conjunction with one of the universities in the area, such as the New York State College of Forestry. In all, it was estimated that the president ended up planting 220,000 trees on his Hyde Park property.[10] Of his tree planting he told reporters, "I am practicing what I preach . . . that is stopping erosion."[11] And it was such comments as these that continued to give Roosevelt favorable press coverage for his own conservation efforts and those of his administration. As one writer pointed out, "Throughout the years 1933–42, there were always articles appearing that commended the national resource policy."[12]

Franklin Roosevelt at first had little support from the Democratic Party for his conservation proposals, but he worked hard to bring party leaders into his confidence. When he became the Democratic Party's nominee on July 2, 1932, for example, he made it quite clear that he was in the process of planning a Civilian Conservation Corps' public works project to put people back to work and put them to work in the national parks and forests,[13] this despite the fact that the 1932 Democratic platform had only a limited number of references to the environment, including a statement concerning the need to expand federal programs for "adequate flood control and waterways" and one statement regarding the advocacy of conservation, and use of the nation's water power.[14] In the 1936 Democratic platform there was bare mention of Roosevelt's desire to "continue to improve the soil conservation and domestic allotment program with payments to farmers."[15]

The Democratic Party platform of 1940, however, was quite different. For the first time the party platform looked like one that Roosevelt had put together, as it stressed the need to "continue the broad program launched by his Administration for the coordinated development of our river basins through reclamation and irrigation, flood control, reforestation and soil conservation, stream purification, recreation, fish and game protection, and low-cost power, and rural industry."[16]

Legislative Leadership

While few presidents are strong leaders of Congress, having a Democratic Congress in full support of the president's legislative objectives gave Roosevelt more leverage than most presidents enjoy. Those first one hundred days for Roosevelt was a period of productivity that has not been replicated by any other modern president. FDR was able to encourage Congress to pass fourteen major pieces of legislation including legislation involving two major environmental and energy production projects, namely, the Tennessee Valley Authority and the Civilian Conservation Corps.

FDR spoke several times during his time in office about the importance of the TVA. In 1933, for example, he explained how the TVA was to be used as an instrument of conservation. As he stated, it should be charged with the broadest duty of planning for the proper use, conservation, and development of the natural resources of the Tennessee River drainage basin and its adjoining territory for the general social and economic welfare of the nation."[17] President Roosevelt suggested in his 1945 State of the Union message that the Tennessee Valley Authority would "add new and fertile territories to the United States." He then indicated that TVA was just the beginning.[18]

A lot rested on the success of the TVA project. As Roosevelt indicated, "If we are successful here we can march on, step by step, in a like development of other great natural territorial units within our borders."[19] Looking beyond the TVA to other river basins, the president suggested that similar development to those other river basins would "provide the same kind of stimulus to enterprise as was provided by the Louisiana Purchase and the new discoveries in the West during the nineteenth century."[20] Roosevelt saw the development of the river basins as a means to develop "integrated plans to conserve and safeguard the prudent use of waters, water-power, soils, forests and other resources of the areas entrusted to their [the people's] charge."[21]

The desperate state of the economy, with millions unemployed, proved to be an opportunity for Roosevelt to combine the need to put people back to work with his passion for preserving the environment. The two million people who accepted government employment in the national parks and national forests enabled the president to respond to two crises—unemployment and preservation of the environment—at once. FDR also hoped the involvement with the CCC would build confidence, strengthen character, and save the lives of the corps workers. As he noted that year, "I had determined even before Inauguration to take as many of these young men as we could off the city street corners and place them in the woods at healthful employment and sufficient wage so that their families might also be benefited by their employment."[22]

Later in his term, he sent legislation to Congress covering six primary areas related to the environment including: forests, minerals, water, soil, wildlife, and recreational resources.[23] Roosevelt insisted that his legislative program related to the environment be orderly and integrated, rather than chaotic and haphazard. One of the most important legislative acts related to his conservation program was the National Industrial Recovery Act of June 16, 1933, which called for some $3.3 billion to cover the development of natural resources and water power, the redirection of rivers and harbors, the implementation flood control, the purification of water, and the prevention of coastal and soil erosion.[24] It also employed thousands of workers.

On March 14, 1938, Franklin Roosevelt addressed Congress regarding the state of forestry in the country, recommending that Congress look for new ways to protect the national forests. He made it a point to add protected forest lands each year of his presidency so that by 1941, more than 177 million acres were protected, an area that stretched over forty-two states and into two territories.[25] Moreover, as Riesch Owen noted of Roosevelt's conservation program, "every aspect of the conservation of natural resources was integrated." This is what made FDR's conservation focus more effective than other presidents' efforts. In fact, Riesch Owen concluded that "the conservation accomplishments during the Roosevelt administration far surpassed those of any previous presidential administration."[26] What was clear throughout was that whenever changes were necessary to respond to the conditions of the time, the president often relied on conservation.

Administrative Actions

Roosevelt's administrative actions also helped to strengthen his conservation program. His budget requests often had the environment as its primary focus, despite the fact that funding for the environment had to be significantly reduced during the war years. In 1935, for example, as much as 10.79 percent of his budget was devoted to the environment, but by 1944 allocations for the environment dropped to its low of 0.56 percent.[27] While this was FDR's lowest budget percentage devoted to the environment, it was still comparable with that of other presidents who would follow him.

As chief executive President Roosevelt was a *balancer* of interests. On assuming office after the 1932 election, Roosevelt had to respond to the depressed economy, crises among farmers and railway personnel, and the need to reverse the loss of confidence citizens felt in the nation's future as a result of the Depression. While never forgetting his interest in conservation, at times it understandably had to await crisis resolution.

One of the most important things Roosevelt did on the road to economic recovery was to place environmental activists in administrative positions who would carry out Roosevelt's bidding. Those closest to Roosevelt, in fact, were persons who shared his interest in environmental reform and who closely advised him on approaches he could use to achieve his objectives. The two most important persons he appointed were Harold Ickes, who served as Roosevelt's long-term secretary of the interior, and Henry Wallace, FDR's secretary of agriculture, who later would serve as his vice president during his third term as president, and even later as FDR's secretary of commerce. Though Harold Ickes did not have environmental experience prior to his appointment, as a Progressive Republican he had supported FDR and played a crucial role in attracting moderate voters to the president and his programs. Henry Wallace, on the other hand, was trained in plant genetics and brought this expertise with him into the Department of Agriculture.[28] Other persons in his administration who supported his conservation objectives included Forest Service head F. S. Silcox, National Park Service director Arno Camerer, staff adviser Rexford Tugwell, Soil Erosion Service head Hugh Bennett, Bureau of Reclamation head Elwood Mead, and Bureau of Fisheries head Frank T. Bell.

It became quite clear that whomever Roosevelt appointed to his administration, they would have to be supportive of the administration's conservation program. For instance, December 1941, at the end of the first year of FDR's third term, Claude R. Wickard, Roosevelt's second secretary of agriculture, could report that "the increased war demands for timber could be met without impairing the productivity of the forests."[29] Unlike almost every other president, with perhaps the exception of Theodore Roosevelt, conservation lay behind most of what this administration did. The difference between the administrations of the two Roosevelts was that Franklin Roosevelt had to deal with a much larger and more complex government, but he had the luxury of doing so in conjunction with a very supportive Congress, particularly during his first term.

Although FDR was the first modern conservationist president, there was still a limited number of conservation issues upon which he could focus his attention and resources during his years in office. More specifically, he devoted his energies to expanding and developing national forests, increasing the number of national parks, protecting and managing public lands, preserving wildlife, conserving natural resources, and devising new ways to conserve clean water. More recent presidents have not always been able to be so selective in what environmental issues they chose to focus on, given the state of the environment. Most presidents since Jimmy Carter, for example, have not only had to respond to the issues Roosevelt dealt with, but they have also had to be concerned with air pollution, endangered species, trade, toxic waste, recycling, wilderness preservation, and the many global environmental issues.[30]

In 1933 Congress also gave Roosevelt an advantage few other presidents have enjoyed, namely, the authority to reorganize government for two years without any congressional oversight.[31] This allowed him a virtual free hand in establishing a government structure that would also facilitate the carrying out of his environmental objectives. Structural additions to government put into place by Franklin Roosevelt included the Soil Erosion Service, the National Resources Board, the Soil Conservation Service, the Works Progress Administration, the Federal Emergency Administration, the Division of Grazing Control, as well as the previously mentioned Civilian Conservation Corps. The Public Health Service also became involved with environmental issues in 1938, creating the first division of water pollution that provided funding to state and local areas for treating sewage problems. Other agencies important in strengthening FDR's conservation efforts were, in particular, the National Power Policy Committee and the Rural Electrification Administration.

The environment continued to be an important focus of attention after Roosevelt's first term. Even during the height of World War II, FDR made it a point to reserve some budgetary funds exclusively for conservation purposes, and he encouraged each governmental department to adopt a conservation approach whenever possible.[32]

Environmental Diplomacy

Franklin Roosevelt, like his cousin before him, had few international environmental achievements to his credit. He did, however, negotiate two treaties related to the environment in 1935 and 1936. With Canada, FDR signed a treaty to clean up an area affected by mining and smelting in British Columbia, and with Mexico, the United States negotiated a migratory bird treaty that Roosevelt felt was essential to the success of his national wildlife restoration program.[33]

In addition, administration representatives attended several important international conferences during FDR's term in office including a 1934 trade meeting in Rome, a 1935 World Power Conference, and a 1936 North American Wildlife Conference.[34] But since Roosevelt's primary concerns during his first term were by necessity domestic, his environmental involvement overseas was limited.

In 1940–41 Roosevelt urged Congress—in many cases successfully—to remember that conservation of resources was an important part of America's defense needs. In 1942 Roosevelt's forest policy served to caution Congress to avoid regulating forest practices on private lands, and to limit any increases in "insect and disease control" during the war.[35] In general, FDR made it quite clear that the American citizens were to hold to reasonable conservation principles even under the "stress of war."[36]

In the month of his death, plans were being made to hold a World Conference on Conservation that would be a part of the United Nations Economic and Social Council. Governor Gifford Pinchot submitted his rough draft proposal for the conference on April 17, 1945, five days after Franklin Roosevelt had died.[37] Franklin Roosevelt's importance to the conservation movement was recognized by another president, John F. Kennedy, in a 1962 speech: "What this country needs is a broad, new conservation effort, worthy of the two Roosevelts, Theodore and Franklin, who lived in New York, and who helped build the West; an effort to build up our resource heritage so that it will be available to those who come after us."[38]

Harry S. Truman

One might presume, on first glance, that Harry Truman should have been better prepared than he was to meet the immediate environmental challenges he faced as president. After all, he had served as vice president to one of the premier conservation presidents. Truman surely would have shared those same values that FDR advocated, to conserve and preserve, given how careful Roosevelt had been in selecting members of his administration. Truman must have participated in some of those decisions affecting conservation. In fact, this was not the case. Harry Truman had served as FDR's third vice president for only three months—from January to April of 1945—before Roosevelt's death.

Thus, Harry Truman became a conservationist not because of his association with FDR, but because he realized that conserving resources was the key to ensuring a viable economy and a strong position for America abroad. This was the primary reason Truman saw himself as a conservationist. There is some evidence, however, that Truman did his best to carry out some of Roosevelt's last wishes. In a letter to Cordell Hull on October 24, 1944, Roosevelt wrote: "In our meetings with other nations I have a feeling that too little attention is being paid to the subject of the conservation and use of natural resources. I am surprised that the world knows so little about itself.... It occurs to me, therefore, that even before the United Nations meet ... it might do much good to hold a meeting in the United States of all of the united and associated nations.... I repeat again that I am more and more convinced that Conservation is a basis of permanent peace. I think the time is ripe."[39]

After Roosevelt's death, Truman went ahead and sent a proposal for the conference, held in 1949, called the Conservation and Scientific Conference. According to Cornelia Bryce Pinchot, who was familiar with both Roosevelt's and Truman's objectives, the conference did not achieve the objective of educating those in attendance to what conservation was all about: "Suffice it to say that the moral and social, the economic and political objectives of Conservation, its democratic significance were rigidly ignored by the men of little faith and many fears who organized the conference. Even more unbelievable, all mention of peace and war in relation to conservation was deliberately and definitely excluded from the agenda."[40]

In a speech in 1950, Truman pointed out that "natural resources are the cornerstone of a strong, free democracy. As such, they must be used to advance the well-being and the prosperity of all the people. This philosophy holds that it is necessary for democratic government to make sure that our land and water, our forests and our minerals are used wisely, and not exploited for the benefit of the few."[41] Three years later he was still adhering to that philosophy. In a special message to Congress regarding land and water resources, he stated: "These resources [land and water] are a foundation, upon which rest our national security, our ability to maintain a democratic society, and our leadership in the free world."[42]

During his years in office, President Truman focused most of his attention on the management of land and on water resources. As he explained, he was "vitally interested" in four power projects, those being developed on the Colombia River, on the Snake River, in the Central Valley of California, and on the rivers of the Southeast, which included the state of Arkansas and portions of Missouri and Oklahoma.[43]

With regard to conservation, Harry Truman's Fair Deal domestic program was more orderly than Roosevelt's environmental priority had been. Truman pleaded for a unified conservation policy rather than an ad hoc approach to each program. His reflection on his visit to Grand Coulee Dam exemplifies this quite well. He said that the dam stood for

> the wise use of the natural resources with which God has endowed us for the benefit of all the people; it stands for the use of water for two purposes essential to the growth of the West—irrigation and power; it stands for the industrial development of the West, which is so vital for the growth of this whole Nation; it stands for the courage and determination of farsighted citizens, who kept up the fight for the construction of this dam until that fight was won; it stands for the use of the powers of the Federal Government to promote the welfare of its citizens; and finally, it stands for the great heart and the great vision of one who did so much to make it possible—Franklin D. Roosevelt.[44]

Political Communication

Harry Truman was a loyal Democrat, one who tried constantly to remind people that what they had from government they owed to the Democratic Party. He was particularly critical of the Republicans for their criticism of his environmental program. As he indicated, Republicans had been especially critical of the Soil Conservation Service for being too regimented and "socialistic." Truman was quick to point out that it was the Democrats and not the Republicans who had been, and now were, the "stewards of the land" for the interests of all the people. In 1948 in a speech in Salt Lake City, he said, "I stand and the Democratic Party stands for rapid and uninterrupted development of the land and the forest and the water and the mineral resources of the West, in the interest of the people." He wanted to make it quite clear that "we are fighting with all our strength to prevent the gluttons of privilege from swallowing up the country. We are fighting the battle of the West, because it is the battle of all the country."[45]

Truman was perhaps most effective when he was aggressively defending a cause. He was asked on a regular basis to defend his conservation program. Thomas E. Dewey, the Republican candidate for president who ran against Harry Truman in 1948, charged that Truman's program was "careless," that the administration's agriculture programs were designed to "boss farmers around," and that the Republican Party would be the party that would "really save our forests" while at the same time ensuring a "steady timber supply."[46] Truman's response was that such charges were nothing but "fake . . . just like all the other Republican claims are fake." He mentioned in particular how Republicans had voted against the Tennessee Valley Authority programs, against the Social Conservation and Domestic Allotment Act, against the agriculture conservation program, and overall had "voted to cripple the conservation program." He wondered how with this record the Republican Party could take so much credit for such programs. He then added, "It reminds me of the flea that was on the back of a donkey crossing a bridge. When they got across, the flea said to the donkey, 'Boy, we sure did shake that bridge, didn't we?'"[47]

Legislative Leadership

Truman also had problems with Republicans attempting to block his congressional efforts. His attitude toward the Republicans had changed from a relatively conciliatory tone in 1947 to a more challenging style of rhetoric in 1948 with the Eightieth Congress, which he had labeled the "Do-Nothing" Congress.

Truman did not mind personally lobbying interest groups that worked with Congress, congresspersons who were involved with those causes he felt most keenly about. The St. Lawrence Seaway project was one of those causes that Truman kept pressuring policy makers to accept, hammering away at it over the years. Truman wanted Congress to consent to join with Canada in the venture to build the seaway, and in 1949 he became particularly irritated with Congress's reluctance to approve the seaway.[48] By 1952 he again put it plainly to Congress: "It seems inconceivable to me now that this project is on the eve of accomplishment, that the Congress should allow any local or special interest to divest our country of its rightful place in the joint development of the St. Lawrence River in the interest of all the people of the United States."[49] It was not until 1954, under Dwight Eisenhower, that Congress finally did consent to assist in the building of the project.

In 1950 Truman signed Senate Bill 3409, which created a new Grand Teton National Park made up of all of the old park while adding a large portion of the adjoining land that was known as Jackson Hole National Monument. The remainder of the Jackson Hole area that was not incorporated into the new park was included in the National Elk Refuge and the Teton National Forest.[50] Still another bill the president felt was important was House Resolution 6578, a bill that would allow government to enter into a cooperative arrangement with private industry on research on purification of salt and brackish water. Truman saw this as a possible answer to a major problem faced by many countries around the world.[51]

Budgetary figures showed that Truman was serious about his environmental concern, particularly during the latter years of his presidency. An examination of all governmental expenditures directed at the environment from 1945 through 1952 reveals that Truman's budget outlay for the environment continued to increase. In 1945 only .58 percent of the budget was directed to the environment. By1951 it had risen to 5.4 percent, which stood at the highest level during the Truman years.[52]

On January 19, 1953, before Truman left office, he delivered one final special message to Congress concerning land and water resources. He looked back at Theodore Roosevelt's initial leadership of the conservation movement and affirmed his important role in furthering the progress of the conservation movement. He indicated that although TR's leadership was important, "the legislation enacted to conserve and to develop our water and land resources for the most part was broadly supported by both parties."[53]

Administrative Actions

As chief executive, Harry Truman appointed a Water Resources Policy Commission in January 1950 to make recommendations to him for legislation and policies on water.[54] The commission acted as a major adviser to Truman. He gave the commission credit for developing a "coordinated national program for the development of our water resources."[55]

The president also organized in 1950 a temporary interagency committee made up of representatives from the Departments of Interior, Army, Agriculture, and Commerce, the Federal Security Agency, and the Federal Power Commission. The committee was to look at power generation, forest management, fish and wildlife conservation, flood control, mineral development, industrial water supply, pollution control, and recreation and soil conservation in the New York and New England area.[56] This committee was both temporary and limited in scope, and as a result it did not protect environmental concerns as it might have done.

Truman also became concerned about air pollution. He organized on May 3, 1950, the United States Technical Conference on Air Pollution and invited all those working in this area to the conference. His intent, he said, was to "exchange specialized information," and he hoped that coming out the conference would be "prompt initiation of corrective measures."[57]

President Truman did shape the structure of government in one way that is still critical today to the conservation effort, namely, by establishing the Bureau of Land Management (BLM), which was created when the General Land Office and the Grazing Service of the Department of Interior were consolidated. It was given authority for soil and water conservation and fire protection, and for assisting other agencies with land management, surveying, and examining range use.[58]

Truman's appointments of administrative persons working in the environmental area varied in quality and showed relative instability. The president at first tried to keep Harold L. Ickes from the Roosevelt administration as his secretary of interior, but Ickes soon resigned in protest over another appointment that Truman had made as undersecretary of the Navy. After Ickes left the Interior Department, Truman appointed J. A. Krug, who served until 1949. Truman's final appointment to Interior was Oscar L. Chapman, who served as secretary from 1949 to 1953. For secretary of agriculture, Truman looked to Claude R. Wickard from the Roosevelt years until he resigned in 1945. Truman then appointed Clinton P. Anderson, who served until 1948. His final choice for secretary of agriculture was Charles F. Brannan of Colorado, who probably did the best job for Truman and remained until Truman left office.

Truman also dedicated the sixteenth in the Tennessee Valley Authority group of dams across Tennessee. With the dedication of the Kentucky Dam on October 10, 1945, Truman made it quite clear that the TVA project was not just a project for Tennessee but for the United States as a whole for providing flood control, navigation, and recreation. He also hoped to see the construction of similar TVA developments in the Columbia, Colorado, and Missouri river systems and in the rivers of the Central Valley in California.[59] But those developments did not occur.

One of the high points of his presidency was the opportunity he had to dedicate the Everglades National Park on December 6, 1947. He used the occasion to point out how this national park, like others, has its unique features, but "not lofty peaks ... no mighty glaciers or rushing streams." Here he found a "land, tranquil in its quiet beauty, serving not as the source of water but as the last receiver of it." He saw the national park system as "one part of the national effort to conserve our natural resources."[60]

Environmental Diplomacy

Harry Truman engaged in more international actions that had environmental consequences than did Franklin Roosevelt. Some of those consequences grew out of the Truman commissions. The Materials Policy Commission, for example, reported on international cooperation on resource development, on international trade in raw materials, and on resources and needs throughout the entire free world.

The primary international concern of the Truman administration, however, dealt with the construction of the St. Lawrence Seaway. As we have seen, Congress all but refused to become involved in the project with Canada and moved very slowly on it. It had been deadlocked for nearly twenty years from the time it was first proposed in 1934.

The United States made several other agreements with Canada. One of the more important ones provided both countries with additional water from the Niagara River for power purposes.[61] In addition, the president signed a treaty with Canada to establish an international commission to conserve the Great Lakes fisheries.[62] There were few sanctions provided, however, for those countries that would violate the guidelines of the convention, but it was a beginning.[63]

In January 1949 the White House hosted a conference of eleven countries to focus on the problems of fisheries in the northwest Atlantic Ocean. From that conference came a formal agreement between the United States, Canada, Iceland, and the United Kingdom to establish a formal commission, which now involves eighteen different nations.[64] And in 1952 Truman became part of a conference whose purpose was to manage the treatment of fur seals.[65]

As chief diplomat, Harry Truman became a visible environmentalist. In 1948 the president addressed the first Hemispheric Conference on the Conservation of Natural Resources, where he stressed the point that conservation was the key to peace and prosperity in Latin America.[66] Truman had gained somewhat of a positive reputation as a conservationist, and a year later, in August 1949, he was invited by the United Nations to open a science conference in the United States on the conservation of resources.[67] At the meeting were some seven hundred scientists representing forty-four different countries.[68] The fact that Truman had suggested the conference and the United Nations had supported it indicated that Truman was taken seriously as a conservationist on the world scene.

In March 1952 Truman delivered a special message to Congress on mutual security in which he revealed that the United States had technical and economic "missions" to forty countries. These missions often involved conservation assistance such as the digging of "wells for irrigation and clean water in Iran and Iraq."[69]

President Truman was also very concerned about what World War II had done to the supplies of minerals. He admitted that during the war period, mineral resources were nearly depleted, and that the national park system was, in his words, "maintained on virtually a custodial basis only."[70] Speaking of the approaching Korean War, he said: "Many projects must be cancelled or deferred, but those necessary for defense and essential civilian needs must go forward. If we allow our agricultural and range lands and our forests to deteriorate, and if we misuse critically needed minerals and supplies of water, we shall become weaker each year instead of stronger. If we do not expand the use of some of these resources . . . we cannot expect to reach the full potential of our industrial strength."[71]

Conservation for Truman often had implications for national security, as his last message to Congress in 1953 reveals: "As I leave the office of President, I should like to call to the attention of the Congress several recent actions designed to provide a better basis for the development of our water and related land resources. These resources are a foundation, upon which rest our national security, our ability to maintain a democratic society, and our leadership in the free world."[72]

Summary and Conclusion

Of what importance were the presidencies of Franklin Roosevelt and Harry Truman to the revitalization of the conservation movement? Franklin Roosevelt is given credit, and deservedly so, for introducing the "golden age of conservation."[73] Conservation was a high priority of his, as it had been for his distant cousin Theodore Roosevelt. FDR did his best to enhance the conservation of resources despite the budget demands of the Great Depression, and later, World War II. What better way for an environmental president to resolve the unemployment crisis of the depression than to put the unemployed to work in national parks and forests? Moreover, given that Franklin Roosevelt was in office for twelve years, far longer than any other president, it was critical for the environmental movement that conservation as a policy issue served as such a high priority for him. For FDR there was a connection between maintaining a strong environment and the strengthening of America. He also considered himself a *balancer* of the needs of the environment with other societal needs, and his successful balancing of interests allowed him to respond to both domestic turmoil and the war crisis while at the same time supporting environmental policies as a priority focus.

Roosevelt used all of the president's powers, packaged in personal charm, to sell the public and Congress on the need to protect America's resources. Under *this* Roosevelt, the Democratic Party replaced the Republican Party of his cousin TR to become the leading environmental party during the 1930s and 1940s. The party, the public, and Congress benefited from his untiring efforts. We can sum up his efforts as follows:

1. Franklin Roosevelt's conservation focus was on a handful of issue areas that have long been of concern to conservationists, namely, clean air and water, land management, preserving forest lands, protection of wildlife, conserving of natural resources, and the creation of national parks and monuments.

2. Roosevelt was skilled in finding institutional means to protect and develop many of these resources, as he demonstrated by establishing the Tennessee Valley Authority, which was designed not only to develop and preserve water resources of the Tennessee Valley but also to be the prototype for the development of other river basin areas, and by establishing the Civilian Conservation Corps to provide employment and at the same time build up an infrastructure in the national parks and monuments.

3. FDR's ability to communicate with the people made the public well aware of the importance of the effort he was making to shore up the conservation movement. On Roosevelt's death, Harry Truman carried on the interests of conservation, but with a new emphasis on the need to conserve resources as the key to national security. It was vital to America becoming a world power.

We can sum up Harry Truman's efforts in the following way:

1. Public land and water resources most benefited from Truman's efforts. As he looked back on his years in office, the president was particularly pleased by several of his environmental achievements such as adding some 2.7 million irrigated acres of farmland; supplying irrigated water to 135,000 farms in the West; improving navigable waterways, adding 1,296 new Soil Conservation Districts, and offering flood protection to two million acres, with the promise that in the future more than seven million acres would be protected.[74]

2. Truman was also known for his efforts to counteract the advantages of excessive riches and privilege in America. This led him to divert part of his energies to protect public land from the intrusion of rich interests and private development of public lands.

3. Truman's program made a greater effort than had FDR's policies to look at conservation as a whole. But he was not always as successful as had been Roosevelt with his emphasis on conservation because of frequent confrontations with Congress. Party opposition from congressional Republicans, in both the House and Senate, during the years 1947 and 1948, when Republicans controlled the Congress, slowed Truman's progress, in his own estimation, from doing more to advance the environmental movement.

4. In many ways Truman's interests lay in the international arena, both in times of war and peace. While the Korean War proved to be a most difficult period for him, the Marshall Plan and the Berlin Airlift showed Truman reaching out to conserve life in other nations through America's supplies and concerns, and to protect various aspects of the global environment through treaty and executive agreement. In addition, Truman was able to work through the newly created United Nations to lend support to the conservation movement. Truman also spent many years trying to convince Congress of the need to build the St. Lawrence Seaway between the United States and Canada. He felt it was critical to America's security, its industry and commerce.

All in all, the New Deal–Fair Deal period showed us two presidents exerting a great deal of energy for and in behalf of the environment with different objectives in mind, followed by a different pattern of success. For Roosevelt, conserving natural resources was based on a deep-seated internalized priority; for Truman it was more a need to encourage policy protection for natural resources to ensure America's place in the world. FDR, with a supportive Congress and public, had greater success domestically in achieving progress in the environmental domain than did Harry Truman, but Truman's approach better mirrored what future presidents would be facing in the world at large. While the emphasis of these two presidents was different, in both of their presidencies one could see the worth of government involvement to stabilize the conservation of precious resources.

CHAPTER 2

John F. Kennedy and Lyndon B. Johnson

Even though John Kennedy is not the first president most people think of when considering the preeminent environmental presidents, a speech he gave in 1963 indicated that he did feel a part of the conservation legacy. Kennedy asserted, " I want those Americans who live here in 2000 to feel that . . . those of us who inherited it [the country] from Franklin Roosevelt and Theodore Roosevelt will have something to pass on to those who come. . . . So I hope we will harness our rivers. I hope we will reclaim our land. . . . I hope we can provide, through cooperative effort of the farmers and the Government, the kind of program which will give them a hope for security."[1]

John F. Kennedy

While other issues, such as the economy, foreign affairs, and civil rights, dominated his agenda, Kennedy shared several traits with those presidents who are considered leading political figures in the environmental movement. Although he talked only in terms of conservation, he had a firm understanding and vision of not only conservation but of the potential of the environmental movement in the future.

He acknowledged that Rachel Carson's book *Silent Spring* had an influence on the way he thought about conservation, and about pesticides in particular. In the presidential news conference on August 29, 1962, he was asked about the "widespread use of DDT and other pesticides." He was then asked if he was going to have the Department of Agriculture and Public Health Service "take a closer look at this." He replied, "Yes, and I know that they already are, I think particularly, of course, since Miss Carson's book, but they are examining the matter."[2] The popularity of Carson and the book's focus led Kennedy to instruct his science advisory committee to look into the concern over pesticides. The committee's report came back in May 1963 requesting limits on the use of pesticides. As a result, Kennedy ordered its recommendations to be implemented, which led to the Department of Agriculture halting its spray-

ing programs and to the Food and Drug Administration reviewing the acceptable limits of pesticide residue on our food supply. The report also indicated
"until publication of *Silent Spring* by Rachel Carson, people were generally
unaware of the toxicity of pesticides."[3]

Kennedy also instructed Secretary of Interior Stewart Udall, to look at the
broader range of environmental protection.[4] This interest and concern with
pesticides led later, in 1964, to federal regulations. Stewart Udall, in his own
book *The Quiet Crisis and the Next Generation,* suggested that Carson's particular influence on the Kennedy era wasn't because Carson had made many new
discoveries or had put forth an original thesis, but because she had "prophetic
gifts" as a person who "synthesized the insights of other scientists."[5]

Kennedy was also convinced of the distinct role that the 1960s could play
in advancing the environmental cause; he saw that the 1960s were different from the days of either Theodore Roosevelt or Franklin Roosevelt, that
citizens living in the 1960s had a peculiar task to perform to keep the environmental movement alive and strong. Kennedy argued that the 1960s, as
a time of burgeoning population, would put excessive demands on natural
resources, which could result in diminishing resources of timber, water,
minerals, energy, fuels, and topsoil. Kennedy saw that the 1960s generation
would have to do more than just conserve resources. He indicated in a 1963
speech in Wyoming: "It is not enough to put barbed wire around a forest or
a lake, or put in stockpiles of minerals, or restrictive laws and regulations
on the exploitation of resources. . . . Our primary task now is to increase our
understanding of our environment to a point where we can enjoy it without
defacing it, use its bounty without detracting permanently from its value,
and, above all, maintain a living balance between man's actions and nature's
reactions, for this Nation's great resources are as elastic and productive as our
ingenuity can make them."[6]

The ocean was of particular interest to the president. Whenever he had
a chance to speak about conservation he would say something about the
ocean and its resources. In his March 1, 1962, special message to Congress
he talked about the need both to conserve the public shorelines and to understand the rich resources in the ocean. For this he looked to oceanography
in the hope that ocean resources would help to increase our standard of living.[7] In his remarks to a White House Conference on Conservation in 1962,
he referred to the ocean as a source of food and to oceanography as a source
of answers that would enable us to "double the amount of protein which
is available to people around the world." He called this endeavor a "whole

new area of conservation, unknown to those who preceded us but which is now coming into public understanding as a result of your efforts and the efforts of others, and which can make the most profound difference to the lives of people who live rather listlessly because of inadequate protein."[8] And the next year, on September 25, 1963, Kennedy predicted that "one of the great resources which we are going to find in the next 40 years is not going to be the land; it will be the ocean. We are going to find untold wealth in the oceans of the world which will be used to make a better life for our people."[9]

President Kennedy thought of natural resources in the same way that Harry Truman had indicated that a president should. Kennedy felt that preservation of natural resources was key to America's strength in the world: "Today this great gift of material wealth provides the foundation upon which the defense of freedom rests, here and around the world. And our future greatness and our strength depend upon the continued abundant use of our natural resources."[10]

But beyond inflated rhetoric—elegant though it was—how was this all to be done? Kennedy had the political expertise and astuteness from his family upbringing and his years in the Senate to understand how to use government to enhance the environment. He had a plan for the environment that involved three steps. The first step was to "mount a new campaign to preserve our natural environment. . . . Secondly, that we educate our children. And third, that we use every chance we have to promote the peaceful relations between countries so that we can enjoy what God has given us."[11]

Kennedy also valued what science could do for the environment. Science, he indicated, held the key to successful environmental management: "I hope . . . that we will take this rich country of ours, given to us by God and by nature, and improve it through science and find new uses for natural resources, to make it possible for us to sustain in this country a steadily increasing standard of living, and to move out around the world in the defense of freedom."[12] Science, for Kennedy, was to become "the *servant* of conservation" and should be used "to devise new programs of land stewardship that will enable us to preserve this green environment, which means so much to all of us" [italics added].[13]

One area of almost untouched resource potential, he thought, was not to be found on land, but in the ocean. In 1963 he spoke of the "untold wealth in the oceans of the world which will be used to make a better life for our people."[14] To develop the ocean to the point that Kennedy felt necessary would take cooperation from every aspect of society. "It will require the combined efforts of our scientists and institutions, both public and private, and the co-ordinated efforts of many Federal agencies. It will involve substantial invest-ments in the early years for the construction and operation of ship and shore facilities for research and surveys, the development of new instruments for charting the seas and gathering data and the training of new scientific manpower."[15]

Political Communication

Political communication came most naturally for John Kennedy. He had lit-tle trouble expressing himself, and he knew how to deal with the press since he had been a reporter himself. Moreover, he was bright, articulate, and witty as well as charismatic. Not since Franklin Roosevelt had the press had such an engaging personality to deal with as president.

Though his most significant messages on the environment were reserved for Congress, he did talk to the public during bill-signing ceremonies and during dedications he would give for water projects, and he had the public in mind during some of the special messages he delivered to Congress that were covered by the press. For example, in his special message to Congress on agri-culture, he spoke to a more general audience as well: "We have so taken soil conservation for granted in this generation that we forget it is a task which is barely under way."[16]

Because talking to the public was a strength of his, the president made many public appearances. He traveled extensively during his three years in office, and in the West, for example, Kennedy would often focus on the need to conserve water resources. In his speeches, Kennedy made it quite clear that concern for the environment in all its complexities was not just a regional problem. Despite his recognition of this fact, he was very much aware that not all easterners would be sympathetic with the concerns of the West. He was constantly alert to the potential divisiveness that conservation needs might cause between East and West, urban and rural, one region and the next, warning that "as long as we remain divided, with every group, with every interest, with every section, with every section of every State divided against itself, this country will stand still."[17]

Kennedy knew enough about conservation and was an astute enough politician to know what were the most critical conservation needs in vari-ous regions of the country. When he was in the western United States, for example, he focused on the critical need for water. In a speech in Las Vegas on September 28, 1963, he said:

> And I can assure you that from my experience of the last days, however useful it may be to sit at a desk in Washington and read statistics about increasing population and about the need for water, there is no better education for a President, a Senator, a Congressman or a citizen than to fly over the West and see where it is green where water has done its work, and see where it is arid where there is no water, and then you come to understand the truth of what the Governor and the Senator just said: that water is the key of growth, and its wise use essential to the development of the western United States.[18]

Legislative Leadership

As a legislative leader, Kennedy was helped by Democratic Congresses to work with during the three years he was in office. To solicit the support of these congresspersons for environmental policy, Kennedy used several methods. Through special messages he was able to detail his environmental objectives and goals for America. One of Kennedy's most important messages delivered to Congress dealing with the environment was his 1961 special message on natural resources. In it he stressed the immediate need for all citizens to understand, appreciate, and use natural resources wisely so that these resources would be preserved for use by future generations. Kennedy called attention to forests, public lands, and air and ocean pollution, urging Congress to support his conservation plans.[19] Kennedy made clear in this message that he was also going to have his science advisers and the federal Council for Science and Technology assess research activities in the hopes of resolving some of the unanswered questions regarding natural resources.[20]

In his important special message to Congress on conservation in 1962, the president began by stating how population increases were going to put tremendous pressures on natural resources and how citizens needed to be prepared for this, since access to natural resources was the key to sustaining the nation. He made it clear in his message that the public needed to prevent "waste and despoilment," while at the same time "preserving, improving and renewing the quality and usefulness of all our resources."[21] He was concerned that the conservation program be a complete one, covering all resources—

"air, water, and land; fuels, energy, and minerals; soils, forests, and forage; fish and wildlife"—all of which he called a "vital part of American heritage."[22] Yet despite Kennedy's strong endorsement for the need to take action on these concerns, only one important piece of legislation came out of the Congress that year, namely, the Clean Air Act of 1963 (Public Law 88–206).

In addition to the special messages, Kennedy also used the State of the Union addresses, which are some of the most important formal speeches delivered by a president. Whatever the president mentions in this address usually indicates the president's program or agenda during that year. Even though Kennedy mentioned the environment only once in his 1962 State of the Union message, more was said about his environmental concerns. In discussing urban areas, for example, Kennedy talked about the need to make a greater effort to control air and water pollution in new ways. In his 1963 State of the Union address, Kennedy made another reference to the environment, this time cautioning against overcrowded national parks and recreational areas and warning that an anticipated big increase in park visitors would continue to overburden the parks' existing facilities.[23]

Letters were a second important instrument used by Kennedy to convey his concerns about the environment to congressional leaders, principally to the vice president, who was, of course, president of the Senate, and to the Speaker of the House. These letters were often quite elaborate and allowed him to explain again, in written form, the goals and objectives he had for his environmental programs. In one letter he wrote in 1961 to the vice president and the Senate, he urged Congress to support recent findings in the field of oceanography. The president saw that more expansive knowledge and a larger body of research into the ocean was needed if the nation was to survive, because of the great potential wealth and nutritional resources as well as minerals in the ocean depths.[24]

A third way the president used in getting his message across to Congress and the American people was in what he said during bill-signing ceremonies held after the successful passage of a piece of legislation. In 1961, for example, President Kennedy set aside his first seashore area when he signed the bill establishing the Cape Cod National Seashore Park.[25]

The president's final technique of influence was in the support he gave for important environmental legislation, and in his signing that legislation into law. For example, one of the bills, encouraged by Secretary Udall, was the Wilderness and Conservation Fund Bill, which included the creation of Canyonlands National Park, Fire Island National Seashore, and the Ozark Na-

tional Scenic Riverways. Unfortunately, the president was assassinated before these laws were passed.[26]

One of the primary pieces of legislation of the era was the Wilderness Act of
1964. It had been supported by three presidents and their administrations—
by Eisenhower (weakly) and by Kennedy and Johnson (strongly). The act itself established 9.1 million acres of federally protected wilderness in national
forests. It also defined "wilderness" for the first time, stating that it is "recognized as an area where the earth and its community of life are untrammeled
by man, where man himself is a visitor who does not remain."[27] It prevented
any roads or structures of any kind to be built on those acres.[28] Though it took
eight long years to finally pass, it was a landmark piece of legislation. Passage
took such an extended time because western Senators and House members
took great care to make sure that the legislation did not interfere with state
authority over water rights and that the act would "respect existing mining
claims and established grazing uses." Yet western politicians recognized the
need to protect watersheds as an absolute need to ensure clean water supplies, which was described as "the lifeblood of California's ranching and agricultural sector, our thriving cities and towns, and the economic well-being
of our entire Nation."[29]

Administrative Action

One can tell a lot about a president's intentions and policy preferences by
looking at whom he selects for his staff. Two in particular—Orville Freeman,
Kennedy's secretary of agriculture, and Stewart L. Udall, Kennedy's secretary
of the interior—were essential to this administration's positive environmental record. Freeman had been recognized while governor of Minnesota for
encouraging conservation efforts in that state.[30] Secretary Freeman had been
active in both soil and water conservation. He was asked in 1966 when he
was in the Johnson administration to speak at the Pan American Soil Conservation Congress in São Paulo, Brazil, on April 16, 1966.[31] Conservationists
from Minnesota, including persons from the Minnesota Conservation Federation, the Izaak Walton League, and the Natural History Society of Minnesota, appealed to Freeman to prevent logging, snowmobiles, and motor-
boats from disturbing the Boundary Waters along the border of Minnesota
and Ontario. To study the matter, Freeman set up a special Boundary Waters
Canoe Area Review Committee on May 21, 1964, but it was superseded
by the 1964 Wilderness Act passed by Congress and signed by President
Johnson.[32]

Stewart Udall was a proven conservationist from Arizona who had been important to the movement in past years. He would be seen as the real leader in the conservation efforts of both the Kennedy and Johnson administrations, though his job was made easier because none of Kennedy's appointees could be seen as anti-environmentalist in their views. He was convinced that conservation was closely tied to improvement of "the quality of life."[33] In his book *The Quiet Crisis*, written in 1963, Stewart Udall pointed out that the United States was in a critical period when decisions needed to be made to keep conditions from deteriorating environmentally: "We live in a land of vanishing beauty, of increasing ugliness, of shrinking open space, and of an overall environment that is diminished daily by pollution and noise and blight."[34] Kennedy and Johnson were fortunate to bring in such a knowledgeable conservationist as Udall. John Kennedy's foreword to *The Quiet Crisis* suggests how he had been influenced by Mr. Udall: "Our economic standard of living rises, but our environmental standard of living—our access to nature and respect for it—deteriorates. A once beautiful nation, as Mr. Udall suggests, is in danger of turning into an "ugly America." And the long-run effect will be not only to degrade the quality of the national life but weaken the foundations of national power. The crisis may be quiet, but it is urgent . . . we must expand the concept of conservation to meet the imperious problems of the new age."[35]

As chief executive, a president has several instruments of authority that he can use to protect the environment. One of the most important is the executive order, "a directive issued to executive-level agencies, department heads, or other employees from the President under the President's statutory, or constitutional powers." The executive order becomes a law thirty days after it is officially published in the Federal Register.[36] Between 1961 and 1963 John Kennedy issued nineteen executive orders protecting the environment. Three of these dealt with radioactivity; four with public land use; nine with national forests and parks; and three of them dealt with environmental issues in general.[37]

Executive proclamations are another instrument of power belonging to the president, but it does not carry the weight of law. A proclamation may be either "ceremonial in nature or deal with issues of trade and may or may not carry legal effect."[38] Kennedy used three of the five proclamations issued in 1961 to create national monuments or expand on existing ones, for example, when he expanded Bandelier National Monument (New Mexico) and created the Russell Cave National Monument (Alabama).

Presidents can also create additional governmental structures to facilitate the passage or execution of environmental policy. One instrument Kennedy found of particular worth was the creation of the Youth Conservation Corps—an idea that originated in 1960 with Senator Hubert Humphrey of Minnesota. The Youth Conservation Corps was to be patterned after Franklin Roosevelt's Civilian Conservation Corps. In a speech to delegates of the Northern Great Lakes Region Land and People Conference on September 24, 1963, President Kennedy indicated that the Youth Corps would be a way to put thousands of younger men to work while benefiting the state and national forests at the same time. As he stated, "The young men joining this corps will be working for our country, getting a chance to develop some skills, leaving something behind them which will be memorable, instead of being on a street corner waiting for a job that doesn't come."[39] The Youth Corps would be involved in activities that maintained and preserved public lands, waters, forests and recreational areas.[40]

Other agencies Kennedy established included the Presidential Advisory Committee on Natural Resources under the Council of Economic Advisers and the Bureau of Outdoor Recreation within the Interior Department.[41] In 1962 he urged the creation of a land conservation commission, which was to be staffed by the secretary of the interior, the secretary of agriculture, and the secretary of the army and would advise the president on how user fees would be distributed on federal land and water areas.[42] That same year he proposed shifting the focus of the Department of Agriculture from increasing production, the traditional emphasis, to examining the problems of water and soil, forest resources, forage production, protection of plants and animals against diseases, and watershed protection.[43]

Another important proposal of Kennedy's was the creation of a land conservation fund to raise more money for the federal government to acquire more land and water areas for recreational purposes. The idea of this fund was to acquire land in order to protect it from being controlled by state and private interests.

Environmental Diplomacy

In a speech given on May 25, 1962, Kennedy indicated in a set of remarks to the White House Conference on Conservation that he saw the United States in a position to educate the peoples of the world about conservation: "I think more and more we are placing, quite properly, emphasis in our aid programs upon the development of resources abroad. Whether it may be how we can teach better water irrigation in Bolivia or build a dam in Pakistan, more and more we are emphasizing to the people of the world the great gain that can come to them by the wise use of their own resources which may be inadequate in many cases but which in nearly every case are underdeveloped."[44]

In 1963 President Kennedy also urged the United Nations to put more emphasis on its conservation program: "A worldwide program of conservation could protect the forest and wild game preserves now in danger of extinction for all time, improve the marine harvest of food from our oceans, and prevent the contamination of air and water by industrial as well as nuclear pollution."[45] He indicated to the United Nations how important a knowledge of the ocean would be to all countries. He saw the possibility of international cooperation in sharing information about the oceans.[46]

One of the most important powers a president shares with the Senate is the treaty power, as well as his own authority to structure executive agreements. The most important treaty that Kennedy was involved with concerned nuclear energy. He signed the Treaty Banning Nuclear Weapons Tests in the Atmosphere in 1963 which had consequences for the environment both atmospherically as well as in stopping potential damage underground.[47] The test ban treaty went into effect after a favorable vote by the Senate on October 1, 1963.[48]

Like other presidents before him, Kennedy found that handling negotiations with Native American tribes also fell under environmental diplomacy. In 1961 the Seneca Nation had complained that they wanted the federal government to halt its construction of the Kinzua Dam on the Allegheny River because the project was displacing some tribal members. While Kennedy turned down their request to halt dam construction, the federal government was willing to assist those displaced members of the tribe in finding other accommodations. The administration offered to purchase other tracts of land for them, to encourage them to share in the profits that would be made from the potential recreational value of the dam, and to offer counseling services or other guidance in moving from their homes.[49]

One of the most dramatic programs devised by the Kennedy administration was the encouragement and support that the president gave to the space program. Certainly an important aspect of it had to do with the possible consequences to the environment. Just before Kennedy was assassinated, he delivered a speech on the space program, suggesting that "space research may open up new understanding of man's relation to his environment." He then surmised that "when you study the effects on our astronauts of exhaust gases which can contaminate their environment, and seek ways to alter these gases so to reduce their toxicity, you are working on problems similar to those we face in our great urban centers which themselves are being corrupted by gases and which must be cleared."[50]

All of these efforts and desires to conserve resources and make more available he realized were going to cost money. And so on May 25, 1962, in a White House Conference on Conservation, he encouraged the idea of creating a conservation fund that could be added to over the years. But he indicated that even if the fund was slow in coming, "if we spend that money now and spend it wisely it will be a great economy for us and it will also be a great benefit to those who come after us."[51]

Lyndon B. Johnson

Lyndon Johnson had some attributes in common with his predecessor, John Kennedy, in that he knew what the conservation movement needed to be successful; but unlike Kennedy, Johnson had a long list of conservation successes that far exceeded John Kennedy's actual accomplishments. Lyndon Johnson was a very different sort of conservationist from John Kennedy. Where Kennedy could be seen as a more reflective president who could see the conservation movement as a whole, Johnson focused on single aspects of the movement itself. Johnson had an uncanny ability to work with the Congress for and in behalf of conservation. Because of his previous experience in the Congress as one of the most accomplished Senate majority leaders the Democrats ever produced, Johnson had mastered the way to get things done. He had carried his legislative expertise over into the White House to advance conservation. He contributed a great deal of time and energy into fashioning and executing environmental policy proposals.

Lyndon Johnson, like Franklin Roosevelt before him, limited himself to a workable number of issues on which to focus. These issues included air and water pollution, flood control, desalination of water, preserving national parks, protection of fishing rights, atomic energy, and a primary focus on beautifying America.

When it came to emphasizing the serious nature of his campaign to beautify America, LBJ stated: "The task of creating a more beautiful America, of making it a more pleasant place in which to live, is not and cannot be the job of the Federal Government alone. We must have the enthusiasm, the concern, and the cooperation of every level of government—states, counties, cities, and precincts."[52] As part of this campaign, he felt, cities had an important role to play. Johnson was particularly concerned about the cities of America, and he saw that they could be revitalized: "Tomorrow we should take the first great forward step in this rich land of ours to restore and to revitalize our cities. Our streets, I think, will be lined with trees and gardens, and the city and the countryside will bloom with parks. . . . Once upon a time America was beautiful. All America, city and country, can be beautiful again."[53]

Johnson had a name for his efforts working with people to conserve public land. He called it "'new conservation'—enlightened and progressive conservation for recreation." He then explained that the fifty-three thousand acres that the Johnson administration had assisted states and communities to acquire in 1966 were for recreational purposes, and he indicated that "28 percent [of those acres] are less than an hour from a big city. Fifty-five percent of these are less than 2 hours from a big city. Three-fourths of our new national parkland is within an hour drive from a city. And 96 percent of the new national forest land is that close."[54] This sort of conservation was the type that would reach out to all Americans regardless of where they lived.

Political Communication

Concerns for the environment in both 1960 and 1964 were bipartisan. Lyndon Johnson felt comfortable in advocating his environmental agenda in this sort of atmosphere. For example, in his "Great Society Speech," given at the University of Michigan on May 22, 1964, he indicated that the "Great Society" he foresaw building during his years in office would begin "in our countryside." He further said, "We have always prided ourselves on being not only America the strong and America the free, but America the beautiful. Today that beauty is in danger. The water we drink, the food we eat, the very air that we breathe, are threatened with pollution. Our parks are overcrowded, our seashores overburdened. Green fields and dense forests are disappearing." And he concluded with the two sentences that have most often been quoted: "A few years ago we were greatly concerned about the 'Ugly American.' Today we must act to prevent an ugly America."[55] While this idea did not immediately register with the public, the environment continued to be an important consideration for the people, particularly by the 1970s.[56]

A reading of LBJ's State of the Union addresses reveals that he said nothing about conservation until his 1966 address, when he talked of the "poisoning of our rivers and our air" and expressed the need to come up with ways to end the pollution.[57] In his 1967 address, he indicated one of the solutions to air pollution would be to set up "regional airsheds"—areas where polluting emissions could be monitored—throughout the country to overcome the manmade boundaries that air and water do not respect.[58] In 1968 he briefly alluded to his desire to further explore the "ocean depths," he indicated how widespread air and water pollution were, he shared how the he planned to institute new safeguards to "insure the quality of fish and poultry," and finally, he made clear his high priority to save the redwoods of California.[59]

Johnson's "Report on Natural Beauty in America" in 1965 was an important environmental document that explained what his administration might be able to do to further environmental protection. In this speech, in which he talked of the direction that "new conservation" must take, he sounded more like a reflective John Kennedy: "I said that new conservation would have to be required to deal with these new problems if we are to protect the countryside, save it from destruction, and restore what has been destroyed. And I also said that this conservation must be not just the classic conservation of protection and development, but a creative conservation of restoration and innovation."[60]

Not only did Lyndon Johnson mean to protect natural resources in the traditional sense, but he also wanted to "promote natural beauty" in streams and rivers, in the countryside, at historical and scenic sites, and in wildlife areas. Johnson even proposed that beautifying nature applied to "local neighborhood projects" and recycling efforts in local schools.[61] Beauty, for LBJ, touched the spirit and lifted people up. Ugliness did the opposite. As he suggested, beauty is one of the "most precious possessions that Americans have," whereas "ugly surroundings breed warped and shrunken spirits."[62]

President Johnson also consistently expressed his worries about the long-term effects of pollution. As he described it in 1965: "Pollution now is one of the most pervasive problems of our society. With our numbers increasing and with our increasing urbanization and industrialization, the flow of pollutants to our air, soil, and waters is increasing. This increase is so rapid that our present efforts in managing pollution are barely enough to stay even, surely not enough to make the improvements that are needed. . . . I intend to give high priority to increasing the numbers and quality of the scientists and engineers working on problems related to the control and management of pollution."[63] Though he worried about pollution, that it had been created by human activities, he was convinced that it could be resolved by "enlightened man."[64]

Legislative Leadership

Lyndon Johnson also showed a great deal of strength as a legislative leader. He communicated his environmental agenda through special messages to Congress. In his special message to Congress on preservation, delivered on February 23, 1966, he began by suggesting that America needed to pay attention to history and think about those societies that have been devastated by decay in the past through "careless neglect of the nature that fed them." He then pointed to how our population puts great demands on our resources.[65]

In his special message to Congress in 1967, Johnson pointed to one environmental concern he wanted to do something about—air pollution. He stated, "Polluted air corrodes machinery. It defaces buildings. It may shorten the life of whatever it touches—and it touches everything."[66] Air pollution became one of the issues on which he focused his attention.

In 1968 President Johnson warned Americans, "Conservation's concern now is not only for man's enjoyment—but for man's survival."[67] He felt that, through some of the important conservation measures that had been passed since he came into office , the country was heading in the right direction. These included the Water Quality Act of 1965, the Clean Water Restoration Act of 1966, the Clean Air Act of 1965, and the Air Quality Act of 1967, as well as the Solid Waste Disposal Act of 1965 and the Highway Beautification Act of 1965. He then outlined a conservation agenda that included purification of water and ensuring its plentiful supply, cleaning up the air over the cities, bringing outdoor recreation to all Americans by bringing the parks closer to them, and furthering the exploration of the ocean, and he concluded by suggesting that "our environment can sustain our growth and nourish our future."[68]

The president was able to use his bill-signing events to educate the public and policy maker. In 1964, on signing the Pesticide Control Bill, Johnson gave a tribute to Rachel Carson, who had died on May 12, 1964, one month before the signing of the bill: "I am sorry that one voice which spoke so often and so eloquently for measures like this—the voice of Rachel Carson—is still today. She would have been proud of this bill and of this moment. We owe much to her and to those who still work for the cause of a safer and healthier America."[69]

The next year, LBJ again mentioned Rachel Carson at the signing of the Clean Air Act Amendments and Solid Waste Disposal Bill of 1965. In describing the Solid Waste Disposal Bill, he said, "This bill creates a Federal research and technical assistance program to seek ways of disposing of the millions of tons of solid wastes that we generate each year. This bill gives us the tools to halt pollution before it starts in new industries."[70] He then quoted Carson in her book *Silent Spring:* "In biological history, no organism has survived long if its environment became in some way unfit for it. But no organism before man has deliberately polluted its own environment."[71] In response, Johnson indicated to the members and leaders of both parties that "this morning I join you in saying that together we intend to rewrite that chapter of history. Today we make our beginning."[72]

In signing the Clean Air Act Amendments and the Solid Waste Disposal Bill of 1965, LBJ was very clear in terms of what these bills were designed to do: "We have now reached a point where our factories and our automobiles, our furnaces and our municipal dumps are spewing more than 150 million tons of pollutants annually into the air that we breathe—almost one-half million tons a day."[73]

In signing the Colorado River Basin Project Act on September 30, 1968, Johnson reviewed his accomplishments as a conservationist: "It is a landmark bill, a proud companion of the other 250 separate conservation measures that I have signed in the White House since I became President."[74] He continued to assess his administration's accomplishments when on October 2, 1968, in signing four conservation bills, he spoke of how many acres he had added to the National Park System: "There are now 24 million acres in our National Park System. . . . 2,400,000 acres—or at least ten percent of the total acreage that the Nation has—has been put into that park system since 1961. That compares with fewer than 30,000 acres that were acquired in the entire previous decade." And he was particularly proud of Public Law 90–545 since it would protect the redwood trees of California.[75]

President Johnson was very willing to remind the Congress of the words of Aldo Leopold, one of the most important conservationists of the time, and one that all students of the wilderness are very familiar with. In his 1969 message to Congress, Johnson quotes Leopold: "Wilderness certainly cannot be built at will, like a city park or a tennis court. . . . Neither can a wilderness be grown like timber, because it is something more than trees. . . . If we want wilderness, we must foresee our want and preserve the proper areas against the encroachment of inimical uses."[76]

Johnson went on to chide Congress for not acting on the thirty submissions to the National Wilderness Preservation System he had presented during the beginning of the Ninetieth Congress. He indicated that only four of them had been "accomplished the last year. Another was added in connection with legislation for Washington's North Cascades." He then submitted another thirteen wilderness proposals. One, he indicated, "would designate about 323,000 acres within the Ashley and Wasatch National Forests of Utah" whereas the other twelve would create wilderness areas "within several different wildlife refuges." He urged "early and favorable action on the new proposals as well as on those I submitted previously."[77]

Administrative Action

Johnson appointed several key persons of importance to his administration that would have a positive impact on the environment. To begin with, Lyndon Johnson wisely retained Stewart L. Udall of Arizona from the previous administration as his secretary of interior. LBJ appointed Frank DiLuzio as Udall's assistant secretary of interior and made him responsible for a new Interior Department program responsible for alleviating water pollution.[78] With Udall in the cabinet, much legislation enhancing the Great Society was passed due to his leadership. In addition to Udall's two 1964 acts, the Clear Air, Water Quality, and Clean Water Restoration acts and the landmark Wilderness Act of 1964 bore the Udall imprint. In 1965 two other laws were passed by Congress, the Land and Water Conservation [Fund] Act of 1965 and the Solid Waste Disposal Act of 1965. The next year, the very important Endangered Species Preservation Act of 1966 was passed, and in 1968, the National Trail System Act and the Wild and Scenic Rivers Act were passed.

In 1966, when President Johnson appointed former Pennsylvania congressman James M. Quigley to head the Commission of the Federal Water Pollution Control Administration, he made it quite clear that Quigley would become a "civilian general" in an "all-out attack on water pollution in our rivers, lakes, and streams."[79] Other environmentalists were appointed to the Atomic Energy Commission and to establish the Land and Water Conservation Fund.

The president also established the President's Recreation Advisory Council and appointed a twelve-person Citizens' Advisory Committee on Recreation and Natural Beauty on May 4, 1966, to advise the council. These groups were set up to generate ideas and make recommendations to the president.

Conservation projects certainly were not ignored in the Johnson budget. About the fiscal year 1965 budget, Johnson wrote, "This is 11 percent more than Fiscal Year 1964 appropriations, which in turn equaled those for

Fiscal year 1963."[80] As far as expenditures were concerned, Johnson in his 1964 budget message said, "We must manage and develop our natural resources wisely, to meet the needs of an increasing population and growing economy . . . within the limits of a restrictive budgetary policy. . . . Federal cash payments of $2.7 billion are estimated in 1965 for these purposes."[81]

Only once, in 1969, did President Johnson hold back on his support for a conservation project, and it was one of the last requests made of him. He had been asked to enlarge Mount McKinley National Park in Alaska, to set aside the Sonoran Desert area in Arizona, and to make a national park above the Arctic Circle in Alaska. Instead, he chose to give this decision to the appropriate committees in the House and Senate.[82]

Environmental Diplomacy

Johnson continued his activist approach in matters related to the global environment. He became more involved in the international arena than Kennedy had been, signing or otherwise supporting 1,112 international agreements including treaties, executive agreements, conventions, and protocols. Twenty-two percent of those, or 247, dealt with the environment. This was a better record than either Kennedy or Nixon achieved. On average, only 14 percent of JFK's agreements dealt with the environment, while 19 percent of Nixon's agreements were related to the environment.[83]

A treaty that Lyndon Johnson felt had important environmental consequences was the Outer Space Treaty, written to protect space from nations using it for military purposes. In 1967 some sixty nations joined the United States in signing it, and the Senate ratified it on April 25 of that year. Johnson felt this was the most important international agreement since the 1963 Limited Test Ban Treaty negotiated by Kennedy. Johnson stated, "It puts in treaty form the 'no bombs in orbit' resolution of the U.N. It guarantees access to all areas and installations of celestial bodies. This openness . . . should prevent warlike preparations on the moon and other celestial bodies."[84]

Lyndon Johnson also appointed a number of persons to diplomatic posts. In at least one case, the appointment reflected Johnson's interest in the environment. As he stated in a news conference: "I am sending a fact-finding mission to the Federal Republic of Germany next week to study natural resource management, with a very special emphasis on environmental pollution. Secretary of Interior Stewart Udall will head the mission. . . . This trip marks the first round of what Chancellor Erhard and I envision as a continuing consultation between the two Governments of our countries on common matters."[85]

A number of Johnson's executive agreements also had conservationist consequences, such as the King Crab and Fishing Operations Agreement of 1964, the Protocol on Northwest Atlantic Fisheries of 1966, and the Harp and Hood Seals Agreement of 1966.[86]

In August 1964 President Johnson gave a speech to the Third Conference on the Peaceful Use of Atomic Energy in which he asserted that "a single desalting plant powered by nuclear energy will produce hundreds of millions of gallons of fresh water and large amounts of electricity every day."[87] The next year, Johnson organized the First International Symposium on Water Desalination. Fifty-four countries sent delegates.

Summary and Conclusion

Laborer-philosopher Eric Hoffer in the 1950s drew a distinction in his classic work, *The True Believer*, between "men of words," or those who pioneer a movement, and "men of action," those who consolidated the movement. These roles, Hoffer argued, should be "played by different men succeeding each other as conditions require."[88]

In an environmental context, we can make such a distinction between the New Frontier and Great Society eras:

1. John Kennedy, although a conservationist, was primarily a "man of words," a president with environmental vision, one who had a curiosity that took him from the mysteries of outer space to the depths of the ocean. He reflected on what the 1960s could contribute to the conservation movement to ensure that future generations would enjoy the environment that citizens in the 1960s were able to experience. Kennedy felt that to do what needed to be done at the time would require "concerted action, purposefully directed, with vision and ingenuity."[89]

2. Kennedy also argued that science and full cooperation from every aspect of society were essential to establish maximum strength for the conservation movement. While this did not all happen during Kennedy's three short years in office, his rhetoric revealed a president who was able to sense the contributions his era could make toward stabilizing the environment for future generations.

3. John Kennedy also reflected a competence in knowing what would have to be done if the environmental movement were to make

progress in the 1960s and beyond. In stressing the need to put more focus on the seas and oceanography, Kennedy encapsulated what it would take to move the entire environmental program ahead. It would require "concerted action, purposefully directed, with vision and ingenuity. It will require the combined efforts of our scientists and institutions, both public and private, and the coordinated efforts of many Federal agencies. It will involve substantial investments in the early years for the construction and operation of ship and shore facilities for research and surveys, the development of new instruments for charting the seas and gathering data and the training of new scientific manpower."[90] This statement exemplifies Kennedy's ability to see what such a movement would need in the future to be successful.

4. Lyndon Johnson, on the other hand, was different in many ways from John Kennedy, but both were leaders in the conservation movement in their own individual ways. Johnson was a president of unlimited energies, a "man of action," if you will, who after the assassination of John Kennedy followed up on a number of Kennedy's environmental proposals as well as launching his own.

5. Few presidents were as productive as Johnson in terms of important conservation legislation signed and other policy accomplishments, but it was Johnson's uncanny political ability to "work the system" for his purposes that showed his real strength. It took his legislative strength to persuade, encourage, cajole, and in some cases literally force members of Congress to back the president's environmental objectives in order to advance the movement in the late 1960s.

6. A number of the organizations and agencies that Lyndon Johnson had established were consolidated during Richard Nixon's presidency when the latter established the Environmental Protection Agency.

7. One conservation program that included both President Johnson and Lady Bird Johnson was the "Beautification of America" program. Both the president and First Lady spoke eloquently about the need to "beautify America." One can today see the results of their efforts in the new bridges built, the highways laid, the parks and dams constructed, as well as the beaches set aside.

8. The increase in the public's awareness of the environment in the late 1960s could well have been attributed to President Johnson's efforts with the public. One study, during the latter half of the 1970s, indicated that public interest in the environment rose in the latter

half of the 1960s, peaked in the early 1970s, and then declined during the latter half of the 1970s.[91] Both Lyndon Johnson and, later, Richard Nixon can take some credit for mobilizing the public's interest in the environment during the 1970s. The environmental decade of the 1960s profited from both the "vision" of John Kennedy as well as the lasting policy accomplishments of Lyndon Johnson. In short, it was the "president of words" followed by the "president of action" that gave real vigor to the environmental movement in the 1960s, and society benefited from the combination.

CHAPTER 3

Richard Nixon

The 1970s absolutely must be the years when America pays its debt to the past by reclaiming the purity of its air, its waters, and our living environment. It is now or never.

There is an urgency in this message from Richard Nixon's 1970 State of the Union address that is rarely heard today. Policy makers, as well as the lay public, were in total agreement in the 1970s regarding the need to improve the environment. This decade was unusual in that it was one of the most productive decades for environmental activism. One author indicated that Richard Nixon, in recognition of this, declared the 1970s to be the "decade of the environment."[1] So what accounts for this unusual turn of events?

Circumstances are part of the story. Richard Nixon came into office the same year that newspaper headlines and other media sources made voters well aware of the critical nature of the environment. The public observed, if not experienced, the death and damage to bird life in the oil spill off Santa Barbara, California. The event caused Interior Secretary Walter Hickel to threaten Union Oil with closure. As he asserted to reporters: "They're not going to operate again, and I'm calling them to tell them that. I'm not asking them; I'm telling them."[2] But this was not the approach the administration favored, and it was indicated to Hickel that he needed to soften his approach.

That same year voters noted another environmental disaster that occurred. In Ohio a slick of industrial waste—primarily oil pollution—covered the Cuyahoga River and accidentally caught fire.[3] The symbol of an excessively polluted river ablaze with fire immediately caught national attention and increased environmental awareness.[4] Public awareness of environmental problems could also be seen in the increased number of new environmental interest groups organized during the 1970s, including the Friends of the Earth, the League of Conservation Voters, and the Environmental Action and Natural Resources Defense Council.[5]

Given the visibility of these environmental events, along with the concern people expressed regarding them, it is no wonder that politicians began looking beyond mere conservation to the environment in a broader perspective. Yet researchers of Richard Nixon still wondered at how he found himself in the position of becoming one of our most productive environmental presidents. Jonathan Aitken argued that it basically was timing: "Nixon became an environmental reformer because he was in power at the right moment."[6] David Sive of the National Resources Defense Council expanded on that view, suggesting that Nixon was "there when it began, he signed all the basic legislation, he appointed some absolutely wonderful people."[7] In his 1970 State of the Union address, Nixon indicated what a unifying factor the environment might be when he noted that "restoring nature to its natural state is a cause beyond party and beyond factions."[8]

For President Nixon there were also several ideological and issue-oriented pressures that moved him to recognize the need to protect the environment while also supporting states in their involvement with the environment, but at the same time strengthening federal control over the states and over environmental issues. Most presidents come into office having an idea as to what the relationship between state and federal government should be. Richard Nixon was no exception, calling the relationship he saw between the levels of government "New Federalism," which suggested that his opposition to "big government" was accompanied by his desire to "restore political authority to the local level."[9] It was his intention to use the power of the presidency to bring this about. Yet once Nixon noted the overwhelming popularity of the first Earth Day and the "millions [who] gathered in communities around the nation" supporting it, he realized what political leverage it might give him if he were to *appear* to exert leadership in the environmental movement.[10] It was at that time that he became convinced that *this* issue should most properly be controlled at the federal level. As he stated on October 21, 1972, "I share the view of the Administrator of the Environmental Protection Agency that environmental problems are essentially national in scope, and that most problems, even though they may appear to be local in nature, really affect many other States and localities as well."[11]

This was not always an either-or situation, with the president obligated either to give his full support to the state governments to control the environment, or to place all environmental restrictions at the federal level. He was quite willing, in fact, to encourage the federal and state governments to work together to solve the problems of pollution. On February 8, 1971, in a special message to the Congress, Nixon advocated that federal and state governments should work together for water quality and that this cooperation should be extended to cover "all navigable waters and their tributaries, ground waters and waters of the contiguous zone." Moreover, he proposed that the federal-state water quality standards should be revised to "impose precise effluent limitations on both industrial and municipal sources."[12]

If it was not possible for the two governments to work together, however, the president was not reluctant to instruct the states as to what they should do regarding environmental policy. For example, in a special message to Congress outlining the 1972 environmental program, Nixon told the states to establish local and regional agencies having the authority to operate regulatory programs to "control sediment affecting water quality from earthmoving activities such as building and road construction." But Nixon made it quite clear that if states were unwilling to implement these environmental programs, the federal government would force their compliance without the states' input.[13]

On other occasions President Nixon was fully in support of the states stripping local governments of control over zoning decisions. As Nixon's undersecretary of the interior John C. Whitaker would suggest, in looking at this environmentally oriented Republican president, "it was out of character for a Republican administration to assert the radical proposal of giving federal funds to the states and encouraging them to override, in some case, local zoning decisions." Whitaker further wrote, "Here was a conservative President, elected primarily by white middle-class suburbia, asking Congress for federal grants to help the states reassert control over land development decisions with greater than local impact."[14] But any relationship between states and the federal government was likely to be chaotic, noted William Ruckelshaus, Nixon's first Environmental Protection Agency (EPA) administrator. The states often complained to EPA personnel that the EPA was "pushing us around too much; you're trying to dictate what ought to happen; we can handle this stuff ourselves; just give us more money, more federal grants; stay out of our hair." Some of the states even suggested that the EPA was "really a gorilla in the closet." As Ruckelshaus explained, "So long as we didn't come out of the closet and we let the states alone, the gorilla could help induce compliance."[15] Ruckelshaus went further to suggest that the relationship became most intense when the EPA exerted its oversight function to ensure that "adequate bureaucratic mechanisms" were in place before new programs were introduced. "The states," he suggested, "thought we dictated too much, were too intrusive."[16]

These sentiments make it clear that Nixon and his administration exhibited no consistent pattern in dealing with states and their role in environmental protection. This tension between levels of government seemed to have been determined by particular circumstances.

Political Communication

The question that must be asked regarding Nixon's "greenness" is how much he really invested in becoming one of the "greenest presidents" of the twentieth century? Given the overall support for the environment in the country at the time, he did not have to work very hard to win over the public interest, since it was already there. John C. Whitaker examined both the Gallup polls and White House polls and indicated how public opinion had become increasingly supportive of the environment. In May 1969, for example, only 1 percent of the public felt that protecting the environment was important, but by May 1971 that figure had increased to 25 percent. In addition, Whitaker further noted that Gallup polls showed that a concern for air pollution and water pollution increased from tenth place in 1969 to fifth place two years later in 1971 and, Whitaker contended, the environment was seen as being more important than "'race,' 'crime,' and 'teenage' problems, but not as important as the perennial poll leaders, 'peace' and 'pocketbook' issues."[17] During Nixon's first term in office, 53 percent of the people felt that environmental quality was the most important concern for the nation in 1970.[18] Seeing the importance of this issue, President Nixon determined that he would focus his attention on it and hope to capitalize on it much as Franklin Roosevelt had done previously. Nixon would direct his attention to assuring that the United States would have clean air and water, that citizens would enjoy an increase in the number of natural parks as well as expanded open space.[19] In his 1970 State of the Union address, Nixon said, "Clean air, clean water, open spaces—these should once again be the birthright of every American. If we act now, they can be."[20] Jonathan Aitken described the importance of this one statement as representing the most "far-reaching environmental agenda ever set by a President."[21]

Since the State of the Union address is the most important speech a president delivers to the public and to Congress, it is always important when a president stresses aspects of the environment in this address. In 1970 Nixon was one of the first presidents to devote portions of his State of the Union address to the environment.[22] In it, Nixon placed heavy emphasis on the environment, devoting nearly 44 percent of it to concerns about the environment, explaining that his program would be "the most comprehensive and costly program in this field in America's history."[23]

While later years saw less frequent mention of the environment in Nixon's State of the Union addresses, he did pledge in his 1971 address that the environmental quality of the nation would be the third primary goal of the

"New American Revolution"—his "new approach" to government based on
the ideas of the American Revolution.[24] In his "New American" statement, he
indicated that he would propose a "strong new set of initiatives to clean up
our air and water, to combat noise, and to preserve and restore our surroundings."[25] He also stated in inflated terms that he would encourage Congress
to adopt the most "extensive program ever proposed by a President of the
United States to clean up the environment and preserve parks."[26]

One can easily sense the attention Nixon was paying to the environment
when one examines the president's minor speeches; 69 percent of the 126
minor speeches he delivered between the years 1969 and 1974 dealt with
the environment.[27] A Louis Harris poll found the public quite supportive of
Nixon's focus on the environment, with 54 percent of the people willing to
pay fifteen dollars more a year in taxes in order to finance a federal program
to control air and water pollution in 1970, and 59 percent willing to do the
same in 1971.[28]

In his inaugural addresses the president referred to the environment, but
it was not a primary focus. Nixon mentioned in his first inaugural address
the need for cleaning up the environment, but in his second inaugural address he said less, except for an acknowledgment of the need to finish what
had been left undone the year before.[29]

Had the environment not become such a politically critical issue, it seems
clear that Richard Nixon never would have paid much attention to it.[30] Several who have written about the Nixon years agreed that before coming into
office, Nixon had little knowledge of the environment. As Tom Wicker wrote,
"Richard Nixon was no more an environmentalist than a racial activist when
he entered the White House; he had only a dim view of the environment as a
political issue and delegated the subject largely to [John] Ehrlichman."[31] Stanley I. Kutler, in his 1992 book, *The Wars of Watergate: The Last Crisis of Richard
Nixon*, argued persuasively that early in Nixon's first term, the president admitted that he had never really been attracted to the environment but found
it politically expedient to become interested since it was a way to secure an
important element of the voting public.[32] William Ruckelshaus said much
the same thing. As he indicated, the EPA had been created, in essence, "because of public outrage about what was happening to the environment. Not
because Nixon shared that concern, but because he didn't have any choice."
As Ruckelshaus observed, Nixon himself was "very uninvolved [with the en-
vironment]. . . . Most of the presidential pronouncements that Nixon made
about the environment, many of which were *quite* good, originated in his

Council on Environmental Quality [CEQ]." Russell Train, Nixon's first chairman of the CEQ, and later administrator of the Environmental Protection Agency, along with those who worked with Train, became "the final authors of much of what the president said about the environment in those days."[33] Ruckelshaus continued, "Every time I'd meet with him [Nixon], he would just lecture me about the "crazies" in the agency and advise me not to be pushed around by them. He never once asked me, "Is there anything wrong with the environment? Is the air really bad? Is it hurting people?" . . . Nixon thought the environmental movement was part of the same political strain as the anti-war movement: both reflected weaknesses in the American character."[34] Nixon also indicated to John Ehrlichman, assistant to the president for domestic affairs, and an environmentalist himself, that he felt environmentalists were all "'overrated,' and that they served only the 'privileged.'"

The environment, as an issue, Nixon continued, "was just 'crap,' and for 'clowns,' and 'the rich and [Supreme Court Justice William O.] Douglas.'"[35] On April 27, 1971, in a recorded discussion with Henry Ford II and Lee Iacocca, Nixon indicated that both consumers and environmentalists are a "group of people that aren't one really damn bit interested in safety or clean air. What they're interested in is *destroying the system.* They're enemies of the system."[36] And in a 1972 taped conservation, the president strongly voiced the opinion that he thought the public really did not "give a shit about the environment."[37] In his memoirs, Nixon placed the environment in a category of less significance than other concerns: "Cleaning up the air and the water and the streets is not going to solve the deepest problems that concern us all. Those are material problems. They must be solved. They are terribly important."[38]

Michael R. Vickery felt that the environment was merely used by President Nixon to elicit policies popular with the people: "The mechanistic definition of environmental problems and the faith Nixon seemed to place in entrepreneurial values is unmistakable. It helps us understand how 'the environment' was used by Nixon as a salient rhetorical token and how this token was translated into policies and institutional structures consistent with Nixon's core political philosophy."[39]

Yet, on the basis of a 1991 contact Nixon had with William Reilly at the Plaza Hotel in New York City, J. Brook Flippen thought Nixon had finally come to the realization of the significance of the environment as public policy. Nixon confronted Reilly, saying, "I know . . . you're at EPA, and I founded EPA. I'm an environmentalist too." Flippen concluded from this conversation that quite possibly "Nixon had finally come to realize the true magnitude of environmental issues, and, as such, the importance of his own administration."[40]

Regardless of Nixon's real feelings about the environment as a policy issue, the president, as the ever astute "political animal" he was, recognized this issue's popularity among the public and in Congress, and made up his mind to follow public opinion closely.[41] Conditions were right for the president to succeed as an environmental president. He used both his own powers as president as well as the support of key legislation to establish himself as a premier environmentalist. On April 22, 1970, he created Earth Day, using his own authority in an executive agreement, but never expected the day would become as popular as it did.[42] At first Nixon ignored and even opposed the crowds that turned out to celebrate the day and was not even going to acknowledge Earth Day as a special day, but it became too popular for him to ignore.[43]

As this example points out, the environment, as a public policy issue, was not an issue Richard Nixon easily supported, since not only did he have continual doubts about its intrinsic worth, but also his own party gave him little encouragement. While there was an environmental plank in the Republicans' 1968 party platform, the plank said little about environmental interests. There was a general statement of belief about conservation and natural resource development, and another statement expressing a desire to add and improve national parks, wilderness areas, monuments, and recreational areas, and to improve watersheds and increase sea exploration.[44] It was also clear from what the Democrats had said in their 1968 platform that the environment, as a political issue, was considered to be their issue, as it traditionally had been over the years since the days of Franklin Roosevelt.

By 1972, however, the Republican Party platform revealed Nixon's influence in that his first-term environmental achievements made the party an "eco-friendly" party. Republicans could now list the agencies Nixon helped create, like the Environmental Protection Agency, and mention the $2.4 billion budget for the environment, which was an all-time high. Other Nixon actions taken that were mentioned in the 1972 Republican platform included the federal government's use of low-lead gasoline in government vehicles, the use of recycled paper throughout federal agencies, the increase in prosecutions of polluting industries, and the assistance given to the restoration of the Everglades National Park. In addition, the platform advocated the need to establish cleaner air standards, to create urban parks, to initiate recreational trails in parks and outdoor areas, to sign an international agreement on water use with both Canada and the Soviet Union, to support a ten-year moratorium on whaling, and to support the United Nations' effort to create an international environmental assistance program for those nations that could not afford to develop such assistance. That platform was clearly a *Nixon* platform.

This Republican platform also listed the party's goals for the next four years including adding a department of natural resources to the cabinet, establishing greater control over chemical substances, and creating the Gateway national recreational area (in and around the state of New York and New Jersey) and the Golden Gate national recreational area in San Francisco. In addition, the 1972 Republican platform listed Nixon's hope to set aside thirty-six new wilderness areas, and in addition, the platform encouraged states to use land more wisely. Nixon would also encourage more exploration of the sea, and make more of an effort to protect the oceans and marine mammals. Finally, the language of the 1972 platform expressed the desire to develop coastal zone management, exert better flood control, and engage in a comprehensive pollution control program as well as make an added effort to protect endangered species.[45]

All these accomplishments left the Democrats with little more to do in their 1972 platform than accuse the Nixon administration of voicing elaborate promises without accompanying action.[46] Richard Nixon, the Republican president, succeeded in refashioning his party's environmental plank in such a way as to erase any advantages the Democrats might have had in making the environment a Democratic issue. The president had done this, as Tom Wicker observed, as a "pragmatist, as well as opportunist. He recognized that he had little choice in the face of the 'environmental revolution' but to act; the force of public opinion was too great to resist. . . . Presidents are elected to make such judgments, and devise acceptable means of doing the necessary."[47] And he chose to sell the Republican Party as well as the public on this as a "centrist," choosing the "middle course." As Tom Wicker recalls, the level of auto emissions Nixon proposed was both "higher than that put forward by Detroit but lower than that approved by a 'credit card' Congress," and when he established the Environmental Protection Agency, Nixon made sure that "the Office of Management and Budget had significant power over it," and finally, when he "signed environmental legislation, he tried to limit the spending Congress was willing to approve."[48]

Legislative Leadership

Despite the fact that Nixon faced a Democratic Congress in both houses during his years in office, and perhaps because of it, there is some question as to how important Nixon's input was in the passage of some or any of the more important environmental bills such as the National Environmental Policy Act (NEPA) of 1970. Robert A. Stanley argued, for example, that "leadership in environmental policy, generally, has been acceded to Congress rather than to the presidency, particularly in the areas of air and water pollution, land use, strip mining, and the development of the National Environmental Policy Act of 1970."[49] Nixon was politically astute as ever, and as J. Brooks Flippen indicated, even though he had not participated in any way in the passage of NEPA, he realized how popular it would become and "sought to cast it as his own, portraying it as a demonstration of his personal concern for environmental quality."[50]

Nixon was continually sparring back and forth with Congress and with the leading environmentalists such as Senators Muskie and Jackson, always looking for ways to encroach on their efforts in passing environmental legislation. In John Whitaker's words, "the administration's relations with Congress were antagonistic at best."[51] Yet Nixon was able to claim credit for supporting the passage of more environmental legislation in the 1970s than had been passed in any other comparable period in the modern-day Congress.[52] As a legislative leader, President Nixon saw twenty-five pieces of environmental legislation become law, and all but four were passed during his first term.[53] The National Environmental Policy Act of 1970 was the most sweeping, making environmental protection a primary focus for all governmental agencies. In addition, this law required that all government projects have environmental impact statements before any work is done. This law also established the Council of Environmental Quality in the Office of the President to coordinate environmental efforts from the president's office.

Because Congress was so much involved in the writing and passing of environmental legislation, Nixon found he was frequently coming in conflict with the leading Senate environmentalists—Democratic senators Edmund Muskie (D-Maine) and Henry "Scoop" Jackson (D-Wash.). Nixon wanted at first to veto the legislation, but he felt he could not do this and still convince the voters that he was really the one in control of the environmental legislation that had passed in Congress. He thus signed the legislation.[54]

Other acts passed during his first term included the Water Quality Improvement Act (1970) and the National Clean Air Act of 1970. Congress and the president both worked to see that the Clean Air Act, which regulated air emissions, was strong and passed Congress. It provided for major cuts in automobile carbon monoxide as well as reductions in hydrocarbon emissions standards up to 90 percent. There was also a penalty of ten thousand dollars per vehicle for those manufacturers that refused to comply with the law. To make sure that everyone knew that this was Nixon's bill and not a bill that came from Congress, Senator Edmund Muskie, the primary author of the bill, was completely ignored by the White House, and was not even invited to the bill-signing ceremony.[55]

In addition to the legislation passed in 1970, Nixon delivered nineteen congressional messages and issued thirty-one statements on the environment during his presidency. One message, written April 15, 1970, urged Congress to clean up the Great Lakes along with the oceans. Nixon proposed legislation that would at least begin the process of cleanup.[56] In another special message delivered five months later, Nixon urged legislative cooperation between Congress and the president. As he stated on September 11, 1970, "We can chose to debase the physical environment in which we live, and with it the human society that depends on that environment, or we can choose to come to terms with nature, to make amends for the past, and build the basis for a balanced and responsible future."[57]

In 1971 the Senate passed a water pollution bill that was far too strong for Nixon; the president therefore asked his party's leaders in the House of Representatives to amend the bill to tone it down somewhat.[58] The next year, Congress passed a broadened Federal Water Pollution Control Act Amendment of 1972 (Public Law 92–500). This caught the president off guard and he ended up vetoing it, describing its cost as "staggering" and the bill's effect as "budget wrecking."[59] The bill was indeed more far-reaching and comprehensive than any other piece of environmental legislation introduced in Congress that year. Not only did Nixon not want such comprehensive legislation becoming widespread but he also felt uneasy when congressional leaders tried to take control of the environment from him. In fact, Nixon frequently found himself in a position of both urging passage of environmental legislation and at the same time supporting a weaker version of that same bill that Congress finally adopted as its own, as was the case with the Clean Air Act of December 31, 1970.[60]

During Nixon's second term, five important bills passed with his signature including the Federal Water Pollution Control Act (1972) and the Resource Recovery Act (1972), as well as the Endangered Species Act of 1973 and the Safe Drinking Act of 1974.[61] The one disappointment for environmentalists during this term was when Richard Nixon signed the Trans-Alaska Oil Pipeline Act into law on November 16, 1973.[62] Nixon's environmental focus was clearly more domestic than international, but he did on several occasions speak to Congress concerning such global concerns as unchecked population growth, although he did not seem to see this as an environmental problem.[63]

In supporting legislation that cleaned up the environment, Nixon gained a real reputation as a "protector of the environment."[64] But this did not mean that the president always achieved comity with Congress. For example, when he vetoed the Clean Water Act on October 17, 1972, Congress overrode it, but Nixon, in response, impounded the funds for the bill that he felt would cause higher taxes and prices, making it impossible to spend the allocated funds. This situation also led to Nixon creating the "Quality of Life Review" that would demand cost-benefit assessments for all future environmental measures.[65] The Supreme Court limited the impoundment power of the president in the case of *Train v. City of New York* (1975),[66] finding that Congress had not given the president the discretion that would allow him to determine whether or not to distribute allocated funds.

Administrative Actions

One of the more creative attempts by Richard Nixon to control government and governmental decision making was in his efforts to create his "super cabinet" where four "super" departments would be formed. One of these was to be the Department of Environment and Natural Resources. This department, had it been approved, would have weakened the current Department of Interior and Department of Agriculture. From Interior, this new department would have taken the antipollution programs, and from Agriculture it would have removed the Forest Service. Nixon's eventual resignation precluded this "reorganization" from ever coming about.

While his "super" cabinet reorganization failed, Nixon's creation of additional environmental agencies became a permanent part of government including the establishment of the Environmental Protection Agency, the Council on Environmental Quality, the Citizens' Advisory Committee on the Environment, the National Oceanic and Atmospheric Administration, and the National Industrial Pollution Control Council. The most successful of these agencies was the Environmental Protection Agency (EPA), created by Executive Order 1102 on December 4, 1970.[67] The EPA was established as an independent agency designed to both protect and safeguard public health and the environment. While there was opposition to Nixon's plans for the EPA, some of that opposition came from genuine conservationists in Congress who wanted a more powerful agency. John Dingell (D-Mich.), for example, was one such conservationist. He pushed for a cabinet-level Department of Environmental Quality. He was concerned that if an Environmental Protection Agency was established, it would be taken over by the same special interests it was designed to oversee. To protect against this, once the EPA was established in 1970, Nixon put two strong persons in charge of the agency. From 1970 to 1973 William D. Ruckelshaus headed the agency as its first strong administrator, while environmentalist Russell E. Train chaired the newly created White House Council on Environmental Quality. It was Train himself who became the second director of the EPA in 1973, remaining in that office under Gerald Ford until 1977.[68]

During Richard Nixon's second term, he was not as supportive of the EPA's function as he had been in his first term since an agreement with the Ford Motor Company compromised Nixon's earlier efforts working with the EPA. The president urged John Ehrlichman, White House adviser and a specialist in land-use law in Seattle, to tell the EPA to "say a number of things designed to shock the consumer into a realization that the cost of the environment will be very high and that the air quality laws are very impractical." The EPA conformed with Nixon's wishes, and a number of the strict standards that automobile makers had opposed were reduced or delayed.[69] When he appeared before executives of Ford Motor Company, Nixon made it quite clear that the administration was supportive of business: "Whether it's the environment or pollution or Naderism or consumerism, we are extremely pro-business."[70]

President Nixon made a number of the environmental changes as chief executive through executive orders, orders that are legally binding based on executive authority. For example, in 1969, Nixon's Executive Order 11472 created the Environmental Quality Council and the Citizen's Advisory Committee on Environmental Quality. With Executive Order 11523, Nixon established the National Industrial Pollution Control Council, and he created the Energy Policy Office in 1973 by Executive Order 11726. In the same year, the president established the Federal Energy Office through Executive Order 11748.

But a president's executive order can also delegate authority to other officials to carry out the president's wishes. In 1971, for example, President Nixon, through Executive Order 11629, granted authority to the secretary of state to protect migratory birds and animals, and in 1973 Nixon granted the secretary of state presidential powers via Executive Order 11742 to negotiate international agreements related to the environment.[71]

Given the environmentalists that Richard Nixon brought into his administration—chief advisor for domestic affairs John Ehrlichman; his first secretary of the interior Walter J. Hickel; CEQ chair Russell Train; advisor and later undersecretary of the interior John Whitaker; CEQ chair and later director of the EPA William Reilly; first EPA director and later FBI director William Ruckelshaus—it should have been quite easy for the president's administration to make the environment a priority focus. But critics did not always see it that way. For example, in 1969 critics accused Nixon of making Vietnam his primary concern, which was out of step with the rest of the country's "concern for the environment." It was further asserted that Nixon did "little more than create a token Environmental Quality Control Council, consisting of Cabinet members who have other matters on their minds and rarely meet to discuss the environment."[72]

As far as funding programs to solve environmental problems, President Nixon did not give much financial support to the environment in 1969, but by 1970 the president generously provided funding for the environment. But by 1973 Nixon turned away from the environment cutting back on spending when he impounded some six billion dollars in water cleanup funds.[73]

In terms of Nixon's appointments, the president selected as secretary of the interior Walter J. Hickel, former governor of Alaska. Hickel had an admirable environmental background in Alaska and was familiar with land and natural resources from his days as governor. Yet he wished to encourage passage of legislation dealing with both oil and water pollution. A number of environmental interest groups, including the Sierra Club, opposed Hickel's nomination, feeling he was less of an environmentalist than they would like. On confirmation, Secretary Hickel encouraged the expansion of the National Park Service and supported other environmental legislation such as laws to reduce coastal pollution.[74] But Hickel's independence soon came in conflict with Nixon's environmental thrust. In his responses to situations, he was too aggressive for the president. Some persons within and outside the administration accused Hickel of "showboating" when he masqueraded as an Everglades "poacher" to make his point regarding the need to protect the

Everglades. But Hickel felt that the most effective way to change the nation's attitude about the environment was not only to use protective laws but to find "guys with guts" and "men with an attitude." Hickel had both.[75] But he found he did not have a cabinet job after coming in conflict with Nixon for two years.

To replace Hickel, Nixon appointed Rogers C. B. Morton, the first easterner ever appointed as secretary of the interior. Morton, for many environmentalists, had a mixed record. As Rogers Morton stated at his confirmation hearing, "I am convinced that the priority of our environment must be brought into equity with that of our economy and our defense. Otherwise at some point in time . . . there will be no economy to enjoy and practically no reason for defense."[76] Nixon had Morton, as interior secretary, report to John Ehrlichman, a pro-environmental land-use attorney serving as Nixon's adviser on domestic affairs.[77] Stephen Ambrose indicated that a memo Nixon wrote to Ehrlichman about the economic impact of pollution control suggested that Nixon was saying, "We have gone overboard on the environment, and are going to reap the whirlwind for our excesses—get me a plan for cooling off the excesses."[78]

Russell W. Peterson served as the chair of Nixon's White House Council on Environmental Quality and remained in this position until Gerald Ford became president. He was a former governor of Maryland and had a respected environmental background. Peterson had the support of Friends of the Earth, an important environmental interest group, which pointed to Peterson's record in Maryland as "worthy of emulation throughout the nation."[79]

One of the more important advisers to Richard Nixon was John C. Whitaker who in 1969 was appointed as a deputy assistant to the president. He helped the president to maintain an environmentally friendly agenda. Whitaker also served as undersecretary of interior. His background in geology and his "people skills" allowed him to reach out to the public and provide a pro-environmental image for the administration while at the same time drawing strength from the voters.

Earl Butz, who later became Nixon's secretary of agriculture from 1971 until 1975, was at first appointed as Nixon's natural resources counselor. This man was not sympathetic to the environment. Nixon asked Butz, however, to be supportive of the president's position on the environment—but it was not until the president became less supportive of the environment that Earl Butz could firmly support the president.

William Ruckelshaus, as Nixon's first EPA director, was more doubtful than were others about Nixon's leadership on the environment, but he stayed with the administration until Nixon left office.

Environmental Diplomacy

Although Richard Nixon could not be labeled a foreign policy president when it came to the environment, he and his immediate staff did interact with world leaders in some international conferences where environmental issues were on the agenda. While the president did not take the occasion to attend the United Nations Conference on Humans and the Environment in 1972, he did send Environmental Protection Agency spokespersons to the conference.[80] The president was particularly interested in impressing other nations with the environmental progress that the U.S. had made under his leadership. Indeed, the president saw many of his efforts pay off and become adopted by other nations at the 1972 UN Conference.[81] For example, détente with the Soviet Union was one way Nixon chose to ease the tensions between the two countries. The president, along with EPA administrator Russell Train, sat down with the Soviets and exchanged environmental information and research.[82] Not surprisingly, it did not seem too difficult to involve other nations in adhering to U.S. law when it came to requesting that such animals as leopards and tigers be added to the endangered species list.[83] Concern for climate change, as well, was an issue the United States and other nations could discuss.

Not all of Nixon's overtures in international affairs pleased environmentalists, however. Environmentalists expressed displeasure with Nixon when he ordered the Trans-Alaskan Pipeline System—the world's largest pipeline—to bring oil from the Alaskan North Slope to Prudhoe Bay. Environmentalists did not feel the pipeline was necessary, and they feared that bringing oil that far would possibly damage the environment.[84] Those opposed to the pipeline felt that the trans-Canadian energy corridor, considered safer all around, would have been a better choice since it avoided potential earthquake areas and wildlife preserves, and would have avoided possible future oil spills, but Nixon did not consider this environmental warning when he made his choice for the pipeline.[85]

In 1972 the president sent representatives to the International Biological Weapons Convention, and to the Convention on the Prohibition of the Development, Production, and Stockpiling of Bacteriological and Toxin Weapons. Nixon sent other representatives to the 1973 Convention on Trade in

Endangered Species of Wild Fauna and Flora, a conference that was to protect some endangered species from being over exploited by focusing on import and export permits.[86] The year was so good to the president that reference to these treaties were duly noted in the 1972 Republican platform, which attributed them as some of Nixon's major environmental achievements.[87]

In addition, the United States in 1972, at Nixon's urging, was one of thirty-two nations participating in the important Convention on the Prevention of Marine Pollution by Dumping of Wastes and Other Matter. The document that came out of this convention, adopted on November 13, 1972, did prevent the dumping of certain hazardous materials and required special permits to dump other materials.[88] Richard Nixon was also instrumental in organizing the International Ocean Dumping Convention, and when he was involved in the Moscow Summit of 1972 he encouraged the Soviets to cooperate environmentally.[89] The president also appealed to NATO's Committee on the Challenges of Modern Society to encourage nations to terminate all "intentional discharges of oil and oily wastes from ships into the oceans by 1975, if possible, and not later than the end of this decade."[90]

The year 1972 also found the United States as one of the participant nations signing a document to protect Antarctic seals.[91] The important document was adopted February 11, 1972, to protect six seal species found in the Antarctic. The convention recognized that "this resource should not be depleted by over-exploitation, and hence that any harvesting should be regulated so as not to exceed the levels of the optimum sustainable yield."[92]

The next year, the president turned to the State Department to carry on the task of talking with other countries about global environmental concerns.[93] Several executive orders, as noted previously, granted greater authority to the secretary of state to negotiate with foreign leaders for and in behalf of the president.[94]

Finally, in 1974 Richard Nixon signed an important treaty with Mexico concerning the Colorado River Basin Salinity Control Act that culminated after two years of discussion with the Mexican president. Since the Colorado River is essential to the agricultural well-being of both countries, this treaty ensured that the water supply would be protected from oversalination.[95]

Summary and Conclusion

Despite the belief by liberals as well as conservatives that "Nixon was less a true believer than an opportunist" on all issues including the environment,

Richard Nixon, in his first term, showed environmental leadership, but much of it was undercut in his second term when some of the same programs he had supported were ignored by the Congress.[96] On leaving office, Nixon did little to support and advance the environment. In fact, it was John C. Whitaker, his former adviser and undersecretary of the interior, who, on visiting the former president at his home in San Clemente, indicated to Nixon that he felt that the president would not be remembered so much for Vietnam or his foreign policy accomplishments, but would be remembered primarily for his domestic policies, principally environmental policies. Nixon responded: "For God's sake, John . . . I hope that's not true."[97]

So what impact did Richard Nixon have on the presidency and environment? The 1970s was so important a time for the environment that Nixon felt comfortable in declaring it the "decade of the environment," and felt that he personally could take credit for the following series of accomplishments he either initiated, supported, or assumed ownership:

1. In refocusing the Republican Party and broadening its reach to cover multiple environmental issues, Richard Nixon made the Republican Party an "eco-friendly" party, going even beyond the Republican Party of Teddy Roosevelt, which was a more limited conservationist party. In effect Nixon also dislodged the Democratic Party from its position of dominance over the environment.

2. Nixon used presidential powers, as well as supporting legislative authority, to largely create a political structure to both protect and safeguard the public health and environment that included the formation of the Environmental Protection Agency, the White House Council on Environmental Quality, the Citizens' Advisory Committee on the Environment, the National Oceanic and Atmospheric Administration, and the National Industrial Pollution Control Council. In other words, he was instrumental in creating structures to institutionalize the "environmental presidency."

3. Nixon either persuaded Congress or gave full support to Congress's initiative in forming a major eco-legislative base on which future presidents and Congress could rely as the basis of environmental accomplishments. This legislative base included passage of the broadly based National Environmental Policy Act of 1970, which made environmental protection a primary focus for all government agencies. Other critical bills and acts passed during Nixon's first term included the Water Quality Improvement Act of 1970 and the National Clean Air Act of

1970. It was legislation of this sort that provided the legislative authority for future presidents' environmental accomplishments.

4. Nixon brought into his administration a number of strong environmentalists including William Ruckelshaus as the first EPA director; Russell Train as head of the White House Council on Environmental Quality and later Nixon's second EPA director; Russell W. Peterson, who served as chair of the White House Council on Environmental Quality; and John C. Whitaker who in 1969 was appointed deputy assistant to the president, and was the person who kept Nixon's agenda environmentally friendly.

5. Nixon made the world aware of the United States' focus on the environment by sending effective and environmentally sympathetic spokespersons to international conferences including the 1972 United Nations Conference on Humans and the Environment, and the 1972 Convention on the Prevention of Marine Pollution by Dumping of Wastes and Other Matter. Nixon personally appealed to NATO's Committee on the Challenges of Modern Society to have the NATO nations cease the discharging of oil and oily substances from ships into the ocean.

6. Finally, Nixon did not have to be personally committed to the environment to become one of the most successful presidents in promoting environmental priorities.

In reflecting on Nixon's involvement with the environment, Patricia Limerick, co-founder of the Center of the American West in Boulder, Colorado, observed: "A number of ingredients, including a public outcry to stop pollution, a talented and dedicated group in the executive branch to put forth legislative proposals, a Congress whose majority was ready to act, and a president ready to accept comprehensive recommendations that often ran counter to the wishes of his cabinet officers, all of this combined to produce the best conservation and environmental record since Theodore Roosevelt."[98]

CHAPTER 4

Jimmy Carter

Jimmy Carter campaigned for the White House as an "outsider" who intended to use the power of the presidency to bring change to Washington politics. He began his administration in 1977 by developing a list of nineteen water projects that he felt were "environmentally unsound and fiscally unjustified," and which he believed should be deleted from the federal budget.[1] His failure to understand the need to consult congressional leaders and key Democratic committee chairs as well as consider the political impact of these cuts led to problems between Carter and legislators representing primarily western states. One key Democratic leader in the Senate, furious with the president's action and its direct threat to his state, railed, "My name is Russell Long, and I am chairman of the Senate Finance Committee."[2] As Charles O. Jones observed, "What President would have begun his term by cutting water projects believed by members to be so vital to their districts (and their own political careers")?[3]

Stuart Eizenstat, domestic policy advisor in the Carter administration, characterized Jimmy Carter as having a "first-rate analytical and intellectual capability and rigor," yet as president he "disdained politics in governing as tawdry," and instead of "thinking too small, he thought too boldly at times, wanting more than the political system could produce." Speaker of the House Tip O'Neill encouraged the new president to develop his relations with key members of Congress.[4] After all, Carter had a potential advantage since his party controlled both houses of Congress. Yet Carter was compelled to speak directly to the people via television in an effort to push his agenda.

Although Carter started out with a favorable relationship with the media, once problems arose, conflict persisted in media coverage of the president. As journalist Haynes Johnson explained, President Carter "never seemed at ease around reporters, and he had been unable to conceal his distrust, even disapproval, of the press while campaigning."[5] Once in office, despite employing both traditional and novel ways of communicating with the media and the American public, his relationship with the media increasingly deteriorated. Moreover, Carter had difficulties interacting with a Congress with Democratic majorities in both houses, resulting in a "negative press portrait" early in his term in office.[6]

Carter assumed the presidency with many ideas but no single focus for his administration. Yet environmental protection was one policy area that benefited from his deep interest and concern. As a governor and as president, Carter used the power resources of the state and national executive office to further environmental goals. A concern for the environment predated his executive experience. In his book *An Outdoor Journal* he reminds us that as a Georgia state legislator he was one of the founders of the Georgia Conservancy and that while campaigning for governor his "campaign speeches . . . frequently emphasized my concerns about pollution to Georgia's air, water, forests, marshlands, and other natural areas."[7]

When he entered office, Carter was at the center of centrifugal forces as the expectations of environmental groups were heightened while business and industry felt that their economic interests were threatened. Benjamin Kline explains that, on the one hand, "environmentalists found increased influence in the White House. The Carter administration seemed to welcome them and their cause," while on the other hand, "business coalitions, such as the Business Roundtable, attacked regulations established by the EPA and the Occupational Safety and Health Act, declaring that they cost too much, caused inefficiency, and hurt business morale."[8]

Although Carter supported an activist role for the federal government in environmental policy making, he also saw the value of integrating the states as partners in this effort. For example, he saw conservation efforts as relevant to the states in terms of the control over auto emissions and the conservation of energy use. In a major address to the nation in 1977 about energy conservation, he acknowledged, "One of the side effects of conserving gasoline, for instance, is that State governments that have a limited amount of tax per gallon collect less money through gasoline taxes. To reduce their hardships and to ensure adequate highway maintenance, we should compensate States for this loss through the Highway Trust Fund."[9] Moreover, from the moment he assumed the presidency, water policy was a major element of Carter's environmental agenda. In announcing his administration's water policy in 1978, he observed that "enhanced Federal-State cooperation" was needed in water policy planning.[10] Two integral aspects of the approach he announced included conservation efforts and federal dollars to assist states in their planning process.

He also made his position clear in 1978 when he stated that "environmental laws were fashioned State by State, and then it became obvious that when one State had strict environmental laws and an additional State had weak environmental laws, that industry began to go to the State with the weak laws.... And eventually the Federal government had to provide some kind of uniformity and guideline so that on a nationwide basis, environmental laws could be fair and fruitful and equitable."[11]

In his 1979 State of the Union address, Carter referred to the important role played by the states in response to the landmark National Environmental Policy Act (NEPA) passed during the Nixon administration. He stated that he was "pleased the United States has pioneered laws to protect our air, water and land. I believe our leadership has proved its worth. Since the National Environmental Policy Act was passed, at least 25 States have adopted 'little NEPA's' patterned after the Federal model."[12]

Political Communication

When Jimmy Carter assumed the governorship of Georgia, he gave considerable attention to the environment in his gubernatorial inaugural speech, as much, in fact, as he gave to fighting illiteracy and improving educational opportunities and race relations, other important issues for Carter. As he stated quite forcefully: "Georgia is a state of natural beauty and promise, but the quality of our natural surroundings is threatened because of avarice, selfishness, procrastination and neglect.... Our challenge is to insure that such activities avoid destruction and dereliction of our environment. The responsibility for meeting the challenge is our own. As Governor, I will not shirk this responsibility."[13]

During his run for the presidency in 1976, the Carter campaign received a boost from the League of Conservation Voters, that recognized his commitment to the environment while in office as governor of Georgia.[14] Yet despite this kind of endorsement, he was unable to effectively mobilize American public opinion as president or work effectively with Congress. As his chief of staff, Hamilton Jordan, explained after Carter's loss to Reagan in 1980, "We never clearly fixed in the public mind a sense of our priorities.... We never clearly presented to the American people a short agenda of our country's problems and our solutions to those problems."[15] Instead, President Carter presented a comprehensive list of urgent priorities to Congress and the people.

Carter's attempts to reach out to the public and other policy makers through television and radio were clearly problematic. As reported by Hunter and Noonan, Carter had quite an impressive record regarding environmental speeches he delivered. When compared with other presidents from Kennedy to Reagan, Carter gave the largest number of speeches about the environment, averaging forty-eight per year.[16] However, "Carter, unlike Nixon, did not use his power to propose legislation to Congress. Instead, he made public speeches, suggested measures he hoped Congress would consider and tried to put environmental concerns on the public agenda through general speeches."[17] In the view of Austin Ranney, Carter's preference for appealing to and working with the American people resulted in "poor relationships with Congress and Washington 'insiders.'"[18] In an effort to stress the importance of the energy crisis, for example, Jimmy Carter went on television numerous times to make his case for conservation and other actions. As former Speaker of the House Tip O'Neill described Carter's first major energy address, delivered in February 1977, Carter was wearing a "cardigan sweater and spoke from the White House library, in front of a fireplace."[19] Despite his employment of linguistic and symbolic images attempting to communicate with the public, he was unable to convince most Americans that there was indeed an "energy crisis."

One common theme throughout Carter's nationally broadcast addresses was his commitment to conservation. In his first State of the Union message in 1978, Carter spoke about energy, public lands, mining, and oil spills, among others. He stressed that the passage of energy legislation was his highest priority. He argued that since the United States spends too much on foreign oil, Americans must "increase production" domestically in order to create a "national energy program" . . . and that the "task at home this year, with energy a central element, is the Nation's economy."[20] The issue of public lands, especially in Alaska, was also important to Carter, which is reflected by an impressive public lands legacy when he left office. As he stated in his State of the Union message: "Last year, I sent Congress a proposal for use of Federal lands in Alaska. I hope Congress will adopt these measures, which are needed this year to preserve the unique natural treasures of Alaska and, at the same time, permit the orderly development of Alaskan resources."[21]

In his second State of the Union address, delivered in January 1979, Carter again directed the nation's attention to a variety of environmental issues including natural resources, energy, water policy, Alaska, and overall environmental protection.[22] In doing so, he emphasized that there must be a balance between environmental protection and a healthy economy. He also encouraged conservation and establishment of a viable solar energy program. The following year, Carter spent most of his attention on foreign and defense issues. Still, he continued his call for conservation efforts, a viable solar energy program, nuclear power and synthetic fuels, and at the same time more domestic fossil fuel production.[23]

In his final State of the Union message in 1981, Jimmy Carter submitted a lengthy (sixty-six-page) report in which energy and the environment received considerable coverage both in terms of content and in terms of the number of issues to be dealt with in the environmental domain; furthermore, the latter portion of this document included state actions and recommendations that could be taken in the future.[24] Notwithstanding his commitment to this environmental agenda, the "energy crisis" consumed much of Carter's attention. He delivered four major speeches about the energy crisis, stressing how serious it was and how the American people could respond to it. As he stated in the first of these addresses delivered in 1977: "The energy crisis has not yet overwhelmed us, but it will if we do not act quickly. It is a problem we will not be able to solve in the next few years, and it is likely to get progressively worse through the rest of this century. . . . Our decision about energy will test the character of the American people and the ability of the President and the Congress to govern this nation. This difficult effort will be the 'moral equivalent of war,' except that we will be uniting our efforts to build and not to destroy."[25]

While the public initially responded favorably to the program he set forth, Carter quickly realized that he would face a great deal of opposition from members of Congress once he introduced those measures in Congress. As he stated in his memoirs, "It was impossible for me to imagine the bloody battles we would have to win before the major campaign was over. Throughout my entire term, Congress and I struggled with energy legislation."[26] The decision to give a fourth speech about energy in July 1979 was shrouded in controversy. Without providing any rationale for his actions, Carter canceled the speech a mere thirty hours prior to its broadcast to a national audience. As Burton Kaufman described the problem, Carter was given advice from a variety of advisors and ultimately decided to focus on a "crisis of confidence" theme rather than practical concerns of American citizens—energy and economic problems—that had been encouraged by Vice President Walter Mondale.[27]

As he eventually stated to the American people, "I want to talk to you right now about a fundamental threat to American democracy. . . . The threat is nearly invisible in ordinary ways. It is a crisis of confidence. . . . The erosion of our confidence in the future is threatening to destroy the social and political fabric of America."[28] He continued: "Energy will be the immediate test of our ability to unite this Nation, and it can also be the standard around which we rally. On the battlefield of energy we can win for our Nation a new confidence, and we can seize control again of our common destiny."[29] Yet the public response was tepid, persuading Carter and his advisers to forgo the opportunity to give a fifth speech on energy policy. His pollsters indicated such an effort would be fruitless.[30] And yet, in his last year in office, Carter was proud to report to the nation that his efforts in promoting conservation was having a salutary influence on the behavior of American citizens as gasoline and oil consumption declined.[31]

Although the issue of energy was one of several that dominated Carter's public agenda, he did make numerous minor speeches about a variety of environmental issues. For instance, at the close of his third year in office, he stressed the efforts of his administration in the area of biodiversity: "The bill I am signing [Endangered Species Act Amendments] strengthens our endangered species protection program by including plant, as well as animal, species in the emergency listing and international cooperation provisions."[32] The following year, the president was proud to sign the Alaska Lands Act. He jubilantly stated, "We are setting aside for conservation an area of land larger than the state of California. By designating more than 97 million acres for new parks and refuges, we are doubling the size of our National Park and Wild Refuge System. . . . By classifying 56 million acres of some of the most magnificent land in our Federal estate as wilderness, we are tripling the size of our Wilderness System."[33]

That same year, he drew attention to the interconnections of environment and energy policy at the signing of the Energy Security Act in 1980. Carter stated that the legislation "recognizes that energy and environmental problems are closely interrelated, both very serious problems. Under the provisions of this act, we will complete a comprehensive study of the problem of acid rain and the other impacts of fossil fuel consumption on our environment, our economy, and on our society."[34]

Legislative Leadership

Before discussing Carter's relationship with Congress it is important to examine, if only briefly, Carter's experience as governor and his relationship with the Georgia state legislature. Jimmy Carter's political experience consisted of four years as a state legislator and one term as governor of Georgia. His approach to leadership as governor would be repeated when he reached the White House. Carter himself said, "As an engineer and as a governor I was more inclined to move rapidly and without equivocation and without the long interminable consultations and so forth that are inherent, I think, in someone who has a more legislative attitude, or psyche, or training, or experience. So for all of these reasons, I think there was a different tone to our Administration."[35]

In terms of his approach to policy making, Carter established a pattern in Georgia that would reemerge when Carter was president. For instance, Fred Greenstein informs us that as governor, Carter took his case to the people, bypassing the state legislature.[36] As governor, Carter also exhibited a tendency toward submitting a large volume of legislative proposals to the legislature, avoiding prior consultation with members of the state legislature concerning important legislation.[37]

It is important to take account of the changing dynamics of Congress as a legislative institution to fully understand Carter's personal and political idiosyncrasies and his approach to public policy making. When Carter arrived in Washington, Congress was also undergoing change. Carter faced a Congress that was "more dispersed" and "more fragmented" as organized interests proliferated and exercised their influence while individual members became "more assertive" and "more individualistic."[38] As Hill and Williams put it, "Jimmy Carter arrived in office at a time when the presidency as an institution had been severely weakened and the problems of coalition-building in Congress had become formidable. Any president in his place would have encountered similar problems.[39]

Thirty days into his administration the stage was set for a major confrontation between the president and Congress. Carter placed the nation's energy policy near the top of his political agenda, he appointed a task force on national energy policy, and he submitted a massive energy bill to the Congress. However, where Lyndon Johnson would employ careful attention to the progress of the legislation and consultation with members of Congress, Carter provided broad, comprehensive legislation, expecting legislators to support it while failing to consult with key legislators and then ignoring congressional leadership and going straight to the people to promote his energy program. Carter's failure to work and cooperate with members of Congress resulted in much of the legislation getting bogged down in committee and never coming to the floor for a vote.[40]

Moreover, Carter's emphasis on conservation, a goal supported by environmentalists, placed him at odds with fellow Democrats when he targeted nineteen water projects that we noted earlier. As Charles Jones explains, "For President Carter, the 'unnecessary dams and water projects' represented the 'worst examples' of the 'pork barrel.' Members of Congress were spending government money to win votes. Often the projects themselves did 'more harm than good.'"[41] Yet when faced with considerable opposition by members of Congress who benefited from water projects, Carter was forced to reconsider his threat to veto the water bill. Reluctantly he signed the legislation in 1977, succumbing to legislative will. As Carter himself lamented several years after leaving office, "I had several serious disagreements with Congress, but the issue of water projects was the one that caused the deepest breach between me and the Democratic leadership."[42]

The following year Carter did not acquiesce to congressional sentiment regarding water projects that were good for their constituents as well as re-election considerations. In 1978, midway though his presidential term, he decided to veto a public works bill presented to him by Congress. His veto that year of the annual public works legislation increased tension between the president and Democratic members of Congress, showing that the president must be sensitive to the needs of congressional partisans.[43] Again, many Democrats received political rewards resulting from the benefits being distributed to their respective constituents. However, what Carter saw as waste or inefficiency, legislators in western states saw as benefits for their constituents. The result was two institutions in conflict despite the fact that the president's party controlled both houses of Congress. Clearly, this issue demonstrated that presidents and legislators, despite a common partisanship, often view public policy in very different ways.

Along with the water projects, energy policy continued to drive a wedge between the president and Congress. Once again, Carter prepared a proposal without taking into consideration the sentiments of the members of Congress. In short, what might have resulted in a successful compromise over energy policy between the executive and the legislative branches of government, instead turned into an unnecessary political conflict arising over procedures and goals.

As a result of the energy crisis that began in 1973, Nixon, Ford, and Carter responded with presidential action. Nixon's approach was his "Project Independence" initiative that centered on increasing domestic production of oil resources and encouraging reliance on nuclear power. In contrast, Jimmy Carter's National Energy Plan of 1977 included a variety of initiatives including fuel efficiency, development of renewable energy sources, and promotion of energy conservation. In a major address to the nation, Carter used the prestige of the presidency to call attention to the energy crisis that he referred to as the "moral equivalent of war." After his "war speech," Carter introduced a comprehensive energy package early in his first term. However, as a result of his approach to the problem and his unfavorable relations with Congress, his program ran into numerous obstacles. At this early point in his presidency, Carter had again created a scenario where his plan to do what he thought was right resulted in political conflict with Congress. In the process, he had put his presidency on the line when he "identified the energy program as *the* initiative by which his first year in office would be judged."[44]

In initiating his national energy plan, Carter recruited James Schlesinger to construct an energy proposal that was to be produced in three months (an exceptionally short time) and shielded from congressional involvement.[45] The resulting energy plan included a multitude of proposals that would attempt to have an impact on the total energy policy process—namely, "reduce demand for energy, increase its supply, and distribute the costs and gains from the energy crisis in a way that the administration regarded as more equitable than would have resulted under the free-market approach."[46] However, to paraphrase one observer of the process, Carter alienated energy companies who saw threats to their production and incentives; he offended Democrats and Republicans in Congress who disliked a policy that was created in secret; he undercut Congress in general for his failure to consult with its leaders and members regarding such an important legislative package; and finally, he irritated his cabinet, the White House staff, and the public, all of whom were excluded from the process.[47]

Carter's energy plan was received differently in the House than in the Senate. In the House, the president received help from Speaker Tip O'Neill who engineered a plan to circumvent the numerous House committees that had jurisdiction over the bill. As O'Neill explained his strategy to assist Carter's energy plan, "The only way to score on this play was to do an end run around the existing committees of jurisdiction, and the only way to do *that* was to create a whole new committee just for this bill."[48] Although the bill finally passed the House it ran into difficulty in the Senate where Democrats refused to take the same approach as their colleagues had in the House to get the legislation passed. Another year would pass before the Senate gave its approval to Carter's energy plan.

The Congress produced an energy bill in 1978—but it was quite fragmented as a result of the various Senate committees that had worked on it prior to passage. According to James Pfiffner, Carter received less than he wanted in the final energy package in part because he showed "disdain for bargaining with Congress and communicated this in his dealings with its members. He felt that his policy proposals were best for the country and that members of Congress ought to support them on their merits without special efforts by him to court their votes or bargain for support."[49]

In 1979 when a second "energy crisis" occurred, Carter proposed several initiatives: instituting a windfall profits tax—a tax that would both "decontrol" oil prices while at the same time reclaiming some funds from oil companies, establishing an Energy Mobilization Board that would encourage the development of power plants, developing a synthetic fuels program, rationing and conserving gasoline, and using solar energy.[50] Carter was successful in this effort except for the creation of the Energy Mobilization Board, which was rejected by the Congress. As Carter stated in his memoirs, the purpose of this board was to "expedite high-priority projects by cutting through government red tape."[51] However, environmentalists were concerned about the authority and mandate of this board, since from their perspective it would have included development of nuclear power plants.[52]

The Carter administration also took on the problem of threats posed by toxic chemicals and hazardous waste. A 1978 investigation of Love Canal, New York, discovered that the residential neighborhood had been knowingly constructed on an old industrial chemical waste site.[53] It soon became clear that Love Canal was not an isolated case. Numerous sites around the country from Kentucky to the Hudson River to Missouri and Times Beach, Michigan, among others, reflected the danger posed by toxic chemicals. As a result of this threat to people and the environment, President Carter supported and Congress passed the Comprehensive Environmental Response, Compensation, and Liability (Superfund) Act in 1980 to provide federal funds for cleanup and disposal of toxic waste at sites around the country.[54]

After four years in office, Carter was very successful in establishing a pro-environmental legislative agenda. Among his accomplishments were the 1977 Strip Mining Act, 1977 Amendments to the Clean Air and Clean Water Acts, 1977 Surface Mining Reclamation Act, 1977 Federal Mine Safety and Health Act, 1978 National Energy Act, 1978 Endangered American Wilderness Act, 1978 Federal Environmental Pesticide Control Act, 1978 National Parks and Recreation Act, 1980 Alaska Lands Act, and the 1980 Comprehensive Environmental Response, Compensation, and Liability (Superfund)

Act. The number of bills dealing with environmental legislation was quite impressive given his stormy relationship with Congress, which proved that when it came to the environment, Carter was able to work with a Democratic majority in pushing his environmental agenda.

Administrative Actions

An important means by which the president can influence public policy is the appointment process. For better or for worse, Carter is remembered for his "Georgia mafia" comprised of supporters from his days as governor. Once he reached the White House, however, one legacy of Jimmy Carter is the tremendous effort he made in the appointment of environmentalists to his administration. His effort led one environmental activist to assert that Carter was subjected to some "of the fiercest attacks" that "have been mounted by the oil, timber, and mining industries because the President appointed so many environmentalists to key policy posts—something that had never happened before."[55]

Carter selected Minnesota senator Walter Mondale as his vice presidential running mate. In his memoirs, Carter stated that he had narrowed his choice to Mondale and Maine senator Ed Muskie, an environmentalist. He was impressed with Mondale because he "had excellent ideas about how to make the Vice Presidency a full-time and productive job" and because the two "were personally compatible."[56] While in the Senate, Mondale had a respectable record on environmental policy. In fact, the League of Conservation Voters strongly endorsed Mondale in terms of his previous Senate record on environmental issues and the environmental agenda of the Carter-Mondale ticket.[57]

Carter also made important appointments at the Department of the Interior, Environmental Protection Agency, and the Department of Energy. He appointed former Idaho governor Cecil Andrus as secretary of the interior. In Idaho, Andrus had been known as a conservationist governor. He was concerned about protecting public lands from pollution and preserving them for future generations. As interior secretary, Andrus was intimately involved in protecting public lands, especially in Alaska. Andrus explained that he encouraged Carter to use the power of the proclamation backed by the 1906 Antiquities Act to set aside over 50 million acres of Alaskan lands.[58] Further, he promoted the idea of an Alaskan arctic wildlife refuge, which would later become a point of contention between environmentalists, the

George W. Bush administration, and the energy industry. Andrus characterized the value of an Arctic wildlife refuge as follows: "In some places, such as
the Arctic Refuge, the wildlife and natural values are so magnificent and so
enduring that they transcend the value of any mineral that may lie beneath
the surface. Such minerals are finite. Production inevitably means changes
whose impacts will be measured in geologic time in order to gain marginal
benefits that may last a few years."[59] Andrus was also proud of his role in
encouraging Congress to pass the 1977 Federal Surface Mining and Reclamation Act, which was vetoed in 1974 by President Ford, and which included a
provision for the establishment of an Office of Surface Mining Reclamation
and Enforcement. The legislation was important in addressing the impact of
mining operations on wildlife, habitat, forests, and streams.

Prior to his appointment by Jimmy Carter as administrator of the Environmental Protection Agency in 1977, Douglas Costle served on the President's Advisory Council on Executive Organization where he was in charge
of the study that eventually resulted in the creation of the EPA during the
Nixon administration, as commissioner of the Connecticut Department of
Environmental Protection, and as assistant director for natural resources and
commerce in the U.S. Congressional Budget Office.[60] As Landy, Roberts, and
Thomas explain of Costle's appointment, he was a "successful administrator"
who would fit nicely with Carter's effort to address "administrative reform
and enhanced efficiency."[61] With Costle at the helm, the EPA became a public
health as well as an environmental agency.[62]

Carter was involved in the creation of a new Department of Energy. This
new department eliminated several existing energy-related agencies and
commissions and consolidated energy programs already dispersed among
twenty different executive agencies.[63] Former Nixon administration defense
secretary James Schlesinger was approached by Carter to serve first as energy
advisor and then as secretary of energy. Schlesinger appeared to be an odd
choice for the energy appointment given his background. However, he was
a Washington insider with government experience and an understanding of
the policy making process.[64] He played a key role in Carter's national energy
plan proposed in the spring of 1977. However, he was often at odds with interior secretary Cecil Andrus regarding the Arctic National Wildlife Refuge
in Alaska since Schlesinger favored exploration of oil in the coastal plain.
Schlesinger served in the Carter cabinet for two-and-a-half years until he was
replaced by Charles Duncan Jr. who previously served as deputy secretary of
defense. Carter's recruitment of Schlesinger to serve as energy secretary sug-

gests that Carter viewed the "energy crisis" as a national security issue as well as an "environmental security" issue. Yet at the same time, the underlying basis of Carter's approach to the energy issue was a focus on conservation, an environment-specific principle.

Moreover, Carter made frequent use of proclamations in order to shape environmental policy. He directed his attention in particular to conservation and education related to energy use, public land preservation, and the establishment of numerous national monuments. He also proclaimed Earth Day and Earth Week.

Environmental Diplomacy

Jimmy Carter began and ended his presidential term by placing the importance of the global environment on the political agenda. In his 1977 environmental message to Congress, he articulated his concern about problems that threatened the domestic and global environment and also directed the federal government to take action and prepare a report to the president to form the basis for global environmental policy making. In his message, he stated:

> Environmental problems do not stop at national boundaries. In the past decade, we and other nations have to recognize the urgency of international efforts to protect our common environment. As part of this process, I am directing the Council on Environmental Quality and the Department of State, working in cooperation with the Environmental Protection Agency, and other appropriate agencies, to make a one-year study of the probable changes in the world's population, natural resources, and environment through the end of the century. This study will serve as the foundation of our longer-term planning.[65]

After the report was submitted to the president in 1980, Carter issued the following statement: "Never before had our government or any government attempted to take a comprehensive long-range look at interrelated global issues such as world population, agriculture, water resources, forest resources, energy needs, and the overall environmental quality of the Earth we live on. The Global 2000 study is now complete. . . . These findings point to developments related to the world's peoples and resources that our prompt attention can begin to alleviate."[66] The findings of the report were profound—on the one hand, the global environment needed much attention due to deteriorating conditions. On the other hand, the United States was considered an activist political entity in an effort to achieve international cooperation to address global environmental problems. For instance, Executive Order 12114, issued by Carter a year earlier, concerned the actions of the federal government "to further the purpose of the National Environmental Policy Act with respect to the environment outside the United States, its territories and possessions."

On a regional level, Carter was successful in focusing on cross-national air and water problems with Canada. In 1979 the Carter administration, Canada, and thirty-three other countries adopted the Convention on Long Range Transboundary Air Pollution. While one could argue that the parties to the agreement had good intentions in an effort to address transboundary air pollution, critics argued that it failed to include substantive instruments to "regulate emissions" and the "transboundary fluxes of acid rain."[67] Nonetheless, toward the end of his tenure in office, Carter addressed the acid rain problem in two ways. First, he raised the issue in a message to Congress when he called acid rain "a global environmental problem of the greatest importance."[68] Second, he and Canadian prime minister Pierre Trudeau signed a bilateral agreement—the Acid Rain Memorandum of Intent—in 1980. However, although the Carter administration made an effort to address U.S.-Canadian air pollution problems, the subsequent Reagan administration, while acknowledging that acid rain was a problem, refused to engage in a positive collaborative effort with the Canadian government (see chapter 9).

International environmental issues gained the attention of the president although he was already involved in several other important foreign policy issues including relations with the Soviet Union, the Soviet invasion of Afghanistan, and Americans taken hostage in the Middle East. He signed several treaties related to the environment including the Convention on the Prohibition of Military or Any Other Hostile Use of Environmental Modification Techniques in 1977, the Convention on Future Multilateral Cooperation in the North-West Atlantic Fisheries in 1978, the Convention on the Physical Protection of Nuclear Material in 1980, and the Convention on the Conservation of Antarctic Marine Living Resources in 1980.[69]

Carter supported the biodiversity concept and submitted the Treaty for the Conservation of Migratory Birds and Their Environment to the U.S. Senate for ratification. This treaty added to previous agreements involving migratory birds dating back to Franklin Roosevelt's years in office. Moreover, the United States has been a strong supporter of the International

Whaling Commission and the effort to protect whales. In 1979 Carter, in conjunction with the Australian government, used the office of the presidency in support of this effort by calling for a global ban on commercial whaling.[70]

The Carter administration can also be credited with a heightened sense of interest in the impact of human activities on climate change. Such interest led to the creation in 1978 of the National Climate Change Program Act, which increased funding for this important field of research.[71] It is important to note that the following year, when global climate change had still not yet appeared on the global environmental agenda, scientists from the United States as well as other countries met at the first World Climate Conference held in Geneva.

Carter was also very supportive of the international effort to protect the oceans. One approach employed by the global community began in 1958 with the United Nations Conference on the Law of the Sea (UNCLOS), which addressed protection of the oceans and marine resources. Carter appointed Elliot L. Richardson as the special representative of the president to the third UNCLOS, held during 1973–82. Indicating the importance of the protection of the oceans, the president said, "The oceans comprise over two-thirds of the Earth's surface. But we have been slow to appreciate their increasing importance—the importance of their environmental integrity to our quality of life; their vast potential as a source of minerals, energy and protein; and the essentiality of their freedom of use for the security and well-being of all nations."[72]

Although UNCLOS did not obtain its first signatories until 1982, many feel that the United States would have joined with the other nations of the world in signing the treaty had Carter been reelected in 1980. However, Carter's successor, Ronald Reagan, resisted committing the United States to the international treaty because he opposed limitations on U.S. seabed mining. He also felt that third world countries were too influential in negotiating the treaty and that it was written too "contrary to America's interests."[73]

Summary and Conclusion

When he entered the White House, Jimmy Carter was committed to improving the quality of the environment. Domestically, he expended a considerable amount of political capital in an effort to elicit the support of Congress and the people in order to gain passage of his top legislative priority, his energy program. Both as a governor and as a president, Jimmy Carter valued the environment and he was personally committed to its protection. As governor, Carter attempted to balance the economic growth of a southern state while maintaining protection of Georgia's environment and natural resources. For Carter, we "were grossly wasting our energy resources and other precious raw materials as though their supply were infinite," and he demonstrated early on his concern about the environment when he lamented that "we are still floundering and equivocating about protection of our environment. Neither designers of automobiles, mayors of cities, power companies, farmers, nor those of us who simply have to breathe the air, love beauty, and would like to fish or swim in pure water have the slightest idea in God's world what is coming out of Washington next! What does come next must be a firm commitment to pure air, clean water, and unspoiled land."[74] As a president, he had more successes than failures.

1. As we discussed earlier in this book, both Theodore Roosevelt as well as Franklin Roosevelt protected millions of acres of public lands, converting many acres to national forests, national parks, and national monuments. Jimmy Carter added to this public land legacy through his active support for protecting public land, especially in Alaska.

2. Carter used the State of the Union message and environmental messages in support of environmental initiatives. However, in his effort to use the bully pulpit to promote an energy agenda, he met with only moderate success.

3. Although well-meaning, Carter's inadequate legislative skills created problems for him with Congress. Nonetheless, his list of legislative successes had a salutary impact on the environmental movement. For instance, in his memoirs Carter states, "There have been few more pleasant occasions in my life than when I signed the Alaska National Interest Lands Conservation Act."[75]

4. Carter brought into his administration individuals who had strong "green" credentials. Among them were Vice President Walter Mondale, interior secretary Cecil Andrus, and EPA administrator Douglas Costle. Both Mondale as a senator and on the Carter-Mondale ticket received strong support from the League of Conservation Voters. Andrus was known as a conservationist governor of the state of Idaho and was instrumental in promoting an Arctic wildlife refuge while advising Carter on public lands issues. Costle assumed the helm of the EPA with a background in service involving environmental affairs both at the national and state level. He also promoted public health as well as environmental protection while heading the EPA.

5. During his first year in office, Carter put the global environment on the international agenda with the announcement of a study that would be published in 1980 as *The Global 2000 Report to the President.* This comprehensive study of international environmental conditions alerted world leaders to the need for collective efforts in support of the global environment.

6. In the end, Carter's environmental policy can best be summed up in his own words after leaving the White House: "When I look at how fragile the natural world is, I can understand the feeling of Henry David Thoreau: 'The earth was the most glorious instrument and I was audience to its strains.'"[76]

CHAPTER 5

Bill Clinton

In the 1992 election, the public put into office a president and vice president who had a great deal of support from environmentalists. Environmentalists had been quite frustrated during the twelve years of Presidents Reagan and George H. W. Bush; thus their expectations were very high as they saw Bill Clinton and Al Gore come into office despite Clinton's rather uncertain record as an environmentalist during his years as governor of Arkansas.[1] Clinton was thus seen, in Michael Weisskopf's words, as the "great green hope."[2] The public seemed to agree with this assessment, and when they were asked in a 1992 Gallup/CNN/*USA Today* poll to point to Clinton's future focus, 64 percent indicated that it would be "improving the quality of the environment."[3] After the election, Carl Pope in *Sierra* magazine described the Clinton-Gore team in even more exaggerated terms, seeing them as the environmentalists' "best and perhaps last hope to help move the country from devastation to stewardship, from depletion to sustainability."[4]

Bill Clinton saw himself as a genuine environmentalist. The environment was important to him. As he once said, "I believe maybe if there's one thing that unites our fractious, argumentative country across generations and parties and across time, it is the love we have for our lands."[5] Environmentalism was furthered by his promise, during his first term, to use the "presidential pen" to make government "the greenest in history."[6]

The euphoria environmentalists felt for the Clinton presidency soon dissipated during Clinton's first term, due to the high expectations that led to hesitancy to act on his part. A number of environmental interest groups soon became dissatisfied with the president's lack of effort in that first term, feeling that the president was too willing to give away too much to those opposed to environmental concerns, and was too eager to compromise his position on the environment. Defenders of Wildlife, one of the more active environmental groups, found that the Clinton performance, after one year, was only "fair" and thus gave him a "C–" grade on ancient forest protection, a "B" on endangered species, an "A–" on biodiversity, a "B–" on public lands subsidies, and a "D" on wildlife and trade.[7] The League of Conservation Voters, by contrast, gave Clinton a grade of "C+" with a mild reprimand suggesting that he might not be "living up to his potential."[8] The Sierra Club saw Clinton as weak in the face of special interests and political opposition, while the National Audubon Society indicated in an open letter to Clinton that he and his administration "needed to be *charged* to produce results"—a reference to the need for a "jump start."[9]

Despite what appeared to be a rather mediocre record on the part of the president during his first term, Clinton still retained an interest in having the environment as an issue on his social agenda. In his remarks on Earth Day, April 21, 1993, he talked about three principles that were key to his environmental philosophy: (1) creating a healthy environment dependent on a healthy economy, (2) protecting both the domestic and the global environment, and finally, (3) moving beyond the negative criticisms of the environment expressed by business, government, and individuals.[10]

Bill Clinton, like FDR before him, had an environmental plan that stressed balance, equalizing the needs of the economy with the needs of the environment. The balancing approach was used to both save the California gnatcatcher in Southern California and to try and resolve the long-lasting conflict between loggers and timber interests and environmentalists in the Northwest. Clinton's staff made every effort to bring together interested environmentalists, local government persons, and local industries to save the gnatcatcher, an endangered bird. The result was a compromise, as one might expect, where the California gnatcatcher was listed as a "threatened" species, its ecosystem was given some protection, and local developers were given limited access to the area.[11]

An even more important example of this balance took place in 1993 during the "timber summit" in the Northwest. The summit came about due to the campaign pledge Clinton had made that he would do his best to resolve the conflict that had lasted for five years between the loggers and those attempting to enforce federal laws protecting the forests and endangered species. Clinton asked some sixty persons representing all sides of the issue to meet together for one day in Portland, Oregon, in the hope that through dialogue people might "reason together" to resolve the difficulty.[12]

Included among the participants in the summit, in addition to the loggers , were academics, environmentalists, scientists, fishermen, some Native American tribal leaders, as well as Portland community leaders. President Clinton brought Vice President Gore, along with members of the cabinet and staff who dealt with environmental concerns. Clinton made it clear that he and the administration spokespersons were in Portland to "listen and to learn" from those who had been most affected in the conflict.[13] The president thought it was a success to be able to sit and talk together "in a conference room, not a courtroom."[14] And the administration assured those in the meeting that a compromise solution would result which responded to all those concerned within sixty days after the conference ended. The resulting package included 1.2 billion dollars over a five-year period that would ensure a sizeable reduction in lumber being cut compared to that which was cut in the 1980s.[15]

While most of those in attendance at the summit were satisfied that their concerns had been heard, few of them were satisfied with the way the plan came about. Although the administration had promised transparency in resolving the conflict, few outside the administration saw the final resolution to be anything but what the administration had wanted all along. The forest management plan itself showed signs of an ecosystem approach, which allowed the building of old-growth reserves around waterways and limited thinning in the forests, allowing the owls and other species to survive.[16] Some of those who had been at the original meeting felt they had been "betrayed" by the administration who had promised a more open-ended decision-making process. The Northwest Forest Resource Council, a group representing the forest industry, even filed suit in federal court to void the plan.[17] Interior secretary Bruce Babbitt, on the other hand, felt that the plan was justifiable because "it was the right thing to do."[18]

Not all forest interests were dismayed by the administration's plan, however. An editorial in *American Forest* called the Clinton plan a "courageous, constructive, responsible attempt to make a horrible situation better," and while not perfect, it was an "enormous improvement over the situation that existed on April 1, 1993—the day before the President convened the historic 'forest summit' in Portland, Oregon."[19]

The administration's timber summit did result in the strengthening of the "wise-use movement," a major opposition crusade that was begun in 1988. The summit succeeded in uniting mining interests, loggers, drilling interests, and motorized recreation interests, among other opponents to environmental protection.

Ron Arnold, wise-use movement founder, asserted that movement leaders and followers are the " real environmentalists." After all, he argued, they are the "stewards of the land. We're the farmers who have tilled that land and we know how to manage this land because we've done it here for generations.

We're the miners and we're the ones who depend on our livelihood on this land." He then accused the genuine environmentalists of being "elitist" because they "live in glass towers in New York City. They're not environmentalists. They're part of the problem. And they're aligned with big government. And they're out of touch."[20]

Many a citizen would confuse some of the groups affiliated with the wise-use movement, given the names these groups bear. For example, there is the Environmental Conservation Organization and its member organization, the National Wetlands Coalition, both of which are interested in draining wetlands for development. And Champion Paper and MCI fund the Evergreen Foundation, which spreads the word that "forests need only clear-cutting and healthy doses of pesticides to become places of 'beauty, peace and mystery.'"[21]

The movement itself has made every effort to prevent preservation of public lands. The primary basis of the movement's public lands policy was best stated by Henry Yake, president of the Blue Ribbon Coalition, who argued that there is no inherent value in wilderness areas since they have "no economic value, no timbering, no oil and gas production, no mining, no livestock grazing, no motorized recreation."[22]

Wise-use proponents have also become involved in an educational effort to win public support. One of the groups affiliated with the movement, Alliance for America, has as its major purpose to "put people back in the environmental equation."[23] Wise-users have tried with much effort to strengthen private control over public lands; to support petroleum development in the Arctic National Wildlife Refuge in Alaska; and to develop a national timber harvesting system allowing more cutting of timber on public lands. The movement has also been a major supporter of mining and grazing on federal lands and has encouraged off-road vehicle trails to be built in formally roadless areas, which would prevent these areas from falling under the protection of the Wilderness Act.[24]

President Clinton's successor, George W. Bush, supported the wise-use movement and appointed a number of persons who were eager supporters of the movement, including Gale Norton as secretary of the interior, Ann Veneman as secretary of agriculture, and Veneman's chief of staff, Dale Moor, as well as her undersecretary for natural resources and the environment, Mark Rey, who was a former lobbyist for the timber industry.[25] In addition, Vice President Dick Cheney sat on the board of directors for the Center for Defense of Free Enterprise, which was a Ron Arnold association.[26]

Another important element at the heart of Clinton's environmental effort was his "ecosystem" approach to the environment. Rather than focusing on only one environmental issue, this approach took account of all relationships among humans, animals, and plants living in harmony with the soil, the air, the water, and the climate that might affect the environment.[27] Protecting the ecosystem was the main instrument used to help save such species as the spotted owl in the Pacific Northwest.[28] One observer, impressed with this approach, described it as "the most significant reform in the history of the U.S. land policy."[29] A related project with which interior secretary Bruce Babbitt was pleased involved the restoration and protection of the Florida Everglades wetlands from the sugar interests and the real estate developers. Babbitt described this plan as "the largest, most ambitious ecosystem restoration ever undertaken in this country."[30]

There were occasions when state and local residents rebelled against Clinton's efforts to preserve land spaces. The best—or perhaps worst—example of this was in the politics that surrounded the creation of the Grand Staircase–Escalante National Monument in Utah just prior to the 1996 elections. Clinton saw this as the most impressive environmental accomplishment of his two terms in the White House.[31] Southern Utah residents did not share in his exuberance. In fact, they saw it as an intrusion by an uncaring Democratic president into a solidly Republican state to wrongfully acquire Utah land from resident Utahans in order to politically secure the environmentalists' vote and endorsement for the 1996 elections. Those living closest to the affected area were furious.

While this new national monument did impress environmentalists, helping to secure their support for Bill Clinton during the 1996 election, it also showed the president how effectively he could use the Antiquities Act of 1906 to "protect federal lands of extraordinary cultural, historic, and scientific value." After all, he had done no more nor less than President Theodore Roosevelt had done in using this act to set aside national forests, game preserves, bird reservations, reclamation projects, and national parks and monuments.[32]

The effect of this partisan acrimony in Utah, ironically, was the beginning of a very positive record that Bill Clinton would leave as part of his environmental legacy during his second term. The act of forcing the federal government to confront an antagonistic state government resulted in negotiations conducted by the governor of Utah, Michael Leavitt,[33] and interior secretary Bruce Babbitt, who were able to sit down and work out some financial and land exchanges satisfactory to both sides. The result was a pattern established for creating national monuments that has served as a model for other states as to how land can be so designated without excessive disruption to the state or the federal government.

Political Communication

Clinton's Earth Day speeches were important statements of the president's regarding the yearly "state of the environment" that tended to both inform and, in some cases, inspire policy makers, environmentalists, and lay persons. In his speech on April 21, 1993, for example, Clinton indicated that he would sign five executive orders that would commit the federal government in various capacities to reduce the release of damaging substances into the air. Clinton appeared forthright and strong in his advocacy with the people in behalf of the environment.[34]

Besides these speeches, Clinton used town meetings, television talk shows, and news conferences at home and abroad to communicate with both adults and children about the environment. In intimate circles, as well as public gatherings, few presidents could rival Bill Clinton in his ability as an effective communicator in reaching out to the people. In addition, he took advantage of the photo opportunities he had by making announcements of environmental achievements from outdoor locations that enhanced his environmental interests. For example, when he declared that the Grand Staircase–Escalante landscape in Utah was going to become a national monument, he announced it from the rim of the Grand Canyon in Arizona. He did not pick a Utah setting because he felt it politically unwise for him to do so since Utah was so firmly under the control of the Republican Party.

Yet Bill Clinton did not take the opportunity to use his State of the Union addresses to focus America's attention on the environment. In his 1993 address to the joint session of Congress, for example, he devoted only one percent of his message to the environment.[35] He talked of becoming involved in "the most ambitious environmental cleanup of our time," using the financial resources of the Superfund. His 1994 State of the Union message was longer overall but no more words were devoted to the environment. Here he made reference to the need to invest in "environmental technologies" that would create additional jobs. He also indicated the need to have a Safe Drinking Water Act and a "revitalized" Clean Water Act, as well as a "reformed" and financially strengthened Superfund. In reflecting on the world scene he did point to the "severe environmental degradation" around the world and indicated a need to promote "environmentally sustainable economic growth."[36] In his longest State of the Union message in 1995, which lasted 80 minutes, Clinton used only twenty-eight words to talk about the environment.[37]

While the president did not make great use of the State of the Union speeches to echo his concern for the environment, he did use other means of communication to call attention to many of the environment's pressing issues including offshore drilling, expanding the use of natural gas, introducing light rail, reducing carbon dioxide emissions, avoiding the use of nuclear energy, recycling, directing our attention to the Arctic wilderness, depleting the ozone layer, and urging Americans to protect the ancient forests.[38]

Legislative Leadership

For a president to be an effective legislative leader, he must assertively use all of his individual skills as a negotiator and persuader, since a president has little real authority over Congress. Bill Clinton, in working with the 103rd Congress, was relatively successful. He showed a personal skill for legislative combat and won 86.4 percent of the 191 roll call votes—double that of George H. W. Bush in 1992—which was one of the highest percentages for any president.[39] Yet his successful legislative leadership in the 103rd Congress did not make him a successful environmental leader. In fact, competency in some situations during the latter part of Clinton's first term fell to such a low point that conservative think tanks were suggesting that some of the national parks, troubled with overcrowding and expenses, should be sold and turned over to private interests. In addition, three critical environmental acts—the Clean Water Act, the Clean Air Act, and the Endangered Species Act—were all under attack from the Republican Congress. Conservative Republican senator Larry E. Craig of Idaho, opposed to the attempt to save three species of salmon spawn under the Endangered Species Act, thought the act interfered with the lifestyle of Idaho citizens and echoed the threat, "We'll bring the human species back into the equation. Without that, it [the Act] ought to be abolished."[40]

During the 103rd Congress, the president enjoyed only two major successes in terms of land procurement, namely, the California Desert Protection Act and the Everglades water-flow bill.[41] The Desert Protection Act, while securing some 7.7 million acres of public land, still allowed grazing, mining, trapping, and hunting as well as recreational vehicles on public land.[42] Clinton's second success was persuading Congress to pass an Everglades water-flow bill—Public Law 103–219—to help maintain the Florida Everglades. This bill provided a comprehensive restoration plan and 7.8 billion dollars to repair the damage to this everglade marsh caused by a century of drainage pollution.[43]

The 1994 midterm elections were worse for the administration, since Republicans gained control of both the House of Representatives and Senate. This situation forced Bill Clinton, to "lead" by veto, rather than provide positive legislative declarations. As White House lobbyist Patrick Griffin suggested in 1995, the "veto has always been real to us. The only difference now is it's becoming more evident that it will manifest itself in the process."[44] In a speech to the League of Conservation Voters in 1998, Clinton explained how he would use the veto to protect efforts on the part of the Republican Congress to undercut its effectiveness. He said he would veto any spending proposal that would "do unacceptable harm to the environment."[45] Many of Clinton's thirty-seven regular vetoes during his two terms in office were thus used to protect the environment from efforts made by the congressional Republicans to undercut the advances Clinton and the Democrats had made. A number of vetoes were used against appropriations bills as Republicans attempted to cut back on government expenses.

The 104th Congress was even more difficult for Clinton because of the firm bond enjoyed by Republicans bound by their "Contract with America," a ten-point statement of Republican principles and goals that served to bind together the House Republicans, under the leadership of Speaker Newt Gingrich, in common purpose. The contract said nothing specifically about the environment, but therein lay the problem. It did argue in support for risk assessment and cost benefit analysis in assessing the cost to the private sector of all federal regulations to protect property rights. This placed a barrier in front of those policy makers desiring to pass environmental laws; as *Business Week* magazine stated, the Contract with America was the "GOP's Guerrilla War on Green Laws."[46] The Clean Water Act was an example of the Republicans attempting to undercut a piece of environmental legislation as they granted waivers from pollution restrictions to such polluters as the oil, mining, and the paper industries.[47] Risk assessment, cost benefit analysis, and peer review all became obstructions to environmental advancements.

Environmental interest groups kept pushing the administration to do more than they were doing despite the congressional Republican opposition. The Defenders of Wildlife wanted the Clinton administration to encourage a stricter Endangered Species Act, for more extensive protections under the General Agreement on Tariffs and Trade (GATT), and for the reintroduction of the wolf to Yellowstone National Park. Another environmental group, Greenpeace, asked the administration to grant more money to strengthen the Endangered Species Act, halt nuclear testing of all kinds, cease burning all toxic waste, and stop the purchase of privately owned forest areas. The Sierra Club insisted the administration raise fees for grazing and encourage recycling through an investment tax credit, while Friends of the Earth wished to see the federal expenditure doubled on the environment by 1997.[48]

The coming of the 104th Congress made Clinton much more defensive and less assertive and creative in the environmental arena than he had been during the 103rd Congress. This became clear in his Earth Day speech of April 21, 1995, a day set aside to commemorate the twenty-fifth anniversary of Earth Day. Most of his speech dealt with what he was going to *veto* in order to preserve the environmental advances that had been made up to this point in his presidency. Clinton pledged in this speech that he would not allow lobbyists to rewrite environmental laws to benefit polluters, asserting in a colorful but frustrated way, "Reform, yes; modernize, you bet; but roll back health and safety? No. Let DDT into our food again? Not on your life. Create more tainted water or toxic waste . . . Never. No. Say no, folks. Say no. Just say no to what they are doing."[49] The president had clearly lost the initiative; it had been emasculated by the Republican leadership in the House.

A *New York Times* editorial in May 1995 attempted to offer some support to Clinton's efforts to counteract some of the environmental reversals he feared. It urged him to "invoke his irreversibility principle in answer to the Republican efforts to defang the National Forest Management Act, the National Environmental Policy Act, the Clean Water Act and the Endangered Species Act." The editorial concluded that without an environmentally sensitive president taking some sort of protective action over our "natural areas," they will be "wounded far into the future if not lost forever."[50]

A few of Clinton's successes during his first term came as a result of avoiding Congress altogether through his use of the Antiquities Act of 1906, the same act that Teddy Roosevelt had so effectively used in countering Congress at the turn of the century. Clinton, in his use of the act, was able to set aside some three million acres of federal land as national monuments including the Grand Staircase–Escalante National Monument in Utah, the Pinnacles National Monument in California, and the Grand Canyon–Parashant National Monument in Arizona.

Administrative Actions

President Clinton's administrative actions were much more impressive. Mark Dowie estimated that Clinton hired about "two dozen environmentalists,"[51] placing them throughout government in agencies and departments—such as the State Department, National Security Council, and the Office and Management and Budget—that had previously never had environmentalists as part of their working staffs.[52]

Perhaps his most important appointment was Vice President Al Gore who had been an advocate of the environmental movement in the Senate and had written about it in his 1992 book, *Earth in the Balance: Ecology and the Human Spirit.*[53] The appointment of Gore served as a way for President Clinton to attract environmentalists' support at both the federal and state level, but unexpectedly, his appointment of Gore may also have had a negative effect on the Clinton presidency in his first term in that it further elevated environmentalists' expectations as to what this administration was going to do.

A second appointment, almost as important, was that of Bruce Babbitt as interior secretary. Babbitt also raised expectations on the part of environmentalists since he had long been an activist in the environmental movement, and in June 1993 he made environmentalists very hopeful when he stated that "the stars are aligned . . . All of a sudden, all those things we have been advocating for so many years are possible. We should seize the moment!"[54] Clinton praised Babbitt in guiding the Interior Department "by the unifying purpose of stewardship."[55]

The Environmental Protection Agency would become one of the effective instruments that Clinton would use to achieve the goals of his global agenda. Certainly the primary reason for its effectiveness was due to Carol Browner, who was appointed administrator of the EPA and stayed for the full eight years, becoming the longest-serving administrator the agency has had. While much of her effort was directed to the domestic arena, the EPA did assist those who were working on global concerns.[56]

Others who effectively placed the administration's global environmental policies high on their priority list included Kathleen (Katie) McGinty, who was chairperson of the Council on Environmental Quality and Clinton's senior advisor on environment and natural resources issues. The environmental aspect of most decisions was testimony to her importance in the administration. She was first appointed in 1994 and left the administration in 1998.

Timothy Wirth, a former U.S. senator from Colorado, became President

Clinton's assistant secretary of state for global affairs. He spent much of his time advocating proposals that might be adopted to relieve the threat posed by global warming and climate change. Although he tried to raise support for the Kyoto Protocol, the U.S. Senate refused to ratify the international agreement.

Hazel O'Leary, who served as secretary of energy, was highlighted in the president's 1994 statement in which he recalled his first Earth Day speech: "A year ago on Earth Day, we made a commitment to reduce greenhouse gases which cause climate changes, from global warming to increasingly severe hurricanes. In October, we produced a plan to cut greenhouse gases to 1990 levels by the year 2000. . . . Last night, Energy Secretary Hazel O'Leary signed an historic agreement with virtually the entire electric utility industry to cut greenhouse gases. That means some of our largest industrial polluters are going to clean up their act and clean up our air."[57]

In reflecting on the efforts of his "environmental team," Clinton said, "Thanks to their work, our air and water are cleaner; our food is safer; we've cleaned up twice as many toxic waste sites in these eight years as in the previous twelve. We've protected more land in the lower forty-eight states than any administration since that of Theodore Roosevelt, and have supported research, development, and deployment of energy conservation, technologies, and clean energy sources, demonstrating, I believe convincingly, that we can have environmental protection and economic growth hand in hand."[58]

Whereas Clinton's environmental appointments were impressive, the number of new environmental agencies created were few in number. They included the National Biological Service, created to count and monitor biological resources to determine which species should be protected; the White House Office on Environmental Policy, an office used to coordinate environmental policy; and the President's Council on Sustainable Development, an advisory group of twenty-five, made up of five cabinet members, along with leaders from industry, labor, and the environmental and civil rights arenas.[59] The president also tried to elevate the Environmental Protection Agency to cabinet-level status, but this plan failed as a result of an increasingly hostile Congress.

In addition to the creation of offices, the president also dismantled one very troublesome office, namely, George H. W. Bush's Council on Competitiveness, an organization that had been directed by Vice President Dan Quayle to bolster businesses' strength at the expense of environmental regulations.

Closely associated with Bill Clinton's idea of federalism is his concept of *environmental justice*—"justice" for all citizens regardless of where they happened to live. Accordingly, a special emphasis of environmental justice was minorities and low-income populations who could not afford to live in cleaner and safer communities, and it proposed to take measures to improve their conditions.[60] The president identified environmental justice as a "top administrative priority."[61] On February 18, 1994, Clinton issued Executive Order 12898, which stated that "all Americans have a right to be protected from pollution—not just those who can afford to live in the cleanest, safest communities."[62] Clinton then indicated, "I am therefore today directing that all department and agency heads take appropriate and necessary steps to ensure that the following specific directives are implemented immediately: . . . each federal agency shall analyze the environmental effects, including human health, economic and social effects, of Federal actions including effects on minority communities and low-income communities, when such analysis is required by . . . NEPA."[63] Clinton further explained, "When we talk about environmental justice, we mean calling a halt to poisoning and pollution of our poorest communities, from our rural areas to our inner cities."[64] This was a concept that pledged a clean environment for all citizens, rich or poor, regardless of their living conditions.

While environmentalists could certainly anticipate support from the Clinton presidency, it should be made clear that not everything that Bill Clinton did while in office was supported by environmentalists. In March 1995, for example, the president came out with his plan to consolidate government as a part of the administration's "reinvention" of government. Among those agencies that sustained loss of employees and structural cutbacks in the reform measure was the Interior Department. It was to lose some two thousand persons; moreover, the very agency that collected royalties on oil reserves—the Minerals Management Service—was to be eliminated.[65] The administration's argument for these changes was that the reductions would improve the overall efficiency of government.

Many of Clinton's administrative accomplishments during his second term were instigated through his use of executive orders. This way he did not have to go to Congress for permission to act. As of August 2000, Clinton had signed "more than 450 executive orders and proclamations, which allowed him to escape Congressional oversight since they do not require congressional approval. Many involved minor matters, but some dealt with important and critical concerns. In the year 2000, for example, the president invoked the Antiquities Act to create the Grand Canyon–Parashant, Giant Sequoia, Agua

Fria, and California Coastal national monuments, all in the West."[66] He also signed an executive order to protect some twelve hundred miles of U.S. coastlines, as well as the coral reefs in northwest Hawaii. As Clinton described it, "It was the biggest conservation step I had taken since preserving 43 million roadless acres in our national forests, and a needed one, since ocean pollution was threatening reefs the world over.[67]

Environmental Diplomacy

In the international arena, Clinton still faced a number of barriers centered in Congress that prevented him from finalizing some of his international initiatives. One of those agreements was the Convention on Biological Diversity. While this treaty provided no firm regulations over those countries that signed it, it did commit the countries to develop national policies to identify, monitor, and conserve species, initiate research involving them, train personnel in species diversity, and generally educate the public of the need to conserve biological diversity. Bill Clinton signed the treaty on June 4, 1993 and it was then sent to the Senate where the Senate Committee on Foreign Relations recommended ratification on July 11, 1994. But once the Senate changed political leadership from Democrat to Republican, Senator Jesse Helms, opposed to the treaty, became chair of the Senate Foreign Relations Committee and blocked its final ratification.[68]

President Clinton expressed his interest and concern in global affairs in remarks he made on Earth Day, April 21, 1994, that ranged from his concern about the air we breathe, the dangers posed by lead paint, the need to clean up polluted streams, the need for action against toxic waste dumps, the concern for diseased children, and the need to prevent more fisheries from dying.[69] This list of Clinton's environmental concerns also pointed to what made his response to the environment so much more difficult than that of Franklin Roosevelt. While Clinton's environmental concerns extended worldwide, his authority was frequently frustrated by Senate efforts. For example, some thirty-five Senate Republicans objected to the Clinton administration's interpretation of our obligations under the biodiversity treaty, and a sizeable faction in the Senate refused to support an agreement the United States had made with Egypt—the Cairo Population Conference—since the Senate felt that this agreement focused too much on the abortion question.

Of all of Bill Clinton's international environmental concerns, he was probably most interested in doing something regarding global warming. One of the oldest and most important agreements that President Clinton encouraged was the Kyoto Protocol. Of the Global Climate Change Convention signed in 1992 by George H. W. Bush, Clinton stated, "When the nations of the world gather again in December [1997] in Kyoto for the UN Climate Change Conference, all of us, developed and developing nations, must seize the opportunity to turn back the clock on greenhouse gas emissions so that we can leave a healthy planet to our children."[70] Clinton made it quite clear that the United States should be "committed to realistic and binding limits on greenhouse gases." As he further suggested, "It is obvious that we cannot fulfill our responsibilities to future generations unless we deal responsibly with the challenge of climate change. Whenever the security of our country has been threatened, we have led the world to a better resolution. That is what is at stake here."[71] While Clinton felt the Kyoto Protocol was a good but not yet perfect agreement, he indicated, "It is environmentally sound. It's a huge first step. And I did not dream when we started that we could get this far. We should be very very proud of this." He did, however, wish that it was a "little stronger on developing nations' participation. But we opened the way, the only way we can get there, through joint implementation of projects in those countries."[72]

As of December 2006, policy makers from 169 countries around the world had signed the Kyoto Protocol.[73] Katie McGinty, then Clinton's chair of the White House Council on Environmental Quality, indicated that she felt the protocol was "a momentous step forward for the United States and for the world in grappling with the issue of climate change. Every element that the president announced as a key part of the United States' plan of action was adopted by the international arena."[74] McGinty praised the leadership exhibited by Bill Clinton, Al Gore, and other U.S. policy makers in encouraging world leaders to support Kyoto.[75] Clinton was so convinced that something had to be done about the global warming problem that in June 2000, the president used his influence to persuade President Vladimir Putin of the Russian Federation to sign a Joint Statement of Cooperation to Combat Global Warming. The statement read: "President of the United States Clinton and President of the Russian Federation Putin reaffirm the commitment of the United States and the Russian Federation to cooperate in taking action to reduce the serious risks of global warming."[76]

Bill Clinton signed the Kyoto Protocol for and in behalf of the United States, but he never submitted it to the Senate for the necessary ratification, fearing that it would end in certain defeat in the hands of the Republican

Senate, given that the Senators in 1997 had already sent the president a clear message of opposition to it in a 95–0 vote (on the Byrd-Hagel Resolution), that he should not sign the protocol until that document also restrained developing countries' emissions.[77] Eileen Claussen, who served as an assistant secretary of state for oceans and international environmental and scientific affairs from 1993 (by virtue of a recess appointment) until her official appointment in 1996, left the administration the following year. As assistant secretary of state for oceans she focused her attention on coordinating such global environmental policies as climate change, forest management, biodiversity, fisheries, and wildlife, making recommendations to the president and secretary of state that would provide policy guidelines affecting foreign policy.[78] In this capacity, she became quite critical of the approach the Clinton administration had taken toward the Senate, in failing to work with sympathetic and supportive senators in an effort to ratify the Kyoto Protocol.[79]

In 1999, after Claussen stepped down, David Sandalow was asked to serve as assistant secretary of state for oceans and international environmental and scientific affairs. Sandalow worked in the administration until January 2001. He was also asked by the president to serve at the same time as senior director for environmental affairs, as associate director of the global environment, and as a member of the White House Council on Environmental Quality. In these positions he was able to focus his attention on biotechnology, marine conservation, global warming, and establish "environmental standards of export credit agencies," and have input on environmental concerns when Clinton interacted with foreign countries—especially with China, India, Africa, and Latin America.[80] As a result he probably had more overall input on global environmental affairs than any other appointee during those last few years.

While Clinton was unable to comply with the wishes of the Senate before he left office, this did not dampen his enthusiastic endorsement of the protocol. He felt that it was important enough for the United States to continue to offer support and leadership to other nations wishing to support the protocol.

Journalist Scott Allen did notice a change in Bill Clinton's approach to global environmental concerns after his reelection in 1996. He observed that Clinton became "increasingly bold on environmental issues. Now, the president has taken international leadership on reducing global warming, and the administration has declared that environmental protection will be near the top of the U.S. foreign policy agenda."[81] On April 22, 1999, in his last Earth Day speech, Clinton said, "A new century brings new environmental

challenges—perhaps the greatest is global warming. There is no clearer re-
minder that we are, indeed, all members of one global community. Only by
acting together—as a nation, and in partnership with other nations—can we
avert this common threat."[82]

Despite Clinton's signature on the Kyoto Protocol and his efforts to win
support for it from other countries, George W. Bush had quite a different
view of the protocol, calling it "fatally flawed," and he renounced it in March
of 2001. Where Bill Clinton had relied on scientific consensus and collaborative international diplomacy to come to his conclusion regarding the protocol, President Bush pursued a unilateralist, antiregulatory approach to the
Kyoto Protocol, in opposition to the interests of the global community but in
favor of the domestic fossil fuel industry.

The Montreal Protocol on Substances presented a different scenario.
This protocol committed each signatory state to reduce certain pollutants
that were depleting the ozone layer. It was first adopted on September 16,
1987, and was afterward amended five different times, in 1990, 1992, 1993,
1997, and the last in 1999. The Senate passed each one of the amendments.
Those signing the document were committed to reducing certain of the
chlorofluorocarbons (CFCs) by 50 percent by 1999. A number of controls
were to be implemented on some of the CFCs as well. Clinton stated in his
message to the Senate: "Early ratification by the United States is important
to demonstrate to the rest of the world our commitment to protection and
preservation of the stratospheric ozone layer and will encourage the wide
participation necessary for full realization of the Amendment's goals."[83] As of
January 16, 2007, 190 nations had ratified the Montreal Protocol.[84]

Few presidents have made an effort to meet with Native American tribes,
and even fewer presidents have met with them regarding environmental
concerns. President Clinton was the exception. One of the concerns Native
American tribes had during Clinton's time in office was their inability to use
eagle feathers in their religious service because of the restrictions in the Endangered Species Act. Clinton announced on April 29, 1994, that there would
be an exception made for Native American ceremonies: "This Administration has undertaken policy and procedural changes to facilitate the collection and distribution of scarce eagle bodies and parts for this purpose."[85]

Although Bill Clinton may not have been as successful in working with
Congress on the acceptance of the Kyoto Protocol, he did accomplish more in
the international arena during his first and second terms than people give him
credit for. Quite often the Clinton presidency has been criticized for being an

environmental "do-nothing" during his first term. However, if one takes note
of the international environmental agreements negotiated by the administration, one begins to see quite a different picture emerging. In terms of the
sixty global environmental agreements and protocols approved—including
forty-six agreements, ten protocols, and four amendments—thirty-eight of
the agreements were accepted between the years 1993 and 1996 (Clinton's
first term), compared to twenty-two of them that received approval between
the years 1997 and 2000, during Clinton's second term. The agreements included those affecting forestry, chemical weapons, fisheries, marine pollution, border environmental cooperation, timber interests, weather concerns,
nuclear safety, mineral transportation, migratory birds, sea turtle preservation, waste management, humane trapping of mammals, air pollution, pesticides, military environmental matters, and polar bear management.[86] The
president maintained that sort of energy and focus on the global environment until the end of his second term.

Summary and Conclusion

As the first Democratic president since Franklin Roosevelt who served two
consecutive terms, Clinton had a number of important environmental
accomplishments:

1. Despite his lackluster first term, Clinton saw himself as an accomplished environmentalist, given the diversity and the number of issues
   he dealt with, establishing a pattern for presidents quite different from
   that of Franklin Roosevelt, who dealt with only a few limited issues
   during his twelve years in office. Moreover, much of Clinton's actions
   in support of the environment came during the latter part of his last
   year in office.[87] As he stated of his own accomplishments: "We have
   adopted the strongest air quality protections ever, improved the safety
   of our drinking water and food, cleaned up about three times as many
   toxic waste sites as the two previous administration combined . . . And
   yes, we have tried to protect a lot of our Nation's precious treasures. . . .
   It seems to me that these last seven years should finally have put to
   rest the idea that you can't have a strong economy and a cleaner, safer,
   more balanced environment. And I hope we will never have that
   debate again."[88]

2. More specifically, Bill Clinton can take credit for establishing twenty-
   two national monuments comprising some six million acres. In addi-

tion there were forty-two wildlife refuges created. And one environmentalist reminds us there were also 84 million acres underwater set
aside in the Hawaiian Islands.[89] This has made him the president who
preserved more land in national monuments in the lower forty-eight
states than any other president since Theodore Roosevelt.[90]

3. In addition, President Clinton banning the building of roads in more
   than 58 million acres of forest land in thirty-nine different states, protecting this forest land from development.

4. The president was also able to increase protective regulations over
   air and water, as well as restrict mining and grazing on public lands,
   allowing him to claim partial victories over some of the same environmental issue battles he had lost in his first term.[91]

5. Critics of these environmental accomplishments saw, however, that
   the president was somewhat inconsistent in what he did. In answer to
   this criticism, Paul Wapner suggested of Clinton's efforts that he was a
   president who made a promise to reduce greenhouse gases in his first
   Earth Day speech, yet it was still an even larger problem on his leaving
   office. Wapner then asked, What kind of "green" president does this?
   Wapner's answer to his own question was, "A real one." He indicated
   that both Carter and Clinton showed that "progressive presidents can
   enact good policies and accomplish much to enhance collective well-
   being. But when it comes to deep, structural challenges, they often
   make little progress. Like all presidents, they are beholden not simply
   to special interests but to broader paradigms that constrain their actions."[92] Yet, despite these problems, or perhaps because of them, the
   League of Conservation Voters, in assessing Clinton's environmental
   accomplishments, could still proclaim him as "one of the best of any
   president."[93]

6. Unquestionably, Clinton's overall interest in the environment over
   time is well established, as is his understanding of the complexity
   of environmental issues. As he stated in a speech to the League of
   Conservation Voters in 1998: "We've had a lot of exceedingly complex, as well as difficult—politically difficult but also intellectually
   complex—decisions we've had to make, working out our position on
   climate change, on how to deal with the northwest forest challenge,
   on whether we could figure out a way to save Yellowstone, on figuring
   out the genuine equities that lay underneath the big decision on Grand
   Staircase Escalante."[94]

7. While President Clinton's understanding of environmental policy making could not be criticized, his political strength and the leverage he had with Congress could be questioned and even labeled as insufficient to overcome Republican dominance of the policy process. Thus his environmental legacy often depended on finding ways to encourage policy acceptance while avoiding party confrontation within the Congress.

PART TWO

Presidents Having a Mixed Impact on the Environment

CHAPTER 6

Dwight D. Eisenhower

When Dwight Eisenhower became president, he exhibited what Fred Greenstein called a "hidden hand" political style where he preferred to work behind the scenes rather than get directly involved in partisan politics.[1] As the leader of the Republican Party, he emphasized a commitment to what he called the "New Republicanism," indicating early on that he would not further expand the role of the federal government. Among the characteristics Eisenhower brought with him into office was his emphasis on frugality and close attention to limiting federal spending. In the few cases where Congress supported a federal role in protecting the environment, Eisenhower's approach was to ensure that federal expenditures were limited and his preference was to see public-private partnerships prevail, although he was likely to support private interests over public interests. As reflected in a letter to his longtime friend Everett E. "Swede" Hazlett, Eisenhower preferred economic development to the arguments put forth by the conservationists.[2] Moreover, as Dennis Soden and Brent Steel argue, "Eisenhower clearly established a Republican inclination that would reappear with Ford, Reagan, and Bush (father and son). He favored development over the causes of the growing environmental protection and preservation movements."[3]

In contrast to the two Roosevelts and Harry Truman before him, Eisenhower favored a limited federal role in responding to environmental policy and preferred that conservation efforts be addressed at the state and local levels of government. For instance, several states including Texas and Louisiana claimed jurisdiction over oil-rich submerged lands off their coast. The Truman administration, backed by a Supreme Court decision (*United States v. California*, 1947), had asserted federal authority over these important resources.[4] Eisenhower's campaign rhetoric in an October 1952 speech supported the state's authority over federal control.[5] In an attempt to secure some form of state control over offshore lands, Republicans in Congress used the legislative process to promote their cause. The issue became a bitter conflict between Democrats and Republicans in Congress. Democratic senator Wayne Morse of Oregon filibustered for hours, arguing that the Republican pledge

was a "giveaway" of public (federal) lands to the states.[6] Republican senator Robert Taft of Ohio, on the other hand, argued the party's position that
submerged lands were under the authority of the states and that Supreme
Court opinions to the contrary were wrong.[7] President Eisenhower eventually signed the Submerged Lands Act. The act established what he considered
to be a valid and historical basis for the statement about submerged lands in
the 1952 Republican party platform, which promoted Eisenhower's states'
rights philosophy preventing federal encroachment.[8]

Another example of Eisenhower's environmental philosophy that supported state control rather than federal responsibility was in the way he dealt
with natural resources. While he would suggest the need to conserve limited
resources, he made it quite clear that he was more seriously concerned with
maintaining fiscal responsibility at the federal level rather than ensuring environmental quality. Consequently, the environmental policy arena would
involve a partnership between the federal and state governments as well as
private interests. As he stated in his annual budget message in 1955, "An important policy of this Government is to encourage an increased sharing by
State and local governments of our long-range development projects.... This
budget proposes the start of several new construction projects under such
partnership arrangements. Thus, we are continuing to develop our natural
resources at less cost to the Federal Government."[9]

Eisenhower's philosophy of limiting the federal role in environmental
affairs in deference to the states was further reflected in his opposition to
the Tennessee Valley Authority (TVA). The TVA, established by FDR during
the 1930s, was a major economic development and environmental project.
For FDR, the TVA served a dual environmental purpose, both providing an
important source of low-cost energy for American citizens during a time of
economic distress and creating employment opportunities in order to improve the depressed Tennessee Valley region.[10] It also reduced the environmental damage to the Tennessee Valley that resulted from lack of planning.
At the same time, millions of trees were planted in the process of building the
TVA. In the words of Andrea Gerlak and Patrick McGovern, "Within a decade
over seven hundred miles of the river were made navigable, two hundred
million trees had been planted in the upland areas, and low cost electricity
had been provided to almost every rural dweller in the region."[11] Yet Eisenhower viewed the TVA with outright disdain since it was a federal project
that should have been constructed and managed at the state level. In fact, his
first presidential budget "cut TVA's operations to the bare bones."[12] For Eisen-

hower, the TVA was an example of "creeping socialism," and as he admitted, "No one has worked harder than I have to stop the expansion of the area of TVA."[13] Moreover, when the issue of expanding the TVA emerged in the mid-1950s, Eisenhower repeated his often quoted philosophy that he "urged that either through state, municipal, or private enterprise" a new plant be built.[14]

Although later presidents would confront serious new environmental problems such as global warming and stratospheric ozone depletion, environmental policies during the 1950s were limited to issues related to public lands and emerging air and water quality concerns. The focus on public lands, in particular, was not a surprise to any student of the environment. As we discussed in the introduction, Theodore Roosevelt had set aside millions of acres of public land for national forests, national parks, and national monuments for future generations. This public lands legacy was continued by Franklin Roosevelt during his "golden age of conservation."[15]

The "Mission 66" public lands program, which was an initiative to improve the country's national park system for the public's benefit, became Eisenhower's primary environmental success story (discussed later in this chapter). However, Eisenhower did not show the same sentiment for wilderness areas. Thus a value conflict arose over an emerging wilderness bill that was being debated in Congress. It was attacked from the beginning by the U.S. Chamber of Commerce, by resource extraction interests such as the logging, mining, and cattle grazing lobbies, and by members of Congress from both parties who were sympathetic to these groups. While the Forest Service and the National Park Service opposed the bill, it was supported by the Fish and Wildlife Service and the Kennedy administration, resulting in an eight-year battle until President Johnson signed the Wilderness Act in 1964 (see chapter 2).[16]

Another area of conflict arose over the construction of reservoirs and dams to generate hydroelectric power in the Upper Colorado Basin. Groups including the Wilderness Society and the Sierra Club engaged in active opposition to some of these projects. Conservationists and Eisenhower were involved in an ongoing philosophical conflict.[17] Conservationists were concerned about the impact of constructing reservoirs and dams on land controlled by the national park system, and with the flooding of Echo Canyon in Utah's Dinosaur National Monument in particular. According to Christopher McGrory Klyza, the "preservation movement viewed this proposal as a critical threat to what they had achieved in terms of protecting nature. If a dam could flood this national monument, no national park, no national monu-

also enthusiastically supported statehood for Alaska, seeing it as an abundant source of natural resources. Consequently, it would not be until the next decade, with the rise of postindustrial society, that Americans would begin to focus on quality of life issues that included environmental protection.[28]

Political Communication

Dwight Eisenhower won election in 1952 and reelection in 1956. As Tatalovich and Wattier explain, while the 1952 presidential campaign was concerned primarily with the "Korean War, corruption, and communism," his reelection in 1956 "was essentially a personal victory largely devoid of issues."[29] Although Eisenhower expressed his concern about the conservation of natural resources, his political communication revealed that his attention was centered on other domestic and foreign policy issues.

Mary Stuckey argues that Eisenhower was a popular president in part because he employed a positive approach when directing his attention to the American viewer on television.[30] However, as Samuel Kernell characterized the president's communication style, "Eisenhower's famous syntactical convolutions left reporters scratching their heads and conferring among themselves after a [press] conference to determine what the president had said.... Eisenhower's press conference sputterings were hardly telegenic. After the novelty wore off, the networks rarely broadcast the entire conference."[31] In any event, Eisenhower was a pioneer in employing the media in ways useful to his presidency. Innovative media-driven instrumental acts included setting up a television studio in the White House and using New York media consultants and televised fireside chats and press conferences.[32]

During Eisenhower's first term in office, he used the annual State of the Union message to convey several of his concerns, such as the need to develop a partnership between federal and state governments and local communities and the importance of developing fiscal responsibility in government spending and balanced budgets. His concern about the conservation of natural resources and their wise development fit within the environmental philosophy that he articulated in his first State of the Union message delivered on February 2, 1953. Here he informed the nation about his preference for public-private partnerships: "The best natural resources program for America will not result from exclusive dependence on Federal bureaucracy. It will involve a partnership of the States and local communities, private citizens, and the Federal Government, working together."[33]

Eisenhower was reelected in 1956 and began his second term with an emphasis on a healthy economy, fiscal responsibility, and foreign policy. In the words of Lammers and Genovese, his election "was more a reaffirmation of his strong emphasis on foreign policy and his personal popularity than evidence of support for new initiatives."[34] As far as the environment was concerned, Eisenhower continued to limit his concern to the issue of natural resource conservation although the need to preserve water resources began to emerge in his speeches. However, he reiterated his philosophy of limiting the federal role and encouraging public-private partnerships. As Eisenhower indicated in his first State of the Union message of his second term in office: "Our soil, water, mineral, forest, fish, and wildlife resources are being conserved and improved more efficiently. . . . But they must not be the concern of the Federal Government alone. State and local entities and private enterprise should be encouraged to participate in such projects. . . . Domestic and industrial uses clearly demand the closest kind of cooperation and partnership between municipalities, States and the Federal Government."[35]

Eisenhower spent the majority of his 1961 farewell address discussing the progress that had been made during his administration in domestic and foreign policy. He encouraged his contemporaries to think about the future of the nation's resources: "As we peer into society's future, we . . . must avoid the impulse to live only for today, plundering, for our own ease and convenience, the precious resources of tomorrow."[36]

Unlike other modern presidents to his time, Eisenhower never fully used the power resources of his office to speak on behalf of the environment. Research by Susan Hunter and Victoria Noonan informs us that Eisenhower delivered few speeches about the environment, and when he did they were limited in their scope."[37]

Legislative Leadership

During Eisenhower's first two years in office, Republicans controlled both houses of Congress. It was a period when few, if any, environmental initiatives emerged on the legislative agenda. Subsequent to the congressional elections of 1954, Democrats gained majorities in the House and the Senate and maintained these majorities throughout Eisenhower's years in office. During this time, three important pieces of environmental legislation became law—namely, the 1955 Air Pollution Control Act, the 1956 Federal-Aid Highway Act, and the 1956 Federal Water Pollution Control Act Amendments.

The 1955 Air Pollution Control Act, while important, was limited in certain ways. Air quality was not a new issue to government and health officials, but by the mid-1950s the federal government was compelled to take some action to preserve clean air. This action was encouraged by several major public health events that had occurred. In 1930 sixty-three people died in Belgium due to a thermal inversion, while in 1948 twenty persons succumbed in Donora, Pennsylvania, to the adverse affects of poor air quality. Four years later, sixteen hundred people died in the dangerous fog of London.[38] In January 1955, when Eisenhower presented a special message to Congress about public health, he included a provision to increase financial support for research into the impact of air pollution on public health. When Congress responded to the air pollution issue by passing the 1955 Air Pollution Control Act, Eisenhower signed it, implicitly acknowledging a limited federal role, while putting the burden of addressing the problem on states and municipalities.

The interstate highway system that emerged in the 1950s was an important infrastructure improvement as it increased the linkages across the country. The Eisenhower administration considered the interstate highway system—later known as the 1956 Federal-Aid Highway Act—to be a successful program.[39] However, congressional testimony included little, if any, commentary concerning the impact of the highway system on current and future conditions of the environment including wilderness and wildlife domains.[40] Moreover, the enhancement of the highway system, along with a growing automobile industry, set the stage for increasing dependence on fossil fuels and the onset of air quality problems.

Up until the late 1940s, water policy was considered a state and local problem. However, as water pollution problems intensified, the federal government became inexorably drawn into the water quality debate. In 1948 Congress passed and President Truman signed the Water Pollution Control Act, which established a federal presence in water pollution policy making, although it was limited to technical assistance and providing limited financial contributions for research.[41] In 1955, Congress debated the merits of renewing the legislation. Despite concerns raised about extending grants versus loans to local communities to build sewage treatment plants and the extent to which the federal government should be involved in water pollution policy making, as well as concerns raised by industry over establishing water quality standards, Congress passed and Eisenhower signed the Federal Water Pollution Control Act in July 1956. Although citing the importance of the legislation, Eisenhower stated at the signing of the bill that he felt the legislation went beyond what he preferred regarding the federal government's role in providing grants to local communities. In doing so, he stated that "I urge that no community with sufficient resources to construct a needed sewage treatment project without Federal aid, postpone that construction simply because of the prospect of a possible Federal grant."[42]

Eisenhower's approach in limiting the federal role in policy making and the issue of water pollution met head-on with congressional efforts to increase federal funding for municipal sewage treatment plants. Three years after the president signed the 1956 Federal Water Pollution Control Act, both the House and Senate sponsored legislation to support sewage plant projects in communities around the country, an action that contradicted Eisenhower's preference to reduce the federal role in support of sewage treatment plants altogether. When congressional leaders realized that Eisenhower would probably use a pocket veto in response to the legislation, they decided to wait until the following year to submit the legislation for formal approval of the president. When he eventually refused to sign the bill, Eisenhower stated unequivocally that "because water pollution is a uniquely local blight, primary responsibility for solving the problem lies not with the Federal Government but rather must be assumed and exercised, as it has been, by State and local governments."[43] Although a majority of Democrats opposed Eisenhower's position, they were unable to obtain the required two-thirds vote to override his veto of the legislation.

Congress and the president did work together to pass several other bills that, although limited in their impact, continued the role of the two national institutions in environmental policy. Eisenhower signed the Outer Continental Shelf Act in 1953 that ensured that mineral resources under the ocean floor (as far as twelve miles from the U.S. coastline) would be under the authority of the federal government. The following year, he signed the Water Facilities Act. This legislation established a nationwide program (originally limited to seventeen states in the West) to deal more effectively with water conservation. The new program provided loans for farms and ranches. Eisenhower saw this legislation as groundbreaking, stating that "this legislation... establishes for the first time a nation-wide program of conservation practices based on the concept that farms, streams, forests, and towns are all interrelated parts of a watershed."[44]

Administrative Actions

During the Eisenhower administration, environmental appointments had a profound effect on the environmental policy domain. Sherman Adams, selected as chief of staff, became a powerful "assistant president." Adams, former governor of New Hampshire, had an environmental philosophy that paralleled that of Eisenhower. He supported conservation measures related to natural resources but agreed that regulatory measures should be carried out by states and localities rather than the federal government.

The Department of the Interior and the Department of Agriculture were the primary centers of environmental activity. Eisenhower appointed Douglas McKay to serve as secretary of the interior during Eisenhower's first term. McKay was succeeded by Fred Seaton during Eisenhower's second term. The president appointed Ezra Taft Benson of Utah to the position of secretary of agriculture. Benson served in this position through both terms of the Eisenhower presidency. Within the Department of Agriculture, Richard McArdle served as chief of the Forest Service.

Douglas McKay, an automobile dealer and governor of the state of Oregon, was selected to run the Interior Department since he was familiar with the politics of the West, a region so important to the nation's resource base. Eisenhower selected McKay because he needed someone familiar with the conflict over water resources particularly in the West and saw him as one of two westerners who "would be deemed by its people to be impartial in his administration of the affairs of the department and in helping to settle these differences."[45] Nonetheless, McKay exhibited personal traits and policy preferences that created problems for the administration. As McKay was characterized by two observers of the Eisenhower administration, "He suffered from foot-in-mouth affliction, depended on his subordinates to run the department, and proved to be an ineffective defender of administration programs."[46] McKay was a central figure in two embarrassing appointments involving his department. The first was Tom Lyon, who on the advice of McKay was appointed by the president to the position of director of the Bureau of Mines. Eisenhower was confronted by immediate public protest and controversy. In addition to opposition to his appointment by the United Mine Workers, Lyon's testimony before the Senate's Interior and Insular Affairs Committee revealed his inability to enforce mine safety regulations with which he disagreed. Instead, Lyon preferred that regulatory action take place at the state level rather than the federal government.[47] Moreover, Lyon's association with the Anaconda Copper Company suggested a financial relationship that tainted his objectively and ultimately his nomination, which was withdrawn by the president.[48] The second controversy involved Marion Clawson, director of the Bureau of Land Management, a holdover from the

Truman administration. As reported by Herbert Parmet, McKay removed Clawson from the position and then he publicly stated that Clawson had resigned and that he would be given a secondary position in the administration.[49] Clawson publically argued that he had not resigned from his position. Eisenhower was compelled to change his organizational procedures in response to these kinds of embarrassing instances of executive agency nominations and appointments.

During his tenure as secretary of the interior, McKay also came under fire from Democrats who criticized his prodevelopment orientation. McKay became known as "Giveaway McKay" as he tried to terminate several wildlife refuges and hand over Nevada's fish and game department control to the Desert Game Reserve. Not being a strong advocate of public power projects, McKay also attempted to turn over public energy resources to the private sector.[50] Although Eisenhower stood behind his interior secretary's efforts, he was somewhat relieved when McKay decided to leave his post in 1956, after his unsuccessful run for a Senate seat.

One area where McKay received favorable reviews from environmentalists was his involvement with the Mission 66 public lands program, named in honor of the fiftieth anniversary of the founding of the National Park Service. The idea of improving land conditions in the nation's parks began in 1954 when Eisenhower heard of concerns about the parks. In a letter to McKay in 1955, Eisenhower expressed "considerable ignorance" about the national park system and the problems of overuse.[51] On the basis of a substantive conversation with the president, McKay began a thorough review of the national park system. According to White House deputy cabinet secretary Bradley Patterson, those operating the National Park Service wanted time to put together a ten-year nationwide plan to present to the cabinet. When the park service administrators were ready to make their presentation in 1956, National Park Service director Connie Wirth, along with several park staff, made a compelling presentation to interior secretary McKay. McKay was impressed with the presentation and asked the president to revise his recently submitted budget to increase funding for the new Mission 66 program to improve and preserve the national park system. Patterson points out that "park service veterans still talk of the 1956–66 period as one of the most exciting times of improvement in the national park system.[52]

McKay's successor, Fred Seaton, a midwestern media mogul, had occupied several administrative posts prior to his appointment as secretary of the interior during Eisenhower's second term. According to Pach and Richardson,

Seaton was a supporter of Eisenhower's notion of Modern Republicanism, and was able to provide a balance between environmentalists and resource interests in an effective manner.[53] As interior secretary, Seaton was very involved in an important environmental and geographical change facing the country—namely, statehood for the vast territory of Alaska. As Eisenhower characterized the movement toward statehood: "Proponents of Alaskan statehood pointed to its size . . . and to its resources . . . forests . . . hydroelectric potential . . . coal. . . . Beyond this, an intensified search for oil by American companies, operating under enabling legislation and governmental leases, began in the mid-1950s. . . . By May of 1958, private oil companies had spent more than $30 million on exploration in the territory. Alaskans began to argue that Alaska's emergence from territory to state would spur the development of these enormous natural resources."[54]

Alaskan statehood was viewed by the Eisenhower administration as an important addition to the United States due to its critical geopolitical location for national security as well as its store of natural resources. Moreover, in a nod toward Alaskan officials and reflective of the administration's philosophy regarding the relationship between the federal and state governments, interior secretary Seaton articulated his views about conflicting governmental responsibility for Alaska's natural resources in a letter to budget director Maurice Stans. In supporting statehood for Alaska (requiring presidential action on congressional legislation to that effect), Seaton stated that it was the intention of the Interior Department that "administration, management, and conservation of these resources in the national interest" be transferred from Washington to the State of Alaska.[55]

In addition to the Interior Department, the Department of Agriculture served as the other "twin pillar" of Eisenhower's environmental governing apparatus. Agricultural secretary Ezra Taft Benson was a conservative member of the Council of the Twelve Apostles of the Church of Jesus Christ of Latter-day Saints (the Mormon Church) and had a background in farm cooperatives and agricultural marketing. However, he was considered an unpopular and divisive figure within the administration.[56] When given a choice between development and conservation, Benson sided with development. Practically, he supported industrial interests over those of environmental or public health concerns. His primary interest in agriculture was in research and farm production, allowing "departmental scientists to continue to develop chemicals and methods for increasing productivity. Little interest or concern was given to the toxic effects these substances were contributing to rivers and streams, thus contaminating fish and wildlife."[57] As Schapsmeier and Schapsmeier argue, "At a time when ecology was not yet a popular subject, the established scientists in the Department of Agriculture defended the use of pesticides and weed control sprays as both safe and necessary" while agriculture secretary Benson "sincerely believed that with proper safeguards there was no danger involved from residues that remained in the water or soil.[58] In another instance, at a meeting arranged by chief of staff Sherman Adams, Secretary Benson met with representatives of the Forest Industries Council, National Lumber Manufacturers Association, American Paper and Pulp Association, and the American Pulpwood Association, who were concerned about regulatory pressures on their industries.[59] The outcome of the meeting was that the Forest Service was to eliminate regulation and cooperate with the interested industries.

Benson's environmental philosophy was also demonstrated by actions regarding two other issues—namely, grazing policy and a soil bank plan. The former involved stock owners who wanted to expand grazing rights on public lands and who sought support from Benson for a Uniform Federal Grazing Act. According to Forest Service chief Richard McArdle, Benson stated to the assistant secretary of agriculture, "These are our friends. Give them what they want."[60] However, protests by conservationists and timber interests that felt threatened succeeded in compelling Secretary Benson and chief of staff Adams to protect the public lands from the grazing interests.

The soil bank plan dealt with agricultural surpluses and farm prices. One part of the plan involved government payments to farmers who set aside crop acreage. The plan was supported by Eisenhower but opposed by Benson, who was concerned about the impact of government payments to farmers and the impact on the federal budget.[61] The second part of the plan involved a conservation reserve program where millions of acres of cropland were set aside by farmers on a voluntary basis. This part of the program focused on cropland that was set aside for a specified period of time and used for "conservation practices" including the planting of trees and grasses.[62] On the one hand, some observers of the program argued that wildlife, in particular grassland birds, benefited from the new habitat that had been created. On the other hand, critics of the program argued that it resulted in increased soil erosion due to more intensive use of existing croplands.[63]

Before serving as Eisenhower's chief of the Forest Service, McArdle had served as the dean of the College of Forestry at the University of Idaho and had worked in the Forest Service. McArdle was associated with an important piece of legislation related to public lands—namely, the Multiple Use–Sustained Yield Act of 1960. Over the years, different resource users, especially the timber industry, sought to secure priority within the public lands domain. The Multiple Use Mining Act of 1955 provided the Forest Service with the authority to protect timber reserves that were not related to mining.[64] This act, along with multiple-use legislation offered by Senator Hubert Humphrey in 1956, set the stage for the codification of public land use. During the legislative debate, conservationist Democrats were successful in ensuring that conservation was given priority over sustained yield in the legislation that was eventually passed by Congress and signed by President Eisenhower.[65] The legislation set forth the principle that national forests would be administered for outdoor recreation, range, timber, watershed, and fish and wildlife. More importantly, in the words of one observer of the process, "The Multiple Use law was intended not only to give legislative sanction to long-standing programs and policies but also to forestall the timber industry from continuing to demand first priority, as it had ever since 1897."[66]

Environmental Diplomacy

The Eisenhower administration's involvement in international politics was oriented primarily toward Cold War issues. As Richard Neustadt has argued, "Throughout Eisenhower's years in office there can be no doubt that peace, in the sense of a fundamental easing of the threat of war, was the broad objective he had most in mind, the one that stirred and interested him most, the one for which he felt himself particularly fitted."[67] At the same time, Eisenhower was well aware of the attendant problems associated with a world power that was also an increasingly consumption-oriented society. The United States required the material resources to support its internationalist orientation and its military establishment. In this regard, as Eisenhower stated to a friend, "No other nation is exhausting its irreplaceable resources so rapidly as is ours. Unless we are careful to build up and maintain a great group of international friends ready to trade with us, where do we hope to get all the materials that we will one day need as our rate of consumption continues and accelerates?"[68] Yet while acknowledging his concerns about what he saw as a rapid diminution of the country's natural resources, he suggested that he was more concerned about resource development and consumption rather than conservation.

During Eisenhower's tenure in office, several important international environmental treaties were signed by him and ratified by the U.S. Senate. These treaties included the 1954 International Convention for the Protection of Pollution of the Sea by Oil, the 1958 Convention on Fishing and Conservation of the Living Resources of the High Seas, and the 1959 Antarctic Treaty. While the first two treaties dealt with pollution and marine life, the latter agreement concerned the establishment of a nonmilitarized use of Antarctica where international scientific research and cooperation would occur.

The 1959 Antarctic Treaty was an important step in terms of both environmental and national security concerns. As Steinar Andresen reports, science and diplomacy followed parallel tracks in the late 1950s that resulted in a treaty acceptable to the twelve countries scientifically and politically interested in Antarctica.[69] The treaty was preceded by the International Geophysical Year (1957–58) that involved scientific activities and eventually set the stage for consultations and eventually a treaty between the twelve interested parties.[70] The treaty affecting Antarctica was a diplomatic effort to ensure peaceful scientific exploration of Antarctica. While the international agreement prohibited nuclear explosions and the storage of radioactive waste in the area, its significant environmental impact was a commitment by the signatories to work toward the "preservation and conservation of living resources in Antarctica" mandated in Article IX of the treaty. As Long, Cabral, and Vandivort explain, the "Antarctic Treaty laid the cornerstone for a series of agreements composing the Antarctic Treaty System, an international regime that was especially significant because the agreements served as preventative measures designed to address environmental issues in advance of potential threats."[71]

Summary and Conclusion

In the words of two political observers of Eisenhower's presidency, "During his eight years in office Eisenhower had many opportunities to act on his preference for dealing with foreign rather than domestic issues."[72] When Dwight Eisenhower assumed the presidency in 1953, the United States was involved in a Cold War with the Soviet Union and engaged in combat on the Korean peninsula. Eisenhower was now occupied with maintaining an internationalist orientation for the United States and with maintaining a healthy economy at home. This included containment of the Soviet Union abroad and management of domestic concerns about alleged communist infiltration of government at home. Such concerns had been raised by Senator Joseph McCarthy, a Wisconsin Republican who argued that communism had infiltrated the U.S. government.

Eisenhower's commitment to environmental protection reflected a cautious approach in this policy domain. During his two terms in office, the president was more involved with other domestic and foreign priorities. Eisenhower's record can be summarized as follows:

1. The president's environmental philosophy reflected his preference that the federal government should support the states and localities and limit its direct involvement in environmental policy making.

2. Eisenhower used the State of the Union message to convey and reaffirm his philosophy of supporting public-private partnerships while limiting federal involvement in environmental policy.

3. Although he signed air and water pollution legislation, Eisenhower did so with little fanfare. He is remembered for his comment that water pollution, in particular, was a uniquely local blight, thus reaffirming his emphasis on putting the burden of environmental policy making on state and local governments. Moreover, although Eisenhower considered the 1956 Federal-Aid Highway Act that established the interstate highway system a successful program, he failed to consider or understand the implications of more automobiles, dependence on fossil fuels, and air quality issues.

4. The president brought into his administration individuals who lacked strong environmental credentials. These appointments included Douglas McKay as secretary of the interior and Ezra Taft Benson as secretary of agriculture. Both McKay, who became known as "Giveaway McKay," and Benson were characterized by their overt prodevelopment orientation.

5. Although Eisenhower supported several important international environment agreements, including the 1959 Antarctic Treaty, his environmental philosophy was tied to his primary objective as president—namely, to promote and ensure international peace. Hence, his limited attention given to the conservation of natural resources could be seen as an indirect outcome of his international diplomacy.

6. Despite the progress made during the administration of Franklin D. Roosevelt, environmentalism in the 1950s could be considered an issue that was not a primary concern of Eisenhower. A broad commitment to environmental protection would have to await the publication of Rachel Carson's *Silent Spring* in 1962, the rise of the modern environmental movement of the 1960s, and a more progressive president who would be willing to address important environmental issues.

CHAPTER 7

Gerald Ford

Gerald Ford could in many ways be thought of as a *balancer*, weighing the need to respond to environmental concerns, on the one hand, against the necessity to seek additional energy resources and to stabilize the economy, on the other. Yet more often than not, Ford would allow those other concerns to outweigh environmental needs. As he pointed out, "Even with a strong conservation program, we will still have to mine more coal, drill for more oil and gas, and build more power plants and refineries. Each of these measures will have an impact on the environment . . . yet this can be minimized . . . [by] careful analysis and planning, with broad public participation."[1]

Although environmental concerns did not always appear to be Gerald Ford's top priority, this president's interests in nature, unlike Nixon, lay in conserving basic resources rather than tackling a full range of environmental issues. His concerns reflected more those of the conservationist presidents who served prior to Richard Nixon. He was particularly concerned about preserving clean air and water and protecting public lands in a proper balance with other needs. Ford's approach to the environment was best captured in a speech he gave on July 3, 1975, when he dedicated the National Environmental Research Center built by the federal government on the campus of the University of Cincinnati. As he stated in the dedicatory speech: "I cherish the out-of-doors, and I stand with those who fight to preserve what is best in our environment." Now if the president had ended his speech with this phrase, one would have concluded that he was fully in support of conserving natural resources, but he then added a modifying caveat, suggesting that as president he could "never lose sight of another insistent aspect of our environment—the economic needs of the American people. Your security, your well-being must enter into every decision I make—and it does." Then he went on: "I pursue the goal of clean air and pure water, *but* I must also pursue the objective of maximum jobs and continued economic progress. . . . If accomplishing every worthy environmental objective would slow down our effort to regain energy independence and a stronger economy, then of necessity I must weigh all factors involved [italics added]."[2] Conservation, in other words, did not seem to be Ford's highest priority. Gerald Ford is the only modern-day president, as far as we can tell, who considered the economy as an integral part of the environment.

This is not to say that the environment was not an honest concern of this president. For example, during the dedication of the facility in Cincinnati, Gerald Ford gave his audience some insights into how much the environment was really worth to the Ford administration. The president indicated that the newly built research facility cost thirty million dollars to construct, or approximately 113 million dollars in current-day dollars. Though this single project was not a great percentage of the federal budget, it represented one of the few projects in 1976 that Ford had fully funded. There were additional aspects of the environment on which he wanted to have some impact. The president hoped, for example, that through the 1970s his administration would make a "cleaner and healthy environment a matter of the highest national priority," and then he added for illustrative emphasis: "And I should add, as long as I have anything to say about it, this country's symbol will never be an empty beer can in a river of garbage."[3]

Despite what Ford claimed, we could not call Gerald Ford a Richard Nixon "environmentalist"—a president who will be remembered as the quintessential environmental president who had made major contributions to the environmental movement, despite his own questioning of the overall importance of environmentalism and environmentalists' contribution to public policy. Ford could best be thought of as a conservationist president of modest accomplishment.

One reason why President Ford may not have put more focus on environmental preservation was because of what he felt the immediate seriousness of the other events he was facing at the time. The 1973 oil crisis, the high levels of inflation, and the ensuing recession posed a constant challenge to his presidency. The energy and oil crisis of the 1970s began in October 1973 as the Organization of the Petroleum Exporting Countries (OPEC) announced that it would not sell oil to nations that had supported Israel in the conflict that had previously arisen between Israel and Syria and Egypt. OPEC also used its price-setting capabilities to raise the price of oil several times higher than the rate of inflation to compensate for their simultaneous decrease in oil production.

As a result of the energy crisis, consumer demand grew for more fuel-efficient products.

To meet this new demand for energy, taxes were levied on gas, conservation programs were implemented, and domestic drilling options were explored. President Ford submitted legislation to allow more power plants to convert to coal. He felt that the United States could engage in "greater coal use without sacrificing cleaner air goals."[4] Ford used his own authority as president to raise prices on imported oil and other petroleum products. In addition he launched a new program to encourage oil production from the outer continental shelf and from the Naval Petroleum Oil Reserves in Alaska. This was his primary priority, feeling that the environmental risks tied to either of these programs was negligible.[5]

So eager was Gerald Ford to do something about inflation, he made a mass appeal calling on all citizens to united in response against inflation. To lead this "war" against inflation, Ford established a citizens' committee to come up with strategies to win the war, and he also coined that now-famous acronym for the campaign—"WIN," the acronym for "Whip Inflation Now!" It was a campaign complete with red-and-white "Win Buttons," one of which the president wore to address the people and Congress. The buttons and phrase were soon discarded, however, since they too frequently became a focus of late-night comedian's jokes. A relieved chair of the citizens' committee, Sylvia Porter, observed: "As an acronym it is dead and God bless it."[6]

President Ford felt that doing anything meaningful regarding the environment would take more than the federal government going it alone. As he stated on July 3, 1975: "I am convinced that an active partnership between the Federal, State, and local agencies is the proper formula for assuring the future success of our environmental efforts. This is not idle theorizing. Such cooperation has already brought about in many, many areas of our country a remarkable improvement in air and water quality."[7] Ford, like so many other Republican presidents, was also reluctant to support federal regulation if it interfered with the states' efforts to improve the environment. He thus insisted on standards to preserve the environment that were initiated by the states.

The president did show that he was not alone in his attitude of encouraging governments at all levels to respond to the environment. He was, in fact, in full harmony with the Republican position on the environment as stated in the 1976 party platform. The platform stated that Republicans supported what the Supreme Court had stated in the 1970s regarding air pollution, namely, that the solution to this environmental dilemma should come from "the level of government closest to the problem."[8] The platform further

stated, "We are proud of the progress that the current Republican Administration has made toward bringing pollution of water, land, and air under
control. We will meet the challenges that remain by stepping up efforts to
perfect our understanding of pollutants and the means for reducing their effects. Moreover, as the nation develops new energy sources and technologies,
we must insure that they meet safe environmental standards."[9] This portion
of the platform convinced Gerald Ford that he would probably have no difficulty in securing support for his efforts from his fellow Republicans. It would
be the Democrats and the environmentalists that would offer the most opposition to the Ford position.

Consistent with his attitude toward government's involvement in protecting the environment, President Ford proclaimed Earth Day on March 21,
1975, stating, "The earth will continue to regenerate its life sources only as
long as we and all the peoples of the world do our part to conserve its natural
resources. It is a responsibility which every human being shares. Through
voluntary action, each of us can join in building a productive land in harmony with nature."[10] Ford also saw Earth Day as an opportunity to instruct
the people individually concerning the environment, asking that "special
attention be given to educational efforts directed toward protecting and enhancing our life-giving environment."[11] He hoped that if the public were fa-
miliarized with environmental preservation, each individual would become
more responsible for his or her immediate environment, relying less on the
federal government. To President Ford, this education also meant "striving
for an environment that not only sustains life but also enriches the lives of
people everywhere—harmonizing the works of man and nature."[12] But Ford
went beyond what Nixon had done and not only reinstated Earth Day but
created Earth Week as well, declaring the week of April 22–28, 1976, to be set
aside as Earth Week, asking all government officials, civic organizations, and
businesses to engage in "at least one new effort during this week for a cleaner,
safer, healthier environment."[13]

Political Communication

By the time Gerald Ford became president, conditions had changed from the
Nixon years. No longer was the public in overwhelming support of the environment. Public interest in environmental protection had, as one author put
it, "declined or remained stagnant" compared to what it had been during the
1970s.[14] Nor was the public any longer fully in support of the presidency

after Ford had issued the presidential pardon to Richard Nixon. In August 1974, when Gerald Ford first took office, public support for the president reached 71 percent, but by April 1975, eight months after the pardon was issued, public support for him had dropped to an all-time low of 37 percent. Ford's average support from the American public as of 1976 was an unimpressive 46 percent, which, as Jeffrey Jones contends, was "one of the lowest since World War II."[15] Ford's approval rating even among rank-and-file Republicans was so low that it opened up a spirited challenge from Ronald Reagan for the 1976 Republican nomination. Reagan wanted to see the party move farther to the political right, and given his advanced age of sixty-five, Reagan felt this might be his last opportunity to put his imprint on the party. While Ford led Reagan by 61 percent to 35 percent among Republicans in general, he scored only a narrow victory over Reagan among the convention delegates.[16]

Of the many differences voiced during the primary campaign between Ford and Reagan, conservation was not one of the issues. Rather, Republican conservatism, détente with the Soviet Union, the Strategic Arms Limitation Talks (SALT I), relations with China, and Ford's pardon of those who had avoided the Vietnam draft were the principle issues that divided the two opponents.[17] Reagan was so successful that he came within 117 delegates of unseating a sitting president at the Kansas City convention.[18] These primary election battles between the two of them, Ford long felt, was the major reason for his defeat at the hands of Jimmy Carter. In addition, of course, it strengthened the hold that Ronald Reagan had on the Republican Party, allowing him to establish himself for the next presidential contest in 1980 as the candidate to defeat. In addition to the challenge offered by Reagan, voters questioned whether Ford's actions in pardoning Richard Nixon was in exchange for Nixon facilitating his becoming president. This speculation was fueled further by a meeting that Nixon's chief of staff, Alexander Haig, had with Ford while the latter was still vice president, regarding the actions that Ford might take respecting Nixon.[19] There does not seem to be confirming evidence, however, that Ford was willing to comply with such a request.[20]

Ford's stated reason for pardoning Richard Nixon, he insisted, was his belief that a Nixon trial would disrupt the "tranquility to which this nation has been restored" and that such a trial would "cause prolonged and divisive debate over the propriety of exposing to further punishment and degradation a man who has already paid the unprecedented penalty of relinquishing the highest elective office of the United States."[21] While this pardon led to Ford's own political downfall, it did give him greater freedom of movement to focus attention on other policy matters including the environment.

While the environment to President Ford was not as pressing a concern as energy development or the maintaining of a strong economy, it was not something he could totally ignore. He did express particular concern for the environment when pollution posed a potential threat to the children of America, yet it was still unclear how troubled he really was when a polluted environment came in conflict with the need to find oil and produce energy. The president indicated, "We care about the air you breathe, the water you will drink, the land that you will need. It is a message about environment that says to all of us: America—handle with care!"[22] Ford's central message here was that the environment must be "handled with care" by future generations. Yet it was unclear whether this meant he was eager to spend the allotted money to fully protect the environment for the future, or whether he was more interested in encouraging Americans to do what he praised Alaskans for doing, namely, seeking "self-sufficiency in energy" and to "produc[ing] more oil in harmony with appropriate environmental concerns." He did not detail what these "environmental concerns" really were.[23]

In his 1975 State of the Union address, Gerald Ford gave us another example of this conflict between preserving the environment and seeking sources of energy. In it, he talked of the need to use coal: "Use of our most abundant domestic resource—coal—is severely limited," he indicated. "We must strike a reasonable compromise on environmental concerns with coal. I am submitting Clean Air [Act] amendments which will allow greater coal use without sacrificing clean air goals."[24] It was not always clear whether that sort of balance would protect the environment. In fact, if the environment got in the way of energy development, President Ford would make certain his decision supported energy. In 1974 Ford met with coastal state governors concerning oil and gas development on the outer continental shelf. In his statement to the governor, President Ford stated, "I believe that the Outer Continental Shelf (OCS) oil and gas deposits can provide the largest single source of increased domestic energy during the years when we need it most. The OCS can supply this energy with less damage to the environment and at a lower cost to the U.S. economy than any other alternative. We must proceed with a program that is designed to develop these resources."[25] Ford was careful to adopt the program that would "increase our domestic production of oil and gas" in response to the energy crisis, while at the same time protecting the environment from "unacceptable risk."[26]

As party leader, Gerald Ford confronted a struggling post-Watergate political party. The platform for 1976 supported the idea that Ford had previously indicated, namely, that he should be a *balancer* of interests. The platform stated that "environmental concern must be brought into balance with the needs for industrial and economic growth," which Ford held to firmly. Elsewhere in the platform it was reemphasized that "public land areas should not be closed to exploration for minerals or for mining without an overriding national interest."[27] The platform also promised a "clean and healthy natural environment" as the "rightful heritage of every American." To guarantee this, the Republicans pledged to "provide for proper development of resources, safeguards for clean air and water, and protection and enhancement of our recreation and scenic areas."[28] Ford was fully in support of this aspect of the Republican platform.

Legislative Leadership

President Ford delivered a limited number of speeches to Congress that focused on the environment. In those speeches, he usually always added the caveat that the president needed to pay attention to other concerns in addition to the environment. His speech of December 12, 1974, was typical. The president said, "Today, millions of our citizens share a new vision of the future in which natural systems can be protected, pollution can be controlled, and our natural heritage will be preserved. . . . The crusade to improve the quality of our human environment has begun." But undercutting those words, he added, "Another valuable lesson was learned during the energy crisis last winter when . . . it became clear that we cannot achieve all our environmental and all our energy and economic goals at the same time. . . . By rejecting the extremes—by accepting the need for balance—we held fast to the accomplishments of the past and looked with new perspective toward the imperatives of the future."[29]

We must add, however, that some important environmental legislation did come about during the Ford years as a result of the president's own efforts. As a former National Park ranger,[30] for example, Gerald Ford set aside additional public lands as wilderness areas, but he did so rather carefully. As he stated to Congress on December 4, 1974: "Today we reach another milestone in this unfolding story. The Executive Branch has now completed the initial, decade-long review prescribed by law in 1964, and as a result of this survey, I am hereby proposing 37 new additions to the Wilderness System. If accepted by the Congress, these recommendations would add an additional nine million primeval acres to the system."[31] But when he created a wilderness area within a national forest in Colorado, he was even more cautious. In signing the bill in December 1975, he hesitated and explained that he had three concerns about creating "wilderness areas" in national parks. He did not favor designating forest areas as wilderness if people were interested in using the land in some other way, nor did he want to name a segment of public land as a wilderness area if it did not have boundaries and follow "recognizable natural features and be located to facilitate protection of the wilderness." Finally, he suggested that in the National Forest System that "wilderness" ought to be a category that can be "traded off" for other more valuable resources such as "recreation," "wildlife," or "mineral resources."[32]

President Ford ended his presidency having protected 3.1 million acres of public land, which was far less than had been protected by a number of other presidents. For example, Lyndon Johnson set aside 9.9 million acres in public land, while Jimmy Carter secured 60 million acres of land for the United States.[33]

In addition to the wilderness protection Gerald Ford secured in 1974, he also signed legislation that focused on the need to protect clean water, including the Safe Drinking Water Act of 1974, a bill that allowed the Environmental Protection Agency to set standards for drinking water, and the Deepwater Port Act of 1974, an act that authorized the secretary of transportation to issue licenses to construct, own, and operate deepwater ports for the importing of oil. In addition, Ford signed an energy act that same year—the Energy Research Reorganization Act—that established the Nuclear Regulatory Commission (NRC), the Energy Resource and Development Administration (ERDA), and an energy resource council made up of members from the ERDA, the budget office, and the secretary of the interior.[34] This bill was aimed at continuing research on alternative energy sources derived from nuclear materials and fossil fuels, as well as helping to "expand a program of environmental control technology and assessment of environmental and health effects of energy technologies."[35]

Two years later Gerald Ford signed a more diversified number of bills that reached out even further to support various areas of the environment. The most important of these acts was the Coastal Zone Management Act Amendments of 1976, which granted the states additional funding to protect any of the economic, environmental, and social consequences of gas development on the outer shelf.

Several other bills he signed supported more traditional conservation issues including wildlife, public lands, forests, and natural resources. The National Wildlife Refuge System legislation shifted management responsibility for wildlife protection to the Interior Department's Fish and Wildlife Service from the Bureau of Land Management (BLM). The public lands and forest bills he signed into law included the Land Conservation Fund legislation, which allowed for federal land additions to the National Park System, and the more controversial National Forest Management Act of 1976, which offered limited protections to national forests, allowing some clear-cutting within the national forests themselves. This, as one might imagine, raised questions among environmentalists. The final act among the more traditional bills was the Federal Land Policy and Management Act of 1976, a bill that gave the secretary of the interior authority to establish land use plans for natural resources that previously were administered through the Bureau of Land Management.[36]

In addition to these bills passed and signed in 1976 there was also the Toxic Substances Control Act of 1976, which authorized the Environmental Protection Agency to require industry to submit to pretesting of industrial and commercial chemicals for potential dangers to people's health and to the environment. Also signed by Ford that year was the Solid Waste Utilization Act, which prohibited the dumping of large amounts of solid wastes and hazardous wastes. Finally, the president signed a bill that focused attention on electric cars—The Electric Vehicle Research, Development, and Demonstration Act—which established a research administration that was to bring together into one agency all federal development programs focused on energy research.[37]

The Democratic Congress's failure to approve all of Ford's environmental legislation stemmed from an antagonistic and partisan relationship it had with the president—one in which each actor had differing goals and was suspicious the other. The relationship between Congress and the White House had first deteriorated with the Watergate scandal, which turned the locus of power to the Congress. During the first months Ford was in office, relations between Congress and the President had initially thawed, but when the president pardoned Richard Nixon the Congress would have nothing more to do with the president.[38] Many Democrats and environmentalists were further disappointed in the new president as he "showed signs of being less sympathetic to environmentalists' goals than was his predecessor, Nixon."[39]

Although he had been quite a popular minority leader in the House, once

he became president, Ford confronted a Congress that was heavily Democratic. Democrats in 1971–72 controlled 254 seats, but by 1975–76, Democrats controlled 289 seats.[40] This provided Congress with another excuse to
oppose Ford's Republican policies, which made it difficult for the president
to prevail. Ford thus responded to Congress in much the same way that Harry
Truman had confronted the "do-nothing" 1948 Congress. Ford charged the
heavily Democratic Congress with failing to act on his programs. He thought
he could safely do this, since Congress was even more unpopular than Ford
was in 1975. At that time Congress had the support of only 32 percent of the
people, while the president had a popularity rating of 39 percent.[41]

As a result of the difficulty President Ford faced from both congressional
Democrats and a number of congressional Republicans, Ford felt his only
way to govern was to freely use his presidential veto. And use it he did. In the
short time he served in office, he vetoed sixty-six different pieces of legislation, with twelve of those vetoes being overridden by Congress. With 18 percent of his vetoes being overridden by Congress, Gerald Ford placed second
among all presidents in terms of the frequency of vetoes overridden.[42] This
is significant considering that all the other presidents—with the exception
of Ford and Andrew Johnson—on average have had only about 3 percent of
their vetoes overridden.[43] Other Ford vetoes that were nearly overridden included two bills dealing with strip mining regulations—one in December
1974 and the other in April 1975. One bill demanded recovery of land, insist-
ing that states adopt some minimal standards against strip mining or divest
control of that land to the federal government; the other bill would have put
a tax on coal mining to reclaim abandoned mines. In both instances Ford vetoed these bills, alleging that they would bring a slowdown if not a halt to
coal-mining efforts.[44] Of his sixty-six vetoes, four of them were issued in support of environmental causes, while seven of his vetoes could be considered
anti-environmental.[45]

President Ford indicated in 1975 his view that "the veto is not a negative,
dead end device. In most cases, it is a positive means of achieving legislative
compromise and improvement—better legislation, in other words."[46] It is unclear whether Ford really believed this or suggested this only to make his veto
record look more acceptable. Ford's vetoes were particularly important since
sixty-one of his sixty-six vetoes were on important public bills—bills that
normally deal with larger, more comprehensive national concerns—rather
than the more limited private bills that are restricted to individuals or organizations.[47] President Ford's critics, in response to his use of the veto, charged

him with vetoing legislation without proposing alternative solutions.[48] This was the case when in 1976 the Ford administration contributed to the defeat of the most important environmental bill of the year, "a compromise measure amending the 1970 Clean Air Act."[49]

Gerald Ford took the occasion of the campaign debate with Jimmy Carter on October 22, 1976, to sum up his own successes as a legislative leader, pointing out some of what he considered to be very positive positions on the environment. He said that he had added funding for the environment, approving money for water treatment plants and for water and land conservation programs, and diverting 12 million dollars to the National Park Service. He also claimed in the same debate that he had added more wilderness areas and scenic river areas than any other president up to 1976.[50] Jimmy Carter, however, saw those accomplishments of the Ford administration somewhat differently, pointing out that it had actually held back funding that could have been used to enforce air and water pollution standards. Carter further accused both Nixon and Ford of impounding those funds that could have been used to control pollution. While Carter did acknowledge that Ford had signed some important legislation to protect public land and wilderness areas, as well as protecting the national parks, he indicated that Ford had also seen it necessary to seriously reduce funding for environmental agencies.

While environmental activists, including those in Congress, approved of some of Ford's actions, they basically held that Ford "offered few initiatives in the area [of the environment] and was similarly disposed to side with industry in clashes over environmental issues."[51] Viewing President Ford's involvement in this light, environmentalists sided with the Democratic presidential nominee, Jimmy Carter, who had a much better record on environmental protection than did Ford.[52]

Administrative Actions

President Ford received mixed reviews on those he brought into his administration to handle environmental concerns. He appointed Rogers C. B. Morton as his first secretary of interior. Morton was a man who had served Richard Nixon in a similar capacity, and a man whom Ford felt close to since both shared a similar view on the environment. Both Ford and Morton saw that it was necessary whenever policy makers considered protecting the environment to balance the environment against other concerns. Sierra Club president Phillip S. Berry reacted to Morton's appointment by suggesting his nomination reflected "at best apathy toward the environment and at worst outright hostility."[53] President Ford soon showed that a concern for energy was really more important to him than a concern for the environment since he released Rogers Morton from his position as secretary of interior and made him a chief energy adviser in the executive branch.

The president also appointed Frank G. Zarb as executive director of Energy Resources Council, giving the Ford administration a strong energy team. Replacing Morton as interior secretary was Stanley Hathaway, a former two-term governor of Wyoming who was appointed by Ford in 1975 but who served for only three months and twenty-six days. While governor, Hathaway had supported environmental controls over the minerals industry, had established Wyoming's environmental quality department, and had signed legislation to protect the air and water.[54] Ford thought that Hathaway looked strong as a potential interior secretary, but the administration's vetting process proved inadequate. What Ford and Hathaway were unprepared for were the two-month-long Senate hearings during which senators were relentless in questioning Hathaway on his views on strip mining, on oil shale, and on the alleged favoritism he showed as governor to certain engineering firms and industries regarding water rights allowed from the Tongue and the Powder rivers near Yellowstone National Park.[55]

Once finally winning Senate approval, Hathaway, as secretary, began the demanding work of overseeing the operation of 540 million acres of federal land. But the pressures on him for his past actions as governor, and his own work schedule as secretary, seemed too much for Hathaway, causing him to become ill and to tender his resignation. Ford, however, refused at first to accept his resignation, recommending instead that his own personal physician attend to the secretary. Once the president's physician ordered Hathaway to Bethesda Naval Medical Center, indicating that he was suffering from both exhaustion and "reactive depression," Ford relented and accepted the Hathaway resignation on July 23, 1975.

Hathaway was replaced by Thomas Kleppe from North Dakota, who served from 1975 until 1977. Kleppe was considered by Congressman Morris Udall (D-Ariz.), who was sympathetic to environmental needs, to be "qualified for a lot of jobs, but not Secretary of Interior."[56]

Russell Train, as EPA director, was the only accomplished environmentalist in the Ford administration and was one in whom Richard Nixon had had a great deal of confidence. Yet Ford gave Train little decision-making authority. Train soon proved more environmentally friendly than was Ford, causing the two to often come in conflict over decision making. The frequent clashes eventually led to Russell Train leaving government service.

Ford also kept Russell W. Peterson on as chair of the White House Council on Environmental Quality. Peterson was one who felt that there was no conflict between the environment and energy production. "We can and must have them both," he stated.[57]

Ford also found it was necessary to cut the budgets of most of the environmental agencies, along with cuts in the defense budget, in order to deal with inflation.[58] To make matters even more difficult for these agencies, 1975 was also the year that Congress implemented a limit on deficit spending, which reduced the amount that could be appropriated to social programs and the environment. On several occasions the president made both budgetary and environmental appeals to the public, such as: "I think it is time for responsible men and women of all political persuasions—Republicans, Democrats, Independents—to come together, not in an effort for a political advantage, but in a spirit of true American patriotism, to whip problems like inflation, energy, the environment, to strengthen our successful foreign policy by the restoration of bipartisanship. And it is also time for the American voter, whatever his views, to demonstrate by the ballot that he supports a responsible and responsive anti-inflation policy; that he opposes wasteful Government spending; that he demands a strong, secure national defense program; and most important, that he wants elected representatives who feel the same way."[59] Ford was making a case that he could be both committed to environmental preservation as well as support a stable economy without doing damage to either.

One appointment that should be mentioned because of the difficulty it posed for Ford was another holdover from the Nixon cabinet, namely, Earl Butz, who served as secretary of agriculture from 1971 until 1976. Butz got into several policy conflicts with President Ford when he tried to sell some 500 million dollars' worth of grain to the Soviet Union. Ford reacted by overruling him since he felt such action would be inflationary. Butz's dismissal came during the 1976 presidential campaign when he told some off-color jokes directed at African Americans. Despite a public apology, Butz was asked to leave the administration.[60]

Volunteerism was Gerald Ford's preferred approach to environmental needs rather than reliance on governmental regulation. When the president proclaimed Earth Day in 1975, for example, he asked that "special attention be given to personal voluntary activities and educational efforts directed toward protecting and enhancing our life-giving environment."[61] The environmental public immediately responded, as 20 million people organized demonstrations and thousands of schools and communities participated in environmental awareness activities. This support was reflected in extensive media attention given to the demonstrators. As a result of the president's Earth Day proclamation, there was a decided increase in grassroots attention paid to environmental concerns.

Gerald Ford seemed quite satisfied with the governmental structure that dealt with environmental decision making. No new environmental agencies were created during Ford's years in office. Unlike President Nixon, Gerald Ford never had any desire to reconstitute the Department of Natural Resources, that proposed new department that had been a part of Nixon's "super cabinet" reform. The plan was to allow this new department to centralize all environmental efforts under one "super secretary," giving the secretary added authority. To Nixon this department represented the greatest potential of any new structure for handling concerns of the environment. Ford's attitude in refusing to follow up on this proposal or to even consider how new government structures might better respond to challenges posed by the environment irritated environmentalists.[62]

Environmental Diplomacy

President Ford was actually more involved in the international arena with environmental relations than he had been domestically. The president's primary international accomplishment involving the environment consisted of the treaties and agreements he signed protecting exotic animals. Agreements with China, Canada, Mexico, United Kingdom, Germany, and France were designed to penalize the trade or possession of endangered species.[63] In September 1976 Ford also ratified an agreement with Canada, Denmark, Norway and the Soviet Union to protect the polar bear in the Arctic regions.[64] In that same year, six species of Antarctic seals were protected through an agreement with the United Kingdom and Northern Ireland.[65]

Two years earlier, the United States and Japan signed an agreement to protect endangered birds, with Gerald Ford issuing an executive agreement to formalize the action taken.[66] Migratory birds also received similar protection from an international agreement Ford made with the Soviet Union in 1976, which included all birds that shared the flyways and the feeding and the breeding grounds between the two countries.[67] Finally, the United States and Poland began negotiations that encouraged both countries to cooperate on pollution abatement, on the control of radiation, and on protecting flora and fauna.[68] This agreement began a three-decades-long relationship that also eventually led to the United States and Poland jointly reaching a technological coopera- tive agreement encouraging support of one another in the fields of "cancer research, emerging and infectious disease research, joint research training programs, nanotechnology, biotechnology, and environmental sciences."[69]

In addition to the formal agreements signed, the United States also par- ticipated in several international conferences during Ford's years in office, including the 1972 United Nations Conference on Human Environment at Stockholm that established what later became known as the United Nations Environmental Program.[70] This conference was important since it encour- aged greater activity at the national and international levels to limit "the impairment of the human environment." Practically speaking, it led to the establishment of a number of international environmental institutions, the expansion of the environmental agenda, and countries' increasing ac- ceptance of the international monitoring of the environment.[71] The United States also attended a United Nations conference in Bucharest that focused on world population needs. This conference encouraged developed nations to conserve their resources, resulting in reduced consumption on their part in the name of "international equity."[72]

Summary and Conclusion

Some of the same persons who were important to the environmental move- ment under Richard Nixon stayed on through the Ford administration, but Ford clearly did not enjoy the same sort of legacy as did Nixon, and he approached environmental needs quite differently:

1. While Ford proved to be more oriented toward conservation of natural resources than taking on the complexity of other environmental issues, he was a president who believed in "balancing" conservation with other concerns such as energy and his desire to ensure a stable economy. At times, of course, this meant "balancing away" environ- mental improvements in favor of these other concerns. While he an- nounced that he would "fight to preserve what is best in our environ- ment," he was quick to indicate that the economic needs of the people were just as important, if not more important, than any concern for the environment.[73]

2. As a result, there was frustration among environmentalists in the ad- ministration, such as EPA head Russell Train, who was concerned with

the direction President Ford was taking his conservation efforts. Once Ford saw fit to remove Rogers Morton as secretary of interior, appointing Stanley Hathaway for a short three months, and then unthinkingly appointing Thomas S. Kleppe, who had no background to serve in this position, conservation was decidedly weakened as a top priority in the remaining years of the administration.

3. While Ford did have some domestic conservation successes in adding two national monuments, six historic sites, three historic parks, two national preserves, two recreation areas, and protecting three other areas,[74] the president shared much in common with Dwight Eisenhower in terms of carefully focusing his administration's efforts on a limited few environmental concerns, and then not putting much effort into assuring that the environment would receive added protections. Both of these presidents resisted federal regulations, wanting the federal government to exercise limited authority in tailoring governmental policy.

4. President Ford did appear somewhat more active in the international arena, engaging in treaties and agreements with Canada, Mexico, several western European countries, and China regarding endangered species. Agreements to protect birds were also made with Japan and the Soviet Union.

5. Because Gerald Ford was in office such a short time—from August 1974 until he retired January 1977—his overall effect on the presidency and on conservation was limited. Nevertheless, one can speculate as to what might have happened had President Ford lost to Ronald Reagan in the Republican Convention, or if Ford had won in the general election against Jimmy Carter in 1976. In the first instance, given Ronald Reagan's anti-environmental record once he became president in 1980, had Reagan won in 1976, defeating Carter, conservation would have been set back a number of years. On the other hand, had Ford defeated Carter in the general election, it is hard to see that conservation would have made the same sort of advances it made under Jimmy Carter, given Carter's interest in preserving the lands in Alaska.

CHAPTER 8

George H. W. Bush

A fter serving two terms as vice president, George H. W. Bush[1] vigorously campaigned in 1988 as the Republican Party nominee who intended to carry forward the Reagan agenda. However, he chose a different course regarding the environment. Bush 41 made a concerted effort to distance himself from Reagan's environmental policies, since President Reagan had earned a reputation for being the only modern "anti-environmental" president. Bush 41, on the other hand, indicated during the 1988 campaign that he wished to be a "Republican president in the Teddy Roosevelt tradition. A conservationist. An *environmentalist*."[2] He added, "I am an environmentalist; always have been and always will be."[3] It was John Greer who suggested that Bush 41, in taking this position, attempted to "co-opt classic Democratic issues by telling voters that he would be the 'education' and 'environmental' president."[4] In fact, eight months after assuming the presidency, his administration produced a "White House Fact Sheet on Environmental Initiatives" that was a comprehensive description of environmental actions that both the president and Congress had engaged in or would in the future initiate.[5]

It is important to provide a portrait of George H. W. Bush who, as a traditional conservative, found himself caught between a dedication to conservation and an allegiance to the Republican base of his party. As we will see in the following discussion, the first half of his term as president reflected concern with conservation and environmental politics highlighted by his support of the Clean Air Act Amendments of 1990, while the second half of his presidency reflected a reversal in his commitment to environmentalism demonstrated by his negative actions at the 1992 Earth Summit in Rio de Janeiro.

George H. W. Bush's approach to the presidency reflected, in the words of Burt Solomon, filling "his administration with practical men and women who are generally conservative but not obsessively so, who tend to be—as he is—civil, cautious and conciliatory."[6] As Nelson Polsby characterized Bush 41, here was a president who was a "genuine conservative" who cared "about society and the government that is handed to them."[7] Or, as Erwin Hargrove described him, Bush was a "centrist Republican who desires to manage government well after Ronald Reagan's anti-government and anti-communist activism."[8] During his four years in office, Bush 41, the centrist, walked a line between personal commitment and party loyalty. Here was a president who defined his campaign for president in 1988 as part of the environmental tradition of Teddy Roosevelt yet during his reelection campaign in 1992 he referred to Democratic vice presidential candidate Al Gore as "ozone man," reflecting an "antiregulatory tenor [that] sounded increasingly like that of Ronald Reagan in 1980."[9]

As we will see later in this chapter, Bush 41 found himself affected by the countervailing pressures he set in motion. For instance, through his appointments, he satisfied environmentalists by nominating William Reilly, former head of the World Wildlife Fund, as head of the Environmental Protection Agency, while at the same time appointing former New Hampshire governor John Sununu as secretary of the interior, a man at odds with the environmental movement. Ultimately, Bush 41's administration was "beset by internal divisions represented by individuals who themselves were not environmentally friendly, and who in the end controlled the legislative agenda."[10] In short, as Walter Rosenbaum described the president's dilemma, "President George H. W. Bush awakened expectations of major reform from the environmental movement and brought to the White House a more sympathetic and active environmentalism. . . . Nonetheless, the backslide of Bush environmentalism was equally conspicuous" as his administration increasingly represented a "low priority for environmentalism on the policy agenda."[11]

President Bush was challenged by multiple obstacles regarding his environmental agenda. As Robert Shanley explained Bush's dilemma, the president "inherited an enormous deficit problem, a savings and loan bailout and a nuclear weapons plan cleanup estimated to cost billions of dollars, other neglected environmental problems, and a polarization between Congress and the White House."[12] Consequently, he needed to engage in successful coalition-building by forging an alliance between Democrats and Republicans in Congress and thereby gain bipartisan support for his primary environmental commitment, which came about in his campaign as the effort to pass the Clean Air Act Amendments of 1990. However, Bush's appointment of Manuel Lujan Jr. as interior secretary raised concerns among those in the environmental community over the role of the federal and state governments in protecting the environment. Lujan, a former House member from New Mexico, was viewed by environmentalists as too cozy with natural resource interests in western states. Moreover, while Lujan's supporters saw him pursuing a balanced approach to public lands and wildlife issues, his call for the Endangered Species "God Squad," which would "review the denial of timber permits on Bureau of Land Management property because they threatened the habitat of the northern spotted owl," frightened environmentalists who saw this as an attempt to roll back existing protections for habitat and wildlife.[13] In short, there was a concern that the federal government would defer to natural resource interests within state jurisdictions.

As we mention in chapters 3 and 9, the Nixon and Reagan administrations implemented New Federalism as their approach to intergovernmental relations, which was an attempt to alter the responsibilities of the different levels of government. Unlike the Nixon approach, however, the Reagan and Bush 41 administrations gave more power to state and local authorities but it came with fewer federal dollars to carry out their mandates. Just as the states had difficulty meeting their obligations during the Reagan years, the states found that the new Bush 41 presidency did not make their jobs any easier. Continual budget cuts in the environmental policy domain of the fifty states raised the question whether and to what extent the states could or would replace lost federal dollars with state revenues.[14] The issue of state capabilities or state willingness to contribute funds became a new area for debate. Nonetheless, on March 10, 1989, two months into his presidency, Bush 41 stressed his support for federalism, and he commended the states for meeting, despite tight budgets, their new responsibilities for environmental protection that they gained as power shifted from Washington to the states during the 1980s.[15] He reiterated his position in a speech to attorneys general three days later, stating that although he would be providing "limited" resources for environmental protection and drug control strategies, he believed strongly in federalism. He further noted that during the previous ten years, "States have taken on a key role, the lead I might add, in many areas, in terms of protecting the environment."[16]

As an example of his views on federalism, in his first environmental fact sheet made public in September 1989, Bush outlined a commitment to a far-reaching array of environmental issues, one that highlighted shared responsibility among the different levels of government but also promoted support for voluntary rather than government efforts. One aspect of the broad environmental agenda was reforestation. The fact sheet pointed out that the president had "long been an advocate of reforestation" and that "his personal commitment to planting trees is indicative of his support for the ongoing efforts of Federal, State and local programs, as well as reforestation projects undertaken by private and voluntary organizations."[17]

By his fourth year in office, Bush's views about federalism and policy making continued to shift as he asserted that power should be "moved closer to the people, away from Washington" in order for the "federal government to reduce overhead" and to allow "states to manage more flexibly and efficiently."[18] Notwithstanding innovations and accomplishments at the subnational level, for environmentalists who demanded an activist federal role in the environmental domain, Bush 41's suggestion of increasing state power was discouraging.

Political Communication

George H. W. Bush's environmental posture was firmly supported by the Republican Party in 1988 as revealed in the party's platform. It stated the need to protect the air and water from pollution, improve national parks, protect wildlife, clean up hazardous wastes, and respond to global environmental concerns by protecting against tropical forest destruction, limiting ocean dumping, and assisting in bringing a halt to climate change.[19] In fact, as Raymond Tatalovich and Mark Wattier point out in their assessment of party platforms and environmental issues, "After paying homage to Teddy Roosevelt's pioneering efforts" and listing "their accomplishments," the "Republicans in 1988 covered nearly all the environmental bases, by promising more vigilant enforcement and greater commitment, but there was no call for additional legislative authority."[20] Still, Republicans would argue that their party platform gave more attention to the environment compared to the Democratic counterpart and that it reflected Bush's personal commitment to this policy domain.

Yet from the outset of the Bush 41 administration, an interesting dichotomy arose in terms of the president's political communication—major and minor speeches—about the environment. Sussman, Daynes, and West inform us that although there was "little mention of the environment in his major speeches, one could see his interest in and support for environmental issues in his press conferences and minor speeches.[21] For instance, in his first State of the Union message on January 31, 1990, Bush emphasized the need to make a major structural reform that would benefit the environment: "And there's something more we owe the generations of the future, the safekeeping of America's environmental inheritance. . . . We will elevate the

Environmental Protection Agency to Cabinet rank" in order to demonstrate that "environmental issues have the status they deserve."[22] However, this structural reform never occurred. The president also included a commitment to national parks, wildlife refuges, the planting of more trees, and increased funds for global environmental change research. While this is noteworthy, one might expect that Bush 41 would have given more attention to the environment in all of his State of the Union addresses, which would have reached a larger audience that would demonstrate his commitment to the environmental domain.

Bush 41 did make numerous minor speeches about the environment or referred to the environment in other speeches. For instance, on February 8, 1989, very early in his first year in office, the president articulated his commitment to the domestic environment when he stated at the swearing-in of Manuel Lujan as interior secretary that "I believe, as you do, in clean air and clean water and the protection of America's wildlife. I also want to see our nation's public lands preserved so that this generation and future generations can use and enjoy our national bounty: the great outdoors."[23] Referring to environmentalism at the regional level, the following month he noted the progress that was made with Canada in regard to clean air: "If we're to protect our future, we need a new attitude about the environment.... We must make use of clean coal. My budget contains full funding, on schedule, for the clean coal technology agreement that we've made with Canada. We've made that agreement with Canada, and we intend to honor that agreement."[24] Later in December of that year he expressed his optimism about wetlands protection in North America through an agreement with Canada and Mexico. While thanking the governments of our neighbors to the north and south for their participation in the agreement and their recognition of the "need to protect waterfowl habitat in Northern America," Bush "reiterated [his] pledge to work towards a national goal of 'no net loss' of wetlands."[25] On the one hand, the Bush 41 administration could argue that it gave more attention to the environment in minor speeches than any president, except for Richard Nixon, dating back to FDR.[26] On the other hand, it is ironic that after campaigning that he would be an "environmental" president, he failed to mention the environment at all in his inaugural speech in January 1989.

Bush 41's public discourse did not always result in substantive action, particularly in the areas of climate change and biodiversity issues. In April 1990, for instance, the president outlined his environmental philosophy at a White House conference on climate change. At the conference, his position on the environment became quite clear: "Sort out the science on this complex is-sue, to start with what we know about the Earth and . . . the factors, natural as well as man-made, that cause our environment to change. . . . Address the economic factors in environmental questions . . . [as] all of us must be cer-tain we preserve our environmental well-being and our economic welfare."[27] Thus, two years before the Earth Summit in Rio de Janeiro, while Bush clearly showed that, while factoring in a commitment to environmental protection, economics would take priority over environmentalism and science.

The president had difficulty responding to journalists who questioned his commitment to an "environmental presidency" when he had indicated that he might not attend the Earth Summit.[28] Yet on June 12, 1992, at the Earth Summit, he stated, "There are those who say that the leaders of the world do not care about the Earth and the environment. Well, let them all come here to Rio. . . . Today, I invite my colleagues from the industrialized world to join in a prompt start on the convention's implementation. I propose that our countries meet by January 1st to lay out our national plans for meeting the specific commitments in the Framework Convention."[29] The following day he emphasized the leadership role of the United States when he said, "Let me be clear on one fundamental point. The United States fully intends to be the world's preeminent leader in protecting the global environment. . . . And the fact that we don't go along with every single covenant, I don't think that means a relinquishment of leadership."[30] However, his words were not sup-ported by his actions when he referred to U.S. leadership and the global en-vironment. In fact, Bush 41 failed to show leadership on the global warming agreement and stood alone in his refusal to sign the biodiversity treaty.

In contrast to the first two years of his presidency, when he provided some substance to his public pronouncements about the environment, by the end of his term in office his approach had changed. In October 1992, while offer-ing remarks in Des Moines, Iowa, during a campaign stop, he said, "We've gone too far under regulation and too far under interpretation on some of these statutes" and he referred to "extreme groups" rather than the main-stream environmental movement.[31]

Legislative Leadership

Despite George H. W. Bush's campaign commitment to work on behalf of the environment, the environmental community was suspicious of the presi-dent since he had served for eight years as vice president with Ronald Reagan who had been such an assertive anti-environmentalist. Yet Bush intended to prove those doubters wrong, at least during his first two years in office.

The major obstacle facing the new president was divided government as Democrats controlled both houses of Congress. Although Bush 41 began his presidency with an open and bipartisan approach to Congress, conflict broke out between the executive and legislative branches over a number of issues, resulting in the president having the second-lowest support score in Congress since the 1950s during his final year in office.[32]

Just two months into his presidency, Bush 41 was confronted with the worst oil spill in U.S. history. The *Exxon Valdez* oil tanker ran aground in Prince William Sound off the coast of Alaska, spilling almost eleven million gallons of petroleum. The accident was considered an environmental catastrophe and social disaster for residents as well. What made matters worse was that only two months earlier, the oil tanker *Thompson Pass* leaked 72,000 gallons of oil into Port Valdez, Alaska. Needless to say, the larger *Exxon Valdez* spill became a major media event in 1989. According to the Environmental Protection Agency, "The spill posed threats to the delicate food chain that supports Prince William Sound's commercial fishing industry. Also in danger were ten million migratory shore birds and waterfowl, hundreds of sea otters, dozens of other species, such as harbor porpoises and sea lions, and several varieties of whales."[33] Zachary Smith informed us that "the largest oil spill in U.S. history spread out of control and covered 900 square miles within a week."[34]

Although Exxon Corporation engaged in a cleanup of the oil spill, a lawsuit was filed against it resulting in an award of five billion dollars to the plaintiffs. However, Exxon used its considerable resources to avoid payment of the judgment. The response of the Bush 41 administration was mixed. On the one hand, it came under fire for the delayed response to the crisis. In fact, in the opinion of some state and local officials, "Exxon's campaign contributions during the 1988 presidential election had not been forgotten by the Bush administration."[35] Moreover, although he referred to the oil spill as a "major tragedy" in his public statements, he continued to support offshore drilling and he also stated that he saw "no connection" between his support for oil drilling in Alaska's Arctic National Wildlife Refuge and the *Exxon Valdez* catastrophe, which angered environmentalists.[36] On the other hand, in response to the catastrophic oil spill, the president issued a moratorium on oil and gas exploration in Bristol Bay, Alaska.[37] Moreover, the following year he signed the Oil Pollution Act (OPA) passed by Congress in August, which mandated new federal efforts to protect the environment, especially the oceans from oil spills.

The Oil Pollution Act that became law in 1990 was an important example of legislation that transcended congressional gridlock and gained the signature of the president. As Michael Kraft explains, "After ten years of congressional inaction on oil spill legislation, the *Exxon Valdez* spill prompted Congress to enact the Oil Pollution Act of 1990. It required companies to submit oil spill contingency plans to the Coast Guard and the EPA and to train their employees in oil spill response."[38] Moreover, as described by the Office of Emergency Management of the EPA, the OPA was in response to rising public concern about the threat posed by oil spills.[39] Furthermore, as a result of the *Exxon Valdez* oil spill, the relative strength of political actors involved in this policy domain shifted. Thomas Birkland informs us, "Before the spill, environmentalists had a difficult case to make in their efforts to raise awareness of the dangers of oil spills. After the spill, the environmentalists needed only to turn to the saturation news coverage of the spill to make their claims."[40] In the end, the act approved by President Bush provided an improved federal oversight of maritime interests and enhanced environmental protection, mandating the use of double-hulled oil tankers at a future date while ship owners facing litigation from oil spills would face an increased monetary limit in particular.[41]

The highlight of Bush 41's legislative career was the 1990 Clean Air Act amendments. He had indicated that clean air was a high priority for his administration. In signing the clean air legislation he issued an important statement indicating that "the 13-year legislative logjam has now been broken" and that the "bill will allow the Nation finally to meet air quality standards in every city."[42] Here Bush 41 could identify with his Republican predecessor Richard Nixon, who supported the Clean Air Act of 1970. However, although the Carter administration supported renewal of the act in 1977, it languished during the Reagan years, while public health officials drew attention to the public health problems associated with dirty air arising from emissions from sulfur dioxide, nitrous oxide, and mercury.

By committing himself to support the clean air legislation amendments, Bush 41 brought together a coalition of business and industry leaders, environmentalists, and government officials.[43] This effort at coalition-building was important because it transcended Democratic and Republican differences, and because divisions between Democrats also created problems in the effort to move the legislation forward. For instance, House Democrat

Henry Waxman, who represented heavily populated Los Angeles, supported the legislation while House Democrat John Dingell of Michigan, a state with a large automobile manufacturing constituency, was concerned about protecting local interests. Moreover, in the other congressional chamber, West Virginia senator Robert Byrd was concerned about how the clean air legislation might affect the coal industry in his state. While forging a coalition in support of clean air legislation, Bush 41 relied primarily on four key advisors—Roger Porter (chief domestic advisor), Robert Grady (campaign speech writer), C. Boyden Gray (chief in-house lawyer), and William G. Rosenberg (EPA assistant)—to represent the administration's effort to implement the legislation. Each advisor—drawn from within the White House circle and executive agencies—contributed different skills, talent, and expertise in the effort to secure passage of the clean air bill. The successful effort of the president in securing support for the clean air amendments demonstrated Bush 41's commitment to the issue. As two observers of the process reported, although moderate in its overall impact and facing persistent opposition by business and industry, the clean air act received praise from environmentalists and demonstrated that "presidential influence can indeed affect the initiation, course and outcome of a legislative debate."[44]

Two years later, and just prior to the November presidential election, the Energy Policy Act was enacted. During his first year in office, Bush 41 began preparation for a new effort to reduce domestic reliance on foreign sources of oil through the initiation of a new energy strategy (NES) formulated by the Department of Energy. However, while the president "defended the NES as an acceptable balance of energy production and conservation that might help wean the nation from imported oil by expanding domestic supplies," the final version of the plan received criticism from environmentalists who argued that "too many energy conservation measures were dropped at the pleading of Bush's economic advisors."[45] Against a backdrop of Bush 41's support for opening up the 19 million acre Arctic National Wildlife Refuge in Alaska to domestic fossil fuel exploration, the Energy Policy Act succeeded in restructuring "the electric utility industry to promote more competition, provide tax relief to independent oil and gas drillers, encourage energy conservation and efficiency, promote renewable energy and cars that run on alternative fuels, make it easier to build nuclear power plants, authorize billions of dollars for energy-related research and development, and create a climate protection office within the Energy Department."[46] Although Michael Kraft argued that problems remained with the legislation, including failure to raise Corporate Average Fuel Economy (CAFE) standards and the likelihood that foreign oil dependence would not decline, Jacqueline Switzer contended that the act was the "first time in a decade that Congress has been able to compromise on the most contentious provisions—those dealing with alternative fuels and energy-related tax provisions," yet it only received a "single day's media headlines."[47]

Although attempting to prove environmental doubters wrong about his commitment to the environment, by the end of his term as president, Bush 41 found it difficult to argue that he had a successful legislative agenda that benefited the environment. In contrast to his predecessors, the president could point to only two major pieces of environmental legislation that were passed during his presidency—namely, the Clean Air Act Amendments of 1990 and the Energy Policy Act of 1992. This level of legislative success was minimal compared to Lyndon Johnson, Richard Nixon, and Jimmy Carter, who never claimed to be environmental presidents.

Administrative Actions

One would have expected Bush 41, as an "environmental president," to have issued a considerable number of executive orders in support of environmental issues. However, a study of environmental executive orders dating back to FDR has shown that Bush 41 ranks rather low in this regard.[48] In fact, he issued fewer environmental executive orders than his immediate Republican predecessors (Nixon and Ford) and his Democratic successor, Bill Clinton.

If the president was frugal in issuing executive orders regarding the environment, the same cannot be said about his use of proclamations during the first two years of his presidency. He used this instrument of power to highlight several areas of environmental concern, including Proclamation 6198 declaring National Drinking Water Week in May 1990, Proclamation 6216 designating a Yosemite National Park Centennial year celebration in October 1990, and Proclamation 6420 specifying a National Recycling Day in April 1992. However, as he reached the third and fourth year of his presidency, fewer proclamations were issued that concerned the environment.

At the same time, George H. W. Bush surprised environmentalists with his appointment of several pro-environment individuals to his administration. William Reilly, for example, as head administrator of the Environmental Protection Agency, was a former president of the World Wildlife Fund and Conservation Foundation. Michael Deland, who had previously served as New England director of the Environmental Protection Agency, was selected to serve as chair of the Council on Environmental Quality.[49] The environmental community was not pleased, however, with Bush 41's choice of Richard Darman as head of the Office of Management and Budget, Michael Boskin as economic advisor, and especially Manuel Lujan Jr. as secretary of the interior, who had, prior to his appointment, made it quite clear as a Republican House member from New Mexico that as far as public lands were concerned there would be "no major departures" from the days of Ronald Reagan.[50]

As noted previously, Lujan during his time in Congress was associated with natural resource users including timber and mining interests.[51] Consequently, environmentalists were concerned about his appointment to head the Interior Department. The impact of Lujan on public lands and endangered species issues also had support in the judiciary. Two cases involving the secretary of the interior—*Lujan v. National Wildlife Federation* (1990) and *Lujan v. Defenders of Wildlife* (1992)—found Supreme Court justice Antonin Scalia supporting business interests over environmental concerns where Scalia argued against "standing" for environmental groups.[52] In both cases, Scalia held the position that the courts were not the place to pursue remedies for environmental protection but rather the other two branches of the federal government should be approached in this regard.

Moreover, Bush's vice president, Dan Quayle, was appointed to head the newly created Council on Competitiveness that evaluated environmental initiatives in terms of cost-benefit analysis, ultimately protecting big business at the expense of the environment. The Council on Competitiveness oversaw cabinet activity to remove any regulation that might interfere with business competitiveness.[53] In its short life it became a major deregulatory voice within the administration, as it was involved in environmental issues, including clean air policies, industrial safety laws, automobile emission laws, and food and drug regulations. The council was also drawn into the wetlands policy debate when opponents of the federal government's wetlands policy appealed to the Bush 41 administration. Oil, gas, housing, and farming interests were concerned that they were being harmed by their lack of access to millions of acres of public land under federal protection. Although Bush 41 campaigned in 1988 for "no net loss" of the nation's wetlands, his administration through the Council on Competitiveness proposed to redefine what constituted wetlands and thus reduce federal protection for this environmental domain, a move that angered environmentalists and one that would provide relief to business interests.[54] In the end, Congress was asked to review the problem, and Quayle's council came to an abrupt end when President Clinton in his first full day in office abolished it through an executive order and the Clinton administration began a new assessment of the nation's wetlands policy.[55]

Environmental Diplomacy

When addressing the global environment, Bush 41 had some successes but also engaged in retrenchment when involved in this international policy making domain. The president demonstrated leadership and commitment on several occasions. For instance, in 1989 he signed the North American Wetlands Conservation Act along with Canada and Mexico, agreeing to work together to support the vitality of critical wetlands.[56] The visibility of this habitat protection act was enhanced by its important relationship to the protection of migratory animals. The president also took action on the acid rain problem that affected both the United States and Canada but had been neglected by his predecessor, Ronald Reagan. While the 1990 Clean Air Act amendments had made an initial attempt to deal with the acid rain problem, the United States and Canada went still further and adopted the 1991 U.S.-Canada Air Quality Agreement that more fully satisfied both the United States and Canada. This agreement committed both signatories to reduce sulfur dioxide emissions according to an agreed-upon timetable.

George H. W. Bush had several other opportunities to demonstrate environmental leadership in the global environmental arena. At the Paris Economic Summit in the summer of 1989 he stated that there were "serious threats to the atmosphere, which could lead to future climate changes. We note with great concern the growing pollution of air, lakes, rivers, oceans and seas; acid rain, dangerous substances; and the rapid desertification and deforestation. Such environmental degradation endangers species and undermines the well-being of individuals and societies."[57]

It is ironic that Bush 41's effort in helping to secure passage of the clean air act amendments in 1990 failed to translate into a similar approach at the 1990 World Climate Conference and the 1992 United Nations Conference on Environment and Development (Earth Summit) in Rio de Janeiro. It is noteworthy that Bush 41 failed to offer leadership regarding biodiversity and global warming, in particular, which were central to the important and highly

visible Earth Summit. An environmental president would have used the resources of environmental diplomacy in support of the goals highlighted at
both meetings. In response to Bush 41's behavior at the World Climate Conference, Marvin Soroos observed that Bush reneged on his responsibility as
president regarding collaboration in securing the support of industrialized
countries in responding appropriately to the growing threat of global warming.[58] At the Earth Summit in Rio two years later, as Lawrence Susskind reports, the president waited until three days before the conference to make his
decision about whether to attend, and when he did, he stayed for only three
days.[59] At this gathering of delegates from countries from around the world,
Bush 41 used his influence to convince other representatives to revise the
global climate change agreement. This global warming treaty mandated that
signatories share the costs and technologies regarding climate change and
it also imposed mandatory requirements on these same signatories. Bush 41
agreed to sign this international environmental agreement only after all of
the specific antipollution deadlines and specific target dates for implementation of pollution reforms had been significantly weakened.[60] Thus, Bush 41
responded in support of U.S. domestic interest groups that were putting
pressure on him. In short, the Bush 41 version of the agreement excluded
all binding requirements (goals and timetables) for reducing greenhouse gas
emissions.

Moreover, Bush 41 was the only delegate to refuse to sign the Convention on Biological Diversity, further isolating the United States from the
other delegates attending the Earth Summit.[61] The biodiversity agreement
pushed three main goals: the conservation of biodiversity, sustainable use
of the components of biodiversity, and sharing the benefits arising from the
commercial and other utilization of genetic resources in a fair and equitable
way.[62] Why did Bush 41 oppose the agreement? Here is a case, once again,
where domestic constraints were imposed on the president—in this case, domestic interests that were concerned about the impact of the international
agreement on domestic politics. According to an observer of biological protection in the United States and the United Kingdom, the White House was
concerned that the Convention on Biological Diversity would strengthen
the Endangered Species Act within the United States and wetlands policy that the Bush 41 administration was trying to weaken.[63] Moreover,
domestic pharmaceutical companies became concerned about the impact
of the treaty on their business interests and acquisition of genetic materials. Consequently, the White House responded affirmatively to pressure by

the Industrial Biotechnology Association, the Association of Biotechnology Companies, and the Pharmaceutical Manufacturers Association to reject the treaty.[64]

Although he campaigned that he would be an "environmental" president, Bush 41's behavior at the Earth Summit indicated quite clearly a reversal in his commitment to environmental priorities. He was willing to join with delegates from the global community in signing an international agreement that demonstrated concern about climate change. However, in the words of one political observer of the president, he "gave the impression that the U.S. was more concerned about the interests of the domestic fossil fuel and automobile industries than it was to international cooperation and the warnings of the scientific community about the dangers resulting from human induced climate change."[65] The president's unilateral position with regard to the Convention on Biological Diversity only heightened the concern about international cooperation on environmental issues and reduced Bush 41's self-described goal of being an environmental president.

Summary and Conclusion

In assessing the forty-first president's environmental record, Walter Rosenbaum lamented, "Bush's presidential tenure, despite some important environmental accomplishments, nonetheless disappointed most environmental advocates. [EPA administrator William] Reilly was almost alone among Bush's major executive appointments in outspoken environmental leadership."[66] While starting out on the road toward an environmental presidency, pressure from business and industry and internal dissension within the administration led Bush 41 to oppose the Clean Water Act, the Resource Conservation and Recovery Act, and the Endangered Species Act.[67] In addition, the president's behavior at the 1992 Earth Summit in Rio, attended by more than one hundred representatives from countries around the world, showed the reversal in his commitment to the environment. In short, George H. W. Bush exhibited a pattern of support for environmental affairs during his first two years and opposition to environmental protection during his second two years in office.

   1. George H. W. Bush's connection to environmental affairs can be
       viewed in terms of his rhetoric, with which he raised expectations
       during his campaign for the presidency by stating that he would be
       an "environmental president." Four years later, during his reelection

campaign that downplayed his commitment to the environment, he referred to Democratic vice presidential candidate Al Gore as "ozone man."

2. In contrast to his presidential counterparts, Bush 41 was more likely to use minor speeches and press conferences in support of environmental affairs, but in major speeches, including the State of the Union message, he limited his conviction to protecting the environment.

3. As a legislative leader, the highlight of Bush's agenda was the Clean Air Act Amendments of 1990. He used the power resources of his office to build a coalition of policy makers, business and industry leaders, and environmentalists to ensure passage of the legislation. However, his legislative legacy was quite limited, as the only other major environmental bill passed during his term in office was the Energy Policy Act of 1992. Compared to Lyndon Johnson, Richard Nixon, and Jimmy Carter, Bush 41's legislative record was minimal at best.

4. Bush 41 had a mixed record when it came to making appointments in the environmental policy domain. On the one hand, his appointments included William Reilly, former head of the World Wildlife Fund, as EPA administrator, and Michael Deland, former New England director of the EPA, as chair of the Council on Environmental Quality. On the other hand, he appointed his vice president, Dan Quayle, to head the Council on Competitiveness, which used cost-benefit analysis in evaluating environmental initiatives, ultimately protecting business and industry at the expense of the environment. Manuel Lujan Jr. as interior secretary convened what became known as the endangered species "God Squad," with which he questioned the need to protect every species at the expense of jobs and development and attempted to weaken the Endangered Species Act.

5. During his term in office, Bush 41's environmental diplomacy had some successes, but he is also remembered for his retrenchment in pursuit of environmental protection. The president's support for the 1990 Clean Air Act amendments not only reversed the intransigence on the part of Ronald Reagan on this issue but also helped the United States improve its relations with Canada over the acid rain problem. However, two years later, at the 1992 Earth Summit in Rio, Bush 41 had an opportunity to demonstrate U.S. leadership on two critically important issues—namely, the Global Climate Change Convention and the Convention on Biodiversity—yet he failed. He placed politics

over international cooperation and the warnings of the scientific community.

6. Despite serving for eight years as Ronald Reagan's vice president, George H. W. Bush raised expectations among the environmental movement that he would be a "green" president. Four years later, Bush 41's commitment to environmentalism was called into question. As a result, the League of Conservation Voters, an environmental watchdog group, gave him an overall grade of "D" for his performance.[68]

PART THREE

Presidents Having a Negative Impact on the Environment

CHAPTER 9

Ronald Reagan

Ronald Reagan entered office with an anti-environmental, prodevelopment orientation. Here was a president who could be characterized as acting contrary to bipartisan efforts to support the environment. As Shirley Anne Warshaw informs us, "Reagan had promised business and industry 'regulatory relief' during the campaign, asserting that federal regulation permeated every facet of communications, transportation, the workplace, manufacturing, air, water, and noise standards. He promised to eliminate or repeal many of these regulations and therefore reduce the cost of doing business."[1] In contrast to his immediate predecessor, Jimmy Carter, Ronald Reagan came into office with a tightly defined political agenda—one that was hostile to environmental protection. Moreover, he acted in clear opposition to fellow Republican Richard Nixon, who had established the Environmental Protection Agency, signed the landmark National Environmental Policy Act, and declared the 1970s as the "decade of the environment." Reagan inherited legislation to reauthorize the clean air act, but despite political and public pressure to support it during his term in office, it sat dormant and was ignored.

As he concentrated on economic growth and development, he faced public opinion and opposition in both houses of Congress that favored support for environmental protection.[2] When Reagan assumed a "pro" environmental stance it was usually when he considered it as having no negative impact on the economy or on business and industry. However, more often than not, the environment was secondary to the economy rather than being seen as an integral part of a healthy economy. According to C. Brant Short, "Reagan presented a powerful vision that countered the conservation consensus of the previous twenty years and offered an alternative ideological paradigm to understand nature, wilderness, natural resources, and public land management.... President Reagan and his advisors presented an agenda that challenged the core values that had guided environmental politics in the 1960s and 1970s."[3] As John Palmer and Isabel Sawhill further described Reagan's political agenda, "the administration's regulatory policies emphasized productivity over the protection of health, safety, civil rights, and the environment.... A similar pattern prevailed in its natural resources policies. Production of energy resources took precedence over conservation—whether in the Department of Energy's budget or in the Department of Interior's management of public lands and wilderness areas."[4]

Air quality provided a clear example of Reagan's position toward the biosphere. Richard Nixon had signed the 1970 Clean Air Act and Carter signed the reauthorization of that act in 1977. However, Reagan inherited the legislation and despite political and public pressure to support reauthorization during his term in office, it was ignored until his successor, George H. W. Bush signed the Clean Air Act Amendments of 1990. Moreover, Reagan complicated efforts to deal with acid rain in collaboration with Canada. Although he discussed the issue with Canadian prime minister Brian Mulroney, the acid rain problem was not dealt with in a substantive way until George H. W. Bush signed an air quality agreement with Canada in 1991.[5]

The Reagan administration's attitude toward the environment involved the development of New Federalism, which had first appeared with Richard Nixon. Unlike the Nixon administration's conception, which had promoted more authority for states and communities and less federal intrusion into subnational affairs, New Federalism during the Reagan and Bush 41 eras involved fewer resources to carry out state responsibilities. As Robert Dallek describes New Federalism, Reagan "had hoped to transfer some three-quarters of the federal government's ... domestic responsibilities to state and local governments."[6] In the process of applying this approach to subnational politics during the 1980s, environmental protection activities were decentralized and defunded.[7] As James Lester informs us, "During the Reagan and Bush administrations, the states were subject to substantial budgetary cuts in a number of environmental program areas, including air pollution control, water pollution control, hazardous waste management, pesticide enforcement, wastewater treatment, and safe drinking water."[8]

As a westerner, Reagan identified with the notion of giving states greater influence to control the environment. However, Samuel Hays described the evolution of a new environmental movement in the West that gave the region the "ability to meet federal agencies on their own ground, combat the old economy in the context of turf, and mobilize those with new ideas about what the environment of their region should be. This is a vastly different place, a region transformed, that can well be described as a 'new environmental West.'"[9]

Three decades ago, there was a severe clash between the federal govern-

ment and western interests in what was called the "sagebrush rebellion." It
has been described as "a conflict over the values that are to govern public
land management and use—such as the conflicts between livestock grazing
and wildlife management, extractive resource development and landscape
preservation, and hard and soft recreational uses."[10] The sagebrush rebellion
of the 1970s, along with the privatization movement of the 1980s, found support from a Reagan White House that preferred state's rights over federal control. The Reagan administration actually endorsed the notion of privatizing
public lands. In fact, as Christopher Klyza points out, two of the major proponents of privatizing public lands were David Stockman, head of Reagan's
Office of Management and Budget, and Steve Hanke, a senior economist on
President Reagan's Council of Economic Advisors.[11]

At the same time, of course, the sagebrush rebellion mobilized opposition
through a coalition of interests concerned about the impact on the environment. Included among the opponents of the sagebrush rebellion were environmental groups, public officials at all levels of government, Cecil Andrus,
secretary of the interior under Jimmy Carter, and Arizona governor Bruce
Babbitt (who would later became interior secretary in the Clinton administration) and surprisingly, sporting groups.[12]

All in all, Reagan's approach toward environmental policy making was
to seek ways to reduce the control of the federal government over the environment and to cut back on federal regulation and expenses while giving more responsibility to the states and the private sector.[13] Vice President
George H. W. Bush made the president's position clear at a dinner for congressional partisans in early 1981 when he stated that the Reagan mandate
was an effort to "reverse the trend of recent decades where bureaucratic decision making in Washington increased power at the expense of State, local,
and county governments."[14] He was in alliance with those who embraced the
idea of "environmental federalism," where political authority over the environment, particularly public lands, was transferred from the federal government to the states.[15]

A final comment about President Reagan's attitude toward environmental
protection, both domestically and globally, concerns the dominance of ideology over science. More often than not, Reagan would ignore science when
it conflicted with his political views, especially as they related to economic
growth and development. Moreover, as Norman Miller frames the issue:

As the costs of compliance grew with increasing stringent standards,
that scientific foundation became the target of those whose practices are

subject to environmental regulations. It was, not surprisingly, the Reagan administration that made the first move. By advocating the primacy of risk assessment and cost-benefit analyses in environmental rulemaking, Reagan challenged EPA to justify the science upon which its regulations were based—and dragged science itself into a policymaking role. At the same time that he was publicly raising the stakes for what he regarded as good science, however, he reduced EPA's scientific resources by cutting its budget.[16]

A specific example involves the issue of global climate change. Where President Carter responded to the scientific data with "expanded research" and "proposals for international action," Reagan "attempted to reduce the climate research effort."[17] This controversy involving science, politics, and ideology would return during the administration of George W. Bush.

Political Communication

Ronald Reagan differed from other presidents in that he had a background in broadcast media. At an early age he worked in both radio and television and he developed a personable style and delivery that was effective in the commercial arena and would serve him well when he turned to politics. Thirty years before he entered the White House, he was articulating themes that he would repeat throughout his political career. He would focus on and emphasize the problems created by big government, government bureaucracy, and government regulations.[18] These themes, among others, continued into his presidency beginning with his first inaugural address when he complained about the "size and influence of the federal establishment," the need to distinguish between the "powers granted to the federal government and those reserved to the states or to the people," and the problems associated with government "intervention and intrusion in our lives."[19] These themes would have importance for Reagan's environmental policy making as they could be seen in his attempt to shape environmental policy through budget cuts and his appointment powers. For instance, during his campaign for the presidency in 1980, he criticized the federal bureaucracy and demanded that the government get off the backs of the American people. Accordingly, "Reagan's political metaphors meshed comfortably with the Sagebrush Rebellion's notion that government had locked up the public lands, stifling economic growth and fueling inflation."[20] C. Brant Short informs us of a distinct rhetorical approach to environmentalism employed by Reagan during the 1980 campaign where Reagan refrained from reading a prepared speech about his plans to reform the Clean Air Act and instead "quipped that the Mt. St. Helen's volcano had probably dumped more sulfur dioxide into the air than is released in 10 years of 'automobile driving or things of that kind.' Reagan's decision to ignore a policy statement in favor of ridiculing environmental standards for clean air demonstrated his abiding preference for minimizing governmental involvement in the environment."[21]

While he talked considerably about the environment, his actions were symbolic and lacked a substantive commitment to ensure protection of the environment. Throughout his two terms in office, Reagan's rhetoric about the environment was at odds with public opinion about the environment. For instance, during his presidency fully two-thirds of the American people supported environmental protection over economic growth.[22] Moreover, while Reagan supported market forces and voluntary measures by business and industry to address environmental problems, American citizens held significantly different views. Yet by the time Reagan left office, more than 80 percent of Americans felt that business and industry would take action only if forced to do so by the federal government (up from 70 percent in 1970).[23]

As soon as he assumed the presidency, Reagan pitted the environment against other national issues and found himself defending the policies and actions of his appointees. For instance, after signing the Economic Recovery Tax Act of 1981, Reagan defended the role of interior secretary James Watt: "Jim Watt has been doing what I think is a common sense job in the face of environmental extremism that we've suffered from. And I can assure you Jim Watt does not want to destroy the beauty of America. He just wants to recognize that people are ecology, too. We have some needs, and there has to be provision for us to live."[24]

The following year, Reagan's philosophy about the economy and the environment was made clear and unequivocal in a message to Congress reporting on the Council on Environmental Quality. Once again, the earlier theme of government regulations was central to his argument: "We must create a more innovative and flexible framework in which our environmental programs operate. Regulations should complement, not stifle, market forces in determining the most cost-effective methods of proper environmental management."[25]

At a 1982 swearing-in ceremony for William Ruckelshaus, who succeeded Anne Gorsuch Burford as EPA administrator, who resigned under duress, Reagan stressed the importance of the U.S. role in addressing the problem of acid rain with Canada, its neighbor to the north: "Many of us, both here and in Canada, are concerned about the harmful effects of acid rain and what it may be doing to our lakes and forests. So, I'd like you to work with others in our administration, with the Congress, and with State and local officials to meet this issue head-on. . . . People on both sides of the border must understand that we're doing what's right and what's fair in this area."[26] Sadly, the United States during the Reagan administration squandered its opportunity to work with the Canadian government in making improvements in this policy area. Moreover, the Canadian government became increasingly upset with the Reagan administration for failing to make substantive efforts to work with it in an effective and collaborative way.

During the latter part of his first term in office and into his second term, Reagan continued to articulate a perspective on environmental preservation that differed from the actions of his administration. For instance, as he stated at a dedication ceremony for the National Geographic Society in 1984: "We want, as men on Earth, to use our resources for the reason God gave them to us—for the betterment of man. And our challenge is how to use the environment without abusing it, how to take from it riches and yet leave it rich. . . . As I said in my last State of the Union message: 'Preservation of our environment is not a liberal or conservative challenge—it's common sense.'"[27]

The following year, he boasted that the United States offered leadership at home and in the international environmental domain. As he responded to questions submitted by Canadian reporters in 1985: "We take pride that our Clean Air and Clean Water Acts and our other comprehensive environmental legislation have helped to set international standards. . . . For the future, I believe it is a question of doing what is reasonable and responsible after getting all the facts."[28] In a 1986 message to Congress about America's agenda for the future, the president argued, "Recognizing that environmental problems do not stop at national boundaries, we will continue to collaborate closely with other nations, on issues such as acid rain, to maintain the quality of the global environment and improve the management of natural resources of common interest."[29] In making these comments, Reagan failed to add that environmental successes were due to bipartisanship in Congress, that the Clean Air Act of 1977 languished during his administration, that his administration had cut the budget and environmental agency staff personnel, and that the problem of U.S. transboundary acid rain problems continued with Canada throughout the rest of his term in office.

Reagan's environmental philosophy was reflected in the 1980 and 1984 Republican party platforms. While giving lip service to conservation and wise management of the country's natural resources, the 1980 platform emphasized its concern with the "crushing burden of excessive regulations" and it stressed the need for cost-benefit analysis whereby the environment would be assessed against economic concerns. The 1984 platform focused on what Tatalovich and Wattier called the "need for retrenchment so that environmentalism did not damage the ability to provide energy resources or economic prosperity" while Republicans "took credit for restraining overly zealous actions by the environmentalists."[30] Despite Reagan's "talk" about positive efforts made in the environmental domain during his presidency, the Republican party platforms with which he was associated along with his legislative and executive actions suggested just the opposite.

Legislative Leadership

President Reagan entered the White House with a legislative agenda focused on concerns about big government, high taxes, and a weakened military establishment. Closely linked to these themes was a fundamental political philosophy that was oriented toward reducing the regulatory burden on business and industry and on viewing the environment in terms quite different from his predecessors.

The environmental philosophy of Ronald Reagan reflected his view of government and politics—namely, "government is not the solution" but rather "government was the problem."[31] Also, Reagan "thought environmental protection was fundamentally at odds with economic growth and prosperity."[32] Consequently, it was no surprise that with the passage in 1981 of the Economic Recovery Tax Act and Omnibus Budget Reconciliation Act, environmental programs would suffer along with other domestic programs.

Reagan's environmental legislative career was quite telling. On the one hand, he could take credit for signing the Hazardous Waste and Solid Waste Amendments of 1984, the Safe Drinking Water Act of 1986, and the Ocean Dumping Act of 1988. On the other hand, he opposed several important environmental bills including the Superfund Amendments and Reauthorization Act of 1986, the Clean Water Act Amendments of 1987, and the Nuclear Waste Policy Act Amendments of 1987. Where the environment fared well, one could point to a bipartisanship in Congress that continued the effort to promote environmental protection either with the support of the president or against the will of the president.

If one legislative initiative reflected the "problem of the environment" during the Reagan years, it was clean air legislation. Although bipartisan support within Congress ensured that clean air was an important public policy problem that would be addressed (albeit in incremental ways), the Reagan presidency moved in the opposite direction. Clean air initiatives began at the urban and state level long before the federal government became involved in the issue. By the time Richard Nixon entered the White House the federal government had been moving in the direction of promoting a national solution to the problem. As Gary Bryner reports, not only did the Clean Air Act of 1970 attempt to "protect every American from the health risks of polluted air," but it also had "enforcement powers" and "penalties."[33] After the Clean Air Act Amendments were passed in 1977, balancing the concerns of environmentalists and legislative supporters (stricter guidelines) on the one hand, and the auto industry (a two-year extension on tailpipe emission standards) on the other hand, the legislation languished during the 1980s as Reagan refused to act on the measure, thereby leaving the issue to his successor, George H. W. Bush. In persuading Congress to support his policies, President Reagan had the benefit of partisan control of the U.S. Senate during the first six years of his presidency. When Democrats gained control of the U.S. Senate in 1986, Reagan could still threaten to use the veto to thwart attempts to secure passage of clean air legislation. It is ironic that as a former governor of the most populous state, home to large urban areas with air pollution problems, Reagan failed to address this issue as a legislative leader.

By Reagan's second term in office Congress began to reassert its authority to block many of the president's anti-environmental efforts. For example, congressional opposition to Reagan's environmental agenda resulted in the expansion, reauthorization, or the passage of several significant pieces of legislation during the latter part of the president's second term, including the Safe Drinking Water Act (1986), the Superfund Amendments and Reauthorization Act (1986), and the Clean Water Act (1986).[34]

Administrative Actions

Upon entering presidential office, Ronald Reagan used executive powers to shape environmental policy and undermine the intent of legislation that had been passed by Congress during the 1960s and 1970s. The first day he assumed the presidency, and before settling in to his new job, he sent a clear message to the environmental community regarding how he would address the environment as an important public policy issue—namely, he cut the staff of the Council on Environmental Quality by 50 percent.[35] This action did not come as a surprise to the environmental community. When Reagan ran for governor of California his attitude toward the environment was quite clear. As Reagan biographer Lou Cannon explained, although Reagan as a California rancher was personally sensitive to the environment and wildlife, "he lacked even elemental understanding of what private developers would do to irreplaceable national treasures. Environmentalists sniffed at the lack of appreciation for natural esthetics evidenced in such famous Reagan remarks as his comment during the 1966 campaign [for governor], 'You know, a tree is a tree—how many more do you need to look at.'"[36]

The process employed by Reagan to circumvent Congress and use executive powers has been described by Richard Nathan as an "administrative presidency," wherein Reagan employed appointment, staffing, and budget control measures to implement change.[37] In an attempt to promote his philosophy of limited government and reduced regulatory power, Reagan's administrative strategy was a way to ensure that the values of the administration transcended the executive branch agencies in executing the law.[38] Ronald Seyb described Ronald Reagan's underlying rationale for implementing his administrative strategy in the following way:

> Distrust of and even disdain for the bureaucracy fed a determination to place political loyalty and ideological compatibility before professional competence in making appointments, to cut significantly the force and funding levels of departments and agencies harboring missions and practices he opposed, to construct a centralized system for reviewing agency rules and regulations to ensure their consistency with his program, to reinterpret statutes to allow for sweeping policy changes, and to develop "elaborate managerial control systems" for supervising the activities of executive agencies.[39]

Among the changes implemented by the Reagan administration was the appointment of Vice President Bush to head the new task force on regulatory relief. Hundreds of environmental regulations were reviewed, rescinded, or returned to the EPA to be revised in order to fit the values of the administration.[40]

Reagan also used the executive order as an instrument to control the regulatory process and impede the enforcement of environmental laws. As

Kenneth Mayer reports, Reagan had a tremendous impact on the regulatory process when he issued Executive Order 12291 in February 1981 and Executive Order 12498 four years later.[41] Where the former executive order implemented Reagan's cost-benefit analysis that was to be conducted by all executive agencies, the latter executive order mandated that executive agencies submit to the Office of Management and Budget all proposed regulatory actions that would take place during the following year. These executive orders allowed the administration to control the environmental regulatory process. Consequently, Congress was forced to "take active measures to try and recapture the ground it had lost to the president."[42]

Reagan appointed individuals with a decidedly conservative ideological orientation to high-level positions within the government. In doing so he relied on an old friend, Pendleton James, who was a personnel recruiter in California. Shirley Anne Warshaw explains that James was instrumental in the selection of almost all of Reagan's cabinet appointees except three, which coincidentally involved individuals appointed to positions affecting the environment, namely, James Watt (supported by Senator Paul Laxalt to head the Interior Department), James Edwards (supported by Senator Strom Thurmond to head the Energy Department), and John Block (supported by Senator Bob Dole to head the Agriculture Department).[43] These appointees had one characteristic in common—they "all shared an absolutely clear view of where they wanted to take the government."[44]

Prominent among Reagan's appointees were James Watt, who would become interior secretary, Anne Gorsuch Burford, appointed to assume leadership of the Environmental Protection Agency, and Rita Lavell to be assistant administrator for hazardous waste at the EPA. These individuals reflected an anti-environment, prodevelopment orientation.[45] Watt and Burford, in particular, attracted negative media attention for their overt opposition to environmental protection. James Watt was the center of negative publicity from the moment he was appointed secretary of the interior. Prior to his appointment, he had served as a lawyer in Denver and as president of the Mountain States Legal Foundation, which reflected his antiregulatory, prodevelopment environmental philosophy. Watt did not hesitate in pushing his agenda, which was reflected in his comment, "We will mine more, drill more, cut more timber."[46] In six short months, Watt had alienated major environmental groups and just over one year in office major environmental groups published an indictment of the Reagan administration's assault on the environment.[47] Jacqueline Vaughn Switzer drew a clear distinction between James Watt and Jimmy Carter's interior secretary: "[Watt] perceived environmentalists as 'dangerous and subversive,' suggesting they sought to weaken America and to undermine freedom. He called them extremists and likened them to Nazis. More telling, however, was the comparison of Watt to his predecessor, Cecil Andrus, who had said, 'I am part of the environmental movement and I intend to make the Interior Department responsive to the movement's needs.'"[48] After numerous gaffes, including Watt's opposition to a performance by the Beach Boys on the Capital Mall that embarrassed the president and his wife, Watt was finally asked to resign. He was replaced by William Clark who was later succeeded by Donald Hodel.

Anne Burford's reign as head of the EPA was tumultuous as well. Another appointee from Colorado, Burford arrived with little experience but engaged in significant actions that had considerable impact on environmental policy making, including the mission of the EPA and employee morale at the agency. Burford helped slow the rule-making process, engaged in massive budget cuts that hurt EPA functions, and cut the size of the EPA staff.[49] Burford's downfall occurred over the conflict over appropriate administration of the Superfund. A congressional investigation of Burford and other EPA officials was initiated due to their refusal to disclose documents regarding the progress of the Superfund cleanup. In the autumn of 1982, John Dingell, chair of the powerful House Energy and Commerce Committee, was concerned that the EPA was sluggish in its enforcement of its cleanup obligations and requested that Burford appear before his committee and supply documents concerning hazardous waste.[50] Burford, following the instructions of President Reagan, refused to cooperate with the committee and was ultimately found in contempt by a House vote.[51] Following this she resigned from her office. At that time, Reagan announced at a 1983 news conference that "there is 'environmental extremism' in the United States" and further charged that environmentalists would not be satisfied until "the White House looks like a bird's nest."[52]

Burford was succeeded by William Ruckelshaus, former Nixon EPA administrator. Although Ruckelshaus pursued a more balanced approach between the environment and the economy and argued in favor of increasing resources for environmental protection, the Reagan administration refused to change course or respond affirmatively to the EPA administrator's concerns about acid rain. This soon resulted in Ruckelshaus's resignation in November 1984.[53] Lee Thomas, an assistant administrator at the EPA, was appointed to head the agency and refocus it in light of increased scientific findings and public awareness while at the same time enhancing the existing "risk management" approach already in place at the EPA.[54]

Ronald Reagan's impact on the environmental policy-making process was profound. As Walter Rosenbaum argues, "Over Reagan's eight-year term, his executive appointees quietly and consistently slowed or delayed the implementation of numerous environmental programs, while budget reductions put many environmental agencies years behind in accomplishing important environmental missions."[55] Reagan's use of an "administrative strategy" ensured that efforts to reverse his priorities would take time, effort, a new commitment by Congress, and a new occupant in the White House.

Environmental Diplomacy

If Ronald Reagan pursued an anti-environmental agenda at home, it is no surprise that he would neglect the global environment. As some political observers have argued, "Reagan's strategy toward the environment was mainly directed toward domestic affairs and the progressive weakening of environmental protections. His overall lack of concern for environmental issues and his disdain for environmentalism was also apparent in his international agenda and diplomatic activities. . . . Reagan's declared position was that he would only agree to international treaties if they did not adversely affect the nation's economic interests."[56]

Reagan's diplomatic orientation regarding global environmentalism was clearly biased in favor of business and industry. He was opposed to any regulatory efforts that might hinder domestic developmental interests as they might relate to the international arena. During his first term in office, Reagan did sign several treaties, including the Convention for the Conservation of Salmon in the North Atlantic in 1982, the Convention for the Protection and Development of the Marine Environment of the Wider Caribbean Region in 1983, and the Protocol Concerning Cooperation in Combating Oil Spills in the Wider Caribbean Region, also in 1983.[57] However, other actions on his part displayed a disregard for ensuring protection of the global environment or working in a cooperative way with regional and international partners. For instance, he substituted his own Executive Order 12290 for Jimmy Carter's Executive Order 12264. This, in effect, reversed his predecessor's attempt to ensure safe transport of hazardous waste exported by American companies. Also, he refused to sign the United Nations Convention on the Law of the Sea that had been supported by Carter.[58]

Two key issues illustrate Reagan's orientation toward the global environment—namely, acid rain and the threat to the stratospheric ozone layer. First, the issue of acid rain drove a wedge between the United States and Canada. Due to pollutants from Midwest power plants and fossil fuel plants in the United States, forests and lakes in eastern Canada were degraded. Although Jimmy Carter had signed a memorandum of intent with Canadian prime minister Trudeau in 1980 to address the issue of transboundary air pollution, the new Reagan administration failed to go beyond words in his relationship with Canada. In short, as Daynes and Sussman report, "Although the issue was addressed through direct meetings between Reagan and the Canadian prime minister or through American and Canadian envoys, it remained unresolved until George H. W. Bush assumed the presidency."[59] To illustrate the depth of concern on the part of the United States' northern neighbor, in 1988 Canadian prime minister Brian Mulroney, irritated at Reagan, charged in no uncertain terms that "the United States would be pretty upset with me if I were dumping my garbage in your backyard. That's exactly what is happening, except this garbage is coming from above."[60]

Second, by the seventh year of his administration, Reagan had the opportunity to demonstrate U.S. global leadership by signing an important international environmental agreement—namely, the 1987 Montreal Protocol on Ozone Depletion that was established to reduce the threat to the stratospheric ozone layer. Despite disagreements among the international community, the United States in concert with several partners, including Canada, exercised assertive leadership in signing the protocol. This agreement followed the 1985 Vienna Convention for the Protection of the Ozone Layer (although it lacked mandatory guidelines). What was important about the Montreal Protocol was that opposing parties, including the chemical industry, environmentalists, Congress, and President Reagan, were willing to join together in support of this international environmental agreement. Global leaders, scientists, environmentalists, and corporate leaders alike recognized the threat posed by chlorofluorocarbons (CFCs) and cooperated in an effort to reduce the production of the chemical threat to the ozone layer.

Summary and Conclusion

Ronald Reagan was a man of contradictions who left a legacy of unbounded personal optimism and confidence in the American spirit alongside huge budget deficits and the Iran-Contra affair. For some, he won the Cold War against the Soviet Union and offered a strong presidency in response to Vietnam, Watergate, and Jimmy Carter. For others, his leadership style was an unwise delegation of power that led to problems and scandal. He sought the highest political office in the land only to use his power in an unsuccessful effort to reduce the size of the very government over which he presided, referring to government as the problem, not the solution. In contrast to Jimmy Carter, who wrote in his autobiography about the importance of the environment, Ronald Reagan "did not mention James Watt, the Department of Interior, the Environmental Protection Agency, the 'Sagebrush Rebellion,' national parks or wilderness areas, or any other topics related to his environmental legacy."[61]

Although Reagan considered himself an "environmentalist," he failed to comprehend the impact of his policies in the environmental domain. As reported by *Washington Post* journalist Lou Cannon in his book *President Reagan: The Role of a Lifetime:*

> Ronald Reagan was clearly a product of the American West. He was a former governor of the largest state in the region who was sympathetic to the goals of the Sagebrush Rebellion, a movement that epitomized conflict between the values of development and preservation. Reagan's conservative political philosophy prevented him from supporting federal interests before state interests in the environmental arena. Furthermore, his anti-regulatory approach to government along with his pro-development orientation inevitably had a major impact on his environmental policy in the state, national and global policy making arenas.

1. Ronald Reagan pursued a prodevelopment, antiregulatory, antienvironmental agenda. For Reagan, the environment was a secondary or tertiary issue to the economy and national defense. As Norman Vig argues, "Reagan was the first president to come to office with an avowedly anti-environmental agenda. . . . Reagan viewed environmental conservation as fundamentally at odds with economic growth and prosperity. He saw environmental regulation as a barrier to 'supply side' economics and sought to reverse or weaken many of the policies of the previous decade."[62]

2. Reagan entered the White House with a background in broadcast media, which prepared him for pushing his agenda using the bully pulpit. However, while he spoke often about the environment, and considered

himself an environmentalist, his actions were symbolic, lacked substantive commitment, and were often at odds with public opinion on
environmental protection.

3. Since Reagan's priority upon entering the presidency was to reduce
   the regulatory burden on business and industry, he was less likely
   to support important environmental legislation. A clear example of
   Reagan failing to meet the expectations of a legislative leader involved
   reauthorization of the Clean Air Act of 1977, which languished during
   his term in office. Where Reagan refused to act on this issue, his successor, George H. W. Bush, used the power resources of the White House
   in support of the Clean Air Act Amendments of 1990 (see chapter 9).

4. As we would see again during the administration of George W. Bush,
   Ronald Reagan appointed individuals to positions in his administration who were hostile to the environment. Among them were James
   Watt as secretary of the interior, Anne Gorsuch Burford as administrator of the EPA, and Rita Lavell as assistant administrator for hazardous waste at the EPA. Watt promoted a decidedly antiregulatory,
   prodevelopment environmental philosophy, while Burford had a
   record of cutting the size of EPA staff and the budget in ways that hurt
   EPA functions and slowing the rule-making process. Both Watt and
   Burford were forced to resign. Lavell was fired after it was discovered
   that she was involved in the "mismanagement of cleanup operations
   after discovery of the toxic chemical dioxin in roadways at Times
   Beach, Missouri," who ironically was the "only EPA official to face
   criminal charges."[63]

5. As environmental diplomat, Reagan's international environmental
   policy reflected the same orientation as his domestic environmental
   affairs—namely, opposition to actions that would have any negative
   impact on the economy in general and business and industry in particular. For eight years, Reagan presided over a contentious relationship
   with Canada because of his refusal to deal with the acid rain problem.
   By his seventh year in office, he had the opportunity to demonstrate
   U.S. leadership in the environmental domain when he supported the
   Montreal Protocol on Ozone Depletion.

6. In contrast to his fellow Republican Richard Nixon, who declared the
   1970s the decade of the environment, established the Environmental
   Protection Agency, and signed the landmark National Environmental
   Policy Act, Ronald Reagan was more concerned with seeking regula-

tory relief for business and industry in his effort to promote economic development over environmental protection. As an illustration of Reagan's orientation toward environmental affairs, Walter Rosenbaum reminds us that "Reagan sent a message to environmentalists on his first White House day by eliminating half the staff of the CEQ, thereby confirming that relations between the White House and environmentalist organizations would be deeply distrustful and antagonistic.[64] Moreover, Benjamin Kline informs us that one of the first actions Reagan took when entering the White House was to remove the solar panels that Jimmy Carter had installed on the roof.[65]

CHAPTER 10

George W. Bush

George W. Bush, like his father, began his quest for the presidency suggesting that he would be "eco-friendly." Unlike his father, Bush 43 identified closely with Ronald Reagan, who pushed a decidedly prodevelopment, antiregulatory, probusiness agenda. He equated the environment with energy resources while downplaying the importance of other issues such as air and water quality, conservation, protection of wildlife, and global warming. Among his early presidential initiatives was an increase in domestic energy production and opening up Alaska's Arctic National Wildlife Refuge (ANWR) to oil and gas exploration.

As president, George W. Bush caused environmentalists to question his very approach to the environment. In fact, the administration's prodevelopment stance was so firm that James Furnish, who was deputy chief of the U.S. Forest Service, quit in disgust because, as a senior member representing forestry, he would never be invited to participate with the president in any major decisions involving national forests.[1] Furnish was certainly not the only person to quit the administration over conservation and environmental issues. The most visible resignation was Christie Todd Whitman, administrator of the Environmental Protection Agency, who was described as "often at odds with the Bush White House over environmental issues and a lightning rod for the administration's critics," who left her position on June 27, 2003.[2] In addition, Elizabeth Shogren pointed to others who left government service as a result of working for this administration: "senior lawyers from the Environmental Protection Agency, a state director for the Bureau of Land Management, scientists with years of experience and top bureaucrats in Washington. Some of them left in protest, silent or loud. Others left because they believed the new administration had put them on a shelf, and they refused to stay there."[3] By 2002, three top officials at the EPA—Bruce Buckheit, head of the Air Enforcement Division of the EPA, Rich Biondi, associate director of the Air Enforcement Division of the EPA, and J. P. Suarez, head of the EPA's Office of Enforcement and Compliance—left the agency as a result of frustration with Bush 43's environmental policies.

George W. Bush consistently allowed other interests, especially national security and the war on terrorism, to take precedence over preservation of the environment. This is not surprising given that other presidents have acted in the same manner during times of crisis, but what is troubling is that Bush 43 neglected environmental preservation when there was no reason for doing so. Since the president's popularity was linked to foreign policy and especially the war on terrorism, he made every effort to repeatedly tie his domestic policy agenda and the environment in particular to the war effort. And as Norman Vig explained early in Bush's second term in office, Bush as a "self declared 'war president' . . . was able to dominate the domestic as well as the international scene as few American presidents have done. . . . However, one could argue that President Bush had no mandate for major changes in environmental policy. Polls indicate that most people are entirely satisfied with present levels of environmental protection and do not want to see environmental laws weakened."[4] As a result, as Benjamin Kline pointed out, there was a refocusing of priorities. There was no longer talk of the "'century of the environment,'" Kline wrote, "but instead the government declared that the Alaska Wildlife Refuge must be opened to the oil industry in order to free the nation from its dependence on Middle East oil and that the resources of the nation needed to be utilized to fight a lengthy and costly, but ultimately just, war against 'Terrorism.'"[5]

Other than Ronald Reagan, no other modern American president has been so harshly criticized by the environmental movement as has George W. Bush. One observer of the president went so far as to charge him with practicing "voodoo environmentalism" reminiscent of George H. W. Bush's criticism of "Reaganism" and "voodoo economics," suggesting that Bush 43's belief in "growth-induced conservation" as the primary key to environmental progress was sheer chicanery.[6] Another critic of the administration charged that the president too often tried to "suppress," "ignore," or "preempt" environmental interests in favor of developmental concerns.[7] The National Resources Defense Council was even harsher in its criticism of the Bush 43 administration, suggesting that its environmental policies were a "fundamental threat more sweeping and dangerous than any since the dawn of the modern environmental movement in the 1970s."[8] The Friends of the Earth went even further when it charged Bush 43 with putting "the earth up for sale."[9] In 2001, the League of Conservation Voters' report "Bush and the Environment: A Citizen's Guide to the First 100 Days" characterized Bush 43's environmental policy as "an unfortunate and aggressive anti-environmental approach to public policy."[10] At the end of the president's first year in office, the League of

Conservation Voters gave him a grade of "D–." As reported by the Associated Press, by mid-2003 the League revised its evaluation, giving the president an "F" and arguing that he was "well on his way to compiling the worst environmental record in the history of our nation."[11] During Bush's second term in office, environmentalists continued to criticize his environmental policy, and public opinion was in direct contrast to his environmental agenda.

President Bush 43 emphasized economic growth, the development of natural resources, and energy production. Once in office, he stressed that we could both "develop our natural resources and protect our environment."[12] At the same time, he argued that "we won't conserve our way to energy independence. We must also increase supply."[13] An important aspect of the energy issue concerned Alaska's Arctic National Wildlife Refuge, which the president viewed as a major source of petroleum for the country. He therefore argued that the United States could achieve energy independence by oil exploration on public lands including ANWR. However, environmentalists and many congressional Democrats opposed the effort to open up ANWR to oil drilling. While Bush 43 argued that oil could be extracted with minimal damage to the environment, opponents responded that it was reckless to open up a pristine, unspoiled area to potential damage for a source of oil whose availability and amount were at best uncertain and insufficient.

Environmentalists were very troubled to see how George W. Bush continually tried to undercut and undo many of the environmental achievements made by his predecessor, Bill Clinton—advancements that have been described by one environmentalist as "unrivaled since Theodore Roosevelt set up America's national parks."[14] Moreover, as the *New York Times* reported, "The Bush administration has spent the better part of two years rolling back Bill Clinton's environmental legacy. It has abandoned the Kyoto accord on global warming, weakened protections for wetlands and eased mining laws."[15] The reversal on wetlands, for example, was dramatic. Clinton in March of 2000 had increased the restrictions to protect streambeds from disruption. The Bush 43 administration relaxed the restrictions on all streams that do not flow all year, giving local officials more authority to conduct surface mining operations and refusing to exempt some 20 million acres of wetlands from receiving untreated sewage flows.[16] Moreover, where the Clinton administration opposed snowmobile access to national parks, the Bush 43 administration encouraged it. Where the Clinton administration attempted to increase wilderness areas, the Bush 43 administration worked to reverse this effort.

Philosophically, George W. Bush preferred decision making about environmental concerns to be made at the state and local level. In fact, a *New York Times* article compared him to Ronald Reagan and characterized Bush 43's approach to environmentalism, suggesting that "it seeks to tie environmental protection to other goals that are not always complementary, like economic growth, protection from regulation, increased energy production and deference to local control."[17] Yet it is interesting to note that when state and local officials criticized administration policies they were often ignored. As Barry Rabe argued, although Bush 43's campaign for the presidency in 2000 supported increased state authority over environmental programs, the events of September 11, 2001, may have altered Bush's plans regarding environmental federalism since attention shifted to the role of federal agencies in a new era of the war on terrorism.[18]

Given the position of the Bush 43 administration, it is interesting to note that a 2005 University of Vermont analysis of policies to reduce greenhouse gas emissions by subnational governments found numerous states and localities making an effort to reduce greenhouse gases following the standards of the Kyoto Protocol.[19] As reported by the *New York Times*, despite the position adopted by the Bush 43 administration, 132 mayors rebuffed the president and embraced Kyoto.[20] However, the administration in general, and the EPA in particular, continued to oppose efforts made by the states. Despite a landmark Supreme Court case, *Massachusetts v. Environmental Protection Agency* (2007), the EPA was given authority to regulate carbon dioxide (a major greenhouse gas) as a pollutant using the Clean Air Act, but the Bush 43 administration refused to comply with the decision.[21] The following year, the frustration of state governors toward the administration was captured by California governor Arnold Schwarzenegger. The Republican governor acted as spokesperson and leader of a dozen other state governors, who wanted to impose stricter guidelines on greenhouse gas emissions in their respective states, arguing that "if [the Bush administration] would have done something this year, I would have thought it was bogus anyway. If you don't really have an effect by doing something six months before you leave office . . . it doesn't sound to me believable at all. The sincerity is not there."[22]

In many instances, the problem with the Bush 43 administration's environmental policies could be found in its approach—namely, deferring to politics and ideology rather than science. The 2000 appropriations bill, for example, included an industry-supported data quality act that was opposed by environmentalists and some four thousand scientists—including Nobel laureates—who accused "the [Bush] administration of politicizing science" and argued that the act shifted "authority over the nation's science into the politicized environment of the OMB—a change . . . that will favor big business."[23] In addition, a *Washington Post* report in mid-2002 went further: "The Bush administration's approach to science policy has become increasingly controversial. Some scientists and lawmakers said the White House selectively uses studies to fit its political agenda and to justify its challenge to dozens of environmental rules drafted during the Clinton administration. The debate is highly subjective, frequently turning on nuanced interpretations of complicated scientific research, which makes it difficult to prove or disprove many of the White House claims—or the claims of Bush's critics."[24]

Two years later, during the spring of 2004, another news report pointed out that "top scientists and environmentalists accused the Bush administration . . . of suppressing and distorting scientific findings that run counter to its own policies."[25] The impact of this concern became critical among scientists involved in the global climate change debate (see "Environmental Diplomacy" section below).

Political Communication

Although political communication is a very important element of the president's arsenal of the instruments of power, Fred Greenstein argued, "In the first eight months of his presidency, Bush seemed insensitive to the importance of political communication in presidential leadership. He appeared reluctant to address the public; when he did so, his delivery was unpersuasive; and when he was unscripted, was error-prone."[26] However, as Greenstein continued, in the post-9/11 period Bush 43 improved his capacity to communicate with the American public. He "became a rhetorical activist, addressing the public regularly, forcefully, and sometimes eloquently and handling himself far more effectively in extemporaneous contexts" while at times he "slipped into his former plodding manner, especially when he read routine remarks, but he remained effective in major addresses."[27] More importantly, however, as one reporter argued, "While Bush barely mentioned the environment in his campaign, the environment is clearly an area where he may have the most impact."[28]

As a policy domain with important public health consequences, there was a clear disconnect between Bush 43 and the public over environmental issues. While citizens were relatively aware of the president's position on education and tax policies, for instance, very few were informed about his intentions regarding the environment. An April 2001 Pew Research Center survey of American citizens found that only one out of five Americans knew about the president's rejection of the Kyoto Protocol, and again, only one out of five survey respondents were aware of an "unpopular administration move to decrease regulations on arsenic in drinking water."[29] However, when asked about the Kyoto Protocol, "48 percent of the American public disagreed with the decision not to support it; 56 percent were opposed to drilling in the Arctic National Wildlife Refuge; and 81 percent supported tighter pollution standards for business and industry."[30] In a variety of policy decisions affecting the environment, including power plant emissions, building roads in national forests, and drilling for oil in ANWR, among many others, an observer of the polling data argued that "Bush's actions thus played into the stereotype of a conservative Republican former energy company executive who was too cozy with special interests."[31] In fact, only three months into the Bush 43 presidency, almost two-thirds of American citizens believed that "big business had too much influence over the administration's decisions."[32]

In major speeches to the nation, Bush 43 indicated that the environment is a peripheral issue at best although the administration made great strides in shaping environmental policy especially through an administrative strategy. In his inaugural address to the nation on January 20, 2001, Bush failed to include the environment as an important policy area, as it was not mentioned in the speech. One month later, in his first address to Congress and the people, he stated that his budget would provide full funding for the Land and Water Conservation Fund, increase funding for national parks, and help to improve the environment by cleaning up toxic dump sites.[33]

On Earth Day 2002, the president made a major speech in New York calling for conservation and stewardship. In the speech he tried to make the case that environmentalism was a value that is important for every American: "America understands our obligation much more so than in the years past. That we must be careful of our actions. Americans understand that. Good stewardship is a personal responsibility of all of us. And it's a public value. And that's what's important for Americans to understand, that each of us have a responsibility, and it's a part of our value system in our country to assume that responsibility."[34] While supporting in principle the role of the federal government in promoting environmental progress, in the same speech Bush pushed his Clear Skies Initiative, which raised concern among environmentalists and Democrats in Congress who were troubled that the new plan would weaken the existing Clean Air Act. Moreover, former vice president Al Gore, who lost to Bush in the 2000 election, responded to Bush's speech, arguing that "the Bush administration's so-called 'Clear Skies' initiative actually allows more toxic mercury, nitrogen oxide and sulfur pollution than if we enforced the laws on the books today. It ought to be called the 'dirty skies' initiative."[35]

In his State of the Union addresses in January 2002 and again in January 2003 the environment received variable attention. In the 2002 message, the president barely mentioned the environment, only stating support for a "cleaner environment" while promoting "reliable and affordable energy."[36] Although spending much time on the war on terror and the war in Iraq in the 2003 address, Bush 43 focused considerable attention on energy as it related to the environment.[37] The president indicated to Congress and the American people that one of his major goals was "energy independence" while "dramatically improving the environment." In his effort to demonstrate a commitment to making environmental progress, the president once again promoted his Clear Skies Initiative as well as his Healthy Forests Initiative. Both programs were opposed by environmentalists, in whose opinion the initiatives would have the opposite impact suggested by their names. The president indicated his opposition to command and control regulations, suggesting that market-based and voluntary measures are superior to oversight by the federal government. Ironically, or by intention, the environment received no coverage in the president's final State of the Union message of his first term, delivered in January 2004.

In comparing the first term of George W. Bush with that of his father, George H. W. Bush, and that of his immediate predecessor, Bill Clinton, we find that Bush 43 did not use political communication, in the form of national speeches, as a major means to define his commitment to the environment.[38] An evaluation of references to the environment in major speeches showed that Bush 43 made 25 percent fewer references to the environment than did his father and Bill Clinton. And in terms of the number of speeches he gave that were devoted to the environment, Bush 43 made 15 percent fewer than did Bill Clinton and Bush 41. Moreover, two scholars of the presidency and the environment evaluated radio addresses and the coverage given to the environment compared to the coverage of nine other issues including campaign finance, the economy and jobs, defense, and terrorism, among others.[39] The researchers concluded that the environment accounted for only 5 percent of all radio addresses delivered by the president.

During Bush 43's second term, the environment again received variable and/or repetitive attention in his State of the Union messages. In 2005 and 2006 the president argued that the United States needed to become less dependent on foreign oil.[40] In 2006 he made the powerful and ironic statement that "America is addicted to oil" while setting forth the proposition that technology was the key to "move beyond a petroleum-based economy." Yet no substantive change in energy policy emerged from the Bush administration. Again in 2007 and in 2008, Bush drew attention to the problem of U.S. dependence on foreign oil and the need to pursue new technologies to reverse this dependence and to provide a solution to the global problem of greenhouse gas emissions and climate change. Yet, in practice, he maintained support for a policy of market-based solutions.[41]

In the 2000 Republican Party platform upon which George W. Bush ran, the party made it clear from the outset that their nominee would approach environmental issues at the national level "just as he did in Texas."[42] Ironically, this was the very concern raised by the Texas Public Employees for Environmental Responsibility that pointed to environmental degradation in Texas during Bush's term as governor. Several themes emerged from a careful reading of the Republican platform: advancing economic prosperity and environmental protection hand in hand; basing environmental regulations on the best science; relying on market-based incentives; and pursuing environmental federalism in which decision making would occur primarily at the state and local level. For instance, while stating that national parks are the "crown jewels of the country's environmental heritage," the party platform asserted that they "belong to all Americans and should be accessible to all," which seemed to suggest opening public lands to commercial development and reversing actions taken by the Clinton administration to protect public lands.

Four years later, Bush ran for reelection on a platform that would continue the efforts he made during his first term. Important principles that emerged from the party platform included protecting private property rights; supporting the president's Clear Skies Initiative; relying on state and local governments as laboratories of innovation; passing "common-sense management reforms" for national parks; protecting oceans; continuing opposition to the Kyoto Protocol; and "modernizing" the Endangered Species Act. However, as described below, the only arena in which Bush 43 had a conspicuous accomplishment was that of ocean protection, through his establishment of national monuments in the Pacific Ocean.

Legislative Leadership

Bush 43 dispensed with bipartisanship over environmental policy and was at odds with congressional Democrats and environmentally friendly Republicans from the outset of his presidency. Political conflict arose over several important issues, including his budget priorities, clean air, clean water, allocations for the Superfund, arsenic levels in drinking water, the opening of Alaska's Arctic National Wildlife Refuge (ANWR) to gas and oil exploration, and the government's approach to energy policy.

As a legislative leader, Bush 43 attempted to weaken the National Environmental Policy Act (NEPA) and introduced his Clear Skies Initiative that was designed to replace the Clean Air Act. Passed thirty-two years ago under the Nixon administration, NEPA has been referred to as "the Magna Carta of environmental laws."[43] It is legislation that allows citizen groups and individuals to prevent special interests and public officials from damaging public lands. While the White House Council on Environmental Quality viewed its effort to set up a task force to alter the law as moving "federal environmental analysis and NEPA documentation into the 21st century," environmentalists viewed it as constraining and damaging to the law.[44] While the Clear Skies Initiative set limits on nitrogen oxide, which creates the smog and sulfur dioxide that causes acid rain, and would limit the release of mercury by 70 percent by the year 2018, unlike the Clean Air Act, it would not set uniform national standards compelling polluting companies to comply with the law.[45] Instead, Clear Skies would allow power plants to buy and sell pollution credits, which would allow companies the "right to pollute—among themselves."[46]

Another example of this type of legislative action taken on the part of the president as legislative leader involved reversing the Clean Water Act of 1977. Bush 43's substitute would allow coal companies to deposit mining wastes into streams, wetlands, and waterways without compensation.[47] Bush 43's Healthy Forests Initiative would exempt millions of acres of national forests from environmental review, encouraging logging and timber sales of old growth forests and reversing President Clinton's policies. Such a policy was of concern to environmentalists who saw an increase in logging of old growth forests as threatening, among other areas, the Giant Sequoia National Monument where some individual trees date back some two thousand years.[48] Nonetheless, the Republican-controlled Congress passed the legislation. Furthermore, whereas the Endangered Species Act of 1973 had been used by previous presidents to protect flora and fauna, the Bush 43 administration worked to weaken the law. A study reported in the *New York Times* indicated that whereas President George H. W. Bush added an average of fifty-eight species per year and President Bill Clinton protected an average of sixty-two species per year, George W. Bush determined during his two terms in office that only fifty-nine species should be considered "endangered." [49]

The centerpiece of Bush 43's environmental legislative agenda was energy production. In May 2001 the administration proposed its energy plan while emphasizing that the country faced an energy crisis not seen since the 1970s.[50] The president urged Congress to support more energy production, including increased domestic oil and gas drilling and new nuclear and coal plants.

Another aspect of the energy debate concerned greenhouse gas emissions. The Republican-controlled U.S. Senate rejected a bill to implement mandatory caps on greenhouse gas emissions from industry, automobiles, and power plants, a move that was a victory for the Bush 43 administration. Once again, differences over the science affecting greenhouse emissions came into play, as cosponsor of the legislation John McCain of Arizona argued that science offers "irrefutable" evidence of human-induced climate change while James Inhofe of Oklahoma called into question climate change, dismissing as "flawed science" the underlying rationale of the legislation.

The issue of Alaska's Arctic National Wildlife Refuge was also problematic for the president. Although the Republican-controlled House passed the president's energy plan, it stalled in the Senate. Bush 43 had urged senators to overturn the 1980 ban on oil exploration in ANWR, as Republicans supported energy development and Democrats pushed for alternatives to increased energy use.[51] On April 18, 2002, the Senate rejected the administration's ANWR proposal as forty-five Democrats were joined by eight Republicans to defeat the amendment.

Despite the setback regarding ANWR, the administration continued to pursue numerous other sites in the country, especially the Rocky Mountains, for oil and gas exploration.[52] In November 2003 the Republican-controlled House again passed the administration's energy proposal where two-thirds of the tax breaks went to the fossil fuel industry.[53] However, the Senate once again refused to support it, thus depriving the president of a legislative victory. While the president tried directly or indirectly through the remainder of his term in office to secure support for opening up ANWR to oil and gas exploration, he was unable to gain support in Congress.

During the first year of Bush's second term, as Norman Miller informs us, the Energy Policy Act of 2005 represented "a legislative triumph for the Administration. It appropriated billions of dollars in subsidies to the fossil fuel and nuclear industries, strong supporters of the Republican Party, while allocating a small percentage of that amount to conservation and alternate energy sources. On the other hand, the broad parameters of the energy package introduced in 2007, after the Democratic Party secured modest majorities in both Houses in the 2006 mid-term election, generally reversed these priorities."[54]

Administrative Actions

From the outset, Bush 43's appointments caused concern among the environmental community, beginning with his running mate, Dick Cheney, a former Wyoming senator and petroleum entrepreneur. The appointment of Cheney as head of the administration's energy task force in the early months of the administration resulted in conflict between the White House and Congress over the administration's approach to energy policy and the secret actions of the task force. As two researchers observed about the process: "Allegations were made that the vice president and the task force had met with representatives of business and industry in shaping energy policy, while environmentalists were excluded from the meetings. A potential Constitutional conflict ensued after the administration refused to release the records of the energy task force meetings to the General Accounting Office."[55] A March 2001 e-mail—which was not released by the White House until April 2002—indicated that input from environmental groups would only be considered if it was "consistent" with the policy of the Bush 43 administration.[56] In May 2001 the General Accounting Office (GAO) was asked to investigate the controversy by House Democrat Henry Waxman(D-Calif.) and Senator John Dingell (D-Mich.). Although the GAO asked the vice president for information relating to the secret meetings and a variety of documents relating to the individuals involved in the energy task force, Cheney argued in August 2001 that the GAO lacked authority to investigate the matter.[57] Over one year later, in November 2002, a federal judge ruled that the Bush 43 administration was required to turn over documents to the GAO relating to the activities of the energy task force.[58] The following month, a newly appointed federal district judge rejected the GAO lawsuit which ended the controversy for the foreseeable future.[59]

Where two appointments—Christie Todd Whitman and Fran Mainella—
were nominally sympathetic to the environment, Bush 43 found ways to
structurally limit their decision-making power. Christie Todd Whitman was
generally acceptable to the environmental community, but she served as administrator of the EPA for only two-and-a-half years due to problems with
the administration. As EPA administrator, she lost a great deal of power and
authority within the administration since the president thought nothing of
personally intervening in EPA affairs, as he did in November 2002, to protect
utility companies from clean air regulations that specified that when utility
companies or factories expanded or improved their facilities they would have
to install new antipollution equipment. This sort of presidential interference
made it difficult for the EPA to enforce regulations.[60] As Walter Rosenbaum
observed, "Her environmentalist sympathies . . . quickly made her the administration's odd person out. After a series of highly publicized, protracted
disagreements and frustrations with the White House, Whitman resigned
in early 2003, having satisfied neither environmentalists nor their critics."[61]

Whitman's replacement, former Utah governor Michael Leavitt, argued
that he would be sensitive to environmental issues. One positive outcome
early in his tenure as EPA administrator was determining, for the first time,
that highway motorcycles would be subject to new emission standards and
that small scooters and mopeds would be subject to emission standards.[62]
Although she represented a shade of green within the administration, Fran
Mainella, who was appointed to head the National Park Service, was relatively alone, as most of Bush 43's appointments represented prodevelopment
interests.

Sussman and Daynes point out the importance of Bush 43's appointments in their assessment of the president and the environment in the following way: "The interests represented by George W. Bush's appointments
included the fossil fuel industry, mining, ranching and timber. As heads of
agencies, Bush's appointees were in a position to use their power to appoint
lower-level officials and staff that would most likely share the Bush environmental philosophy."[63] For example, for deputy administrator of the EPA the
president appointed Linda J. Fisher, who had formerly been employed as vice
president of government and public affairs at Monsanto, a company involved
with chemicals and agribusiness.[64] Appointed to serve as chair of the Council
on Environmental Quality was James Connaughton, who previously represented General Electric's interests in protecting toxic waste sites against the
challenges of the EPA.[65]

The Interior Department was also staffed by those supporting Bush's policies on the environment. Gale Norton, a protégé of President Reagan's interior secretary, James Watt, who had a reputation as quite unfriendly to the environment, was tapped to head the Interior Department. Steve Griles, who in the past advocated offshore drilling and who had previously served as a lobbyist for oil and coal interests, was appointed deputy secretary of the Interior Department.

As a member of Congress, John Ashcroft, who was appointed attorney general, regularly voted against environmental protections, while Thomas Sanonetti, who was appointed as assistant attorney general, had been a lobbyist for the coal industry. Bush 43's secretary of agriculture, Ann Veneman, was also on record in opposition to environmental laws while her undersecretary, Mark Rey, was previously a spokesperson for the timber industry. Moreover, Spencer Abraham, secretary of energy, who had previously served as an aide to Vice President Dan Quayle, supported drilling for oil and gas in ANWR and opposed higher fuel efficiency for sport utility vehicles.

Bush 43 followed in Ronald Reagan's footsteps as he implemented an "administrative strategy" regarding the environment (see chapter 9). In promoting an anti-environmental agenda, he criticized a command and control approach to environmental policy, which he argued put an undue burden on business and industry. Here the president implemented an approach that contradicted his own philosophy about government, namely, he implemented a strong federal regulatory process that emanated from the White House, one that drove "the formulation and execution of public policy."[66] In short, the appointment, budget, rule-making, and regulatory processes would be used to shape environmental policy. As two observers of the process explained it, "an administration can employ this subtle aspect of presidential power to implement far-reaching policy changes. Most of the decisions are made without the public attention that accompanies congressional debate."[67] Karen Hult explained how Bush 43 used the appointment power in a negative way to weaken the enforcement power of the agency: "Other times the White House has decided *not* to fill particular vacancies, arguably signaling the priority it gives to certain tasks. For example, the former director of the Environmental Protection Agency's Office of Regulatory Enforcement (who resigned in the spring of 2001 after having worked at the EPA for twelve years) contended that the administration continued its 'stealth attack on environmental protection' by not replacing him for over eighteen months."[68] A 2007 *Washington Post* investigation involving EPA pursuit of criminal cases against polluters discovered that they actually decreased during the Bush presidency. Using data obtained from the EPA and the Justice Department, reporters found that the prosecution of polluters (new cases and convictions) declined by one-third.[69]

Bush 43's actions with regard to clean air illustrates the administrative strategy employed by the president. As we noted earlier, he initially introduced his Clear Skies Initiative as a means to circumvent the Clean Air Act. However, when the 107th Congress failed to pass his Clear Skies program he decided to circumvent the legislative branch and implement an administrative strategy by changing regulatory and rule-making processes related to "new source review" regulations. As Michael Kraft describes it, new-source review regulations, part of the Clean Air Act of 1977, "were intended to force older, coal-fired power plants, oil refineries, smelters and steel mills, pulp and paper mills, and other industrial facilities to install new emissions controls when their plants undergo certain major renovations."[70] As a result of Bush 43's revision of the new-source review rule, the EPA decided in November 2003 that it would ease enforcement of pollution cases. The administration thus "decided not to sue dozens of coal-burning utilities, oil refineries, and other industries for past dirty air violations."[71] Moreover, Bush's position on the Clean Air Act and global warming became quite clear when he completely ignored the Supreme Court's 2007 major decision in *Massachusetts v. Environmental Protection Agency*, which indicated that the EPA had an obligation under the Clean Air Act to regulate greenhouse gases. In defying the court's instructions, the president maintained that the EPA had no obligation to regulate carbon dioxide and other greenhouse gases under the Clean Air Act, and "even if it did, it would not use the authority."[72]

Administrative actions also involved the administration's plan to open up ANWR to oil and gas drilling, which received unwanted press coverage in the spring of 2002 when the U.S. Geological Society (USGS) issued a report based upon twelve years of research that indicated that drilling for oil in ANWR would have harmful effects on wildlife. One week later, the USGS issued a two-page follow-up report commissioned by interior secretary Gale Norton that contradicted the original report suggesting that the Bush 43 administration was shaping the "science" regarding the relationship between oil exploration in ANWR and protection of wildlife and their habitat.[73] The issue of ANWR illustrates the Bush administration's approach to public lands issues. According to an analysis by the *Washington Post*, "rules governing millions of acres of undeveloped federal lands in the West . . . decisively favor energy development at a cost of reduced protections for some of the country's last wild spaces."[74] As the analysis showed, weakened federal policies resulting from administration rule changes opened up over 60 million acres of public lands to potential logging and drilling.

At about the same time, the administration made a small change in rules governing what became known as mountaintop removal resulting from coal exploration, especially in West Virginia. Regulations governing "the practice of dumping mining debris into streambeds" were changed by reclassifying mining debris. What had been labeled "waste" was now called "fill," which resulted in protecting the process—a simple change that had profound consequences.[75]

The Bush 43 administration's approach to environmental protection was best summed up by Russell E. Train, who opposed Bush's reelection campaign in 2004. Train, who served both Richard Nixon and Gerald Ford as head of the EPA, lamented that "it's almost as if the motto of the administration in power today in Washington is not environmental protection, but polluter protection. I find this deeply disturbing."[76]

Environmental Diplomacy

George W. Bush consistently allowed other interests like national security and foreign affairs to take precedence over preservation of the environment. Since his popularity was linked to his foreign policy stance, he made every effort to repeatedly tie his domestic policy agenda and the environment in particular to the events of September 11, the war on terror, and the war in Iraq. In short, he failed to include in his policy agenda a commitment to "environmental security."

One concern particularly troubling to environmentalists was his "go it alone" strategy in foreign affairs and the global environment, which caused some difficulties for the United States in the international arena. One of the first actions taken by President Bush 43 was calling the Kyoto Protocol, signed by Bill Clinton, fatally flawed and renouncing it in March 2001. The president was reluctant to join with other nations in limiting global greenhouse gas emissions that contribute to global warming, an action that irritated leaders throughout the world since the United States is a major contributor of greenhouse gases. It was an attitude that caused anti-American demonstrations in Geneva, Madrid, and Stockholm as well as strong criticism from European officials who had formally ratified the agreement.[77] Instead of working with international partners, Bush 43 proposed a substitute measure that called for voluntary compliance on the part of nations rather than mandatory requirements.

Bush 43's "go it alone" strategy was evidenced again when, in the autumn of 2002, he refused to attend the World Summit on Sustainable Development held in Johannesburg, South Africa, where some 174 countries were represented. U.S. secretary of state Colin Powell attended the conference in place of the president and received criticism from other delegates for the United States position in opposing the adoption of rigid deadlines and timetables to reduce greenhouse gas emissions. Yet the Bush 43 administration continued to promote a policy of consumption and energy production with little if any attention to conservation, while at the same time U.S. automobile fuel efficiency declined.

Despite reports by the Intergovernmental Panel on Climate Change and the U.S. National Academy of Science, the Bush 43 administration opposed substantive efforts to address the problem of global warming. Although more and more scientists attributed the increase in global warming to human activities, especially the burning of fossils fuels, the president maintained a position that opposed the Kyoto Protocol as a first step toward international action and supported instead voluntary rather than mandatory guidelines and timetables. Three weeks prior to the 2004 presidential election, a Reuters report warned that "an unexplained jump in greenhouse gases since 2002" was detected and the "rise in the past two years is quicker than mapped out in UN projections to the year 2100 based on increased human use of fossil fuels like coal, oil, or gas."[78]

As we noted earlier in this chapter, President George W. Bush put himself at odds with the findings of scientific research that ran counter to the administration's political agenda. Global climate change, in particular, had been at the center of an ongoing debate between the scientific community and the Bush 43 administration (along with scientific contrarians in support of the president). Dating back to his first year in office, the National Academy of Sciences, according to the *Washington Post*, "rejected Bush administration skepticism about global warming, declaring that it was a real problem caused at least in part by man-made pollution that could well have a 'serious adverse' impact by the end of the century."[79] By the midpoint of his second term, criticisms from the scientific community intensified. In 2006 scientists at the National Oceanic and Atmospheric Administration argued that they were being muzzled by the administration while scientists, engineers, and staff at the Environmental Protection Agency were pleading with Congress to investigate the agency due to its lax approach to its own greenhouse gas programs.[80] A month before the February 2007 release of the *Fourth Report of the Intergovernmental Panel on Climate Change*, which provided a consensus on the human impact on global warming and climate change, the *Christian Science Monitor* reported, "More than 120 scientists across seven federal agencies say they have been pressured to remove references to 'climate change' and 'global warming' from a range of documents, including press releases and communications with Congress."[81] In short, the Bush 43 administration engaged in activities that created roadblocks to objective, dispassionate scientific inquiry while stifling the scientific community's efforts to report research findings to the American public about human activities and global climate change.

The president moved on several fronts in an effort to exempt the military from environmental laws including waivers on military actions with regard to air pollution laws, protection of endangered species and migratory birds, and harassment of marine mammals. Although Democrats opposed these efforts, the deputy undersecretary of defense for installations and environment argued that environmental laws are "limiting realistic preparations for combat, and therefore, our ability to maintain the combat readiness of America's military forces"[82] For instance, after the events of September 11, the EPA dropped its opposition to the use of Halon 1301 (a gas harmful to the ozone layer) used by Air Force F-16s.[83] Moreover, Bush 43 supported the Navy's demand that it be allowed to ignore requirements of the National Environmental Policy Act, the primary environmental sunshine law that demands justification for agency actions. For instance, the Navy felt it should not have to assess damage to marine life when testing its new low-frequency sonar, a technology that emits a noise comparable to that of "a Boeing 747 engine at takeoff."[84] In July 2002 the Navy won a five-year authorization from the National Oceanic and Atmospheric Administration (NOAA) for exemption from the federal rules protecting marine mammals.[85] However, the decision by NOAA could not avoid court action. A San Francisco federal judge refused to allow scientists to use the Navy sonar system to track gray whales since the sonar system had not been proven safe.[86]

One area in which the president worked with environmentalists involved the use of the island of Vieques for Navy bombing practices. Residents on Puerto Rico, along with environmentalists, so criticized the administration that eventually it agreed to halt military exercises and bombing of the island in May 2003.[87]

To his credit, the president supported (with the encouragement of secretary of state Colin Powell) two important international environmental agreements that showed that the United States was capable of working with international partners regarding the global environment. Bush 43 committed the United States to the Stockholm Convention on Persistent Organic Chemicals (that would restrict the use of twelve lethal chemicals), and he supported the "debt for nature swaps" of the Tropical Forest Conservation Fund.[88] Despite this progress, the administration was criticized by public health and environmental groups for not including in the Stockholm Convention a way to add more pollutants to the list when needed.[89] Bush 43 earned high marks in January 2009 from the *Washington Post* for ocean conservation as a result of his 2006 establishment of the Northwestern Islands Marine National Monument that would protect 140,000 square miles around Hawaii. Two weeks prior to leaving office he established three more marine national monuments that would protect 195,000 square miles in the Pacific Ocean.[90] This designation of a vast area in the South Pacific off the coasts of American Samoa, the Mariana Islands, and the U.S. Central Pacific Islands ensures that the reefs and volcanic landmasses will be protected from poaching, oil spills, and other damage.

Summary and Conclusion

On multiple environmental issues including air pollution, water quality, national forests, wetlands, mercury pollution, and global warming, President George W. Bush received criticism from the environmental community and congressional Democrats and praise from business and industry. A comparison of George W. Bush with his father, George H. W. Bush, shows that the son has not lived up to the standards set by his father (at the same time, his father did not meet the standards set by other presidents including Lyndon Johnson, Richard Nixon, Jimmy Carter, and Bill Clinton, among others).[91] Bush 41 talked more about the environment, expanded more national monuments, signed more pro-environmental legislation and international environmental agreements, and allocated more funding for environmental programs than did his son, Bush 43.

1. One factor that distinguishes President George W. Bush from his presidential counterparts, except Ronald Reagan, was his effort to politicize environmental policy while downplaying, interfering with, or ignoring scientific studies as they related to environmental politics. This was especially true of global climate change. By the end of his

first term in office, scientists at NASA and NOAA complained about censorship imposed at their respective agencies while other scientists, including twenty Nobel laureates, issued a statement "accusing the Bush administration of deliberately distorting scientific findings to further its political aims."[92] In 2007 the *Christian Science Monitor* reported that over one hundred scientists at several federal agencies complained about White House interference regarding global warming studies.[93]

2. Although George W. Bush often misspoke when addressing public concerns, he was also misleading in his rhetoric when he discussed the environment, failing, among other things, to account for scientific findings that would bolster protection. He was vague, at best, when speaking about the environment, yet he attempted to characterize himself as eco-friendly. His actions, and those of others within his administration, however, proved harmful to the environment. Ironically, it was George W. Bush, in the 2000 presidential campaign, who appropriated the environmental issue, making it his own, and became the "environmental candidate," in the eyes of many of the voters. In the process, he was able to outmaneuver his opponent, Al Gore, who was the only proven environmentalist running for president. Despite this, in each of George W. Bush's State of the Union messages, he spoke as a champion of the environment, but his actions supported prodevelopment, antiregulatory values, not the environment. This was the case even with regard to global warming, an issue considered by many to be the primary environmental issue of the twenty-first century. For George W. Bush it was just another environmental issue to ignore and downplay.

3. During Bush's eight years in office, not one major piece of environmental legislation was passed. This was not surprising given his environmental philosophy and a Republican-controlled Congress that was at odds with environmental protection. In fact, the president used the power resources of his office in an effort to reverse the impact of extant environmental bills including the Clean Air Act and the Clean Water Act. Although Bush 43 proposed a Clear Skies Initiative to replace the Clean Air Act he failed to gain congressional support for this initiative. However, his Healthy Forests Initiative, which benefited the timber industry at the expense of protecting the environment, was passed and signed into law. During his tenure as president, Bush 43 along with congressional Republicans made every effort possible to open up

Alaska's Arctic National Wildlife Refuge to oil and gas exploration but failed, as he was strongly opposed by Senate Democrats.

4. Just as Ronald Reagan had done before him, George W. Bush employed an "administrative strategy" to push his anti-environmental agenda. Through the budget and appointments process, he sought to shape environmental policy. Furthermore, with the exception of Christie Todd Whitman, whom he recruited to head the EPA, the president's appointments reflected a pro-industry, antiregulatory orientation.

5. In the global arena, Bush 43 encouraged international cooperation with regard to military affairs. This was particularly true regarding the war on terrorism and the war in Iraq, yet he practiced a "go it alone" strategy when it involved environmental affairs. During his tenure in office, Bush 43 signed only a handful of major international environmental agreements including the Stockholm Convention on Persistent Organic Chemicals and the Tropical Forest Conservation Fund. However, when confronted with global climate change, the primary environmental issue of the twenty-first century, he rejected the Kyoto Protocol even though the United States is one of the world's greatest producers of damaging greenhouse gases. In an op-ed piece in the *Philadelphia Inquirer* in the spring of 2004, respected journalist Walter Cronkite argued that "global warming [was] at least as important as gay marriage or the cost of Social Security. And if it is not seriously debated in the general election, it will measure the irresponsibility of the entire political class. This is an issue that cannot, and must not, be ignored any longer."[94] In September 2004 British prime minister Tony Blair, a staunch ally of Bush 43 in Iraq, challenged the president to join him and the rest of the international community to address the problem of global climate change.[95] However, the president continued to support voluntary measures to address the issue of greenhouse gas emissions.

6. During the twentieth century, several presidents took actions that would move them closer to being considered as genuine environmental presidents. George W. Bush is the first president of the twenty-first century, but his environmental record has demonstrated that he certainly will not be considered an environmental president of this century. On the one hand, he receives credit for several pro-environmental actions. For instance, he supported new "diesel standards" that would reduce truck and bus pollutants by 90 percent and a new "Clean Air Interstate Rule" that would be applied in twenty-eight states in the east-

ern United States geared to reduce nitrogen oxide and sulfur dioxide by 70 percent. On the other hand, as we have stated elsewhere: "When one takes account of George W. Bush's environmental accomplishments and compares them to the damage done to the environment by this president and his Administration, any objective assessment would have to conclude that those actions to undercut environmental protection weighed much more heavily than the very few positive accomplishments to his credit."[96] Furthermore, we stand by our conclusion, namely, that "if 'pale green' describes the bare minimum effort of a president to promote environmental quality since the modern presidency began with FDR, then George W. Bush would qualify—and this becomes his environmental legacy."[97]

Conclusion

Comparing the Modern Presidents' Environmental Policies

We travel together, passengers in a little spaceship ... preserved from annihilation only by the care, the work, and, I will say, the love we give our fragile craft.

ADLAI STEVENSON, 1965

As one of the three major pillars of the U.S. political system, the American presidency is expected to fulfill public expectations in performing domestic and foreign policy making. Over the years, the American presidency has been concerned primarily with the economy, jobs, and foreign and national security policy. Health care, education, civil rights, and domestic and transboundary environmental concerns, among other issues, have received different levels of consideration by different presidents.

Over the last seven decades, the twelve presidents who have occupied the White House can be assessed in terms of their commitment to environmentalism. To what extent did they use the power resources of their office to promote environmental values or to what degree did they favor development over preservation and conservation values? Did they take effective, affirmative action that had a positive impact on the environment, function in a symbolic or cautious manner, or use the power of the White House in a way that had a negative impact on the environmental domain?

Environmental Characteristics of the Modern Presidents

Presidents have played a diverse role in the environmental policy-making process. The characteristics, actions, and accomplishments of the modern presidents regarding the environmental domain are summarized in the table below. When considering the theme of individual administrations and the orientation of individual presidents toward the environment, we find a clear difference between Democrats and Republicans. Conservation efforts tend to be associated with Democratic leadership while Republicans are, on the whole, linked to a prodevelopment, antiregulatory orientation. Franklin D. Roosevelt ushered in the "golden age of conservation" while John Kennedy was instrumental in promoting an environmental legacy for future generations. Lyndon Johnson wanted most to beautify America by cleaning up trash, waste, and pollution. Jimmy Carter spoke often about conservation and alternative sources of energy while Bill Clinton (and Al Gore) emphasized "sustainable development." In contrast, Dwight Eisenhower preferred a limited role for the federal government, George H. W. Bush attempted to balance the economy and environment, Ronald Reagan stressed cost-benefit analysis when evaluating environmental concerns, and George W. Bush maintained a probusiness orientation. Having said this, Richard Nixon was the anomaly, as he declared the 1970s the "decade of the environment."

Presidents don't act in isolation from their political environment, and each has had key individuals who played an important role in influencing presidential action involving the making of environmental policy. From Franklin Roosevelt to Lyndon Johnson, the secretaries of the Department of the Interior and the Department of Agriculture contributed in major ways to defining the parameters of environmental policy making. Harold Ickes, Stewart Udall, Cecil Andrus, and Bruce Babbitt all played an important role in promoting protection of the public lands. In contrast, Douglas McKay became known as "giveaway McKay" during the Eisenhower administration, while James Watt became a lightning rod for environmentalists' wrath during the Reagan years. Beginning with Nixon, the head of the Environmental Protection Agency (EPA) increasingly became a key player. Where Anne Gorsuch Burford exhibited overt preference for business interests over the environment while serving under Reagan, Carol Browner promoted a more balanced approach to the economy versus environment debate during the Clinton years. While Bush 41 raised the hopes of environmentalists by appointing William Reilly as head of the EPA, Reilly's influence was downplayed as Bush 41 was influenced in turn by interior secretary Manuel Lujan. Bush 43 chose Dick Cheney as his vice president, and selected Gale Norton, who followed in the steps of James Watt, while Christie Todd Whitman, viewed as a moderate as EPA head, saw her influence decline within the Bush 43 environmental policy–making process.

Presidents have a variety of methods and instruments of power they can employ in the process of carrying out their policy agenda. First, through political communication, presidents can make a connection with the American public by reaching out to them through a variety of communication outlets. Major speeches, including the State of the Union message, provide the president with the opportunity to outline the priorities of the administration, where, for instance, President Richard Nixon declared the 1970s as the "decade of the environment." The president also disseminates preferences through special messages to Congress and communicates in other settings including talks to organized interests and news conferences.

Table: Characteristics of the Modern Presidents and Environmental Policy

President	Theme	Attitude Toward Environment	Infuence On President	Methods	Major Accomplishments
Roosevelt	Golden Age of Conservatism	Balance environment with economic recovery	Harold Ickes, Secretary of Interior Henry Wallace and Claude Wickard, Secretary of Agriculture	Fireside chats Legislation Executive actions	Civilian Conservation Corps Tennessee Valley Authority Depression and wartime conservation
Truman	Conservation and resource development	Conservation and resource development to establish viable economy and U.S. role in the world	Harold Ickes, Secretary of Interior Claude Wickard, Clinton Anderson, and Charles Brannan, Secretary of Agriculture	Speeches Executive actions	Land and water wartime management
Eisenhower	Public-private partnerships Emphasis on state and local government	Environment secondary to economic growth	Douglas McKay, Secretary of Interior Fred Seaton and Ezra T. Benson, Secretary of Agriculture	Speeches Diplomacy	Mission 66 National Parks program
Kennedy	Conservation	Environment linked to American greatness Pass on a positive conservation legacy to future generations	Stewart Udall, Secretary of Interior Orville Freeman, Secretary of Agriculture	Speeches Legislation Executive actions	Air and water legislation Limited nuclear test ban treaty
Johnson	New conservation	Beautification	Stewart Udall, Secretary of Interior Orville Freeman, Secretary of Agriculture	Speeches Legislation Executive actions	Air, water, wilderness legislation
Nixon	Decade of the Environment (1970s)	Disinterested, but saw political benefits Pragmatism Political opportunism	William Ruckelshaus and Russell Train, EPA Walter Hickel and Rogers C. B. Morton, Secretary of Interior Clifford Hardin and Earl Butz	Speeches Legislation Executive actions	Significant legislation and creation of new agencies including EPA

President					
Ford	Prodevelopment	Disinterested / Willing to cut environmental budget / Economic progress and energy development given priority over the environment	Rogers Morton and Thomas Kleppe, Secretary of Interior / Russell Train, EPA / Earl Butz, Secretary of Agriculture over / Frank Zarb, energy advisor	Speeches / Pro-energy legislation	Public lands conservation / Wilderness preservation
Carter	Conservation	Urgency of domestic and international efforts to protect the environment	Cecil Andrus, Secretary of Interior / Douglas Costle, EPA / Robert Bergland, Secretary of Agriculture	Speeches / Legislation / Executive actions / Diplomacy	Public lands legacy / Significant legislation / Global 2000 Report
Reagan	Prodevelopment	Disinterested / Economic growth top priority / Cost-benefit analysis when evaluating economy and environment	James Watt, William Clark, and Donald Hodel, Secretary of Interior / Anne Gorsuch and William Ruckelshaus, EPA	Speeches / Administrative strategy	Anti-environmental agenda
Bush 41	To be environmental president	Prodevelopment, pro-business and industry	John Sununu, Chief of Staff / Manuel Lujan, Secretary of Interior / William Reilly, EPA	Speeches	Clean Air Act Amendments (1990)
Clinton	Great green hope	Sustainable development	Vice President Al Gore / Bruce Babbitt, Secretary of Interior; Carol Browner, EPA	Speeches / Executive actions / Diplomacy	Public lands legacy / Environmental justice / Endangered species and biodiversity protection
Bush 43	Eco-friendly	Economic growth top priority / Prodevelopment / Probusiness and industry	Vice President Dick Cheney / Gale Norton, Secretary of Interior / Spencer Abraham, Secretary of Energy / Energy industry	Administrative strategy	Anti-environmental agenda

Second, as a legislative leader, the president is involved in a relationship with Congress. Partisan control of one or both chambers can make a big difference in presidential initiatives. For example, where an abundance of environmental legislation passed during the administrations of Lyndon Johnson and Richard Nixon, not one major piece of environmental legislation was passed during President George W. Bush's tenure as president. The president has several instruments of administrative power including the executive order, appointment power, and the creation or reorganization of executive agencies. Bill Clinton, facing a recalcitrant Republican-controlled Congress, used the executive order and proclamations to establish or protect public lands and national monuments. Finally, through environmental diplomacy, the president can play a major or divisive role in the process of creating and implementing regional and international environmental treaties and whether and to what extent the United States should be involved in global environmental conferences. Where John Kennedy signed the Limited Nuclear Test Ban Treaty that reduced the threat to public health posed by nuclear fallout, George W. Bush renounced the Kyoto Protocol and reduced the U.S. role as an international leader on the most important global climate change issue.

In the end, the modern presidents have exhibited a diversity of accomplishments along with cautious behavior as well as efforts to reverse environmental gains. For instance, although Franklin Roosevelt was beset by both domestic economic distress as well as a global war, he engaged in a positive working relationship with Congress and succeeded in producing the Civilian Conservation Corps and the Tennessee Valley Authority, as well as maintaining a focus on conservation during hard times. While directing his energies to the Cold War for eight years, Eisenhower considered his Mission 66 national parks program part of his overall legacy, while John Kennedy's short-lived administration succeeded in promoting the seeds of environmentalism at home and abroad while reducing the threat posed by aboveground nuclear testing. Richard Nixon worked with a Democratic Congress and together were responsible for landmark legislation (including the National Environmental Policy Act) and the creation of the Environmental Protection Agency, while Jimmy Carter established a public lands legacy. The Clean Air Act Amendments stagnated during the Reagan years and become law only after George Bush 41 used the power of the presidency to secure a positive outcome to the congressional debate. Bill Clinton, like Carter before him, established a public lands legacy, although Clinton had to circumvent

FIGURE: **Continuum of Greenness:** The Environmental Legacy of Presidents FDR to George W. Bush

VERY GREEN				PALE GREEN
FDR	LBJ	HST	IKE	RR
RN	JC	JFK	GF	GB 43
	BC		GB 41	

FDR	Franklin Roosevelt	JFK	John Kennedy
RN	Richard Nixon	IKE	Dwight Eisenhower
LBJ	Lyndon Johnson	GF	Gerald Ford
JC	Jimmy Carter	GB 41	George H. W. Bush
BC	Bill Clinton	RR	Ronald Reagan
HST	Harry Truman	GB 43	George W. Bush

a Republican-controlled Congress to do so. The administration of George W. Bush can be identified as having the worst record on the environment.

We now provide a summary assessment of the modern presidents and the environment. In doing so, we use the four evaluative categories employed throughout the book—political communication, legislative leadership, administrative actions, environmental diplomacy—as we direct our attention to environmental leadership and the environmental legacy of the twelve presidents. The figure above presents a "continuum of greenness" (discussed in chapter 1) that separates the presidents in terms of those who had a positive influence (very green or green), mixed influence, or negative influence (pale green) in promoting conservation measures and protecting the domestic and global environment. In short, we find at one end of the continuum the presidents who demonstrated environmental leadership while at the other end are those presidents who promoted an anti-environmental agenda.

Presidents Having a Positive Influence in Shaping Environmental Policy: Franklin Roosevelt, Harry Truman, John Kennedy, Lyndon Johnson, Richard Nixon, Jimmy Carter, and Bill Clinton

Seven presidents can be characterized as "very green" or "green" activists in their political orientation, as they took actions that had a positive impact on the environment. These presidents exhibited a strong commitment to environmental values through their speeches and their support for environmental legislation, and by using executive power on behalf of the environment and also by taking a global view of the environment.

Although serving in the White House during the dark days of the Great Depression, FDR was committed to linking both economic and environmental progress. During the mid-to-late 1960s and early 1970s, an abundance of environmental legislation was passed and then signed into law by Lyndon Johnson and Richard Nixon. Nixon, the lone Republican in this group, did the "right deed for the wrong reason," but the rewards for the environmental movement were notable.[1] Nixon was a politically shrewd politician and he was well aware of the public's attitude toward the environment. Jimmy Carter and Bill Clinton established public land legacies that set aside millions of acres for future generations to enjoy. Finally, where Harry Truman showed the beginnings of a "global environmental" presidency, John Kennedy offered a vision of an environmental legacy both domestically and globally.

Political Communication

Given the nature of the times, which included the Great Depression and World War II, it is understandable that FDR's public discourse focused primarily on these two important events. Still, he used several outlets, including the State of the Union message, press conferences, and radio addresses, to convey his message about the importance of conservation and the wise use of the country's resources. In addition, FDR promoted conservation through informal conversations with the press. Comments about his personal activities related to conservation received favorable coverage by reporters, and as Anna Riesch Owen noted, "Throughout the years 1933–42, there were always articles appearing that commended the natural resource policy."[2]

For Harry Truman the environment assumed importance because it provided the means to ensure a viable economy at home and a strong America abroad. Truman lacked the oratorical skills of his predecessor, FDR, and was therefore unable to convey in a similar way the importance of conservation. Still, Truman reached out to the American public in an effort to demonstrate a commitment to this important issue. He criticized the Republican position on conservation and identified conservation with the Democratic Party.

Although he served in office for only one thousand days, during that short time, John Kennedy reflected a commitment to the environment. Unlike most of his predecessors and successors, political communication was a strength of Kennedy's. He felt comfortable in front of reporters and their cameras and he enjoyed the interaction that occurred during press conferences. Although he did not use the State of the Union address as a primary means to disseminate his commitment to the environment, he did employ other outlets in this regard including special messages to Congress, press conferences, and speeches to organized interests. Kennedy could be viewed as a "man of words" and a "man of vision" on a variety of issues including the environment. For instance, in a letter to the Senate concerning the oceans, he stated that in order for the country to do what needed to be done, it would require "concerted action, purposely directed, with vision and ingenuity."[3] Thus was the nature of the man of words whether talking about putting astronauts on the moon or showing concern for the biosphere. Although JFK never lived to serve a second term, he provided an environmental vision for the future that suggested a second term would have been a progressive environmental effort.

John Kennedy's commitment to the environment was carried on by Lyndon Johnson who articulated the concerns of his administration in a variety of media outlets. In his "Report on Natural Beauty in America" delivered in 1965, for instance, he spoke of the "new conservation" that "would have to be required to deal with these new problems if we are to protect the countryside, save it from destruction, and restore what has been destroyed. And I have also said that this conservation must be not just the classic conservation of protection and development, but a creative conservation of restoration and innovation."[4] Johnson was a superb legislator, and as JFK was a man of words, LBJ could be seen as a "man of action," as he used his legislative skill while in the White House to take ideas and translate them into policy in the legislative arena.

Richard Nixon was a perceptive politician and realized that although the environment was not an important issue to him, it had become an important issue for the American public.[5] As such, he used the power resources of his office in support of environmental initiatives. He spoke often about the issue. For instance, in his first State of the Union address he declared the 1970s as the "decade of the environment" and he devoted more than one-third of his speech to this issue.[6] He also was an astute observer of the American electorate and maintained the issue high on the public agenda with an eye to the 1972 presidential election. He saw the environment as an issue that would provide rewards personally and to the Republican Party.

Jimmy Carter entered the White House with an emphasis on energy and the environment which became dominant issues during his term in office.

For instance, in an effort to mobilize the American public to support his energy plan, he delivered four major speeches and was prepared to make a fifth speech until he was informed that it would be a fruitless endeavor.[7] Carter's style was described by two observers of the presidency and the environment in the following way: "Carter, unlike Nixon, did not use his power to propose legislation to Congress. Instead, he made public speeches, suggested measures he hoped Congress would consider and tried to put environmental concerns on the public agenda through general speeches."[8] Moreover, among the modern presidents from Kennedy to Reagan, Carter delivered the greatest number of speeches about the environment.[9] Carter used each of his State of the Union Messages as a means to focus on a variety of environmental concerns. As a matter of fact, his final State of the Union message was sixty-six pages in length and it included considerable attention to the environment. He also delivered in 1977 and again in 1979 special messages to Congress that dealt specifically with the environment.

As a former governor of a small state not known for environmentalism, Bill Clinton began his administration with little public discussion about this policy issue. During his first term, only his last State of the Union address carried a substantive discussion of environmental issues. Since he believed that the environment would have to share the agenda with the economy, Vice President Al Gore and interior secretary Bruce Babbitt were the primary national voices for the environment. Clinton did make numerous minor speeches about the environment, and he delivered an Earth Day speech every year while in office. Moreover, during the latter part of his second term, he gave increasing attention to the nation's public lands, thus ensuring a public lands legacy for his administration.

Legislative Leadership

FDR's first one hundred days in office set a precedent for modern presidents, as his legislative productivity has remained unmatched. In the area of environmentalism, as A. L. Riesch Owen stated, "Congress did not stop . . . with merely approving the president's legislative proposals during the trying early days of the new administration. It also sought the president's support of additional conservation legislation and federal conservation aid for constituents."[10] Among the fourteen major pieces of legislation passed by Congress during this period were two major environment and energy bills—namely, the Tennessee Valley Authority and the Civilian Conservation Corps. The TVA was viewed by FDR as a "laboratory for the Nation to learn how to make the most out of its vast resources for the lasting benefit of the average man and woman."[11] During his term in office he sent legislation to Congress that covered six major areas—forests, minerals, water, soil, wildlife, and recreational resources.[12]

Harry Truman pursued several environmentally related goals including the St. Lawrence Seaway project and creation of the Grand Teton National Park. He also used the veto on several occasions in opposition to bills with which he disagreed. A major area occupying Truman's attention was the status of the United States after World War II. He was concerned about the depletion of the nation's minerals and resources used in the war effort and he was committed to protecting these resources in order to provide a foundation upon which to build a powerful United States and ensure a healthy economy at home. As he left office in 1953 he encouraged Congress to pursue a conservation agenda in concert with various actors in the political system.

President Kennedy displayed a concern for the environment as legislative leader through special messages to Congress, messages to the scientific community, State of the Union addresses, letters to congressional leaders, and bill-signing ceremonies. For instance, as Kennedy stated in his 1962 State of the Union message, the conservation program should cover all resources from "air, water, and land; fuels, energy and minerals; soils, forests, and forage; fish and wildlife," which he argued were a "vital part of the American heritage."[13] Kennedy focused on air and water pollution in his speeches as well as encouraging Congress to be mindful of the need to protect the country's public lands. As he warned, "If we do not plan today for the future growth of these and other natural assets—not only parks and forests but wildlife and wilderness preserves, and water projects of all kinds—our children and their children will be poorer in every sense of the word."[14] The major piece of legislation passed during his term in office was the 1963 Clean Air Act. Sadly, Kennedy's term in office was cut short and his promise as reflected in his legislative leadership was not to be fulfilled.

In pursuing an environmental agenda, Lyndon Johnson used his considerable legislative skills, including telephone calls, speeches and personal one-on-one meetings with key legislators. He effectively used the State of the Union address as well as special messages to Congress in support of environmental goals. He focused on several key issues including air and water pollution, food safety, waste disposal, and preservation of public lands. For instance, to show Congress and the public the seriousness of the problem of air quality, he stated quite graphically at the signing of the 1967 Air Quality

Act that "today we are pouring at least 130 million tons of poison into the air each year.... That leaves us, according to my evaluation, only one real choice. Either we stop poisoning our air—or we become a nation of gas masks, groping our way through the dying cities and a wilderness of ghost towns that the people have evacuated."[15] LBJ was also successful in promoting preservation of the country's public lands. He signed into law several bills that added to the National Park System and wilderness areas.

In many ways, Richard Nixon was a modern environmental president, because through his legislative leadership, more environmental bills were passed during his administration than any other before or since. He signed into law the landmark National Environmental Policy Act, the Clean Air Act, the Clean Water Act, and the Endangered Species Act, among others. However, some saw his actions reflecting a political opportunism that weighed the benefits he would receive from supporting a policy domain that he himself did not have an interest in, as he was more concerned with foreign policy issues.[16] Having said this, the environment fared well, at least during the first term, as a result of Nixon's legislative leadership.

Although Jimmy Carter had a relatively difficult time with Congress during his four years in office, he did have a successful legislative agenda as it related to the environment. In fact, several important environmental bills were put into effect with his signature including amendments to the Clean Air and Clean Water acts, the Superfund act, and the Alaska Lands act. Carter emphasized the energy issue while in office but had difficulty, however, with Congress (and fellow majority Democrats) in pursuing this program. Although an energy bill eventually passed in 1978, it did not reflect all that Carter wanted, due in part to the way he dealt with Congress. Carter stated in his memoirs that one of the most endearing aspects of his presidency was the preservation of millions of acres of public lands, especially in Alaska. Carter's legacy reflected the creation or expansion of national parks and reserves, national wildlife refuges, and wild and scenic rivers and waterways.[17]

After twelve years of Reagan and Bush 41, environmentalists were encouraged when Bill Clinton entered office in January 1993. However, during 1993–94, when he had a Democratic Congress, Clinton had mixed success at best. The highlight of his term was passage of the 1994 California Desert Protection Act that protected almost eight million acres of public land. In November 1994 the Republicans captured control of both houses of Congress for the first time in forty years. For the next six years, Clinton faced a hostile Congress dominated by the opposition party. The Republican-controlled

Congress used its power to reduce funding for various environmental pro-grams while Clinton was criticized by environmentalists for failing to stand up to the Republican attack on the environment.[18] Beginning in 1995, Clinton began to use the veto as an instrument of power to oppose Republican anti-environmental measures.

Administrative Actions

Once he moved into the White House, FDR was confronted with several major challenges—the Great Depression at home and the rise of the formidable powers in Germany and Japan that threatened the United States. Still, he directed his attention to the environment as he used the power resources of his office to promote a conservation legacy. He used his executive power to influence conservation policy by appointing people that would carry out his conservation plans. Included among his appointments were, in particular, Harold Ickes as secretary of the interior and Henry Wallace as secretary of agriculture. FDR also had the good fortune of having, for two years, a Congress that gave him the authority to reorganize government. Accordingly, he established the Civilian Conservation Corps, Soil Erosion Service, the Natural Resources Board, the Soil Conservation Board, the Public Works Administration, and the Works Progress Administration, among others. In this way, FDR linked the environment with economic recovery by creating a variety of projects and putting people to work.[19] Moreover, during the period 1936–43 he was involved in environment-related activities including grazing districts, flood control, conservation of coal, and protecting national forests.

Harry Truman exhibited a mixed record regarding executive power. On the one hand, his budget allocations for the environment were quite impressive. He felt that federal dollars spent on conservation efforts were dollars well spent.[20] On the other hand, his appointments varied in quality and exhibited relative instability. Truman created one environment-related agency, namely, the Bureau of Land Management still in operation today. He carried on the legacy of FDR's TVA by dedicating the sixteenth dam (the Kentucky Dam) in the TVA group of dams. This action was important since his successor, Dwight Eisenhower, did not look kindly on the TVA, which he saw as representative of "creeping socialism." Truman also drew attention to the increasing problem of air pollution by establishing the United States Technical Conference on Air Pollution in 1950.

In making two important appointments, Stewart Udall as secretary of the interior and Orville Freeman as secretary of agriculture, John Kennedy displayed vision and concern for the environment. Udall, in particular, was a proven environmentalist from Arizona. During the first two years of his administration, Kennedy issued nineteen executive orders that improved the environment. Many of these executive orders dealt with public lands, national forests and national parks, and the increasing threat posed by radioactivity. Moreover, Kennedy used the executive order to create the Peace Corps, a program similar to FDR's Civilian Conservation Corps, where volunteers were involved in environmental projects worldwide. Kennedy saw the importance of creating a Land and Water Conservation Fund to acquire more land and water areas for recreational purposes and to keep these areas free from state control and private interests.

Lyndon Johnson followed Kennedy's lead and appointed environmentally friendly personnel to key positions in the government. He retained the services of Stewart Udall as secretary of the interior and appointed James Quigley as commissioner of the Federal Water Pollution Control Administration, who was given the mandate to pursue an "all-out attack on water pollution in our rivers, lakes, and streams."[21] Johnson, along with his wife, Lady Bird, were both committed to the value of beautification. Accordingly, he established the President's Recreation Advisory Council, a Citizens' Advisory Committee on Recreation and Natural Beauty, and organized a White House Conference on Natural Beauty.

Richard Nixon moved aggressively to promote environmental initiatives administratively just as he did as a legislative leader. The same year the National Environmental Policy Act and Clean Air Act were passed, Nixon established the Environmental Protection Agency and the Council on Environmental Quality. The EPA was an independent agency that aggregated many responsibilities of other agencies while the CEQ advised the president about environmental policy and prepared an annual report that focused on the state of the environment in the nation. Differences were evident, however, in the role that would be played by the EPA, as envisioned by Nixon and others in the environmental movement, and by the CEQ. For Nixon, the EPA would be a balancer between environmental protection and industrialization, while environmentalists expected the EPA to promote environmental values.[22]

Jimmy Carter approached the presidency much as he approached his role as governor of Georgia—his goal was to balance environmental concerns with economic development. Through the appointment process, Carter was able to influence environmental policy. A key appointment to his administration was Cecil Andrus as secretary of interior. Andrus was a proven environmentalist who served as governor of Idaho. Andrus promoted protection of the nation's public lands for future generations and was instrumental in influencing Carter to use his executive powers to protect millions of acres of public lands in Alaska. Moreover, he promoted the idea of the Arctic National Wildlife Refuge that remains a point of contention to this day. Carter appointed Douglas Costle to head the EPA. Costle pursued a policy where the EPA would become a public health as well as an environmental agency.[23] Carter established the Department of Energy and appointed former defense department head James Schlesinger to run the new agency. Carter also issued proclamations for Earth Day and Earth Week as well as a focus on conservation and education related to energy use.

The forty-second president, Bill Clinton, surrounded himself with numerous environmentally friendly appointees. The first selection he made was Senator Al Gore as his vice presidential running mate. He chose Bruce Babbitt of Arizona as secretary of the interior, and Carol Browner as EPA administrator. Moreover, he placed environmentalists in the State Department, the National Security Council, and the Office of Management and Budget.[24] Clinton also organized new agencies including the White House Office on Environmental Policy and the President's Council on Sustainable Development. Since Clinton was faced with a Republican Congress during the last six years of his presidency, he turned to executive orders and proclamations to influence environmental policy. Using these instruments of executive power, Clinton established a public lands legacy that rivaled that of Jimmy Carter and Theodore Roosevelt before him.

Environmental Diplomacy

In FDR's day, most attention was directed to the domestic environment. Still, he can be credited with several important international environmental initiatives. First, he signed two important treaties—one with Canada in 1935 that involved cleanup of mining and smelting areas in British Columbia and one with Mexico in 1936 that involved wildlife restoration in general and migratory birds in particular.[25] Second, during World War II, FDR remained committed to conservation efforts and encouraged Congress that the conservation of resources was needed for national defense. In short, he made it clear that American citizens were to hold to reasonable conservation principles even under the "stress of war."[26] Third, he was committed to the idea of world conferences that dealt with global environmental issues. An example of this was the 1936 North American Wildlife Conference that U.S.

administrative officials attended.[27] Moreover, five days after Roosevelt died, the United States delivered plans to organize a World Conference on Conservation that was to be part of the Economic and Social Council of the newly created United Nations.[28]

Harry Truman followed FDR's lead in promoting U.S. efforts involving the global environment. He worked with Canada to construct the St. Lawrence Seaway and negotiated a treaty dealing with the Niagara River and the development of hydroelectric power. He signed several treaties that dealt with fisheries and the creation of the International Whaling Commission.[29] He also committed the United States to a global environmental presence through participation in several conferences, including the first Hemispheric Conference on the Conservation of Natural Resources in 1948, a U.S.-hosted conference in 1949 that dealt with northwest fisheries, and that same year a United Nations–sponsored science conference on the conservation of resources.[30] Truman was also concerned about the potential depletion of the country's mineral resources during World War II and the coming of the Korean War. His goal was to ensure industrial development of the country as well as a strong defense.[31]

John Kennedy's vision of the environment had an international focus. As he stated in 1963, "a worldwide program of conservation could protect the forest and world game preserves now in danger of extinction for all time, improve the marine harvest of food from our oceans, and prevent the contamination of air and water by industrial as well as nuclear pollution."[32] He focused on the importance of the oceans and the need to implement information sharing between nations. In what some environmentalists considered Kennedy's greatest environmental achievement, he negotiated with the Soviet Union and Great Britain to draw up the Limited Nuclear Test Ban Treaty of 1963 that prohibited aboveground nuclear testing, thus reducing the threat of radioactivity.[33] JFK also promoted the idea of a space program that was integrally linked to the global environment. As he suggested, "Space research may open up new understanding of man's relation to his environment," and he surmised that "when you study the effects on our astronauts of exhaust gases which can contaminate their environment, and seek to alter these gases so to reduce the toxicity, you are working on problems similar to those we face in our great urban centers which themselves are being corrupted by gases and which must be cleared."[34]

Kennedy's successor, Lyndon Johnson, signed numerous treaties that had an environmental focus including the Outer Space Treaty in 1967 that

Johnson felt was as significant as the 1963 Limited Nuclear Test Ban Treaty signed by Kennedy.[35] He also used the power of the executive agreement to protect regional and global fisheries. Finally, Johnson was involved in global environmental concerns including the Third Conference on the Peaceful Use of Atomic Energy and the First International Symposium on Water Desalination (both dealing with the issue of producing clean drinking water).

The domestic environmental agenda of Richard Nixon was extended to the international arena. He used his power resources to establish a global environmental agenda. He signed numerous treaties including the 1971 Seabed Treaty, the Convention on the Prohibition of the Development, Production, and Stockpiling of Bacteriological and Toxic Weapons in 1972, and the important Convention on International Trade in Endangered Species of Wild Fauna and Flora (CITES) in 1973. His administration also played an influential role in forming a UN environmental program and the Man and the Biosphere program.

Jimmy Carter began and ended his administration with a focus on the global environment. In his 1977 environmental message to Congress he raised the issue of global environmental problems and directed the federal government to prepare a report (published in 1980) to form the basis for U.S. global environmental policy making. In his last year in office, he acknowledged the importance of the *Global 2000 Report*, which he said was the first time any government "attempted to take a comprehensive long-range look at interrelated global issues . . . and the overall environmental quality of the Earth we live on."[36] He began important work with the Canadian government to deal with the transnational issue of acid rain. Carter was a strong supporter of the United Nations Conferences on the Law of the Sea and he supported efforts to protect the world's biodiversity. He also showed concern about the threat posed to the oceans from oil pollution.

Although he was considered the "great green hope," Bill Clinton's global environmental agenda was hindered by a Republican-controlled Congress as had been his domestic program. Even though Clinton signed the Convention on Biodiversity, the Senate would not ratify it. Despite the fact that Clinton signed the Kyoto Protocol, his efforts were again frustrated by Republicans and some Democrats who made it clear that the protocol, which changed the earlier Rio Earth Summit global climate agreement from voluntary to mandatory requirements, would never be ratified by the Senate. Consequently, Clinton never submitted it to the Senate. Clinton was successful in gaining

Senate support for treaties that involved increasing restrictions against pesticides and protecting forestry, agriculture, and coastal management from pollution.[37]

Presidents Having Mixed Influence in Shaping Environmental Policy: Dwight Eisenhower, Gerald Ford, and George H. W. Bush

While some presidents are activist in manner, others move cautiously and slowly regarding public policy issues. Dwight Eisenhower, Gerald Ford, and George Herbert Walker Bush fall along the midpoint on the continuum of greenness since they lacked consistency in promoting conservation values and environmental protection. Although their environmental accomplishments fell short of those of FDR, Nixon, and their presidential counterparts discussed above, these three presidents supported some initiatives that helped to achieve environmental progress. Both Eisenhower and Ford made important contributions to the protection of public lands. Although Eisenhower directed his attention primarily to Cold War politics abroad, he supported the Mission 66 program, while Gerald Ford, who was more concerned about energy policy than about environmental concerns, gave modest support to public land conservation and wilderness preservation. George H. W. Bush through his positive actions ensured that he would be remembered for the Clean Air Act Amendments of 1990. However, as he ran for reelection in 1992, his commitment to the environment was increasingly questioned as he promoted economic growth over his original commitment to be an environmental president, thus leaving him with a mixed legacy on the environment.

Political Communication

Dwight Eisenhower used the State of the Union message as a means to identify the importance of conserving the nation's resources, with lesser attention given to air and water pollution. Eisenhower's philosophy was that the role of the federal government should be limited as it worked with state and local governments and private interests involving environmental issues. As he stated, for instance, "Water pollution was a state and local matter." A common theme that ran throughout his speeches during his two terms in office was that contemporary generations needed to consider what they were passing on to future generations and he stressed the need to conserve natural resources.

Nixon's successor, Gerald Ford, did not carry on the Nixon environmental legacy and did not view the environment as important as energy development or a strong economy. As a party leader, Ford found his views in agreement with the 1976 Republican Party platform that stated that "environmental concern must be brought into balance with the needs for industrial and economic growth." Moreover, in the limited number of speeches he gave to the public regarding the environment, it was often an issue area to be "balanced away" with other concerns of the office. A speech he gave in Anchorage, Alaska, in 1974, on the occasion of a severe storm and flood that had hit Nome and the Seward Peninsula, illustrates this point. Ford applauded Alaskans for their efforts to seek "self-sufficiency in energy" and to "produce more oil in harmony with appropriate environmental concerns" although he did not detail these concerns.[38]

During the presidential campaign of George H. W. Bush in 1988, he indicated that he would be an environmental president in the tradition of Teddy Roosevelt.[39] Bush 41's environmental agenda was reflected in the Republican Party platform in 1988, which focused on a variety of environmental issues. Despite his outspoken stance on the environment, environmentalists were suspicious of the rhetoric since he served for eight years with Ronald Reagan. Bush 41 included environmental concerns in his State of the Union messages and included this policy domain in numerous minor speeches he delivered around the country. His position, however, changed over time. When he campaigned for reelection he referred to the Democrats' vice presidential candidate, Senator Al Gore, a respected environmentalist, as "ozone man," in reference to Gore's stance on stratospheric ozone depletion.

Legislative Leadership

The presidency of Dwight Eisenhower saw two major pieces of legislation passed—the Air Pollution Control Act of 1955 and the Federal Water Pollution Control Act of 1956. Nonetheless, the president made it clear that the air pollution bill should reflect a limited federal role. Although he signed the 1956 water pollution legislation, four years later he vetoed a federal water pollution bill due to his concerns about the role required of the federal government. As he stated, "Because water pollution is a uniquely local blight, primary responsibility for solving the problem lies not with the Federal Government but rather must be assumed and exercised, as it has been, by State and local governments."[40] A congressional override attempt failed, and while campaigning for president in 1960 Senator John Kennedy, who supported the override, stated that "I am not part of an administration which vetoed a bill to clean our rivers from pollution."[41]

Gerald Ford's approach to the environment was to reduce the role of the federal government in regulating standards to improve the environment and in letting the states play a larger role. Environmentalists both approved some actions and disapproved others taken by the president. He signed legislation to protect public lands as well as created several new additions to the wilderness system and expanded national parks, but he also severely cut the budget for all environmental agencies.[42] In his speeches to Congress, Ford made a limited number of references to the environment, and when the environment was mentioned, it was balanced against other interests. For instance, in a December 12, 1974, speech to Congress, Ford talked about the lessons learned from the energy crisis and suggested that "even with a strong conservation program, we will still have to mine more coal, drill for more oil and gas, and build more power plants and refineries. Each of these measures will have an impact on the environment. Yet this can be minimized . . . by careful analysis and planning, with broad public participation."[43]

When he entered office, George H. W. Bush gave the impression that he would address the environment much differently than his predecessor, Ronald Reagan. In addition to campaigning as an environmental president-to-be, the party platform on which he ran was also committed to an array of important environmental concerns including air and water pollution, hazardous wastes, ocean dumping, and national parks. As a legislative leader, however, he signed only one major piece of legislation—the Clean Air Act Amendments of 1990—but he used the power resources of his office to ensure passage of this bill. He also signed the Energy Policy Act and supported development of clean coal technology.

Administrative Actions

Dwight Eisenhower's executive role was mixed, when one examines his appointments. Ironically, his greatest legacy and also a source of criticism involved his appointment of secretary of interior Douglas McKay. On the one hand, Eisenhower was proud of the role played by McKay and the Mission 66 national parks program, which envisioned a ten-year plan that would improve conditions at the nation's parks by 1966. On the other hand, McKay also came under fire from congressional Democrats who criticized his pro-development orientation. He became known as "giveaway McKay" as he tried to hand over to private interests public energy resources and attempted to terminate several wildlife refuges.[44] Eisenhower appointed Ezra Taft Benson as secretary of agriculture (the second pillar of Eisenhower's environmental governing apparatus). Benson was a very conservative Republican who, given a choice between development and conservation, chose development while supporting industrial interests over those of the environmental community. Another effort of the Eisenhower administration that had a mixed impact was the creation of the interstate highway system. While the highway system proved an attempt to link a growing country, the highway system also encouraged the growing automobile industry and set the stage for increased use of fossil fuels along with the attendant air pollution.

In order to shape environmental policy, Gerald Ford made several appointments that reflected his environmental orientation. In contrast to Russell Train, EPA administrator who was pro-environment and had the confidence of Richard Nixon, Ford selected Rogers Morton as his secretary of interior, an individual who, like Ford, balanced the environment with other interests. As Morton stated, "Priority of our environment must be brought into equity with that of our economy and defense. Otherwise at some point in time . . . there will be no economy to enjoy and practically no reason for defense."[45] President Ford recruited Russell W. Peterson as chair of the Council on Environmental Quality, a man who felt that there was no conflict between the environment and energy. As he stated, "We must not think in terms of a conflict between energy supply and environmental quality. We can and must have them both."[46] In his effort to deal with inflation, Ford ended up cutting the budgets of most of the environmental agencies as well as funds that would have gone to the Department of Labor and Department of Health, Education, and Welfare. But the president made no cuts in the defense budget.[47]

Similar to Eisenhower, George H. W. Bush had a mixed record regarding executive power. On the one hand, he appointed William Reilly, a proven environmentalist and former head of the World Wildlife Fund, to head the EPA and Michael Deland, former New England director of the EPA, to chair the CEQ. On the other hand, he appointed Manuel Lujan Jr. as secretary of the interior, and vice president Dan Quayle to head the newly created Council on Competitiveness. Lujan indicated that public lands policy would remain similar to that which existed under the Reagan administration, while the Council on Competitiveness would use cost-benefit analysis in its evaluation of environmental concerns, which tended to support business and industry over conservation and preservation. In short, the council oversaw cabinet activity to remove any regulation that might interfere with business competitiveness.[48] Moreover, the council became involved in wetlands issues when it tried to redefine its meaning in response to farmers and developers who wanted wetlands reduced in size.[49]

Environmental Diplomacy

During the administration of Dwight Eisenhower, U.S. attention to foreign affairs focused primarily on the Korean War and Cold War issues. At the same time, he was well aware of the problems of an emerging consumption-oriented society and the increasing use of the nation's natural resources. Yet he was more concerned about resource development than conservation. Eisenhower signed several important international treaties including the 1954 International Convention for the Protection of Pollution of the Sea by Oil, two treaties in 1958 (the Convention on the Continental Shelf and the Convention on Fishing and Conservation of the Living Resources of the Sea), and in 1959 the Antarctic Treaty. He also worked with Canada and Mexico on mutually beneficial projects including development of electric power.

Although he inherited Nixon's environmental legacy, Gerald Ford moved slowly in pushing new initiatives. In response to concerns about the flow of Persian Gulf oil to the United States, he continued Nixon's Project Independence and encouraged conservation along with domestic production. He signed several international environmental agreements that protected endangered species including an agreement with China, Denmark, Norway, and the Soviet Union to protect polar bears in the Arctic regions in September 1976.[50] He also signed a treaty with the United Kingdom to protect Antarctic seals and another with the Soviet Union that protected migratory birds.[51]

Similar to his approach in domestic environmental policy making, George H. W. Bush exhibited both support for and then opposition to global environmental issues. On the one hand, he signed the North American Wetlands Conservation Act with Canada and Mexico and he worked cautiously with the Canadian government to deal with the acid rain problem, resulting in the U.S.-Canada Air Quality Agreement. On the other hand, when the United States had the opportunity to demonstrate leadership on the global arena at the 1992 Earth Summit in Rio, Bush 41 retreated. He almost failed to even attend the international gathering. He signed the Convention on Global Climate Change only after changes were made to incorporate voluntary rather than mandatory guidelines and timetables, and the United States stood alone as the only country to refuse to sign the Convention on Biodiversity. In the Persian Gulf War, Bush succeeded in removing Saddam Hussein from Kuwait, but the environmental disaster that resulted from the conflict raised questions about the United States' concern about the dangers posed to the environment due to massive oil pollution of local and regional waters around Iraq.

Presidents Having a Negative Influence in Shaping Environmental Policy: Ronald Reagan and George W. Bush

In contrast to those presidents who pursued an activist, pro-environmental agenda, some presidents have also been activist but with an anti-environmental agenda. In this case, they engaged in practices to reverse environmental progress or they tried to implement anti-environmental initiatives. Both Ronald Reagan and George W. Bush—"pale green" presidents—fall along this part of the continuum of greenness, since the best that could be said of their actions was that they exhibited disinterest in the environment or benign support for environmental action as long as they felt that it did not have a negative impact on the economy and industry, an outlook that reflected their probusiness, antiregulatory policy approach.[52] Each president served two terms and during that time each had a negative impact on environmental protection. Ironically, the presidency of Ronald Reagan benefited the environmental movement for the wrong reason, by encouraging an increase in the membership of many environmental groups. The positive accomplishments of the Reagan years included his support, in his second term, for the 1987 Montreal Protocol, which was designed to reduce pollutants that threatened the stratospheric ozone layer. George W. Bush prided himself in his support for oil drilling in Alaska's Arctic National Wildlife Refuge at home, and his rejection of the Kyoto Protocol abroad. Bush clearly failed to use the resources of the American presidency in support of environmental protection. Having said that, he gets credit at home for a proposal to increase automobile fuel efficiency standards and supporting new diesel standards that he inherited from the Clinton administration, and abroad, for establishing the Northwestern Islands Marine National Monument in 2006 and three marine national monuments in 2009.[53]

Political Communication

The Reagan presidency pursued a decidedly probusiness, antiregulatory orientation with little attention given to environmental concerns. In fact, his administration was openly hostile to environmentalism, and it set out to reverse years of progress in promoting environmental protection. The environment was almost nonexistent in Reagan's major speeches including his State of the Union addresses, although he included the environment frequently in his minor speeches. However, his comments lacked a substantive commitment to ensure environmental protection. Moreover, he made statements that were considered derogatory by many in the environmental movement.

George W. Bush, like Reagan, fully supported a probusiness, antiregulatory, prodevelopment agenda. He gave little attention to the environment in State of the Union messages, and the environment was not included in his 2004 State of the Union address. He included the environment in minor speeches, but, like Reagan's, the speeches contained little substantive content. He made considerable use of radio addresses, but again, the environment was only nominally mentioned. Two issues, however, received considerable attention by Bush 43—namely, oil drilling in Alaska's Arctic National Wildlife Refuge and global warming. In the case of ANWR, he strongly promoted drilling for petroleum in what has been described as one of the few remaining pristine areas left in the United States. Bush 43 was hesitant about accepting the research findings on global warming of the U.S. National Academy of Sciences and the Intergovernmental Panel on Climate Change, and he promoted an alternative, voluntary program in contrast to the requirements of the Kyoto Protocol.

Legislative Leadership

Ronald Reagan felt that "environmental protection was fundamentally at odds with economic growth and prosperity."[54] Due to the president's position on the environment, Congress had a difficult time but managed to strengthen the Resource Conservation and Recovery Act, enact Superfund amendments, and support the Safe Drinking Water and Clean Water acts, but problems continued on acid rain legislation, the Clean Air Act, and the nation's pesticides law.[55] Problems also arose between Congress and the executive branch due to Reagan's employment of an administrative strategy to deal with the environment

During his two terms in office, George W. Bush did not use the legislative leader role in an effort to promote environmental protection. During this time, not one major piece of environmental legislation was passed. Moreover, he had to respond to congressional concerns about his administration's plan to suspend the Clinton standard regarding arsenic levels in water. Congressional Democrats raised concerns about the composition of the administration's energy task force and how energy policy was being formulated. Congressional Democrats opposed Bush's efforts to open up ANWR to oil and gas exploration. Members of Congress also complained about cuts in various domestic policy areas including the environment.

Administrative Actions

Ronald Reagan employed an administrative strategy to pursue an anti-environmental agenda. As Vig and Kraft point out, Reagan decided to reevaluate all environmental policies within his overall framework of reducing government regulations, shifting responsibility to the states and relying more on the private sector.[56] In the process of passing the Economic Recovery Act of 1981 (tax cuts for individuals and tax breaks for corporations), along with massive defense spending, a huge budget deficit made it difficult to support environmental programs. About this same time, ten environmental organizations issued an "indictment" against the Reagan administration, charging that he had "broken faith with the American people" by taking "scores of [legislative and executive] actions that veered radically away from bipartisan consensus in support of environmental protection that has existed for many years."[57]

In short, rather than responding to environmental needs, Ronald Reagan was more inclined to provide regulatory relief to business and industry.[58] Reagan used budget and appointment powers to influence environmental policy. For instance, he imposed budget cuts that negatively impacted environmental agencies and their personnel. Reagan's appointments clearly represented an anti-environmental agenda. James Watt was appointed to head the Interior Department while Anne Gorsuch Burford was appointed as administrator of the EPA. As heads of important government agencies, both used their influence in favor of development over preservation and in favor of business and industry over environmentalists. Moreover, virtually all second- and third-level appointees came from business, corporations, or legal firms that opposed government regulations in the area of the environment.[59]

Although he suggested he would be an eco-friendly president, George W. Bush's actions defined him as an anti-environmental president. When he was unable to succeed through the legislative process (e.g., opening up ANWR to oil drilling) he implemented an administrative strategy following the lead of Ronald Reagan. In contrast to his father, who appointed individuals with environmental credentials, Bush 43's appointees caused real concern among environmentalists as they saw no person with an environmental background receiving appointments in his administration. His vice president, Dick Cheney, previously served as chief executive officer of Haliburton, a worldwide oilfield service company. As attorney general Bush appointed John Ashcroft, who as a senator had a voting record that was decidedly anti-environment. He appointed Linda J. Fisher, formerly vice president for government and public affairs at the Monsanto chemical company, as deputy administrator of the EPA. At the Interior Department, Bush 43 selected Gale Norton, who learned her trade from James Watt while they were in Colorado. Deputy secretary of interior Steve Griles previously served as a lobbyist for oil and coal interests. For national security advisor he selected Condoleeza Rice, formerly a director at Chevron Oil. Among the few appointees who were identified as having an environmentally friendly approach, Bush 43 would find a way to frustrate their efforts. For instance, when Christie Todd Whitman, appointed as head of the EPA, tried to exercise environmentally friendly actions, Bush would intervene, thus weakening the enforcement authority of the EPA, as he did in 2002, protecting utility companies from clean air regulations. Overall, according to George W. Bush, conservation measures had to be voluntary, not mandatory, and he used his executive powers in this regard.

Environmental Diplomacy

While Nixon expanded his pro-environmental focus from the domestic to the global arena, fellow Republican Ronald Reagan extended his anti-environmental agenda at home and expanded it to the international arena. He failed to refer to the global environment in any of his State of the Union messages except for two brief times in his 1984 speech. While acknowledging that acid rain was a problem, he refused to work with the Canadian government to resolve it, thus weakening the effort begun by President Carter. Reagan only signed international treaties when he felt convinced that there were no negative economic costs imposed on U.S. corporations or on the U.S. economy. For instance, he signed several marine environment treaties during his first term, as discussed in chapter 9. Most importantly for the Reagan administration was when it joined with thirty other countries and supported the Montreal Protocol to reduce production of chlorofluorocarbons (CFCs) that threatened the stratospheric ozone layer.

Following in the footsteps of Ronald Reagan, George W. Bush continued the effort to extend antiregulatory, prodevelopment policies into the international arena. Barely two months in office, he renounced the Kyoto Protocol, thus weakening the effort to address greenhouse gas emissions. Although he signed some environmental agreements, he did so following the rationale of Reagan—the agreement could not have a negative impact on the economy or business and industry. Bush 43 pursued a "go it alone" strategy that caused difficulties for the United States. For instance, on the tenth anniversary of the Earth Summit, he refused to attend the 2002 Johannesburg World Summit on Sustainable Development, sending instead Secretary of State Colin Powell in his place. The United States maintained a position of opposing rigid deadlines and timetables, instead favoring voluntary actions.[60] In the last State of the Union message of his term, he never mentioned the global environment.

Concluding Comments

Five key conclusions are evident from the findings of this study. First, *presidents make a difference.* When presidents are activist and use the power resources of their office, they can have a considerable impact in shaping environmental policy either in promoting a pro-environmental or anti-environmental agenda. For instance, as Richard Nixon ushered in the "decade of the environment" and established the EPA, and as Jimmy Carter and Bill Clinton built a public lands legacy dating back to the actions taken by Theodore Roosevelt, Ronald Reagan and George W. Bush pushed pro-growth, anti-regulatory, anti-environmental agendas.

Second, *presidents do not act in isolation from their political environment.* As we have seen in this study, administration officials have played an important role in the shaping of environmental policy. From FDR to LBJ, the heads of the Department of Interior and the Department of Agriculture provided major roles in defining the parameters of conservation and environmental policy. For example, where Stewart Udall as secretary of the interior had a profound and positive impact on JFK and Lyndon Johnson, James Watt as interior secretary became a lightning rod and an embarrassment for Ronald Reagan. Where Eisenhower's agriculture secretary, Ezra Taft Benson, promoted development over conservation, Jimmy Carter's secretary of the interior, Cecil Andrus, kept the president focused on conservation and environmental matters. Beginning with Richard Nixon, the head of the EPA exhibited a mixed role. Where EPA head Anne Gorsuch Burford exhibited overt preference for business interests over the environment while serving under

Reagan, Carol Browner promoted a more balanced approach to the economy and environment debate during the Clinton years. While Bush 41 raised the hopes of environmentalists by appointing William Reilly as head of the EPA, Reilly's influence was eventually downplayed as Bush 41 was influenced, in turn, by his chief of staff, John Sununu, and interior secretary Manuel Lujan Jr. Christie Todd Whitman, viewed as a moderate as EPA head, saw her influence decline within the Bush 43 administration. Vice presidents can also make a difference in the environmental policy-making process. For instance, where Al Gore became a major voice in support of environmentalism during the Clinton years, Dick Cheney, Bush 43's vice president, ensured that fossil fuel interests and the energy industry would prevail over environmental protection.

Third, we have found that *Democratic presidents tend to be "promoters" and "stewards" where they encouraged an activist, pro-environmental agenda.* Although the administration of FDR was beset by both domestic distress and a global war, he was engaged in a positive working relationship with Congress and succeeded in producing the Civilian Conservation Corps and Tennessee Valley Authority, as well as maintaining a focus on conservation during hard times. Carrying on a tradition dating back to Theodore Roosevelt, Jimmy Carter and Bill Clinton established a public lands legacy although Clinton had to circumvent a Republican-controlled Congress in order to do so. The anomaly is Richard Nixon, who supported a pro-environmental agenda, but for political gain. In contrast, as we have seen in this study, Republican presidents have acted slowly and cautiously or promoted an anti-environmental agenda.

Fourth, *an important and distinguishing characteristic of the administration of George W. Bush was the politicization of science.* Science, under this president, was viewed through the prism of ideology. This occurred in science policy in general and environmental policy in particular. For instance, during the last year of Bush 43's first term, the *New York Times* highlighted the problem by reporting comments by Wolfgang H. K. Panofsky, a retired Stanford University physicist who advised the government on science and national security since the Eisenhower administration. Panofsky said, "I think this is as bad as it's ever been. This is an extremely serious issue. I believe it is true that there is such a thing as objective scientific reality, and if you ignore that or try to misrepresent it in formulating policy, you do so at peril to the country."[61] Four years later, scientists continued to be frustrated with the "White House's morality-based politics that they say ignores scientific evidence, distorts facts and leads to outright censorship of reports and scientists."[62] Given the importance of the subsequent 2008 presidential election, these concerns were captured by members of the scientific community for the next president of the United States. For instance, climate scientist Michael Mann demanded that "the next president also has to listen carefully to his or her top science advisors, allowing hard science, and not politics, to inform policy," and Ken Caldeira, a climate and ecology researcher at Stanford University, wanted to see an "administration that is willing to say: The world is round, life evolved on Earth over billions of years, humans are causing our climate to change, we or our children will need to pay later for what we buy on credit today, and consumption on this planet cannot grow exponentially forever without running into environmental constraints."[63]

Fifth, *the environmental policy domain remains on the periphery of the presidents' policy agenda, which has usually focused on the economy and jobs, foreign policy, and national security.* An argument can be made that had Vice President Al Gore won the 2000 presidential election, the environment would have captured increased attention by the federal government. Having said this, when will "environmental security" be considered a central feature on the policy agenda of the American president? This question has increased in salience as government has acted or has been forced to act in response to environmental concerns domestically and globally. On the one hand, we have seen a flurry of legislative activity during the Johnson and Nixon years in response to environmental problems. On the other hand, we have seen a lack of global environmental leadership during the administrations of Reagan and Bush 43. While some might argue that conservation values and environmental protection have intrinsic value and therefore must be on the government's agenda, we are also seeing the tangible outcomes of environmental degradation on the planet, including air and water quality, hazardous and toxic waste disposal, the protection of wildlife, and stratospheric ozone depletion, among others. Moreover, new research is showing the profound impact of global climate change on public health, biodiversity, weather patterns, energy policy, and national security. While some progress has been made, much more remains to be done. For instance, Madeleine Albright, former secretary of state in the Clinton administration, indicated quite clearly that the environment was a fundamental feature of U.S. foreign policy.[64] Having said that, we have also seen American states responding to environmental concerns due to inaction at the federal level of government. For example, due to obstructionism on the part of the Bush 43 administration, California under the leadership of Governor Schwarzenegger attempted to impose strict guidelines on automobile greenhouse gas emissions that have both a domestic and global impact. Although, as Jacqueline Vaughn Switzer has stated, "Historically, the president has had a limited role in environmental politics,"[65] we have seen in this study that some presidents have pushed an activist, pro-environmental agenda. Nonetheless, whether and to what extent environmental security assumes a central role in presidential policy making in the twenty-first century remains to be seen.

The Forty-fourth President and the Environment: Barack Obama

In concluding comments in their 2000 book, *The Presidency and Domestic Policy*, William Lammers and Michael Genovese asked, "What, then, are the prospects for policy change? Regardless of the strategies they choose, future presidents will face formidable challenges. The job has become tougher, and budgetary pressures may intensify. Yet important strategies will still be available, and a president's strategic choices can make a difference."[66] The third presidential election of the twenty-first century provided an open seat that found several candidates of both major parties vying for the White House. Would the nation's forty-fourth president become the first "environmental president" of the twenty-first century?

Senator Barack Obama of Illinois emerged as the people's choice on November 4, 2008. The new Democratic president was faced with serious economic and foreign policy problems including two wars and a nationwide crisis involving financial institutions, the automobile industry, home foreclosures, increasing unemployment, and high gasoline prices, among others. With so much on his policy-making plate, how has the new president addressed environmental concerns during his first year in office?

It is safe to say that environmentalists were thrilled with the election of Barack Obama. Roger Schlickeisen, president of the group Defenders of Wildlife, captured the sentiment of the environmental movement: "For the first time in nearly a decade, we can look to the future with a sense of hope that the enormous environmental challenges we face will begin to be addressed and that our air, land, water, and wildlife—and the overall health of our planet—will not be sacrificed to appease polluting industries and campaign contributors."[67]

The new president moved quickly on several environmental fronts in an effort to put a "green stamp" on his administration regarding the environment.[68] On March 28, 2009, he announced that he would launch a Major Economies Forum on Energy and Climate that would bring together delegates from seventeen major economies to discuss energy and climate change issues. The forum convened in Italy later that year in July. As a result of discussions taking place at the meeting, President Obama announced that delegates had agreed to set a "goal to limit global warming to levels recommended by scientists" and that a commitment from emerging economies including China "to work for limiting global warming" was secured, although specific targets were not set for these emerging economies.[69] Also at the end of March, President Obama signed the Omnibus Public Lands Management Act of 2009, landmark legislation that would set aside over two million acres of public land in nine states to be protected as wilderness. In May 2009, the president issued an executive order—Chesapeake Bay Protection and Restoration—that would recommit the federal government, working with state and local governments, to restore the health of the nation's largest estuary, the Chesapeake Bay. A draft plan set forth by federal officials was publicized in October that required a sixty-day comment period before action could be taken. The same day, the Obama administration announced a landmark National Fuel Efficiency Policy, bringing together the federal government, state governments, the environmental community, United Auto Workers, and the auto industry to impose new vehicle gas mileage standards that would improve fuel efficiency and cut greenhouse gas emissions that contribute to global climate change.[70] Moreover, President Obama was able to ameliorate the concerns of state officials in California who were at odds with the Bush administration, which opposed California's efforts to impose stricter guidelines than the federal government. Working with the Obama administration, California officials have agreed to forego imposing their own policy at least through 2016.

The Obama administration also moved forward in the international arena.[71] During his first trip abroad as president, Obama met with Canadian prime minister Stephen Harper on May 19 and both announced in a joint press conference that they would work together to "promote the development of clean energy technologies," to "advance carbon reduction technologies," and to "develop an electric grid that can deliver clean and renewable energy in the U.S. and Canada." Two months later, President Obama visited Mexico where he and President Felipe Calderón announced their plan to strengthen "bilateral cooperation by establishing the U.S.-Mexico Bilateral Framework on Clean Energy and Climate Change." The following month, on her first trip abroad as secretary of state, Hillary Clinton visited a low-emissions power plant in China that uses technology from U.S. corporate giant General Electric. Todd Stern, Clinton's climate change envoy, joined her at the plant, which was symbolic of joint U.S.-China efforts to deal with increasing greenhouse gases produced by China. Stern stated, "There is no way to preserve a safe and livable planet unless China plays an important role along with the United States. This is not a matter of politics or morality or right or wrong, it is simply the unforgiving math of accumulating emissions."

Notwithstanding these important actions in the environmental domain, one policy area that generated conflict between the administration on the one hand and environmentalists and some congressional Democrats on the other hand involved protection for gray wolves under the Endangered Species Act. As reported by *The Washington Post*, CBS News, and MSNBC, although environmental groups won a victory in July 2008 when a federal judge opposed a Bush 43 plan to delist gray wolves from the endangered species list, in March 2009, Obama's Secretary of the Interior, Ken Salazar, sustained the George W. Bush era policy when he upheld the January 2009 decision by the U.S. Fish and Wildlife Service to remove protection for gray wolves, a move that surprised and angered environmentalists. The decision affected gray wolves in some of the northern Rocky Mountain states and western Great Lakes states. While a spokesperson for the Interior department reported that Salazar's decision was "based on science," a senior official with Defenders of Wildlife stated, "Making the decision to adopt the Bush administration's flawed delisting proposal the same week that the president pledged his commitment to the Endangered Species Act certainly calls into question whether the Interior Department was coordinating as closely as one would expect to have done with the White House."[72]

While this is a promising beginning, the new chief executive has a variety of foreign and domestic issues and demands to address that will require his attention. Whether President Obama will join the other activist, pro-environmental presidents discussed in this book remains to be seen. Having said that, he has begun in an environmentally impressive way during his first year in office.

Preface

1. Glen Sussman, Byron W. Daynes, and Jonathan P. West, *American Politics and the Environment* (New York: Longman, 2002), xvii.

2. John Kennedy, "Special Message to the Congress on Improving the Nation's Health," February 7, 1963, *Public Papers of the Presidents of the United States: John F. Kennedy, 1963* (Washington, D.C.: Office of the Federal Register, National Archives and Records Service, U.S. Government Printing Office, 1964), 1:141–47.

Introduction

1. Franklin D. Roosevelt, "Radio Address Delivered at Two Medicine Chalet," August 5, 1934, *The Public Papers and Addresses of Franklin D. Roosevelt: The People Approve,* comp. Samuel I. Rosenman (New York: Random House, 1938), 3:359.

2. Richard Lowitt, "Conservation, Policy on," in *Encyclopedia of the American Presidency,* ed. Leonard W. Levy and Louis Fisher (New York: Simon and Schuster, 1994), 1:289.

3. Rachel Carson, *Silent Spring* (Boston: Houghton Mifflin, 1962).

4. Kennedy, "Special Message to the Congress on Improving the Nation's Health," February 7, 1963, 1:141–47 (see preface, n. 2).

5. Although social policy has been defined in various ways over time, it can simply be defined as "public policy that possesses legal authority having the potential of influencing or changing moral practices, individual standards of behavior as well as community values." Byron W. Daynes and Glen Sussman, *The American Presidency and the Social Agenda* (Upper Saddle River, N.J.: Prentice Hall, 2001), 1. See also Raymond Tatalovich and Byron W. Daynes, *Social Regulatory Policy: Moral Controversies in American Politics* (Boulder, Colo.: Westview Press, 1988). In his assessment of American public opinion, pollster Louis Harris has long considered the environment in the same category as other social issues. See Louis Harris, *Inside America* (New York: Vintage Books, 1987), 135–273. George McKenna, in his 1994 study, made it clear that environmental policy should not be considered any different from other social policies as far as how people react to it. See George McKenna, *The Drama of Democracy: American Government and Politics* (Guildford, Conn.: Dushkin Publishing Group, 1994), 435.

6. Michael Satchell, "Clinton's 'Mother of All Land-Grabs,'" *U.S. News and World Report,* January 20, 1997, 42.

7. George Gallup Jr. maintains that moral values today are more important now than at any other time in sixty years of public opinion polling. Peter Hart Research Associates poll issued for Shell Oil Company that found results that would back up this conclusion. They found that 56 percent of citizens identified "moral values" as the most serious problem in the nation, whereas those who answered the

survey selected "standards set by public officials" as the fifth most important reason for the cause of moral decline in the nation. Reasons considered more important included: families not teaching values; increased drug use; parental examples; and portrayal of life in movies and on TV. Compiled by Robert Kilborn and Lance Carden, "Parents Are Key to Raising Moral Values, Survey Finds," http://www.csmonitor.com/1999/0519/p24s3.html (accessed November 17, 2009).

8. Ben J. Wattenberg, "Social Issues Will Elect Our Next President—and Clinton Knows It," *American Enterprise*, January–February 1996, 3.

9. Ronald Inglehart, *Culture Shift in Advanced Industrial Society* (Princeton, N.J.: Princeton University Press, 1990).

10. Robert V. Percival, "Environmental Law in the Supreme Court: Highlights from the Marshall Papers," *Environmental Law Reporter* 23 (October 1993): 10607.

11. Percival, "Environmental Law in the Supreme Court," 10607.

12. Because all presidents up to 2006 have been men, the masculine pronoun is used throughout the book to refer to the president and presidency in general. This usage in no way excludes the possibility or anticipation that in the future women will surely occupy this office.

13. Both Theodore Lowi, in describing regulatory policy, and Raymond Tatalovich and Byron Daynes, in examining social regulatory policies, maintained that one could expect only "modest leadership from the White House" with regard to these policies. Yet some presidents have exerted energetic policy leadership in handling selected social policies, while others have largely ignored or even rejected these same policies. What does seem clear, though, is that not all presidents fit one behavioral

mode. See Tatalovich and Daynes, *Social Regulatory Policy*, and Theodore J. Lowi's foreword to Tatalovich and Daynes, *Social Regulatory Policy*, x–xxi.

14. Susan Hunter and Victoria Noonan point out that media attention to the environment was highest beginning in the late 1960s through the mid-1970s, as measured by the number of *New York Times* articles on environmental issues during the year, and decreased in the late 1970s through the 1980s. Hunter and Noonan, "Energy, Environment, and the Presidential Agenda," in *The Presidency Reconsidered*, ed. Richard W. Waterman (Itasca, Ill.: F. E. Peacock, 1993), 303–4.

15. Lyn Ragsdale, *Presidential Politics* (Boston: Houghton Mifflin, 1993), 363.

16. Barbara Hinckley, *Problems of the Presidency* (Glenview, Ill.: Scott, Foresman, 1985), 230.

17. Fred I. Greenstein, *The Hidden-Hand Presidency: Eisenhower as Leader* (New York: Basic Books, 1982); Sidney M. Milkis and Michael Nelson, *The American Presidency: Origins and Development, 1776–2002*, 4th ed. (Washington, D.C.: CQ Press, 2003).

18. Samuel Kernell, *Going Public: New Strategies of Presidential Leadership*, 2nd ed. (Washington, D.C.: CQ Press, 1993).

19. Jeffrey E. Cohen, "Presidential Rhetoric and the Public Agenda," *American Journal of Political Science* 39 (February 1995): 87–107.

20. Richard E. Neustadt, *Presidential Power and the Modern Presidents: The Politics of Leadership from Roosevelt to Reagan* (New York: Free Press, 1990).

21. Kenneth R. Mayer, *With the Stroke of a Pen: Executive Orders and Presidential Power* (Princeton, N.J.: Princeton University Press, 2001), 4. See also Philip J. Cooper, *By Order of the President: The Use and Abuse of*

Executive Direct Action (Lawrence: University Press of Kansas, 2002).

22. Robert A. Shanley, *Presidential Influence and Environmental Policy* (Westport, Conn.: Greenwood Press, 1992), 9.

23. Elizabeth R. DeSombre, *Domestic Sources of International Environmental Policy: Industry, Environmentalists, and U.S. Power* (Cambridge, Mass.: MIT Press, 2000), 5, 17.

24. William W. Lammers and Michael A. Genovese, *The Presidency and Domestic Policy: Comparing Leadership Styles, FDR to Clinton* (Washington, D.C. CQ Press, 2000); Norman J. Vig, "Presidential Leadership and the Environment," in *Environmental Policy: New Directions for the Twenty-first Century*, ed. Norman J. Vig and Michael E. Kraft, 6th ed. (Washington, D.C.: CQ Press, 2006), 100–123; Greenstein, *Hidden-Hand Presidency.*

25. Charles O. Jones, *The Trusteeship Presidency: Jimmy Carter and the United States Congress* (Baton Rouge: Louisiana State University Press, 1988).

26. James David Barber, *The Presidential Character: Predicting Performance in the White House,* 4th ed. (Englewood Cliffs, N.J.: Prentice Hall, 1992); Richard Nathan, *The Administrative Presidency* (New York: Wiley, 1983); Richard Rose, *The Postmodern President: Bill Clinton's Legacy in U.S. Politics* (Pittsburgh: University of Pittsburgh Press, 2000).

27. Dennis L. Soden, ed., *The Environmental Presidency* (Albany: State University of New York Press, 1999).

28. Vig, "Presidential Leadership and the Environment," 101.

29. Mary E. Stuckey, *The President as Interpreter-in-Chief* (Chatham, N.J.: Chatham House Publishers, 1991), 134.

30. Tarla Rai Peterson, ed., *Green Talk in the White House: The Rhetorical Presidency*

Encounters Ecology (College Station, Tex.: Texas A&M University Press, 2004).

31. See Peterson, *Green Talk,* 20; also see Michael R. Vickery's complete study of Nixon in "Conservative Politics and the Politics of Conservation: Richard Nixon and the Environmental Protection Agency," chap. 4 in Peterson, *Green Talk,* 113–33.

32. Marc Landy and Sidney Milkis, *Presidential Greatness* (Lawrence: University Press of Kansas, 2000), 3.

33. Vig, "Presidential Leadership and the Environment," 103.

34. We note that we could have placed Truman in the Plodders and Shifters category. As Robert Cahn, an original member of the Council on Environmental Quality, argued, Truman was concerned about resource conservation only as a means to rebuild the economy and ensure national security. However, Cahn also indicated that Truman supported many of the New Deal conservation programs. See Robert Cahn, *Footprints on the Planet: A Search for an Environmental Ethic* (New York: Universe Books, 1978), 49–50.

35. Mark Madison, "Birth of a Notion: The American Conservation Movement," DITC Environmental Education Foundation, Inc., http://www.ditc-eef.org/news letternotion.html (accessed April 15, 2009).

36. Lee M. Talbot, "Conservation," *Grolier Multimedia Encyclopedia,* http:// teacher.scholastic.com/scholasticnews/ indepth/upfront/grolier/conservation.htm (accessed April 15, 2009).

37. Stacy J. Silveira, "The American Environmental Movement: Surviving through Diversity," Boston College Law School Student Publications, http://www .bc.edu/schools/law/lawreviews/meta-elements/journals/bcealr/28_2–3/07_TXT .htm (accessed November 6, 2009).

38. Byron W. Daynes, "Two Democrats, One Environment: First-term Efforts of Franklin Roosevelt and Bill Clinton to Shape the Environment," in *New Deal and Public Policy*, ed. Byron W. Daynes, William D. Pederson, and Michael P. Riccards (New York: St. Martin's Press, 1998), 105–23.

39. Theodore Roosevelt Association, "Conservationist: Life of Theodore Roosevelt," http://www.theodoreroosevelt.org/life/conservation.htm (accessed November 20, 2003).

40. James D. Richardson, *A Compilation of the Messages and Papers of the Presidents* (New York: Bureau of National Literature, 1911), 10:7598.

41. Richardson, *Compilation of the Messages and Papers of the Presidents*, 10:7641.

42. Theodore Roosevelt Association, "Conservationist."

43. For Roosevelt's complete explanation of his Stewardship Theory, see Theodore Roosevelt, *Theodore Roosevelt: An Autobiography* (New York: Scribner's, 1924), 357–58.

44. Paul Russell Cutright, *Theodore Roosevelt the Naturalist* (New York: Harper and Brothers, 1956).

45. Theodore Roosevelt, *The Works of Theodore Roosevelt*, ed. Herman Haggedorn (New York: Scribner's, 1926), 353.

46. William H. Harbaugh, *The Life and Times of Theodore Roosevelt* (New York: Oxford University Press, 1961), 318.

47. Theodore Roosevelt, *Addresses and Presidential Messages of Theodore Roosevelt* (New York: G. P. Putnam's Sons, 1904).

48. Lewis L. Gould, *The Presidency of Theodore Roosevelt* (Lawrence: University Press of Kansas, 1991), 40.

49. Theodore Roosevelt, *Social Justice and Popular Rule* (New York: Arno Press, 1974), 23.

50. William Jennings Bryan, *A Talk of Two Conventions* (New York: Funk and Wagnalls, 1912), 289–91.

51. *An Act for the Preservation of American Antiquities*, Public Law 59–209, *U.S. Statutes at Large* 34 (1906): 225.

52. Theodore Roosevelt Association, "Conservationist."

53. Shanley, *Presidential Influence and Environmental Policy*, 13; Carl E. Hatch, *The Big Stick and the Congressional Gavel: A Study of Theodore Roosevelt's Relations with His Last Congress, 1907–1909* (New York: Pageant Press, 1967), 8–9.

54. Hatch, *Big Stick and the Congressional Gavel*, 12.

55. Stephen Skowronek, *Building a New American State: The Expansion of National Administrative Capacities, 1879–1920* (New York: Cambridge University Press, 1982), 172.

56. U.S. House, Office of the Clerk, "Presidential Vetoes (1789–2001)," House History, http://clerk.house.gov/art_history/house_history/vetoes.html (accessed November 11, 2009).

57. The executive proclamation is either "ceremonial in nature or deal[s] with issues of trade and may or may not carry legal effect." The executive order, on the other hand, is "similar to written orders, or instructions the president of a corporation might send to department heads or directors. Thirty days after it is officially published in the Federal Register, an [executive order] becomes law." About.com, "U.S. Government Info," http://usgovinfo.about.com/library/weekly/aa121897.htm (accessed February 6, 2007).

58. Harbaugh, *Life and Times of Theodore Roosevelt*, 313.

59. Paul Russell Cutright, *Theodore Roosevelt: The Making of a Conservationist* (Urbana: University of Illinois Press, 1985), 218–19.

60. Char Miller, *Gifford Pinchot and the Making of Modern Environmentalism* (Washington, D.C.: Island Press, 2001), 4.

61. Theodore Roosevelt, *An Autobiography* (New York: Macmillan, 1913), 451.

62. Charles F. Bennett, *Conservation and Management of Natural Resources in the United States* (New York: Wiley, 1983), 18.

63. Bennett, *Conservation and Management*, 18.

64. Theodore Roosevelt Organization, "Conservation Commissions under the Roosevelt Administration, 1901–1909," http://www.theodoreroosevelt.org/life/conservation.htm#conf (accessed October 25, 2004).

65. Hilary Jan Izatt, "Theodore Roosevelt's Environmental Presidency" (unpublished manuscript, Brigham Young University, 2003), 20.

66. Theodore Roosevelt, *Theodore Roosevelt: An Autobiography* (New York: Scribner's, 1924), 410.

67. Cutright, *Theodore Roosevelt: The Making of a Conservationist*, 231.

68. Gifford Pinchot, "Conservation as a Foundation of Permanent Peace," *Nature* 146 (August 1940): 183–85.

69. Cutright, *Theodore Roosevelt: The Making of a Conservationist*, 223–24.

70. Harbaugh, *Life and Times of Theodore Roosevelt*, 308.

71. Harbaugh, *Life and Times of Theodore Roosevelt*, 317.

72. Theodore Roosevelt Association, "Conservationist."

73. Theodore Roosevelt Association, "Conservationist."

74. See Cutright, *Theodore Roosevelt: The Making of a Conservationist*, 213.

75. Gifford Pinchot, *The Fight for Conservation* (Washington, D.C.: U.S. Government Printing Office, 1908), 94–95.

76. Lowitt, "Conservation, Policy on," 1:289.

77. Donald F. Anderson, *William Howard Taft: A Conservative's Conception of the Presidency* (Ithaca, N.Y.: Cornell University Press, 1968), 230–31.

78. Michael L. Bromley, *William Howard Taft and the First Motoring Presidency, 1909–1913* (Jefferson, N.C.: McFarland, 2003), 198–99.

79. Anderson, *William Howard Taft*, 72–73.

80. "A Hike through History," Sierra Club Bulletin, *Sierra* Magazine, January–February 2000, http://www.sierraclub.org/sierra/200001/bulletin.asp (accessed September 8, 2004); Don Hendershot, "A Presidential Role in Preserving Public Land: Former Presidents Led the Trend towards Today's Conservation," *Smoky Mountain News*, February 21, 2001, http://www.smokymountainnews.com/issues/2_01/2_21_01/out_presidential_roles.shtml (accessed September 8, 2004).

81. Barry Mackintosh, *The National Park Service: A Brief History*, Park Net, 1999, http://www.cr.nps.gov/history/hisnps/NPSHistory/npshisto.htm (accessed September 22, 2004).

82. National Park Service, "The Department of Everything Else: Twentieth Century Headliners and Highlights," http://www.cr.nps.gov/history/online_books/utley-mackintosh/interior13.htm (accessed September 8, 2004).

83. National Park Service, "Department of Everything Else."

84. Robert K. Murray, *The Harding Era: Warren G. Harding and His Administration* (Minneapolis: University of Minnesota Press, 1969), 444.

85. Edward Connery Lathem, *Calvin Coolidge Says: Dispatches Written by Former President Coolidge and Syndicated to Newspapers, 1930–1931* (Plymouth, Vt.: Calvin Coolidge Memorial Foundation, 1972), April 23, 1931, n.p.

86. Keith Easthouse, "The Party that Was Green," *Forest Magazine: For People Who Care About Our Forests*, July–August 2001, http://www.fseee.org/forestmag/0104east.shtml (accessed September 8, 2004).

87. Hendershot, "Presidential Role in Preserving Public Land."

88. Herbert Hoover, "Annual Message to the Congress on the State of the Union," December 3, 1929, *Public Papers of the Presidents of the United States: Herbert Hoover, 1929* (Washington, D.C.: Office of the Federal Register, National Archives and Records Service, U.S. Government Printing Office, 1930), 426.

89. Herbert Hoover, "The President's News Conference of May 15, 1931," *Public Papers of the Presidents: Herbert Hoover, 1931* (Washington, D.C., 1976), 255.

90. Kendrick A. Clements, "Herbert Hoover and Conservation, 1921–33," *American Historical Review* 89, no. 1 (1984): 86.

Chapter 1

1. Anna Lou Riesch Owen, "Conservation under Franklin D. Roosevelt," in *The American Environment: Readings in the History of Conservation,* ed. Roderick Nash (Reading, Mass.: Addison-Wesley, 1968), 150–51.

2. Franklin D. Roosevelt, "Message to Congress on Our Use of Our National Resources," January 24, 1935, American Presidency Project, University of California at Santa Barbara, ed. John T. Woolley and Gerhard Peters, http://www.presidency.ucsb.edu/ws/index.php?pid=14891&st=nature&st1=resources (accessed November 11, 2009).

3. Anna Lou Riesch Owen, *Conservation under FDR* (New York: Praeger, 1983), 105.

4. George McJimsey, *The Presidency of Franklin Delano Roosevelt* (Lawrence: University of Kansas Press, 2000), 111.

5. Lowitt, "Conservation, Policy On," 1:289 (see intro., n. 2).

6. While there is some question as to the exact number of "fireside chats," since the White House did not always label a radio address as a "fireside chat," the best information suggests that there were at least twenty-eight of them. See Franklin D. Roosevelt Presidential Library and Museum, "Fireside Chats," http://www.fdrlibrary.marist.edu/arch.html (accessed May 15, 2004).

7. FDR held a record number of news conferences, averaging 6.9 a month. See Harold W. Stanley and Richard G. Niemi, *Vital Statistics on American Politics* (Washington, D.C.: CQ Press, 1988), 50.

8. Stanley and Niemi, *Vital Statistics on American Politics*, 50; Clinton's press conferences for his first term were obtained from *Weekly Compilation of Presidential Papers* for the years he was in office.

9. Franklin D. Roosevelt, "1936 State of the Union Address," Home Page of Kenneth Janda, http://janda.org/politxts/State%20of%20Union%20Addresses/1934–1945%20Roosevelt/FDR36.html (accessed November 11, 2009).

10. Ted Morgan, *FDR: A Biography* (New York: Simon and Schuster, 1985), 37.

11. Riesch Owen, *Conservation under FDR*, 9.

12. Riesch Owen, *Conservation under FDR*, 183.

13. Riesch Owen, *Conservation under FDR*, 11.

14. "Democratic Party Platform of 1932," American Presidency Project, ed. Woolley and Peters, http://www.presidency.uscb.edu/site/docs/platforms.php (accessed November 7, 2003).

15. "Democratic Party Platform of

1936," American Presidency Project, ed. Woolley and Peters, http://www.presidency.uscb.edu/site/docs/platforms.php (accessed November 7, 2003).

16. "Democratic Party Platform of 1940," American Presidency Project, ed. Woolley and Peters, http://www.presidency.uscb.edu/site/docs/platforms.php (accessed November 7, 2003).

17. Franklin D. Roosevelt, "Message to Congress Suggesting the Tennessee Valley Authority," April 10, 1933, American Presidency Project, ed. Woolley and Peters, http://www.presidency.ucsb.edu/ws/?pid=14614 (accessed November 11, 2009).

18. Franklin D. Roosevelt, "State of the Union Address," January 6, 1945, American Presidency Project, ed. Woolley and Peters, http://www.presidency.ucsb.edu/ws/index.php?pid=16595 (accessed November 6, 2009).

19. FDR, "Message to Congress Suggesting the Tennessee Valley Authority."

20. Franklin D. Roosevelt, "State of the Union Address," January 6, 1945, American Presidency Project, ed. Woolley and Peters, http://www.presidency.ucsb.edu/ws/index.php?pid=16595 (accessed November 11, 2009).

21. Franklin D. Roosevelt, "Message to Congress on National Planning and Development of Natural Resources," June 3, 1937, American Presidency Project, ed. Woolley and Peters, http://www.presidency.ucsb.edu/ws/index.php?pid=15415&st=nature&st1=resources (accessed November 11, 2009).

22. Franklin D. Roosevelt, "Three Essentials for Unemployment Relief (C.C.C., F.E.R.A., P.W.A.)," March 21, 1933, *The Public Papers and Addresses of Franklin D. Roosevelt: The Year of Crisis*, comp. Samuel I. Rosenman (New York: Random House, 1938), 2:82.

23. Riesch Owen, *Conservation under FDR*, 105–6.

24. Shanley, *Presidential Influence and Environmental Policy*, 15 (see intro., n. 22).

25. U.S. Department of Agriculture, Forest Service, "Forests and People," in *Report of the Chief of the Forest Service* (Washington, D.C.: U.S. Government Printing Office, 1942), 27.

26. Riesch Owen, *Conservation under FDR*, 105–6.

27. These figures were based on budget figures of the departments of Agriculture and Interior, as well as budget funds from the TVA, Improvements of Rivers and Harbors, Flood Control, the Federal Power Commission, and the CCC for the years 1933–1944. Figures are from Bureau of the Budget, *The Budget of the United States for the Fiscal Years 1933–1944* (Washington, D.C.: U.S. Government Printing Office).

28. Morgan, *FDR*, 370–72.

29. Franklin D. Roosevelt, *Franklin D. Roosevelt and Conservation, 1911–1945: Use and Abuse of America's Natural Resources*, comp. and ed. Edgar B. Nixon (New York: Arno Press, 1972), 1:543.

30. Daynes, "Two Democrats, One Environment," 116 (see intro., n. 38).

31. This practice ended in 1939 when Congress established the oversight procedures for government reorganizations. See Raymond Tatalovich and Byron W. Daynes, *Presidential Power in the United States* (Monterey, Calif.: Brooks/Cole, 1984), 203.

32. Riesch Owen, "The Objectives of Conservation during the Roosevelt Administration," in *Conservation under FDR*, 92.

33. Daynes, "Two Democrats, One Environment," 116.

34. Daynes, "Two Democrats, One Environment," 117.

35. Riesch Owen, *Conservation under FDR*, 19.

36. Riesch Owen, *Conservation under FDR*, 18–19.

37. Franklin D. Roosevelt, "Proposed Conservation Conference," April 17, 1945, in Nixon, *Franklin D. Roosevelt and Conservation*, 2:646–47.

38. John F. Kennedy, "Remarks in Los Banos, California, at the Ground-Breaking Ceremonies for the San Luis Dam," August 18, 1962, *Public Papers of the Presidents of the United States: John F. Kennedy, 1962* (Washington, D.C.: Office of the Federal Register, National Archives and Records Service, U.S. Government Printing Office, 1963), 2:628–29.

39. "Address by Cornelia Bryce Pinchot at the Dedication of Gifford Pinchot National Forest," October 15, 1949, Forest History Society, http://www.foresthistory .org/publications/FHT/FHTSpring1999/ mrsPinchot.pdf (accessed November 11, 2009).

40. "Address by Cornelia Bryce Pinchot."

41. Harry Truman, "Address in Casper, Wyoming," May 9, 1950, *Public Papers of the Presidents: Harry S. Truman, 1950* (Washington, D.C., 1965), 1:322.

42. Harry Truman, "Special Message to the Congress on the Nation's Land and Water Resources," January 19, 1953, *Public Papers of the Presidents: Harry S. Truman, 1953* (Washington, D.C., 1965), 1:1208–15.

43. Harry Truman, "The President's News Conference of January 5, 1950," *Public Papers of the Presidents: Harry S. Truman, 1950* (Washington, D.C., 1965), 1:13.

44. Harry Truman, "Address in Seattle before the Washington State Press Club," June 10, 1948, *Public Papers of the Presidents: Harry S. Truman, 1948* (Washington, D.C., 1964), 319.

45. Harry Truman, "Address at the Mormon Tabernacle in Salt Lake City," September 21, 1948, *Public Papers of the Presidents: Harry S. Truman, 1948* (Washington, D.C., 1964), 532, 534.

46. Leo Egan, "Dewey Pledges a Program of Conservation to West," *New York Times*, September 22, 1948.

47. Harry Truman, "A Recorded Interview with the President," September 29, 1952, *Public Papers of the Presidents: Harry S. Truman, 1952* (Washington, D.C., 1966), 625.

48. Harry Truman, "Annual Message to the Congress on the State of the Union," January 5, 1949, *Public Papers of the Presidents: Harry S. Truman, 1949* (Washington, D.C., 1964), 5.

49. Harry Truman, "Special Message to the Congress Urging Action on the St. Lawrence Seaway," January 28, 1952, *Public Papers of the Presidents: Harry S. Truman, 1952* (Washington, D.C., 1966), 125–28.

50. Harry Truman, "Statement by the President upon Signing a Bill Establishing a New Grand Teton National Park," September 14, 1950, *Public Papers of the Presidents: Harry S. Truman, 1950* (Washington, D.C., 1965), 635–36.

51. Harry Truman, "Statement by the President upon Signing Bill Providing for Water Research and Development," July 4, 1952, *Public Papers of the Presidents: Harry S. Truman, 1952* (Washington, D.C., 1966), 472–73.

52. All figures were based on pertinent figures from the Departments of the Interior and Agriculture in Bureau of the Budget, *The Budget of the United States Government for Fiscal Year Ending June 30, 1954* (Washington, D.C.: U.S. Government Printing Office, 1953), 1137–38.

53. Truman, "Special Message to the

Congress on the Nation's Land and Water Resources," 1:1208–15.

54. Harry Truman, "Statement by the President Making Public a Report by the Water Resources Policy Commission," December 17, 1950, *Public Papers of the Presidents: Harry S. Truman, 1950* (Washington, D.C., 1965), 748.

55. Harry Truman, "Letter Concerning the Establishment of an Interagency Committee to Study the Resources and Development of New England and New York," October 11, 1950, *Public Papers of the Presidents: Harry S. Truman, 1950* (Washington, D.C., 1965), 666.

56. Paul P. Kennedy, "President Orders Resources Survey: 6 Federal Agencies to Organize Committee for Study to Cover New York, New England," *New York Times*, October 12, 1950.

57. Harry Truman, "Message to the United States Technical Conference on Air Pollution," May 3, 1950, *Public Papers of the Presidents: Harry S. Truman, 1950* (Washington, D.C., 1965), 281–82.

58. Harry Truman, "Special Message to the Congress Transmitting Reorganization Plan 3 of 1946," May 16, 1946, *Public Papers of the Presidents: Harry S. Truman, 1946* (Washington, D.C., 1962), 262–63.

59. Harry Truman, "Address and Remarks at the Dedication of the Kentucky Dam at Gilbertsville, Kentucky," October 10, 1945, *Public Papers of the Presidents: Harry S. Truman, 1945* (Washington, D.C., 1961), 389–94.

60. Harry Truman, "Address on Conservation at the Dedication of Everglades National Park," December 6, 1947, *Public Papers of the Presidents: Harry S. Truman, 1947* (Washington, D.C., 1963), 505–8.

61. Harry Truman, "Special Message to the Senate Transmitting Treaty with Canada Concerning Uses of the Waters of the Niagara River," May 2, 1950, *Public Papers of the Presidents: Harry S. Truman, 1950* (Washington, D.C., 1965), 280.

62. "Fish Treaty with Canada Shaped," *New York Times*, September 21, 1945, http://proquest.umi.com/pqdweb?index=0&did=88297723&SrchMode=1&sid=1&Fmt=10&VInst=PROD&VType=PQD&RQT=309&VName=HNP&TS=1257984422&clientId=9338 (accessed November 11, 2009). In 1946 the United States, under Harry Truman's authorization, joined other nations in a halibut fishing agreement, and Truman also signed the more important International Whaling Convention, which represented one of the first efforts to unite world opinion in supporting the management of threatened wildlife.

63. Carolyn Long, Michael Cabral, and Brooks Vandivort, "The Chief Environmental Diplomat: An Evolving Arena of Foreign Policy," in *The Environmental Presidency*, ed. Dennis L. Soden (Albany: State University of New York, 1999), 196.

64. Northwest Atlantic Fisheries Organization (NAFO), http://www.nafo.int/about/frames/about.html (accessed November 11, 2009).

65. See table 5.3, "The Presidency and International Environmental Diplomacy: Selected Agreements," in Daynes and Sussman, *American Presidency and the Social Agenda*, 133–34 (see intro., n. 5).

66. William M. Blair, "Truman Predicts World of Plenty: President Tells Hemispheric Conference Conservation Is Key to Peace, Prosperity," *New York Times*, September 21, 1948, sec. 1, p. 23.

67. George Barrett, "Truman Again Bid to U.N. Dedication," *New York Times*, June 11, 1949, 5.

68. Thomas J. Hamilton, "Resources

Parley Will Open Today," *New York Times*, August 17, 1949.

69. Harry Truman, "Special Message to the Congress on the Mutual Security Program," March 6, 1952, *Public Papers of the Presidents: Harry S. Truman, 1952* (Washington, D.C., 1966), 186.

70. Harry Truman, "Annual Budget Message to the Congress: Fiscal Year 1948," January 10, 1947, *Public Papers of the Presidents: Harry S. Truman, 1947* (Washington, D.C., 1963), 83.

71. Harry Truman, "Annual Message to the Congress: The President's Economic Report," January 12, 1951, *Public Papers of the Presidents: Harry S. Truman, 1951* (Washington, D.C., 1965), 35.

72. Truman, "Special Message to the Congress on the Nation's Land and Water Resources," 1:1208.

73. Lowitt, "Conservation, Policy On," 1:289 (see intro., n. 2).

74. Harry Truman, "Special Message to the Congress on the Nation's Land and Water Resources," 1:1211.

Chapter 2

1. John F. Kennedy, "Remarks at the High School Memorial Stadium, Great Falls, Montana," September 26, 1963, *Public Papers of the Presidents of the United States: John F. Kennedy, 1963* (Washington, D.C.: Office of the Federal Register, National Archives and Records Service, U.S. Government Printing Office, 1964), 729.

2. John F. Kennedy, "The President's News Conference of August 29, 1962," American Presidency Project, ed. Woolley and Peters, http://www.presidency.ucsb .edu/ws/?pid=8839 (accessed November 22, 2008).

3. Michael Jay Friedman, "A Book that Changed a Nation," U.S. State Department, Bureau of International Information

Programs, March 2007, http://www .america.gov/st/energy-english/2008/May/ 20080602124122eaifaso.7619854.html (accessed November 11, 2009).

4. Adam Rome, "'Give Earth a Chance': The Environmental Movement and the Sixties," *Journal of American History*, 90, no. 2 (September 2003), http://www .historycooperative.org/journals/jah/90.2/ rome.html (accessed November 22, 2008).

5. Stewart L. Udall, *The Quiet Crisis and the Next Generation* (Salt Lake City: Peregrine Smith Books, 1988), 203.

6. John F. Kennedy, "Address at the University of Wyoming," September 25, 1963, *Public Papers of the Presidents: John F. Kennedy, 1963* (Washington, D.C., 1964), 722.

7. John F. Kennedy, "69—Special Message to the Congress on Conservation," March 1, 1962, American Presidency Project, ed. Woolley and Peters, http:// www.presidency.ucsb.edu/ws/index .php?pid=9081&st=west& (accessed November 22, 2008).

8. John F. Kennedy, "216—Remarks to the White House Conference on Conservation," May 25, 1962, American Presidency Project, ed. Woolley and Peters, http://www.presidency.ucsb.edu/ws/index .php?pid=8684 (accessed November 22, 2008).

9. Kennedy, "Address at the University of Wyoming," 722.

10. John F. Kennedy, "Remarks at the Dedication of the National Wildlife Federation Building," March 3, 1961, *Public Papers of the Presidents: John F. Kennedy, 1961* (Washington, D.C., 1962), 148.

11. John F. Kennedy, "Remarks at the Convention Center in Las Vegas, Nevada," September 28, 1963, *Papers of the Presidents: John F. Kennedy, 1963* (Washington, D.C., 1964), 749.

12. Kennedy, "Remarks at the High School Memorial Stadium," 729.

13. Kennedy, "Remarks at the Convention Center," 748.

14. Kennedy, "Address at the University of Wyoming," 722.

15. John F. Kennedy, "Letter to the President of the Senate on Increasing the National Effort in Oceanography," March 29, 1961, *Public Papers of the Presidents: John F. Kennedy, 1961* (Washington, D.C., 1962), 240.

16. John F. Kennedy, "Special Message to the Congress on Agriculture," March 16, 1961, *Public Papers of the Presidents: John F. Kennedy, 1961* (Washington, D.C., 1962), 199.

17. John F. Kennedy, "Remarks at the Air Terminal in Fresno, California, After Inspecting Western Conservation Projects," August 18, 1962, *Public Papers of the Presidents: John F. Kennedy, 1962* (Washington, D.C., 1963), 630.

18. Kennedy, "Remarks at the Convention Center," September 26, 1963.

19. John F. Kennedy, "Special Message to the Congress on Natural Resources," February 23, 1961, *Public Papers of the Presidents: John F. Kennedy, 1961* (Washington, D.C., 1962), 114–21.

20. Kennedy, "Special Message to the Congress," February 23, 1961, 115.

21. Kennedy, "Special Message to the Congress," March 1, 1962, 177.

22. Kennedy, "Special Message to the Congress," March 1, 1962, 177.

23. John F. Kennedy, "State of the Union Message," January 14, 1963, *Public Papers of the Presidents: John F. Kennedy, 1963* (Washington, D.C., 1964), 1:14.

24. Kennedy, "Letter to the President of the Senate on Increasing the National Effort in Oceanography," March 29, 1961, 240–41.

25. John F. Kennedy, "Remarks upon Signing Bill Authorizing the Cape Cod National Seashore Park," August 7, 1961, *Public Papers of the Presidents: John F. Kennedy, 1961* (Washington, D.C., 1962), 551–52.

26. These bills were all passed in 1964 during Lyndon Johnson's presidency: Fire Island National Seashore bill (78 Stat. 928), Canyonlands National Park bill (78 Stat. 934); and the Ozark National Scenic Riverways bill (78 Stat. 608).

27. *Wilderness Act of 1964*, Public Law 88–577 (16 U.S. Code 1131–36), 88th Cong., 2nd sess., September 3, 1964.

28. "The Wilderness Act of 1964," Wilderness.net, http://www.wilderness.net/index.cfm?fuse=NWPS&sec=legisAct (accessed November 11, 2009).

29. U.S. Senate, "40th Anniversary of the Wilderness Act," *Congressional Record*, September 29, 2004, section 17, GovTrack.US, http://www.govtrack.us/congress/record.xpd?id=108-s20040929-17 (accessed January 24, 2009).

30. S. Res. 89, "Honoring the life of former Governor of Minnesota Orville L. Freeman, and expressing the deepest condolences of the Senate to his family on his death," March 13, 2003, U.S. Senate, 108th Cong., 1st sess., THOMAS, Legislative Information from the Library of Congress, http://thomas.loc.gov/cgi-bin/query/z?c108:S.RES.89.ATS: (accessed November 11, 2009).

31. Orville L. Freeman, "Address before the Pan American Soil Conservation Congress," April 16, 1966, Orville L. Freeman References Outside the USDA History Collection, Special Collections of the National Agricultural Library, http://www.nal.usda.gov/speccoll/collect/history/freemref.htm (accessed January 24, 2009).

32. Miron Heinselman, *The Boundary Waters Wilderness Ecosystem: Wilderness*

Ecosystem (Minneapolis: University of Minnesota Press, 1999), 120–21.

33. Rome, "'Give Earth a Chance': The Environmental Movement and the Sixties.,"

34. Stewart Udall, *The Quiet Crisis* (New York: Holt, Rinehart and Winston, 1963), viii, 189.

35. Udall, *Quiet Crisis*, xii–xiii.

36. "Executive Orders," About.com, "U.S. Government Info," http://usgovinfo .about.com/library/weekly/aa121897.htm (accessed June 5, 2004).

37. "John F. Kennedy's Executive Orders: 35th President of the United States, 1961–1963," University of Michigan Library, http://www.lib.umich.edu/gov-docs/jfkeo.html (accessed November 25, 2003).

38. "Executive Orders," About.com.

39. John F. Kennedy, "Address to the Delegates to the Northern Great Lakes Region Land and People Conference in Duluth, Minnesota," September 24, 1963, *Public Papers of the Presidents* (Washington, D.C., 1964), 713.

40. Ann L. Riley, *Restoring Streams in Cities: A Guide for Planners, Policymakers, and Citizens* (Washington, D.C.: Island Press, 1998), 331; John F. Kennedy, "Special Message to the Congress on the Nation's Youth," February 14, 1963, *Public Papers of the Presidents* (Washington, D.C., 1963), 167.

41. Kennedy, "Special Message to the Congress on Natural Resources," February 23, 1961, 114–15; Kennedy, "69—Special Message to the Congress on Conservation."

42. John F. Kennedy, "Letter to the President of the Senate and the Speaker of the House Transmitting Bill to Create a Land Conservation Fund," April 4, 1962, *Public Papers of the Presidents: John F. Kennedy, 1962* (Washington, D.C., 1963), 292.

43. Kennedy, "69—Special Message to the Congress on Conservation."

44. Kennedy, "216—Remarks to the White House Conference on Conservation."

45. John F. Kennedy, "Address before the 18th General Assembly of the United Nations," September 20, 1963, *Public Papers of the Presidents, John F. Kennedy, 1963* (Washington, D.C., 1964), 2:696.

46. Kennedy, "Letter to the President of the Senate on Increasing the National Effort in Oceanography," March 29, 1961, 243.

47. John F. Kennedy, "Televised Address on Limited Nuclear Test-Ban Treaty, July 26, 1963," in *The Speeches, Statements, and Writings of John F. Kennedy*, ed. Theodore C. Sorensen (New York: Delacorte Press, 1988), 294.

48. Dennis L. Soden and Brent S. Steel, "Evaluating the Environmental Presidency," in *The Environmental Presidency*, ed. Dennis L. Soden (Albany: State University of New York, 1999), 328.

49. John F. Kennedy, "Letter to the President of the Seneca Nation of Indians Concerning the Kinzua Dam on the Allegheny River," August 11, 1961, *Public Papers of the Presidents: John F. Kennedy, 1961* (Washington, D.C., 1962), 563.

50. John F. Kennedy, "Remarks at the Dedication of the Aerospace Medical Health Center" November 21, 1963, Air Force Brooks City-Base, http://www .jfklibrary.org/Historical+Resources/ Archives/Reference+Desk/Speeches/JFK/ 003POF03AerospaceMedicalCenter 11211963.htm (accessed November 13, 2009).

51. Kennedy, "216—Remarks to the White House Conference on Conservation."

52. Lyndon B. Johnson, "Statement by the President Making Public a Joint Report

on Natural Beauty in America," October 2, 1965, *Public Papers of the Presidents: Lyndon B. Johnson, 1965* (Washington, D.C., 1966), 1037.

53. Lyndon B. Johnson, "Remarks to Members of the National Recreation and Park Association," October 13, 1966, *Public Papers of the Presidents: Lyndon B. Johnson, 1966* (Washington, D.C., 1967), 1174.

54. Johnson, "Remarks to Members of the National Recreation and Park Association," October 13, 1966, 1175.

55. Lyndon B. Johnson, "Great Society Speech: Remarks at the University of Michigan," May 22, 1964, *Public Papers of the Presidents: Lyndon B. Johnson, 1964* (Washington, D.C., 1965), 705.

56. Frederick Buttel, "New Directions in Environmental Sociology," *Annual Review of Sociology* 13 (1987): 473.

57. Lyndon B. Johnson, "Annual Message to the Congress on the State of the Union," January 12, 1966, *Public Papers of the Presidents: Lyndon B. Johnson, 1966* (Washington, D.C., 1967), 6.

58. Lyndon B. Johnson, "Annual Message to the Congress on the State of the Union," January 10, 1967, *Public Papers of the Presidents: Lyndon B. Johnson, 1967* (Washington, D.C., 1968), 5.

59. Lyndon B. Johnson, "Annual Message to the Congress on the State of the Union," January 17, 1968, *Public Papers of the Presidents: Lyndon B. Johnson, 1968* (Washington, D.C., 1969), 29–30.

60. Lyndon B. Johnson, "Report on Natural Beauty in America," October 2, 1965, *Public Papers of the Presidents: Lyndon B. Johnson, 1965* (Washington, D.C., 1966), 1036.

61. Johnson, "Report on Natural Beauty in American," 1036.

62. Lyndon B. Johnson, "Remarks at the Unveiling of the 'Plant for a More Beautiful America' Postage Stamp," October 5, 1966,

Public Papers of the Presidents: Lyndon B. Johnson, 1966 (Washington, D.C., 1967), 1116.

63. Lyndon B. Johnson, "Statement by the President in Response to Science Advisory Committee Report on Pollution of Air, Soil, and Waters," November 6, 1965, *Public Papers of the Presidents: Lyndon B. Johnson, 1965* (Washington, D.C., 1966), 1101.

64. Lyndon B. Johnson, "Statement by the President upon Arrival in Syracuse: Conservation of the Nation's Water Resources," August 19, 1966, *Public Papers of the Presidents: Lyndon B. Johnson, 1966* (Washington, D.C., 1967), 843.

65. Lyndon B. Johnson, "82—Special Message to the Congress Proposing Measures to Preserve America's Natural Heritage," February 23, 1966, American Presidency Project, ed. Woolley and Peters, http://www.presidency.ucsb.edu/ws/index.php?pid=28097 (accessed November 7, 2009).

66. Lyndon B. Johnson, "Special Message to the Congress: Protecting our Natural Heritage," January 30, 1967, *Public Papers of the Presidents: Lyndon B. Johnson, 1967* (Washington, D.C., 1968), 97.

67. Lyndon B. Johnson, "Special Message to the Congress on Conservation: 'To Renew a Nation,'" March 8, 1968, *Public Papers of the Presidents: Lyndon B. Johnson, 1968* (Washington, D.C., 1970), 355.

68. Johnson, "Special Message to the Congress," March 8, 1968, 97.

69. Lyndon B. Johnson, "341—Remarks upon Signing the Pesticide Control Bill," May 12, 1964, American Presidency Project, ed. Woolley and Peters, http://www.presidency.ucsb.edu/ws/index.php?pid=26245&st=rachel+carson&st1=/ (accessed January 24, 2009.

70. Lyndon B. Johnson, "568—Remarks in the Hospital at the Signing of the Clean Air Act Amendments and Solid Waste

Disposal Bill," October 20, 1965, American Presidency Project, ed. Woolley and Peters, http://www.presidency.ucsb.edu/we/index .php?pid=27316&st=rachel+carson&st1=/ (accessed January 24, 2009).

71. Carson, *Silent Spring*, n.p.

72. Johnson, "568—Remarks in the Hospital at the Signing of the Clean Air Act Amendments."

73. Johnson, "568—Remarks in the Hospital at the Signing of the Clean Air Act Amendments."

74. Lyndon B. Johnson, "Remarks upon Signing the Colorado River Basin Project Act," September 30, 1968, *Public Papers of the Presidents: Lyndon B. Johnson, 1968* (Washington, D.C., 1969), 992.

75. The bill protecting the Redwoods was Public Law 90–545, 82 Stat. 931.

76. Aldo Leopold, "Wilderness as a Form of Land Use," *Journal of Land and Public Utility Economics*, 1, no. 4 (October 1925): 399, as quoted by Lyndon B. Johnson, "700—Message to the Congress Transmitting Annual Report on the National Wilderness Preservation System," January 18, 1969, American Presidency Project, ed. Woolley and Peters, http://www.presidency .ucsb.edu/ws/index.php?pid=29361&st= aldo+leopold&st1=/ (accessed January 2, 2009).

77. Johnson, "700—Message to the Congress Transmitting Annual Report."

78. Lyndon B. Johnson, "The President's News Conference at the LBJ Ranch," July 5, 1966, *Public Papers of the Presidents: Lyndon B. Johnson, 1966* (Washington, D.C., 1967), 704.

79. Lyndon B. Johnson, "The President's News Conference," February 26, 1966, *Public Papers of the Presidents: Lyndon B. Johnson, 1966* (Washington, D.C., 1967), 218.

80. Lyndon B. Johnson, "Letter to the President of the Senate and to the Speaker

of the House Transmitting Reports on Oceanographic Research," March 19, 1964, *Public Papers of the Presidents: Lyndon B. Johnson, 1964* (Washington, D.C., 1965), 401.

81. "Text of President's Message and an Analysis of Federal Budget of $97.9 Billion," *Special to the New York Times*, January 22, 1964, sec. 7, p. 19.

82. Lyndon B. Johnson, 1969, "Statement by the President upon Signing Five Proclamations Adding Lands to the National Park System," January 20, 1969, *Public Papers of the Presidents: Lyndon B. Johnson, 1969* (Washington, D.C., 1970), 1369.

83. Daynes and Sussman, *American Presidency and the Social Agenda*, 133 (see intro., n. 5).

84. Lyndon B. Johnson, "Statement by the President Announcing the Reaching of an Agreement on an Outer Space Treaty," December 8, 1966, *Public Papers of the Presidents: Lyndon B. Johnson, 1966* (Washington, D.C., 1967), 2:1441.

85. Johnson, "President's News Conference," February 26, 1966, 218.

86. Daynes and Sussman, *American Presidency and the Social Agenda*, 179.

87. Lyndon B. Johnson, "Filmed Message to Delegates of the Third International Conference on the Peaceful Uses of Atomic Energy," August 30, 1964, *Public Papers of the Presidents: Lyndon B. Johnson, 1964* (Washington, D.C., 1965), 1024.

88. Eric Hoffer, *The True Believer* (New York: Harper and Row, 1966), 134.

89. Kennedy, "Letter to the President of the Senate on Increasing the National Effort in Oceanography," 240.

90. Kennedy, "Letter to the President of the Senate on Increasing the National Effort in Oceanography," 240.

91. See Buttel, "New Directions in Environmental Sociology," 472–73.

Chapter 3

The chapter epigraph is from Richard M. Nixon, *A New Road for America: Major Statements, March 1970 to October 1971* (Garden City, N.Y.: Doubleday, 1972), 522.

1. Gordon J. McDonald, "Environment: Evolution of a Concept," *Journal of Environment and Development*, 12, no. 2 (June 2003): 160.

2. Walter J. Hickel, *Who Owns America?* (Upper Saddle River, N.J.: Prentice Hall, 1971), 92.

3. Melvin Small, *The Presidency of Richard Nixon* (Lawrence: University Press of Kansas, 1999), 196.

4. Jonathan H. Adler, "Fables of the Cuyahoga: Reconstructing a History of Environmental Protection," *Fordham Environmental Law Journal*, 14 (2002): 90–92.

5. Stephanie A. Slocum-Schaffer, *America in the Seventies* (Syracuse, N.Y.: Syracuse University Press, 2003), 131.

6. Jonathan Aitken, *Nixon: A Life* (Washington, D.C.: Regnery Publishing, 1993), 398.

7. Quoted in Tom Wicker, *One of Us: Richard Nixon and the American Dream* (New York: Random House, 1991), 518.

8. Richard M. Nixon and Congressional Quarterly, Inc., *Nixon: The First Year of His Presidency* (Washington, D.C.: Congressional Quarterly Press, 1970), 2.

9. Public Broadcasting Service, *The American Experience*, "Domestic Politics: Richard M. Nixon, 37th President," http://www.pbs.org/wgbh/amex/presidents/37_nixon/nixon_domestic.html (accessed June 7, 2004).

10. PBS, *American Experience*, "Domestic Politics: Richard M. Nixon."

11. Richard Nixon, "Memorandum of Disapproval of the National Environmental Data System and Environmental Centers Act of 1972," October 21, 1972, Richard Nixon Foundation, http://www.nixonlibraryfoundation.org/clientuploads/directory/archive/1972_pdf_files/1972_0359.pdf (accessed November 13, 2009).

12. Richard Nixon, "48—Special Message to the Congress Proposing the 1971 Environmental Program," February 8, 1971, American Presidency Project, ed. Woolley and Peters, http://www.presidency.ucsb.edu/ws/index.php?pid=3294 (accessed November 13, 2009).

13. Richard Nixon, "51—Special Message to the Congress Outlining the 1972 Environmental Program," February 8, 1972, American Presidency Project, ed. Woolley and Peters, http://www.presidency.ucsb.edu/ws/index.php?pid=3731 (accessed November 13, 2009).

14. John C. Whitaker, *Striking a Balance: Environment and Natural Resources Policy in the Nixon-Ford Years* (Washington, D.C.: American Enterprise Institute for Public Policy Research, 1976), 147–48.

15. U.S. Environmental Protection Agency, William D. Ruckelshaus Oral History Interview, "State Governments," http://www.epa.gov/history/publications/ruck/13.htm (accessed October 8, 2004).

16. U.S. EPA, Ruckelshaus Oral History Interview, "State Governments."

17. John C. Whitaker, "Earth Day Recollections: What It Was Like When the Movement Took Off," *EPA Journal*, July–August 1988, http://earthday.grc.nasa.gov/history/earth_day_recollections-jwhitaker.htm (accessed August 27, 2004).

18. Mary Etta Cook and Roger Davidson, "Deferral Politics: Congressional Decision Making on Environmental Issues in the 1900s," in *Public Policy and the Natural Environment*, ed. Helen M. Ingram and R. Kenneth Godwin (Greenwich, Conn.: JAI Press, 1985), 48.

19. Nixon and Congressional Quarterly, *Nixon: The First Year*, 3.

20. Richard Nixon, "Annual Message to the Congress on the State of the Union," January 22, 1970, *Public Papers of the Presidents of the United States: Richard Nixon, 1970* (Washington, D.C.: Office of the Federal Register, National Archives and Records Service, U.S. Government Printing Office, 1971), 13. This sounds very much like Bill Clinton's discussion with urban residents in which he advocated his concept of environmental justice—where everyone, regardless of where they lived, were deserving of clean air and water. See Conservative Caucus, "The Donnelly Collection of Presidential Executive Orders," http://www.conservativeusa.org/eo/clinton .htm (accessed July 22, 2004), Executive Order 12898, which articulates the federal actions that would address environmental justice in minority populations and low income populations.

21. Aitken, *Nixon*, 397.

22. J. Brooks Flippen, *Nixon and the Environment* (Albuquerque: University of New Mexico Press, 2000), 38.

23. Richard M. Nixon, as quoted in "U.S. Environmental Protection Agency Facts," *Salt Lake Tribune* [online], August 12, 2003; Nixon, "Annual Message to the Congress on the State of the Union," January 22, 1970, 13.

24. Nixon, "Annual Message to the Congress on the State of the Union," January 22, 1971, 50.

25. Nixon, "Annual Message to the Congress on the State of the Union," January 22, 1971, 50.

26. Richard Nixon, "Statement on Signing an Executive Order for the Control of Air and Water Pollution at Federal Facilities," February 4, 1970, *Public Papers of the Presidents: Richard Nixon, 1970* (Washington, D.C., 1971), 78.

27. Daynes and Sussman, *American Presidency and the Social Agenda*, 48 (see intro., n. 5).

28. Louis Harris and Associates, *The Harris Survey Yearbook of Public Opinion 1970* (New York: Louis Harris and Associates, 1971), 58, 262.

29. Richard Nixon, "Inaugural Address," January 20, 1969, *Public Papers of the Presidents: Richard Nixon, 1969* (Washington, D.C., 1971), 1.

30. A number of scholars support the notion that Richard Nixon's interest in the environment was a politically motivated response to public interest. These include Walter A. Rosenbaum, *Environmental Politics and Policy*, 3rd ed. (Washington, D.C.: CQ Press, 1995), 79–80; Jacqueline Vaughn Switzer, *Environmental Politics: Domestic and Global Dimensions* (New York: St. Martin's Press, 1994), 16; Mark K. Landy, Marc J. Roberts, and Stephen R. Thomas, *The Environmental Protection Agency: Asking the Wrong Questions* (New York: Oxford University Press, 1990), 30–33; and Richard E. Cohen, *Washington at Work: Back Rooms and Clean Air* (New York: Macmillan, 1992), 15–16.

31. Wicker, *One of Us*, 507.

32. See Stanley I. Kutler, *The Wars of Watergate: The Last Crisis of Richard Nixon* (New York: W. W. Norton, 1992).

33. U.S. EPA, Ruckelshaus Oral History Interview, "President Nixon," http://www .epa.gov/history/publications/ruck/index .htm (accessed October 27, 2004).

34. U.S. EPA, Ruckelshaus: Oral History Interview, "President Nixon."

35. Kutler, *Wars of Watergate*, 78.

36. Wicker, *One for Us*, 515.

37. Richard Nixon, taped conversation, April 19, 1972, tape 39, 23–46, as quoted in Small, *Presidency of Richard Nixon*, 197.

38. Richard Nixon, *The Memoirs of Rich-*

ard Nixon (New York: Grosset and Dunlap, 1978), 465.

39. Vickery, "Conservative Politics and the Politics of Conservation," 130 (see intro., n. 31).

40. Flippen, *Nixon and the Environment*, 231.

41. Soden and Steel, "Evaluating the Environmental Presidency," 330 (see chap. 2, n. 48).

42. Flippen, *Nixon and the Environment*, 1–2.

43. Flippen, *Nixon and the Environment*, 1–3.

44. "1968 Republican Platform," *Congressional Quarterly Weekly Report* 26, no. 32 (August 9, 1968): 2126–34.

45. "1972 Republican Platform," *Congressional Quarterly Weekly Report* 30, no. 35 (August 26, 1972): 2146–71.

46. "1972 Democratic Platform," *Congressional Quarterly Weekly Report* 30, no. 29 (July 15, 1972): 1726–49.

47. Wicker, *One of Us*, 517.

48. Wicker, *One of Us*, 517.

49. Shanley, *Presidential Influence and Environmental Policy*, 51 (see intro., n. 22).

50. Flippen, *Nixon and the Environment*, 51.

51. Flippen, *Nixon and the Environment*, 129.

52. Michael E. Kraft, *Environmental Policy and Politics: Toward the Twenty-first Century* (New York: HarperCollins, 1996), 71–74.

53. Soden and Steel, "Evaluating the Environmental Presidency," 315–16 .

54. Flippen, *Nixon and the Environment*, 48.

55. James Rathlesberger, ed., *Nixon and the Environment: The Politics of Devastation*, (New York: Taurus Communications, 1972), 9–18.

56. Richard Nixon, "Special Message to the Congress about Waste Disposal,"

April 15, 1970, *Public Papers of the Presidents: Richard Nixon, 1970* (Washington, D.C., 1971), 357.

57. Richard Nixon, "Special Message to the Congress on the Administration's Legislative Program," September 11, 1970, *Public Papers of the Presidents: Richard Nixon, 1970* (Washington D.C., 1971), 719.

58. "Domestic Programs," *Congressional Quarterly Almanac, 1972*, 92nd Cong., 2nd sess., 28:113.

59. "Most Productive Environmental Session in History," *Congressional Quarterly Almanac, 1972*, 92nd Cong., 2nd sess., 28:115.

60. Rathlesberger, *Nixon and the Environment*, 198, 231.

61. Raymond Tatalovich and Mark J. Wattier, "Opinion Leadership: Elections, Campaigns, Agenda Setting, and Environmentalism," in *The Environmental Presidency*, ed. Dennis L. Soden (Albany: State University of New York Press, 1999), 166–67.

62. Richard Nixon, "Statement about the Trans-Alaska Oil Pipeline," *Public Papers of the Presidents: Richard Nixon, 1973* (Washington D.C., 1975), 945.

63. Soden and Steel, "Evaluating the Environmental Presidency,"331.

64. David Greenberg, *Nixon's Shadow: The History of an Image* (New York: W. W. Norton, 2003), 307.

65. Rathlesberger, *Nixon and the Environment*, 59.

66. 420 U.S. 35 (1975).

67. Richard Nixon, "Special Message to the Congress about Reorganization Plans to Establish the Environmental Protection Agency and the National Oceanic and Atmospheric Administration," July 9, 1970, *Public Papers of the Presidents: Richard Nixon, 1970* (Washington, D.C., 1971), 578–86.

68. U.S. Environmental Protection Agency, History Office, 2001, "Russell E.

Train Biography," http://www.epa.gov/history/admin/agency/train.htm (accessed September 24, 2003).

69. Flippen, *Nixon and the Environment*, 192.

70. Wicker, *One of Us*, 556.

71. Richard Nixon, "Executive Order 11742—Delegating to the Secretary of State certain functions with respect to the negotiation of international agreements relating to the enhancement of the environment," American Presidency Project, ed. Woolley and Peters, http://www.presidency.ucsb.edu/ws/index.php?pid=59121(accessed November 13, 2009).

72. *Fortune* magazine editors, *The Environment: A National Mission for the Seventies* (New York: Harper and Row, 1970), 179.

73. Richard Nixon, "Annual Budget Message to Congress, Fiscal Year 1975," February 4, 1974, Richard Nixon Foundation, http://www.nixonlibraryfoundation.org/clientuploads/directory/archive/1974_pdf_files/1974_0032.pdf (accessed November 13, 2009). In addition, see "Solid Waste: Disposal, Refuse Present Problems," *Congressional Quarterly Weekly Report* 31, no. 1 (April 28, 1973): 1019–23; as well as J. C. Davies, *The Politics of Pollution* (New York: Western Publishing, 1982); C. O. Jones, *Clean Air: The Policies and Politics of Pollution Control* (Pittsburgh: University of Pittsburgh Press, 1975); Nixon, "State of the Union Address," *Congressional Record*, January 22, 1970, 739; and Nixon, "State of the Union Address, Part 1: Message on the Environment and Natural Resources," 1973, http://janda.org/politxts/State%20of%20Union%20Addresses/1970–1974%20Nixon%20T/RMN73N.html (accessed November 13, 2009).

74. Flippen, *Nixon and the Environment*, 38.

75. Hickel, *Who Owns America?*, 101, 105.

76. Senate Committee on Interior and Insular Affairs, *Hearings before the Committee on Interior and Insular Affairs on the Nomination of Hon. Rogers C. B. Morton to Be Secretary of the Interior*, 92nd Cong., 1st sess., January 25–26, 1971, 9.

77. Flippen, *Nixon and the Environment*, 28, 201.

78. Stephen Ambrose, *Nixon* (New York: Simon and Schuster, 1987), 2:460.

79. Senate Committee on Interior and Insular Affairs, *Hearing before the Committee on Interior and Insular Affairs on the Nomination of Russell W. Peterson to Chairman of the Council on Environmental Quality*, 93rd Cong., 1st sess., October 30, 1973, 87.

80. Soden and Steel, "Evaluating the Environmental Presidency," 331; Flippen, *Nixon and the Environment*, 172–73.

81. Flippen, *Nixon and the Environment*, 173.

82. Flippen, *Nixon and the Environment*, 173.

83. Flippen, *Nixon and the Environment*, 174.

84. Rathlesberger, *Nixon and the Environment*, 89.

85. Rathlesberger, *Nixon and the Environment*, 89.

86. Richard Nixon, "Message to the Senate Transmitting the Convention on International Trade in Endangered Species of Wild Fauna and Flora," April 13, 1973, *Public Papers of the Presidents: Richard Nixon, 1973* (Washington D.C., 1975), 285.

87. "Republican Party Platform of 1972," American Presidency Project, ed. Woolley and Peters, http://www.presidency.ucsb.edu/ws/index.php?pid=25842 (accessed August 8, 2004).

88. "Convention on the Prevention of Marine Pollution by Dumping of Wastes

and Other Matter, 1972," International Maritime Organization, http://www.imo.org/Conventions/contents.asp?topc_id=258&doc_id=681 (accessed August 28, 2004).

89. Small, *Presidency of Richard Nixon*, 196.

90. Small, *Presidency of Richard Nixon*, 196.

91. Center for International Earth Science Information Network, "Environmental Treaties and Resource Indicators," June 1, 1972, http://sedac.ciesin.columbia.edu/entri/texts/antarctic.seals.1972.html (accessed November 18, 2009).

92. Internet Guide for International Fisheries Law, "Convention for the Conservation of Antarctic Seals."

93. U.S. National Archives and Record Administration, "Federal Register: Nixon's Executive Orders," http://www.archives.gov/federal-register/executive-orders/nixon.html (accessed November 13, 2009).

94. See Executive Order 11629 for 1971 where the president delegates authority to the secretary of state to protect migratory birds and animals; and Executive Order 11742 in 1973 where the president gives authority to the secretary of state to negotiate international agreements with foreign leaders for and in behalf of the environment.

95. Richard Nixon, "Remarks on Signing the Colorado River Basin Salinity Control Act," June 24, 1974, *Public Papers of the Presidents: Richard Nixon, 1974* (Washington, D.C., 1975), 542.

96. Greenberg, *Nixon's Shadow*, 309.

97. From an interview of John Whitaker by J. Brooks Flippen on July 23, 1996, which appeared in Flippen, *Nixon and the Environment*, 220.

98. Patricia Limerick, felt Nixon had done a lot for the environment under

the circumstances he faced. "Headwaters News: Perspective; Insight and Analysis for the Rocky Mountain West," November 19, 2003, http://www.headwatersnews.org/p.whitaker.html (accessed July 17, 2004).

Chapter 4

1. Michael L. Mezey, *Congress, the President, and Public Policy* (Boulder, Colo.: Westview Press, 1989), 101; Garland A. Haas, *Jimmy Carter and the Politics of Frustration* (Jefferson, N.C.: McFarland, 1992), 76.

2. Barber, *Presidential Character*, 437–38 (see intro., n. 26).

3. Charles O. Jones, *Separate But Equal Branches: Congress and the Presidency* (Chatham, N.J.: Chatham House Publishers, 1995), 153.

4. Tip O'Neill with William Novak, *Man of the House: The Life and Political Memoirs of Speaker Tip O'Neill* (New York: Random House, 1987), 308–9.

5. Haynes Johnson, *In the Absence of Power: Governing America* (New York: Viking Press, 1980), 25.

6. Mark J. Rozell, *The Press and the Carter Presidency* (Boulder, Colo.: Westview Press, 1989).

7. Jimmy Carter, *An Outdoor Journal: Adventures and Reflections*, new edition (Fayetteville: University of Arkansas Press, 1994), 140.

8. Benjamin Kline, *First Along the River: A Brief History of the U.S. Environmental Movement*, 2nd ed. (San Francisco: Acada Books, 2000), 98–99.

9. Jimmy Carter, "Address to the Nation: The Energy Problem," *Public Papers of the Presidents of the United States: Jimmy Carter, 1977* (Washington, D.C.: Office of the Federal Register, National Archives and Records Service, U.S. Government Printing Office, 1978), 666.

10. Jimmy Carter, "Federal Water Policy:

Remarks Announcing the Administration's Policy," June 6, 1978, *Public Papers of the Presidents: Jimmy Carter, 1978* (Washington, D.C., 1979), 1043–44.

11. Jimmy Carter, "White House Conference on Balanced National Growth and Economic Development," February 2, 1978, *Public Papers of the Presidents: Jimmy Carter, 1978* (Washington, D.C., 1979), 266–67.

12. Jimmy Carter, "State of the Union Address: Annual Message to the Congress," January 25, 1979, *Public Papers of the Presidents: Jimmy Carter, 1979* (Washington, D.C., 1980), 121.

13. Jimmy Carter, "Inaugural Address, January 12, 1971," Jimmy Carter Library, http://www.jimmycarterlibrary.org/documents/inaugural_address.pdf. (accessed June 30, 2004).

14. Jacqueline Vaughn Switzer with Gary Bryner, *Environmental Politics: Domestic and Global Dimensions*, 2nd ed. (New York: St. Martin's Press, 1998), 51.

15. "Jordan Takes Stock as He Packs Up His Memories," *New York Times*, December 4, 1980, 22.

16. Hunter and Noonan, "Energy, Environment, and the Presidential Agenda," 313–14 (see intro., n. 14).

17. Hunter and Noonan, "Energy, Environment, and the Presidential Agenda,," 317.

18. Austin Ranney, "The Carter Administration," in *The American Elections of 1980*, ed. Austin Ranney (Washington, D.C.: American Enterprise Institute, 1981), 7.

19. O'Neill, *Man of the House*, 319.

20. Jimmy Carter, "The State of the Union: Annual Message to the Congress," January 19, 1978, *Public Papers of the Presidents: Jimmy Carter, 1978* (Washington, D.C., 1979), 116.

21. Carter, "State of the Union," January 19, 1978, 116.

22. Carter, "State of the Union," January 25, 1979, 147–52.

23. Jimmy Carter, "The State of the Union: Annual Message to the Congress," February 23, 1980, *Public Papers of the Presidents: Jimmy Carter, 1980* (Washington, D.C., 1981), 199.

24. Jimmy Carter, "The State of the Union: Annual Message to the Congress," January 16, 1981, *Public Papers of the Presidents: Jimmy Carter, 1981* (Washington, D.C., 1982), 2931–97.

25. Carter, "Address to the Nation: The Energy Problem," 656.

26. Jimmy Carter, *Keeping Faith: Memoirs of a President* (New York: Bantam Books, 1982), 91.

27. Burton I. Kaufman, *The Presidency of James Earl Carter, Jr.* (Lawrence: University Press of Kansas, 1993), 144.

28. Jimmy Carter, "The Crisis of Confidence Speech" July 15, 1979, www.pbs.org/wghb/amex/carter/filmmore/ps_crisis.html (accessed November 20, 2009).

29. Carter, "Crisis of Confidence Speech."

30. Kernell, *Going Public*, 1 (see intro., n. 18).

31. Carter, "State of the Union Address: Annual Message to the Congress," February 23, 1980, 195.

32. Jimmy Carter, "Endangered Species Act Amendments: Statement on Signing S. 1143 into Law," December 28, 1979, *Public Papers of the Presidents: Jimmy Carter, 1979* (Washington, D.C., 1980), 2288.

33. Jimmy Carter, "Alaska National Interest Lands Conservation Act: Remarks on Signing H.R. 39 into Law," December 2, 1980, *Public Papers of the Presidents: Jimmy Carter, 1980* (Washington, D.C., 1980), 2756.

34. Jimmy Carter, "Energy Security Act: Remarks on Signing S.932 into Law," June 30, 1980, *Public Papers of the Presidents: Jimmy Carter, 1980–1981* (Washington, D.C., 1982), 1253.

35. Quoted in Edwin C. Hargrove, *Jimmy Carter as President: Leadership and the Politics of the Public Good* (Baton Rouge: Louisiana State University, 1988), 15.

36. Fred Greenstein, *The Presidential Difference: Leadership Style from FDR to George W. Bush*, 2nd ed. (Princeton, N.J.: Princeton University Press, 2004), 132.

37. Tinsley E. Yarbrough, "Carter and the Congress," in *The Carter Years: The President and Policy Making*, ed. M. Glenn Abernathy, Dilys M. Hill, and Phil Williams (New York: St. Martin's Press, 1984), 178–79.

38. Dilys M. Hill and Phil Williams, introduction to Abernathy, Hill, and Williams, *The Carter Years*, 3; Neustadt, *Presidential Power*, 234–37 (see intro., n. 20).

39. Hill and Williams, introduction to Abernathy, Hill, and Williams, *Carter Years*, 3.

40. Richard A. Watson and Norman C. Thomas, *The Politics of the Presidency*, 2nd ed. (Washington, D.C.: CQ Press, 1988), 254.

41. Jones, *Trusteeship Presidency*, 143 (see intro., n. 25).

42. Carter, *Keeping Faith*, 78.

43. Haas, *Jimmy Carter and the Politics of Frustration*, 75–77.

44. Rozell, *Press and the Carter Presidency*, 49.

45. John C. Barrow, "An Age of Limits: Jimmy Carter and the Quest for a National Energy Policy," in *The Carter Presidency: Policy Choices in the Post-New Deal Era*, ed. Gary M. Fink and Hugh Davis Graham (Lawrence: University Press of Kansas, 1998), 162.

46. Marilu Hunt McCarty, "Economic Aspects of the Carter Energy Program," in *The Presidency and Domestic Policies of Jimmy Carter*, ed. Herbert D. Rosenbaum and Alexej Ugrinsky (Westport, Conn.: Greenwood Press, 1994), 560.

47. Haas, *Jimmy Carter and the Politics of Frustration*, 69.

48. O'Neill, *Man of the House*, 323.

49. James P. Pfiffner, *The Modern Presidency*, 2nd ed. (New York: St. Martin's Press, 1998), 157.

50. Jones, *Trusteeship Presidency*, 174–79; Eric R. A. N. Smith, *Energy, the Environment, and Public Opinion* (Lanham, Md.: Rowman and Littlefield Publishers, 2002), 30.

51. Carter, *Keeping Faith*, 123.

52. Jeffrey K. Stine, "Environmental Policy during the Carter Administration," in *The Carter Presidency: Policy Choices in the Post-New Deal Era*, ed. Gary M. Fink and Hugh Davis Graham (Lawrence: University Press of Kansas, 1998), 191.

53. Roger C. Dower, "Hazardous Wastes," in *Public Policies for Environmental Protection*, ed. Paul R. Portney (Washington, D.C.: Resources for the Future, 1990), 168.

54. Marc Landy, "Ticking Time Bombs!!! EPA and the Formulation of Superfund," in *Public Policy and the Natural Environment*, ed. Helen M. Ingram and R. Kenneth Godwin (Greenwich, Conn.: JAI Press, 1985), 239–57.

55. Brock Evans, "The Importance of Appointments," *Sierra* Magazine 65 (September/October 1980): 22–23. For names and brief backgrounds of appointees with environmental backgrounds, see also Landy, Roberts, and Thomas, *Environmental Protection Agency*, 39–40 (see chap. 3, n. 30).

56. Carter, *Keeping Faith*, 37.

57. Stine, "Environmental Policy during the Carter Presidency," 182.

58. "Cecil Andrus Remembers," *People, Land & Water* (March–April 1988): 48–50.

59. Cecil Andrus quoted in "Statement of David J. Hayes, Deputy Secretary, Department of the Interior, before the Committee on Resources, House of Representatives, on Restricting Domestic Exploration and Development of our Oil and Gas Resources," April 12, 2000, Department of the Interior, Office of Congressional and Legislative Affairs, http://www.doi.gov/ocl/2000/oilandgas.htm (accessed July 7, 2004).

60. "Douglas M. Costle: Biography," Environmental Protection Agency, http://www.epa.gov/history/admin/agency/costle.htm (accessed November 17, 2009).

61. Landy, Roberts, and Thomas, *Environmental Protection Agency*, 39.

62. Landy, Roberts, and Thomas, *Environmental Protection Agency*, 41.

63. Shirley Anne Warshaw, *The Domestic Presidency: Policy Making in the White House* (Boston: Allyn and Bacon, 1997), 82.

64. James W. Riddlesperger Jr. and James D. King, "Political Constraints, Leadership Style, and Temporal Limits: The Administrative Presidency of Jimmy Carter," in Rosenbaum and Ugrinsky, *Presidency and Domestic Policies of Jimmy Carter*, 365.

65. Cited in Gerald O. Barney, *The Global 2000 Report to the President*, Council on Environmental Quality, U.S. Department of State (New York: Penguin Books, 1982), vii.

66. Jimmy Carter, "Global 2000 Study: Statement on the Report to the President," July 24, 1980, *Public Papers of the Presidents: Jimmy Carter, 1979* (Washington, D.C., 1980), 1415.

67. Gareth Porter, Janet Welsh, and Pamela S. Chasek, *Global Environmental Policy*, 3rd ed. (Boulder, Colo.: Westview Press, 2000), 84. An alternative view suggests that sulfur dioxide emissions from midwestern power plants were declining during the last two years of the Carter ad-

ministration. See M. S. McMahon, "Balancing the Interests: Canada and America," in *International Environmental Diplomacy: The Management and Resolution of Transfrontier Environmental Problems*, ed. John E. Carroll (Cambridge: Cambridge University Press, 1988), 163.

68. Jimmy Carter quoted in James L. Regens and Robert W. Rycroft, *The Acid Rain Controversy* (Pittsburgh: University of Pittsburgh Press, 1988), 118.

69. United Nations, *Register of International Treaties and Other Agreements in the Field of the Environment, 1996* (Nairobi: United Nations Environment Programme, 1997).

70. Kristin M. Fletcher, "The International Whaling Regime and U.S. Foreign Policy," in *The Environment, International Relations, and U.S. Foreign Policy*, ed. Paul G. Harris (Washington, D.C.: Georgetown University Press, 2001), 220.

71. Karen Fisher-Vanden, "International Policy Instrument Prominence in the Climate Change Debate," in *Climate Change and American Foreign Policy*, ed. Paul G. Harris (New York: St. Martin's Press, 2000), 152.

72. Jimmy Carter, "Ambassador at Large and Special Representative of the President for the Law of the Sea Conference, Nomination of Elliot L. Richardson, with a Statement by the President," January 25, 1977, *American Presidency Project*, ed. Woolley and Peters, http://www.presidency.ucsb.edu/ws/index.php?pid=1733 (accessed November 5, 2007).

73. Gary Bryner, *From Promises to Performance: Achieving Global Environmental Goals* (New York: W. W. Norton, 1997), 54. See also Zachary M. Petersen, "Critics Assail Law of the Sea Treaty," *Navy Times*, October 4, 2007, http://www.navytimes.com/news/2007/10/navy_lawofthesea_071004w/ (accessed June 2, 2008).

74. Jimmy Carter, *A Government as Good as Its People* (New York: Simon and Schuster, 1977), 47.

75. Carter, *Keeping Faith*, 582.

76. Carter, *Outdoor Journal*, 16.

Chapter 5

1. Bush and his supporters had charged that Arkansas had ranked fiftieth of fifty states as far as protecting the environment, which was based on a study by an Atlanta, Georgia, environmental group. See "President Bush vs. Bill Clinton on the Environment: Sound Accomplishments vs. Failures and Radicalism," September 24, 1992, http://web.mit.edu/gora/Mac-Data/afs/net/user/tytso/usenet/nptn/campaign92/rep/24 (accessed November 9, 2009).

2. Michael Weisskopf, "The Dream Team?" *Outside*, November 1992, 74.

3. The actual question asked the public was "Next, I have some questions about the Clinton administration, which will take office in January. Regardless of which presidential candidate you preferred, do you think the Clinton administration will or will not be able to do each of the following." John Kenneth White, "The General Campaign: Issues and Themes," in *America's Choice: The Election of 1992*, ed. William Crotty (Guilford, Conn.: Dushkin Publishing Group, 1993), 67. The environment had come third, after "improving education," which was named by 69 percent, and "improving conditions for minorities and the poor" was chosen by 68 percent of the public.

4. Carl Pope, "Lead and Learn," *Sierra Magazine* 78 (May–June 1993): 26.

5. David Foster, "Clinton Designates Several National Monuments: With a Presidential Legacy on the Line Clinton Gets Environmental," Associated Press, August 7, 2000, http://abcnews.go.com/Travel/Story?id=118851&page=4 (accessed November 14, 2009).

6. "Remarks on the Observance of Earth Day," *Weekly Compilation of Presidential Documents* 30, no. 16 (April 21, 1994): 868.

7. "Grading Clinton," *Defenders*, Winter 1993–94, 33–36.

8. Mark Dowie, "Friends of Earth—or Bill?: The Selling (Out) of the Greens," *The Nation*, April 18, 1994, 515.

9. "Environmental Fallout: A Tale of Two Countries," *New York Times*, October 13, 1994, 7A; "Open Letter to President Clinton," *Audubon*, July–August 1994, 6.

10. Bill Clinton, "Remarks on Earth Day," April 21, 1993, *Public Papers of the Presidents, of the United States: William J. Clinton, 1993* (Washington, D.C.: Office of the Federal Register, National Archives and Records Service, U.S. Government Printing Office, 1994), 1:469.

11. Ted Gup, "It's Nature, Stupid," *Time*, July 12, 1993, http://www.time.com/time/magazine/article/0,9171,978848,00.html (accessed November 14, 2009).

12. "The President's Radio Address," April 3, 1993, American Presidency Project, ed. Woolley and Peters, http://www.presidency.ucsb.edu/ws/print.php?pid=46401 (November 14, 2009).

13. Bill Clinton, "Remarks on Opening the Forest Conference in Portland, Oregon, April 2, 1993," *Public Papers of the Presidents: William J. Clinton, 1993* (Washington, D.C., 1994), 1:385.

14. "President's Radio Address," April 3, 1993.

15. Timothy Egan, "Oregon, Foiling Forecasters, Thrives as It Protects Owls," *New York Times*, October 11, 1994, http://www.nytimes.com/1994/10/11/us/oregon-foiling-forecasters-thrives-as-it-protects-owls.html (accessed November 14, 2009).

16. Neil Sampson, "Thumbs-up for Clinton Plan—Pres. Bill Clinton's Policy on Timber Harvests on Federal Lands," *American Forests*, September–October 1993, http://findarticles.com/p/articles/mi_m1016/is_n9–10_v99/ai_14536135/ (accessed November 14, 2009).

17. Gregg B. Walker and Steven E. Daniels, "The Clinton Administration, the Northwest Forest Conference, and Managing Conflict: When Talk and Structure Collide," *Society and Natural Resources*, 9 (1996): 88.

18. Former secretary of interior Bruce Babbitt, interview by Byron W. Daynes, March 6, 2009, Stegner Center's Fourteenth Annual Symposium, Salt Lake City, Utah.

19. Sampson, "Thumbs-up for Clinton Plan."

20. Ron Arnold, "Overcoming Ideology," and excerpt from *A Wolf in the Garden: The Land Rights Movement and the New Environmental Debate*, ed. Phillip D. Brick and R. McGreggor Cawley (Lanham, Md.: Rowman and Littlefield Publishers, 1996), Center for the Defense of Free Enterprise, http://www.eskimo.com/~rarnold/wiseuse.htm (accessed March 9, 2009).

21. William Kevin Burke, "The Wise Use Movement: Right-Wing Anti-Environmentalism," *Public Eye Magazine* 7, no. 2 (June 1993), http://www.publiceye.org/magazine/v07n2/wiseuse.html (accessed March 9, 2009).

22. "Policy Objectives of the Wise Use Movement," Wild Wilderness, http://www.wildwilderness.org/wi/wiseuse.htm (accessed March 9, 2009).

23. Burke, "Wise Use Movement."

24. "Policy Objectives of the Wise Use Movement," Wild Wilderness.

25. David Helvarg, "'Wise Use' in the White House," *Sierra* Magazine 89 (September–October 2004), http://www.sierraclub.org/sierra/200409/wiseuse.asp (accessed March 9, 2009).

26. Helvarg, "'Wise Use' in the White House."

27. Brad Knickerbocker, "Clinton Plan Challenges 'Lords' of the U.S. Rural West," *Christian Science Monitor*, March 3, 1993, 4.

28. "Issue: Old-Growth Forests and Spotted Owls," *Congressional Quarterly Weekly Report* 52, no. 43 (November 5, 1994): 3171.

29. Roger Schlickeisen, "Ecosystem Opportunity," *Defenders*, Summer 1994, 5.

30. Alexander Cockburn, "Beat the Devil: Environmental Policies of Interior Secretary Bruce Babbitt and the Bill Clinton Administration," *The Nation* 257, no. 7 (September 6, 1993): 234.

31. Bill Clinton, *My Life* (New York: Knopf, 2004), 727–28.

32. Theodore Roosevelt Association, "Conservationist" (see intro., n. 39).

33. Leavitt would later serve as Health and Human Services secretary in the George W. Bush administration.

34. See Richard L. Berke, "Clinton Declares New U.S. Policies for Environment" and "Clinton Supports Two Major Steps for Environment," *New York Times*, April 22, 1993, 1A.

35. Chuck Alston, "The State of the Address," *Congressional Quarterly Weekly Report* 51, no. 7 (February 13, 1993): 302.

36. "The State of the Union: Clinton Stresses Welfare, Health-Care Reform," *Congressional Quarterly Weekly Report* 52, no. 4 (January 29, 1994): 194–98.

37. William J. Clinton, "Address before a Joint Session of the Congress on the State of the Union," January 24, 1995, American Presidency Project, ed. Woolley and Peters, http://www.presidency.ucsb.edu/ws/index.php?pid=51634 (accessed August 11, 2005).

38. John H. Cushman Jr., "Timber! A

New Idea is Crashing," *New York Times*, January 26, 1995, 5E.

39. Steve Langdon, "Clinton's High Victory Rate Conceals Disappointments," *Congressional Quarterly Weekly Report* 52, no. 50 (December 31, 1994): 3619–23.

40. "Endangered Species Act May Be Revised by Congress," *Provo Daily Herald*, January 30, 1995, 3C.

41. "Various Wilderness Bills Considered by Congress," *Congressional Quarterly Almanac, 1993*, 103rd Cong., 1st sess., 49:278–85; "Many Environment Bills Offered; Few Pass," *Congressional Quarterly Almanac, 1994*, 103rd Cong., 1st sess., 50:254–67.

42. "The 103rd Congress: What Was Accomplished, and What Wasn't," *New York Times*, October 9, 1994, 28; see also "Issue: Wilderness Areas," *Congressional Quarterly Weekly Report* 52, no. 43 (November 5, 1994): 3174–75.

43. Richard Weisskoff, "Missing Pieces in Ecosystem Restoration: The Case of the Florida Everglades," *Economics Systems Researcher* 12, no. 3 (1994): 271–303.

44. David Cloud, "Clinton Holds His Veto Power Over Heads of Republicans," *Congressional Quarterly Weekly Report* 53, no. 22 (June 3, 1995): 1559.

45. John Cushman Jr., "Bipartisan House Rejects Public Lands Measure," *New York Times*, October 8, 1998, 23A.

46. Ed Gillespie and Bob Schellhas, eds., *Contract with America: The Bold Plan by Rep. Newt Gingrich, Rep. Dick Armey, and the House Republicans to Change the Nation* (New York: Random House, 1994), 132; Mary Beth Reagan, "The GOP's Guerilla War on Green Laws," *Business Week*, December 12, 1994, 102.

47. John H. Cushman Jr., "House Republicans Advance in Redoing of Pollution Law," *New York Times*, May 12, 1995, 1A.

48. Brad Knickerbocker, "Environmentalists, Lawmakers Line Up Legislative Wish Lists," *Christian Science Monitor*, February 4, 1993, 2.

49. Bill Clinton, "Remarks on the 25th Observance of Earth Day in Havre De Grace, Maryland," April 21, 1995, *Public Papers of the Presidents: William J. Clinton, 1995* (Washington, D.C., 1996), 1:562.

50. Editorial, "A Presidential Contract," *New York Times*, May 21, 1995, 14.

51. Dowie, "Friends of Earth—or Bill?" 514.

52. "President Names Eileen Claussen to Serve as Assistant Secretary of State for Oceans, Environment, and International Scientific Affairs," Office of the Press Secretary, The White House, July 20, 1995, Almanac Information Server, 19.

53. Albert Gore, *Earth in the Balance: Ecology and the Human Spirit* (Boston: Houghton Mifflin, 1992).

54. Joan Hamilton, "Babbitt's Retreat," *Sierra* Magazine 79, no. 4 (July–August 1994): 53.

55. Bill Clinton, "Remarks on the 150th Anniversary of the Department of the Interior," March 4, 1999, *Public Papers of the Presidents,: William J. Clinton, 1999* (Washington, D.C., 2000), 1:308–11.

56. William J. Clinton, "The President's Radio Address," August 14, 1999, *Weekly Compilation of Presidential Documents* 35, no. 33 (August 23, 1999): 1633 (from the 1999 Presidential Documents Online via GPO Access [frwais.access.gpo.gov][DOCID: pd23au99_txt-2]).

57. William J. Clinton, "Remarks on the Observance of Earth Day," April 21, 1994, *Weekly Compilation of Presidential Documents* 30, no. 16 (April 25, 1994): 865 (from the 1994 Presidential Documents Online via GPO Access [frwais.access.gpo.gov] [DOCID:pd25ap94_txt-24]).

58. Bill Clinton, "Remarks on the Designation of New National Monuments," January 17, 2001, *Public Papers of the Presidents: William J. Clinton, 2000–2001* (Washington, D.C., 2002), 3:2930.

59. William J. Clinton, "Remarks Announcing a New Environmental Policy," *Weekly Compilation of Presidential Documents* 29, no. 6 (February 8, 1993): 159.

60. William J. Clinton, "Statement on the Executive Order on Environmental Justice," *Weekly Compilation of Presidential Documents* 30, no. 7 (February 11, 1994): 283.

61. Evan J. Ringquist, "Environmental Justice: Normative Concerns and Empirical Evidence," in Vig and Kraft, *Environmental Policy: New Directions for the Twenty-first Century,* 4th ed. (Washington, D.C.: Congressional Quarterly Press, 2000), 247.

62. William J. Clinton, "Executive Order 12898—Federal Actions to Address Environmental Justice in Mining Populations and Low-Income Populations," and "Statement on the Executive Order on Environmental Justice," *Weekly Compilation of Presidential Documents* 30, no. 7 (February 11, 1994): 276, 283.

63. Clinton, "Executive Order 12898—Federal Actions to Address Environmental Justice" and "Statement on the Executive Order on Environmental Justice."

64. Bill Clinton, "Remarks Announcing the Creation of the White House Office of Environmental Policy," June 14, 1993, *Public Papers of the Presidents: William J. Clinton, 1993* (Washington, D.C., 1994), 1:845.

65. "Point by Point: Trimming at Four Agencies," *New York Times,* March 28, 1995, 10A.

66. Charles Babington and Joby Warrick, "Clinton Pushing to Build Legacy; White House Plans Onslaught of New Environmental Rules," *Washington Post,* August 25, 2000, 1A.

67. Clinton, *My Life,* 907.

68. Susan R. Fletcher, "Biological Diversity: Issues Related to the Convention on Biodiversity," *CRS Report for Congress,* May 15, 1995, http://ncseonline.org/NLE/CRSreports/biodiversity/biodv-2.cfm. (accessed November 19, 2009).

69. "Remarks on the Observance of Earth Day," April 21, 1994, 866.

70. Bill Clinton, "Remarks to the 52d Session of the United Nations General Assembly in New York City," September 22, 1997, *Public Papers of the Presidents: William J. Clinton, 1997* (Washington, D.C., 1999), 2:1207.

71. Bill Clinton, "Remarks during a Discussion on Climate Change," July 24, 1997, *Public Papers of the Presidents,: William J. Clinton, 1997* (Washington, D.C., 1999), 2:993–95.

72. Bill Clinton, "Remarks on the Kyoto Protocol on Climate Change and an Exchange with Reporters in New York City," December 10, 1997, *Public Papers of the Presidents,: William J. Clinton, 1997* (Washington, D.C., 1999), 2:1745–46.

73. United Nations, Kyoto Protocol, December 13, 2006, "Kyoto Protocol Status of Ratification," http://unfccc.int/files/essential_background/kyoto_protocol/application/pdf/kpstats.pdf (accessed November 17, 2009).

74. Kathleen McGinty, interviewed by Miles O'Brien, *CNN Sunday Morning,* December 14, 1997.

75. U.S. House, Committee on Science, "Statement of the Honorable Kathleen A. McGinty, Chair, Council on Environmental Quality," 105th Cong., 2nd sess., February 4, 1998, http://www.lexisnexis.com.erl.lib.byu.edu/congcomp/getdoc?HEARING-ID=HRG-1998-SCI-0035.

76. Bill Clinton, "Russia–United States Joint Statement on Cooperation to Combat Global Warming," June 4, 2000, *Public Papers of the Presidents: William J. Clinton, 2000–2001* (Washington, D.C., 2001), 1:1074–5.

77. U.S. House, "A resolution expressing the sense of the Senate regarding the conditions for the United States becoming a signatory to any international agreement on greenhouse gas emissions under the United Nations Framework Convention on Climate Change," SR 98, 105th Cong., 1st sess., *Congressional Record* 143, no. 107 (July 25, 1997): S8113–S8138.

78. U.S. Department of State, "Biography: Eileen B. Claussen," http://dosfan.lib .uic.edu/ERC/biographies/claussen.html (accessed July 12, 2006).

79. Eileen Claussen, "American College and University Presidents Climate Commitment Summit," Washington, D.C., June 12, 2007, Pew Center for Global Climate Change, http://www.pewclimate.org/ press_room/speech_transcripts/ec_acupcc (accessed November 15, 2009).

80. SourceWatch, "David Sandalow," December 10, 2007, http://www. sourcewatch.org/index.php?title=David _Sandalow (accessed March 26, 2009).

81. Scott Allen, "President Stakes a Claim on Ecology; Campaign '96," *Boston Globe*, October 23, 1996, 1A.

82. Bill Clinton, "Statement on Earth Day," April 22, 1999, *Public Papers of the Presidents: William J. Clinton, 1999* (Washington, D.C., 2000), American Presidency Project, ed. Woolley and Peters, http:// www.presidency.ucsb.edu/ws/?pid= 57438.

83. "Message to the Senate Transmitting the Amendment to the Montreal Protocol on Substances that Deplete the Ozone Layer," *Weekly Compilation of Presi-*dential Documents* 29, no. 29 (July 20, 1993): 1410.

84. United Nations, United Nations Environmental Programme—Ozone Secretariat, October 13, 2009, http://ozone .unep.org/Ratification_status/ (accessed November 15, 2009).

85. "Memorandum on Distribution of Eagle Feathers for Native American Religious Purposes," *Weekly Compilation of Presidential Documents* 30, no. 17 (April 29, 1994): 935.

86. See University of Oregon, International Environmental Agreements Database Project, 1993–2000, http://iea .uoregon.edu/page.php?query=summary& type=MEA (accessed November 15, 2009).

87. Daynes, "Two Democrats, One Environment" (see intro., n. 38).

88. Bill Clinton, "Remarks on Signing a Proclamation Establishing the Giant Sequoia National Forest in Sequoia National Forest, California," April 15, 2000, *Public Papers of the Presidents: William J. Clinton, 2000–2001* (Washington, D.C., 2001), 720–22.

89. Charles Levendosky, "Clinton Left Us One of the Greatest Land Legacies," *Liberal Opinion Week*, February 5, 2001, 6.

90. President Jimmy Carter, however, holds the record for setting aside the most land in monuments as a result of setting aside some 56 million acres in Alaska, much of which was later converted by Congress to national parks and preserves.

91. William Booth, "A Slow Start Built to an Environmental End-Run: President Went around Congress to Building Green Legacy" *Washington Post*, January 13, 2001, http://www.lexisnexis.com/us/lnacademic/ results/docview/docview.do?docLinkInd= true&risb=21_T7896132719&format=GN BFI&sort=DATE,A,H&startDocNo=1&res ultsUrlKey=29_T7896126795&cisb=22_T

7896130964&treeMax=true&treeWidth= 0&csi=8075&docNo=9 (accessed January 20, 2001).

92. Paul Wapner, "Clinton's Environmental Legacy," *Tikkun*, March–April 2001, http://web.ebscohost.com/ehost/detail? vid=3&hid=111&sid=1cf15a92-dbb2–43b9–946f-0b4400ab24e9%40sessionmgr 111&bdata=JnNpdGU9ZWhvc3QtbG12ZS ZzY29wZT1zaXRl#db=aph&AN=4113401 (accessed November 17, 2009).

93. Wapner, "Clinton's Environmental Legacy."

94. Bill Clinton, "Remarks at the League of Conservation Voters Dinner," October 7, 1998, *Public Papers of the Presidents: William J. Clinton, 1998* (Washington, D.C., 2000), 2:1965–2025.

Chapter 6

1. Greenstein, *Hidden-Hand Presidency* (see intro., n. 17).

2. Robert Griffith, ed., *Ike's Letters to a Friend, 1941–1958* (Lawrence: University Press of Kansas, 1984), 127–33.

3. Soden and Steel, "Evaluating the Environmental Presidency," 326 (see chap. 2, n. 48).

4. 332 U.S. 19 (1947).

5. Frank E. Smith, *The Politics of Conservation* (New York: Pantheon Books, 1966), 285.

6. Robert L. Branyan and Lawrence H. Larsen, ed., *The Eisenhower Administration, 1953–1961: A Documentary History* (New York: Random House, 1971), 1:125.

7. Branyan and Larsen, *Eisenhower Administration*, 125–31.

8. Walter J. Mead, Asbjorn Moseidjord, Dennis D. Muraoka, and Philip E. Sorensen, *Offshore Lands: Oil and Gas Leasing and Conservation on the Outer Continental Shelf* (San Francisco: Pacific Institute for Public Policy Research, 1985), 9–14.

9. Dwight D. Eisenhower, "Annual Budget Message to the Congress: Fiscal Year 1956," January 17, 1955, *Public Papers of the Presidents of the United States: Dwight D. Eisenhower, 1956* (Washington, D.C.: Office the Federal Register, National Archives and Records Service, U.S. Government Printing Office, 1959), 1:93.

10. Andrea K. Gerlak and Patrick J. McGovern, "The Twentieth Century: Progressivism, Prosperity, and Crisis," in Soden, *Environmental Presidency*, 67.

11. Gerlak and McGovern, "Twentieth Century."

12. Smith, *Politics of Conservation*, 232.

13. Chester J. Pach Jr. and Elmo Richardson, *The Presidency of Dwight D. Eisenhower* (Lawrence: University Press of Kansas, 1991), 57.

14. Robert H. Ferrell, ed., *The Eisenhower Diaries* (New York: W.W. Norton, 1981), 299.

15. Sussman, Daynes, and West, *American Politics and the Environment*, 169–70 (see preface, n. 1).

16. Doug Scott, *The Enduring Wilderness* (Golden, Colo.: Fulcrum Publishing, 2004), 50.

17. Kline, *First Along the River*, 72 (see chap. 4, n. 8).

18. Christopher McGrory Klyza, *Who Controls Public Lands? Mining, Forestry, and Grazing Policies, 1870–1990* (Chapel Hill: University of North Carolina Press, 1996), 79.

19. Pach and Richardson, *Presidency of Dwight D. Eisenhower*, 56–57.

20. Mark W. T. Harvey, *A Symbol of Wilderness: Echo Park and the American Conservation Movement* (Albuquerque: University of New Mexico Press, 1994), 211.

21. Harvey, *Symbol of Wilderness*, 211.

22. Harvey, *Symbol of Wilderness*, 213.

23. Harvey, *Symbol of Wilderness*, 273, 278.

24. Scott, *Enduring Wilderness*, 45.

25. Scott, *Enduring Wilderness*, 45.

26. Scott, *Enduring Wilderness*, 46.

27. Dwight D. Eisenhower, "Annual Message to the Congress on the State of the Union," January 6, 1955, *Public Papers of the Presidents: Dwight D. Eisenhower, 1955* (Washington, D.C., 1959), 1:10.

28. Ronald Inglehart, *The Silent Revolution: Changing Values and Political Styles among Western Publics* (Princeton, N.J.: Princeton University Press, 1977), chap. 2.

29. Tatalovich and Wattier, "Opinion Leadership," 173 (see chap. 3, n. 61).

30. Stuckey, *President as Interpreter-in-Chief*, 53–58 (see intro., n. 29).

31. Samuel Kernell, *Going Public: New Strategies of Presidential Leadership*, 3rd ed. (Washington, DC: CQ Press, 1997), 83–84.

32. Craig Allen, *Eisenhower and the Media: Peace, Prosperity, and Prime-Time TV* (Chapel Hill: University of North Carolina Press, 1993), 7–8.

33. Dwight D. Eisenhower, "Annual Message to the Congress on the State of the Union," February 2, 1953, *Public Papers of the Presidents: Dwight D. Eisenhower, 1953* (Washington, D.C., 1960), 1:26.

34. Lammers and Genovese, *Presidency and Domestic Policy*, 166 (see intro., n. 24).

35. Dwight D. Eisenhower, "Annual Message to the Congress on the State of the Union," January 10, 1957, *Public Papers of the Presidents: Dwight D. Eisenhower, 1957* (Washington, D.C., 1958), 1:21–22.

36. Dwight D. Eisenhower, "Farewell Radio and Television Address to the American People," January 17, 1961," *Public Papers of the Presidents: Dwight D. Eisenhower, 1961* (Washington, D.C., 1961), 1039.

37. Hunter and Noonan, "Energy, Environment, and the Presidential Agenda," 310–11 (see intro., n. 14).

38. Zachary A. Smith, *The Environmental Policy Paradox*, 3rd ed. (Upper Saddle River, N.J.: Prentice Hall, 2000), 80.

39. Bradley Patterson, White House Deputy Cabinet Secretary, interview with authors, October 17, 2003.

40. James. N. Levitt, "Networks and Nature in the American Experience," *Forest History Today*, Fall 2002, 6.

41. J. C. Davies and B. S. Davies, *The Politics of Pollution*, 2nd ed. (Indianapolis: Pegasus, 1975).

42. Dwight D. Eisenhower, "Statement by the President upon Signing the Water Pollution Control Act Amendments of 1956," July 9, 1956, *Public Papers of the Presidents: Dwight D. Eisenhower, 1956* (Washington, D.C., 1959), 592.

43. Dwight D. Eisenhower, "Veto of Bill to Amend the Federal Water Pollution Control Act," February 23, 1960, *Public Papers of the Presidents: Dwight D. Eisenhower, 1960* (Washington, D.C., 1961), 1:208.

44. Dwight D. Eisenhower, "Statement by the President upon Signing Bill Amending the Water Facilities Act," August 17, 1954, *Public Papers of the Presidents: Dwight D. Eisenhower, 1954* (Washington, D.C., 1960), 2:725.

45. Dwight D. Eisenhower, *Mandate for Change, 1953–1956* (Garden City, N.Y.: Doubleday, 1963), 86–87.

46. Pach and Richardson, *Presidency of Dwight D. Eisenhower*, 36.

47. Herbert S. Parmet, *Eisenhower and the American Crusades* (New York: Macmillan, 1972), 215.

48. See Parmet, *Eisenhower and the American Crusades*, 215; Branyan and Larsen, *Eisenhower Administration*, 64.

49. Parmet, *Eisenhower and the American Crusades*, 215.

50. Kline, *First Along the River*, 72; William R. Nester, *The War for America's Natural Resources* (New York: St. Martin's Press, 1997), 91.

51. Eisenhower, *Mandate for Change*, 550.

52. Patterson interview, October 17, 2003.

53. Pach and Richardson, *Presidency of Dwight D. Eisenhower,* 182–83.

54. Dwight D. Eisenhower, *Waging Peace: 1956–1961* (Garden City, N.Y.: Doubleday, 1965), 324–25.

55. Branyon and Larsen, *Eisenhower Administration,* 997–1000.

56. Sherman Adams, *Firsthand Report: The Story of the Eisenhower Administration* (New York: Harper and Brothers, 1961), 202.

57. Edward L. Schapsmeier and Frederick H. Schapsmeier, *Ezra Taft Benson and the Politics of Agriculture: The Eisenhower Years,* 1953–1961 (Danville, Ill.: Interstate Printers and Publishers, 1975), 228.

58. Schapsmeier and Schapsmeier, *Ezra Taft Benson,* 228–29. See also Carson, *Silent Spring,* chap. 10 (see intro., n. 3).

59. Harold K. Steen, *The U.S. Forest Service: A History* (Seattle: University of Washington Press, 1976), 270–71.

60. Steen, *U.S. Forest Service,* 275.

61. Adams, *Firsthand Report,* 212–13.

62. See the University of Arkansas, Division of Agriculture, "Agriculture Glossary," http://agglossary.uaex.edu/viewSGlossary1.asp (accessed June 20, 2006).

63. See Department of Natural Resources, State of Wisconsin, "Milestones: 100+ Years of Promoting Clean Water, Healthy Aquatic Ecosystems and Abundant Recreation," http://www.dnr.wi.gov/org/water/division/yow/milestones.pdf (accessed June 19, 2006); Theodore Roosevelt Conservation Partnership, http://www.trcp.org/farmbill_whitepaper.aspx (accessed June 20, 2006).

64. Paul J. Culhane, *Public Lands Politics: Interest Group Influence on the Forest Service and the Bureau of Land Management* (Baltimore: Johns Hopkins University Press, 1981), 52.

65. Smith, *Politics of Conservation,* 289.

66. Michael Frome, *The Forest Service* (New York: Praeger, 1971), 23.

67. Neustadt, *Presidential Power,* 141 (see intro., n. 20).

68. Griffith, *Ike's Letters,* 9.

69. Steinar Andresen, "The Convention for the Conservation of Antarctic Marine Living Resources (CCAMLR): Improving Procedures but Lacking Results," in *Environmental Regime Effectiveness: Confronting Theory with Evidence,* ed. Edward L. Miles, Arild Underdal, Steinar Andresen, Jorgen Wettestad, John Birger Skjaerseth, and Elaine M. Carlin (Cambridge, Mass.: MIT Press, 2002), 406–7.

70. Lynton Keith Caldwell, *International Environmental Policy: From the Twentieth to the Twenty-First Century,* 3rd ed. (Durham, N.C.: Duke University Press, 1996), 196.

71. Long, Cabral, and Vandivort, "Chief Environmental Diplomat," 200 (see chap. 1, n. 63).

72. Lammers and Genovese, *Presidency and Domestic Policy,* 164 (see intro., n. 24).

Chapter 7

1. Gerald R. Ford, "Message to the Congress Transmitting Annual Report of the Council on Environmental Quality," December 12, 1974, *Public Papers of the Presidents of the United States: Gerald R. Ford, 1974* (Washington, D.C.: Office of the Federal Register, National Archives and Records Service, U.S. Government Printing Office, 1975), 740.

2. Gerald R. Ford, "Remarks at Dedication Ceremonies for the National Environmental Research Center, Cincinnati, Ohio," July 3, 1975, *Public Papers of the Presidents of the United States: Gerald R. Ford, 1975* (Washington, D.C., 1977), 910.

3. Ford, "Remarks at Dedication Ceremonies for the National Environmental Research Center, Cincinnati, Ohio," 910.

4. Gerald Ford, "1975 State of the Union Message," in *Ford and the Economy*, ed. Lester A. Sobel (New York: Facts on File, 1976), 73.

5. Lester A. Sobel, ed., *Ford and the Economy* (New York: Facts on File, 1976), 73.

6. Linda Charlton, "Anti-Inflation Group Scraps WIN, a Losing Slogan," *New York Times*, March 9, 1975, 32.

7. Ford, "Remarks at Dedication Ceremonies for the National Environmental Research Center, Cincinnati, Ohio," 910.

8. "1976 Republican Party Platform," Ford Library Museum, http://www .fordlibrarymuseum.gov/library/document /platform/platform.htm (accessed November 15, 2009).

9. "1976 Republican Party Platform," Ford Library Museum.

10. President Gerald Ford, "Proclamation 4356—Earth Day, 1975," March 20, 1975, American Presidency Project, ed. Woolley and Peters, http://www.presidency .ucsb.edu/ws/?pid=23814. (accessed November 18, 2009).

11. Gerald R. Ford, "Statement of the Observance of World Environment Day," June 5, 1975, *Public Papers of the Presidents: Gerald R. Ford, 1975* (Washington, D.C., 1977), 1:779–80.

12. Ford, "Statement of the Observance of World Environment Day," June 5, 1975, 2020.

13. President Gerald Ford, "Proclamation 4435—Earth Week, 1976," April 20, 1976, American Presidency Project, ed. Woolley and Peters, http://www.presidency .ucsb.edu/ws/?pid=816 (accessed November 15, 2009).

14. Deborah Lynn Guber, *The Grassroots of a Green Revolution: Polling America on the Environment* (Cambridge, Mass.: MIT Press, 2003), 60.

15. Jeffrey M. Jones, "Gerald Ford Retrospective: Approval Ratings Low by Historical Standards," Gallup News Service, December 29, 2006, http://www.gallup .com/poll/23995/gerald-ford-retrospective .aspx?version=print (accessed November 15, 2009).

16. Jones, "Gerald Ford Retrospective."

17. Jonathan Martin, "The Moderates' Last Stand: Gerald Ford and the GOP," *National Review Online*, December 28, 2006, http://article.nationalreview.com/ ?q=MjdjYmU3MWQyOWQ5M2I4ZDdh NjliNmM5MGQ3 OGRiMWE (accessed February 27, 2009).

18. Martin, "Moderates' Last Stand."

19. Everett R. Holles, "Haig Denies that He Urged Ford to Pardon Nixon," *New York Times*, September 18, 1974, ProQuest Historical Newspapers: *The New York Times* (1851–2003), 19.

20. Everett R. Holles, "Haig Plea on Nixon Health Linked to Ford's Reversal," *New York Times*, September 17, 1974, ProQuest Historical Newspapers: *The New York Times* (1851–2003), 73; see also David E. Rosenbaum, "Ford Defends Pardon before House Panel and Says There was 'No Deal' with Nixon," *New York Times*, October 18, 1974, ProQuest Historical Newspapers: *The New York Times* (1851–2003), 1.

21. Gerald R. Ford, "Proclamation 4311, Granting Pardon to Richard Nixon," September 8, 1974, *Public Papers of the Presidents: Gerald R. Ford, 1974* (Washington, D.C., 1975), 103–4.

22. Ford, "Remarks at Dedication Ceremonies for the National Environmental Research Center, Cincinnati, Ohio," 910.

23. Gerald R. Ford, "Remarks at Anchorage, Alaska," November 17, 1974, *Public Papers of the Presidents: Gerald R. Ford, 1974* (Washington, D.C., 1975), 615.

24. Gerald R. Ford, "President Gerald R. Ford's Address before a Joint Session of the Congress Reporting on the State of the Union," January 15, 1975, *Public Papers of*

the Presidents: Gerald R. Ford, 1975 (Washington, D.C., 1977), 36.

25. Gerald R. Ford, "Remarks at a Meeting with Coastal State Governors on Outer Continental Shelf Oil and Gas Development," November 13, 1974, *Public Papers of the Presidents: Gerald R. Ford, 1974* (Washington, D.C., 1975), 587.

26. Ford, "Remarks at a Meeting with Coastal State Governors," November 13, 1974, 587.

27. "1976 Republican Party Platform."

28. "1976 Republican Party Platform."

29. Ford, "Message to the Congress Transmitting Annual Report of the Council on Environmental Quality," December 12, 1974, 740.

30. Whitaker, *Striking a Balance*, 198 (see chap. 3, n. 14).

31. Gerald R. Ford, "Message to the Congress Proposing Establishment of New National Wilderness Areas," December 4, 1974, *Public Papers of the Presidents: Gerald R. Ford, 1974* (Washington D.C., 1975), 704.

32. Gerald R. Ford, "Statement on Signing a Bill Designating a National Forest Area in Colorado as the Flat Tops Wilderness," December 13, 1975, *Public Papers of the Presidents: Gerald R. Ford, 1975* (Washington, D.C., 1977), 1968–69.

33. Campaign for America's Wilderness, "People Protecting Wilderness for People," 7, http://www.pewtrusts.org/our_work_report_detail.aspx?id=30695 (accessed November 15, 2009).

34. *Congressional Quarterly Almanac, 1974*, 93rd Cong., 2nd sess., 30:423, 791, 813, 745.

35. Gerald Ford, "Statement on the Energy Reorganization Act of 1974," October 11, 1974, American Presidency Project, ed. Woolley and Peters, http://www.presidency.ucsb.edu/ws/?pid=4452 (accessed September 13, 2004).

36. Almost all of these laws can be found in *Congressional Quarterly Almanac, 1976*, 94th Cong., 2nd sess., 32:101, 107, 102, 143, 177, 192–93. The Solid Waste Utilization Act can be found at Thomas Legislative Information, http://thomas.loc.gov/cgi-bin/bdquery/z?do94:SN02150:L (accessed September 13, 2004). The Federal Land Policy and Management Act of 1976 can be found at Cornell University Law School, http://www.law.cornell.edu/uscode/43/usc_sup_01_43_10_35.html (accessed November 19, 2009).

37. Ford, "Statement on the Energy Reorganization Act of 1974," October 11, 1974.

38. John Robert Greene, *The Presidency of Gerald R. Ford* (Lawrence: University Press of Kansas, 1995), 95.

39. Congressional Quarterly, *Congress and the Nation: A Review of Government and Politics in the Postwar Years*, vol. 4, *1973–1976* (Washington, D.C.: Congressional Quarterly, 1977), 293.

40. "Table 5–4 Number of Committees and Majority Party Chairmanships, 1955–2000," in Harold W. Stanley and Richard G. Niemi, *Vital Statistics on American Politics, 1999–2000* (Washington, D.C.: CQ Press, 2000), 204–5.

41. Jones, "Gerald Ford Retrospective."

42. U.S. House, Office of the Clerk, "Presidential Vetoes (1789 to Present)," House History, http://clerk.house.gov/art_history/house_history/vetoes.html (accessed February 15, 2007).

43. These statistics are calculated from: U.S. House, Office of the Clerk, "Presidential Vetoes (1789 to Present)."

44. Walter A. Rosenbaum, *The Politics of Environmental Concern*, 2nd ed. (New York: Praeger, 1977), 247.

45. The following four vetoes were considered to be pro-environmental in nature:

veto of HR 11873, animal health research legislation, August 15, 1974; veto of HR 11541, National Wildlife Refuge System legislation, October 22, 1974; veto of S. 3537, Willow Creek, Oregon, flood control project legislation, December 18, 1974; and veto of HR 4035, a petroleum price review bill, July 21, 1975. The following seven vetoes were considered anti-environmental: veto of HR 25, a surface mining control and reclamation bill, May 20, 1975; memorandum of disapproval of HR 11929, Tennessee Valley Authority legislation, December 23, 1974; memorandum of disapproval of S. 425, surface mining control and reclamation legislation, December 30, 1974; memorandum of disapproval of S. 3943, a bill to extend funding for rural environmental programs, January 4, 1975; veto of S. 391, the federal coal leasing amendments bill, July 3, 1976; veto of HR 13655, the automotive transport research and development bill, September 24, 1976; and memorandum of disapproval of S. 2081, the agricultural resources conservation bill, October 20, 1976. These eleven vetoes can be found in the following *Public Papers of the Presidents: Gerald R. Ford* volumes: In *Public Papers of the Presidents: Gerald R. Ford, 1974* (Washington, D.C., 1975), HR 11873, animal health research legislation veto, August 15, 1974, 1:15; National Wildlife Refuge System legislation veto, October 22, 1974, 1:447–48; Willow Creek, Oregon, flood control project legislation veto, December 18, 1974, 1:761–62; Tennessee Valley Authority legislation veto, December 23, 1974, 1:774–75; and the memorandum of disapproval of S. 425, surface mining control and reclamation legislation, December 30, 1974, 1:780–81. In *Public Papers of the Presidents: Gerald R. Ford, 1975* (Washington, D.C., 1977), veto of HR 4035, a petroleum price review bill,

July 21, 1975, 2:1007–8. In *Public Papers of the Presidents: Gerald R. Ford, 1975* (Washington, D.C., 1977), veto of HR 25, a surface mining control and reclamation bill, May 20, 1975, 1:693–96; and memorandum of disapproval of S. 3943, a bill to extend funding for rural environmental programs, January 4, 1975, 1:15–16. In *Public Papers of the Presidents: Gerald R. Ford, 1976–1977* (Washington, D.C., 1979), veto of S. 391, the federal coal leasing amendments bill, July 3, 1976, 2:640–41. In *Public Papers of the Presidents: Gerald R. Ford, 1976–1977* (Washington, D.C., 1979), veto of HR 13655, the automotive transport research and development bill, September 24, 1976, 3:2322–23; and memorandum of disapproval of S. 2081, the agricultural resources conservation bill, October 20, 1976, 3:2583.

46. Gerald R. Ford, "Remarks at the White House Conference on Domestic and Economic Affairs in Cincinnati," July 3, 1975, *Public Papers of the Presidents: Gerald R. Ford, 1975* (Washington, D.C., 1977), 910–13.

47. Richard A. Watson, *Presidential Vetoes and Public Policy* (Lawrence: University Press of Kansas, 1993), 32.

48. Mark J. Rozell, *The Press and the Ford Presidency* (Ann Arbor: University of Michigan Press, 1992), 113.

49. *Congress and the Nation*, vol. 4, *1973–1976*, 303.

50. "Presidential Campaign Debate of October 22, 1976," *Public Papers of the Presidents: Gerald R. Ford, 1976–1977* (Washington, D.C., 1979), 2621–49 (accessed November 18, 2009).

51. *Congress and the Nation*, vol. 4, *1973–1976*, 287.

52. *Congress and the Nation*, vol. 4, *1973–1976*, 303.

53. Senate Committee on Interior and Insular Affairs, *Hearing before the Com-*

mittee on Interior and Insular Affairs on the Nomination of Hon. Rogers C. B. Morton to Be Secretary of the Interior, 92nd Cong., 1st sess., January 25–26, 1971, 11.

54. Senator Craig Thomas (R-Wyo.), "Honoring Former Governor Stan Hathaway," Congressional Record, October 7, 2005, http://www.govtrack.us/congress/record .xpd?id=109-s20051007-31 (accessed January 26, 2009).

55. Full text of "Indian Water Rights," Senate, Hearings before the Subcommittee on Administrative Practice and Procedure of the Committee on the Judiciary, 94th Cong., 2nd sess., June 22–23, 1976, http://www .archive.org/stream/indianwaterright-oounit/indianwaterrightoounit_djvu.txt (accessed November 18, 2009).

56. Mark Grossman, Encyclopedia of the United States Cabinet (Santa Barbara, Calif.: ABC-CLIO, 2000), 1:373.

57. Senate Committee on Interior and Insular Affairs, Hearing before the Committee on Interior and Insular Affairs on the Nomination of Russell W. Peterson to Chairman of the Council on Economic Quality, 93rd Cong., 1st sess., October 30, 1973, 87.

58. Marjorie Hunter, "President Asks $46 Billion Cut in Spending Now," New York Times, November 27, 1974, 77.

59. Gerald R. Ford, "Remarks in Los Angeles, California," October 31, 1974, Public Papers of the Presidents: Gerald R. Ford, 1974 (Washington D.C., 1975), 529–36.

60. "Earl Lauer Butz," in Grossman, Encyclopedia of the United States Cabinet, 1:29–30.

61. Gerald R. Ford, "A Proclamation: Earth Day 1975," Office of the White House Press Secretary, March 21, 1975, http://www.wowzone.com/ed75.htm (accessed February 16, 2007).

62. Flippen, Nixon and the Environment, 229 (see chap. 3, n. 22).

63. Department of State, United

States Treaties and Other International Agreements (Washington, D.C.: U.S. Government Printing Office, 1977), vol. 27, pt. 2 (1976): 1087–1361.

64. Department of State, United States Treaties, vol. 27, pt. 4 (1976): 3918–32.

65. Department of State, United States Treaties, vol. 29, pt. 1 (1976–77): 441–91.

66. Department of State, United States Treaties, vol. 25, pt. 3 (1974): 3329–82.

67. Department of State, United States Treaties, vol. 29, pt. 4 (1976–77): 4647–87.

68. Department of State, United States Treaties, vol. 28, pt. 7 (1976–77): 8015–23. These negotiations were later ratified in the United States on September 12, 1977.

69. U.S. Department of State, United States Diplomatic Mission to Warsaw, Poland, "United States and Poland Sign Science and Technology Cooperation Agreement," February 10, 2006, http://poland. usembassy.gov/poland/stca.html (accessed November 18, 2009).

70. Gladwin Hill, "World Is Warned on Resource Use," New York Times, June 6, 1974, 5.

71. Pamela S. Chasek, The Global Environment in the Twenty-first Century: Prospects for International Cooperation (New York: United Nations University Press, 2000), 3.

72. Gladwin Hill, "World Conference Adopts Population Plan of Action," New York Times, August 31, 1974, 47.

73. Ford, "Remarks at Dedication Ceremonies for the National Environmental Research Center, Cincinnati, Ohio," 910.

74. Larry West, "Gerald Ford: President and Park Ranger," About.com, Environmental Issues, http://environment.about.com/ od/activismvolunteering/a/ford_ranger .htm?p=1 (accessed February 21, 2009).

Chapter 8

1. George Herbert Walker Bush will also be referred as "Bush 41," the forty-first

president of the United States, to distinguish him from his son George W. Bush, or "Bush 43," the forty-third president of the United States.

2. John Jolusha, "Bush Pledges Aid for Environment," *New York Times*, September 1, 1988, 9.

3. Robert Bryce, "Cleaning the Air on Father and Son Differences: Bush v. Bush," *Austin Chronicle* 18, no. 39 (May 28, 1999).

4. John G. Greer, "Campaigns, Party Competition, and Political Advertising," in *Politicians and Party Politics*, ed. John G. Greer (Baltimore: Johns Hopkins University Press, 1998), 188.

5. George Bush, "White House Fact Sheet on Environmental Initiatives," September 18, 1989, *Public Papers of the Presidents of the United States: George [H. W.] Bush, 1989* (Washington, D.C.: Office of the Federal Registrar, National Archives and Records Service, U.S. Government Printing Office, 1989), 1212–15.

6. Burt Soloman, "A Gathering of Friends," *National Journal*, June 10, 1989, 1402.

7. Nelson Polsby quoted in Joel D. Aberbach, "The President and the Executive Branch," in *The Bush Presidency: First Appraisals*, ed. Colin Campbell and Bert Rockman (Chatham, N.J.: Chatham House Publishers, 1991), 236.

8. Erwin Hargrove quoted in Aberbach, "President and the Executive Branch," 237.

9. Vig, "Presidential Leadership and the Environment," 107 (see intro., n. 24).

10. Glen Sussman and Mark Andrew Kelso, "Environmental Priorities and the President as Legislative Leader," in *The Environmental Presidency*, ed. Dennis L. Soden (Albany: SUNY Press, 1999), 117.

11. Walter A. Rosenbaum, *Environmental Politics and Policy*, 6th ed. (Washington, D.C.: CQ Press, 2005), 8.

12. Shanley, *Presidential Influence and Environmental Policy*, 131 (see intro., n. 22).

13. Jacqueline Vaughn Switzer, *Environmental Politics: Domestic and Global Dimensions*, 3rd ed. (Boston: Bedford/St. Martin's, 2001), 73.

14. James P. Lester, "Federalism and State Environmental Policy," in *Environmental Politics and Policy*, ed. James P. Lester, 2nd ed. (Durham, N.C.: Duke University Press, 1995), 41–42.

15. George Bush, "Remarks to Members of the National Conference of State Legislators," March 10, 1989, *Public Papers of the Presidents: George [H. W.] Bush, 1989* (Washington, D.C., 1990), 210.

16. George Bush, "Remarks to Members of the National Association of Attorneys General," March 13, 1989, *Public Papers of the Presidents: George [H. W.] Bush, 1989* (Washington, D.C., 1990), 222.

17. Bush, "White House Fact Sheet on Environmental Initiatives," 1215.

18. George Bush, "Annual Message to the Congress on the State of the Union," January 29, 1991, *Public Papers of the Presidents: George [H. W.] Bush, 1991* (Washington, D.C., 1992), 77.

19. "Republican Platform Text," *Congressional Quarterly Almanac 1988*, 100th Cong., 1st sess., 44:63A–64A.

20. Tatalovich and Wattier, "Opinion Leadership," 160 (see chap. 3, n. 61).

21. Sussman, Daynes, and West, *American Politics and the Environment*, 163 (see preface, n. 1).

22. George Bush, "Annual Message to the Congress on the State of the Union," January 31, 1990, *Public Papers of the Presidents: George [H. W.] Bush, 1990* (Washington, D.C., 1990), 132.

23. George Bush, "Remarks at the Swearing-in Ceremony for Manuel Lujan Jr. as Secretary of the Interior," *Public Papers*

of the Presidents: George [H. W.] Bush, 1989 (Washington, D.C., 1990), 67.

24. George Bush, "Address on Administration Goals before a Joint Session of Congress," February 9, 1989, *Public Papers of the Presidents: George [H. W.] Bush, 1989* (Washington, D.C., 1990), 74–81.

25. George Bush, "Remarks on Signing the North American Wetlands Conservation Act," December 13, 1989, *Public Papers of the Presidents: George [H. W.] Bush, 1989* (Washington, D.C., 1990), 1699.

26. Sussman, Daynes, and West, *American Politics and the Environment,* 164.

27. George Bush, "Remarks at the Opening Session of the White House Conference on Science and Economics Research Related to Global Change," April 17, 1990, *Public Papers of the Presidents: George [H. W.] Bush, 1990* (Washington, D.C., 1991), 510–12.

28. George Bush, "The President's New Conference," April 10, 1992, *Public Papers of the Presidents: George [H. W.] Bush, 1992* (Washington, D.C., 1992), 585.

29. George Bush, "Address to the United Nations Conference on Environment and Development in Rio de Janeiro, Brazil," June 12, 1992, *Public Papers of the Presidents: George [H. W.] Bush, 1992* (Washington, D.C., 1993), 925.

30. George Bush, "The President's News Conference in Rio de Janeiro," June 13, 1992, *Public Papers of the Presidents: George [H. W.] Bush, 1992* (Washington, D.C., 1993), 928.

31. George Bush, "Remarks and a Question and Answer Session in Des Moines, Iowa," October 27, 1992, *Public Papers of the Presidents: George [H. W.] Bush,* 1992 (Washington, D.C., 1993), 2009.

32. Daynes and Sussman, *American Presidency and the Social Agenda,* 79 (see intro., n. 5).

33. U.S. Environmental Protection Agency, "Exxon Valdez Oil Spill," Emergency Management Learning Center, Nationally Significant Incidents, http://www.epa.gov/emergencies/content/learning/exxon.htm (accessed November 17, 2009).

34. Zachary Smith, *The Environmental Policy Paradox,* 5th ed. (Upper Saddle River, N.J.: Prentice Hall, 2009), 163.

35. Sheldon Kamieniecki, Matthew A. Cahn, and Eugene R. Goss, "Western Governments and Environmental Policy," in *Politics and Policy in the Contemporary American West,* ed. Clive S. Thomas (Albuquerque: University of New Mexico Press, 1991), 486.

36. Pamela A. Miller, "Exxon Valdez Oil Spill: Ten Years Later," Technical Background Paper, 1999, *Arctic Circle,* University of Connecticut, http://arcticcircle.uconn.edu/SEEJ/Alaska/miller2.htm (accessed February 15, 2007); and Kline, *First Along the River,* 105 (see chap. 4, n. 8).

37. Brian O'Malley and Annie Strickler, "Risk of Oil Spill Disasters Still High, Fifteen Years After Exxon Valdez Tragedy," Sierra Club press release, http://www.sierraclub.org/utilities/printpage.asp?REF=/pressroom/releases/pr2004-03-24.asp (accessed February 15, 2007).

38. Michael E. Kraft, *Environmental Policy and Politics,* 2nd ed. (New York: Longman, 2001), 68.

39. Environmental Protection Agency, Office of Emergency Management, "Oil Pollution Act Overview," http://www.epa.gov/OEM/content/lawsregs/opaover.htm (accessed March 1, 2009).

40. Thomas A. Birkland, *An Introduction to the Policy Process,* 2nd ed. (Armonk, N.Y.: M. E. Sharpe, 2005), 96.

41. See Prince William Sound Regional Citizens' Advisory Council, "Oil Pollution Act of 1990," June 2007, http://www

.pwsrcac.org/docs/d0000200.pdf (accessed March 1, 2009); and Birkland, *Introduction to the Policy Process*, 168.

42. George Bush, "Statement on Signing the Bill Amending the Clean Air Act, November 15, 1990," American Presidency Project, ed. Woolley and Peters, www.presidency.ucsb.edu/ws/index.php?pid=19039 (accessed November 20, 2009).

43. See Glen Sussman and Mark Andrew Kelso, "Environmental Priorities and the President as Legislative Leader," in Soden, *Environmental Presidency*, 119–25.

44. Glen Sussman and Mark Andrew Kelso, "Environmental Priorities and the President as Legislative Leader," 125.

45. Kraft, *Environmental Policy and Politics*, 150.

46. Switzer, *Environmental Politics*, 152.

47. Kraft, *Environmental Policy and Politics*, 152; Switzer, *Environmental Politics*, 143, 152.

48. Jonathan P. West and Glen Sussman, "Implementation of Environmental Policy: The Chief Executive," in Soden, *Environmental Presidency*, 79–82.

49. Norman J. Vig and Michael E. Kraft, ed., *Environmental Policy: New Directions for the Twenty-first Century*, 6th ed. (Washington, D.C.: CQ Press, 2006), 106.

50. Vig and Kraft, *Environmental Policy*, 105.

51. Rosenbaum, *Environmental Politics and Policy*, 311.

52. Daniel A. Farber, "Is the Supreme Court Irrelevant? Reflections on the Judicial Role in Environmental Law," *Minnesota Law Review* 8 (February 1997): 547.

53. Elizabeth A. Palmer, "White House War on Red Tape: Success Hard to Gauge," *Congressional Quarterly Weekly Report* 50, no. 18 (May 2, 1992): 1155.

54. Switzer, *Environmental Politics*, 172.

55. Timothy Noah, "Proposed Legisla-
tion Would Give EPA Broad New Powers," *Wall Street Journal*, February 24, 1993, 3A.

56. Bush, "Remarks on Signing the North American Wetlands Conservation Act," 1699–1700.

57. George Bush, "Paris Economic Summit: Economic Declaration," July 16, 1989, *Public Papers of the Presidents: George H. W. Bush, 1989* (Washington, D.C., 1990), 965.

58. Marvin Soroos, *The Endangered Atmosphere* (Columbia: University of South Carolina Press, 1997), 313–14.

59. Lawrence Susskind, *Environmental Diplomacy* (Oxford: Oxford University Press, 1994), 39–40.

60. Godfrey D. Dabelko, "Clinton, Gore Set for Environmental Push," *Christian Science Monitor*, December 4, 1992, 19; "Four Men and a Planet," *Sierra* Magazine 77 (September–October 1992): 47.

61. Rudy Abramson, Norman Kempster, and James G. Zang, "Bush Will Not Sign Wildlife, Habitat Treaty," *Los Angeles Times*, May 30, 1992, A1; Russell Mittermeier and Peter Seligmann, "U.S. Should Take a Stand on Biodiversity," *Christian Science Monitor*, July 17, 1992, 19.

62. See the Convention on Biological Diversity at http://www.cbd.int/ (accessed November 17, 2009).

63. See Kal Raustiala, "The Domestic Politics of Global Biological Protection in the United Kingdom and the United States," in *The Internationalization of Environmental Protection*, ed. Miranda A. Schreurs and Elizabeth C. Economy (Cambridge: Cambridge University Press, 1997), 49.

64. Raustiala, "Domestic Politics of Global Biological Protection," 50.

65. Glen Sussman, "Like Father, Like Son? Comparing Presidents George H. W. Bush and George W. Bush on Air Quality and Global Climate Change," in *Interna-*

tional Governance and International Security: Issues and Perspectives, ed. Yiannis A. Stivachtis (Athens: Athens Institute for Education and Research, 2004), 299.

66. Rosenbaum, Environmental Politics and Policy, 70.

67. Vig, "Presidential Leadership and the Environment," 85 (see intro., n. 24).

68. Philip Shabecoff, "Shades of Green in the Presidential Campaign," Issues in Science and Technology 4 (Fall 1992): 75.

Chapter 9

1. Warshaw, Domestic Presidency, 118 (see chap. 4, n. 63).

2. Riley E. Dunlap, "Trends in Public Opinion toward Environmental Issues, 1965–1990," in American Environmentalism: The U.S. Environmental Movement, 1970–1990, ed. Riley E. Dunlap and Angela G. Mertig (New York: Taylor and Francis, 1992), 103–5.

3. C. Brant Short, "Conservation Reconsidered: Environmental Politics, Rhetoric, and the Reagan Revolution," in Peterson, Green Talk, 134 (see intro., n. 30).

4. John L. Palmer and Isabel V. Sawhill, "Overview," in The Reagan Record: An Assessment of America's Changing Domestic Priorities, ed. John L. Palmer and Isabel V. Sawhill (Cambridge, Mass.: Ballinger Publishing Company, 1984), 4.

5. George Bush, "Remarks by the President and Prime Minister Brian Mulroney of Canada at the Air Quality Signing Agreement Ceremony in Ottawa," March 13, 1991, Public Papers of the Presidents of the United States: George [H. W.] Bush, 1991 (Washington, D.C.: Office of the Federal Register, National Archives and Records Service, U.S. Government Printing Office, 1992), 254–57.

6. Robert Dallek, Ronald Reagan: The Politics of Symbolism (Cambridge, Mass.: Harvard University Press, 1984), 100.

7. Richard Nathan, Reagan and the States (Princeton, N.J.: Princeton University Press, 1987).

8. James Lester, "New Federalism and Environmental Policy," Publius 16 (1986): 149–65.

9. Samuel P. Hays, Explorations in Environmental History (Pittsburgh: University of Pittsburgh Press, 1998), 170.

10. John G. Francis and Richard Ganzel, "Conclusion: Public Lands, Natural Resources, and the Shaping of American Federalism," in Western Public Lands, ed. John G. Francis and Richard Ganzel (Totowa, N.J.: Rowan and Allanheld, 1984), 29.

11. Christopher McGrory Klyza, Who Controls Public Lands? Mining, Forestry, and Grazing Policies, 1870–1990 (Chapel Hill: University of North Carolina Press, 1996), 95–96.

12. C. Brant Short, Ronald Reagan and the Public Lands: America's Conservation Debate, 1979–1984 (College Station, Tex.: Texas A&M University Press, 1989), 26.

13. Michael E. Kraft, "Environmental and Energy Policy in the Reagan Presidency: Implications for the 1990s," in Energy, the Environment, and Public Policy: Issues for the 1990s, ed. David L. McKee (New York: Praeger, 1991), 22.

14. George Bush, "Remarks of the Vice President at the Annual Republican Senate-House Dinner," April 7, 1981, Public Papers of the Presidents: Ronald Reagan, 1981 (Washington D.C., 1982), 339.

15. Terry L. Anderson and Peter J. Hill, ed., Environmental Federalism (Langham, Md.: Rowman and Littlefield, 1997).

16. Norman Miller, Environmental Politics: Stakeholders, Interests, and Policymaking, 2nd ed. (New York: Routledge, 2009), 134–35.

17. Neil E. Harrison, "Political Responses to Changing Uncertainty in Climate

Science," in *Science and Politics in the International Environment*, ed. Neil E. Harrison and Gary C. Bryner (Langham, Md.: Rowman and Littlefield, 2004), 131.

18. See, for instance, Ronald Reagan, "Your America to Be Free," a commencement address at Eureka College, June 7, 1957, http://reagan2020.us/speeches/Your_America_to_be_Free.asp; "A Time for Choosing," a nationally televised address sponsored by the Goldwater-Miller presidential ticket, October 27, 1964, http://nationalcenter.org/ReaganChoosing1964.html; and "To Restore America," a nationally televised address, March 31, 1976, http://reagan2020.us/speeches/To_Restore_America.asp (all sites accessed November 18, 2009).

19. Ronald Reagan, "First Inaugural Address," January 20, 1981, *Public Papers of the Presidents: Ronald Reagan, 1981* (Washington, D.C., 1982), 1.

20. Short, *Ronald Reagan and the Public Lands*, 43.

21. Short, "Conservation Reconsidered," 145.

22. Sussman, Daynes, and West, *American Politics and the Environment*, 61 (see preface, n. 1).

23. Environmental Defense Fund, "Environmental Poll Compares Attitudes of Baby Boomers and Internet Generation," April 12, 2000, http://edf.org/pressrelease.cfm?ContentID=1274 (accessed November 17, 2009).

24. Ronald Reagan, "Remarks on Signing the Economic Recovery Tax Act of 1981 and the Omnibus Budget Reconciliation Act of 1981, and a Question and Answer Session with Reporters," *Public Papers of the Presidents: Ronald Reagan, 1981* (Washington, D.C., 1982), 711.

25. Ronald Reagan, "Message to the Congress Transmitting the Annual Report of the Council on Environmental Quality,"

Public Papers of the Presidents: Ronald Reagan, 1981 (Washington, D.C., 1982), 953.

26. Reagan, "Remarks at the Swearing-in Ceremony of William D. Ruckelshaus as Administrator of the Environmental Protection Agency," *Public Papers of the Presidents: Ronald Reagan, 1982* (Washington, D.C., 1983), 733–34.

27. Ronald Reagan, "Remarks at Dedication Ceremonies for the New Building of the National Geographic Society," June 19, 1984, *Public Papers of the Presidents: Ronald Reagan, 1984* (Washington, D.C., 1986), 873–75.

28. Ronald Reagan, "Written Responses to Questions Submitted by Maclean's Magazine of Canada," March 6, 1985, *Public Papers of the Presidents: Ronald Reagan, 1985* (Washington, D.C., 1988), 266.

29. Ronald Reagan, "Message to the Congress on America's Agenda for the Future," February 6, 1986, *Public Papers of the Presidents: Ronald Reagan, 1986* (Washington, D.C., 1988), 158.

30. Tatalovich and Wattier, "Opinion Leadership," 158–59 (see chap. 3, n. 61).

31. Reagan, "First Inaugural Address," 1.

32. Norman J. Vig, "Presidential Leadership and the Environment from Reagan and Bush to Clinton," in *Environmental Policy in the 1990s: Toward a New Agenda*, ed. Norman J. Vig and Michael E. Kraft, 2nd ed. (Washington, D.C.: CQ Press, 1994), 76.

33. Gary C. Bryner, *Blue Skies, Green Politics: The Clean Air Act of 1990* (Washington, D.C.: CQ Press, 1993), 83–84.

34. Michael E. Kraft, "Environmental Gridlock: Searching for Consensus in Congress," in Vig and Kraft, *Environmental Policy in the 1990s: Toward a New Agenda*, 105.

35. Walter A. Rosenbaum, *Environmental Policy and Politics*, 6th ed. (Washington, D.C.: CQ Press, 2005), 68.

36. Lou Cannon, *President Reagan: The*

Role of a Lifetime (New York: Simon and Schuster), 529.

37. Nathan, *Administrative Presidency* (see intro., n. 26).

38. Shanley, *Presidential Influence and Environmental Policy*, 23 (see intro., n. 22).

39. Ronald P. Seyb, "Ronald Reagan's Administrative Presidency: Costs, Contradictions, and the Future of Administrative Action," in *Ronald Reagan's America*, vol. 2, ed. Eric J. Schmertz, Natalie Datlof, and Alex Ugrinsky (Westport, Conn.: Greenwood Press, 1997), 519.

40. Vig, "Presidential Leadership and the Environment from Reagan and Bush to Clinton," 77.

41. Mayer, *With the Stroke of a Pen*, 126–30 (see intro., n. 21).

42. Mayer, *With the Stroke of a Pen*, 127.

43. Shirley Anne Warshaw, "The Reagan Administration: White House Control of Domestic Policy," in *The Reagan Presidency: Ten Intimate Perspectives of Ronald Reagan*, ed. Kenneth W. Thompson (Langham, Md.: University Press of America, 1997), 87–89.

44. Warshaw, "Reagan Administration," 89.

45. Landy, Roberts, and Thomas, *Environmental Protection Agency*, 246–51 (see chap. 3, n. 30); Jonathan Lash, Katherine Gillman, and David Sheridan, *A Season of Spoils: The Reagan Administration's Attack on the Environment* (New York: Pantheon Books, 1984), 42.

46. Cannon, *President Reagan*, 531.

47. Friends of the Earth, *Ronald Reagan and the American Environment: An Indictment, Alternate Budget Proposal, and Citizen's Guide to Action* (San Francisco: Friends of the Earth, 1982).

48. Switzer, *Environmental Politics*, 69 (see chap. 8, n. 13).

49. Robert F. Durant, "Hazardous Waste Policy, the Reagan Revolution, and

the 'Democratic Deficit' in America," in Schmertz, Datlof, and Ugrinsky, *Ronald Reagan's America*, 1:179.

50. Lash, Gillman, and Sheridan, *Season of Spoils*, 73–76.

51. Lash, Gillman, and Sheridan, *Season of Spoils*, 76–81.

52. "Transcript of President's News Conference on Foreign and Domestic Matters," *New York Times*, March 12, 1983, 8.

53. Cannon, *President Reagan*, 533–34.

54. Landy, Roberts, and Thomas, *Environmental Protection Agency*, 255–59.

55. Rosenbaum, *Environmental Policy and Politics*, 69.

56. Long, Cabral, and Vandivort, "Chief Environmental Diplomat," 211 (see chap. 1, n. 63).

57. United Nations Environment Programme, *Register of International Treaties and Other Agreements in the Field of the Environment, 1996* (Nairobi: United Nations Environment Programme, 1997).

58. Long, Cabral, and Vandivort, "Chief Environmental Diplomat," 212–13.

59. Daynes and Sussman, *American Presidency and the Social Agenda*, 136 (see intro., n. 5).

60. "Canada Losing Patience with U.S. on Acid Rain," *New York Times*, April 25, 1988, 10A.

61. Short, "Conservation Reconsidered," 137.

62. Vig, "Presidential Leadership and the Environment," 104.

63. Switzer, *Environmental Politics*, 71.

64. Rosenbaum, *Environmental Politics and Policy*, 68 (see chap. 8, n. 11).

65. Kline, *First Along the River*, 101 (see chap. 4, n. 8).

Chapter 10

1. Elizabeth Shogren, "A Natural Split with Bush and Many Quit," *Los Angeles Times*, June 3, 2002 [online].

2. John Heilprin, "EPA Administrator Christie Todd Whitman Resigns," *Washington Post*, May 23, 2003 [online].

3. Shogren, "Natural Split with Bush and Many Quit."

4. Vig, "Presidential Leadership and the Environment," 111 (see intro., n. 24).

5. Benjamin Kline, *First Along the River*, 3rd ed. (Lanham, Md.: Rowman and Littlefield, 2007), 159.

6. William G. Mosely, "Voodoo Environmentalism," *Christian Science Monitor*, February 27, 2002 [online].

7. Mark Engler, "Greenwashing the Truth," TomPaine.com, http://www.tompaine.com/scontent/7502.html (accessed March 31, 2003).

8. Douglas Jehl, "On Rule of Environment, Bush Sees a Balance, Critics a Threat," *New York Times*, February 23, 2003 [online].

9. Andrew Goldstein and Matthew Cooper, "How Green is the White House?" *Time*, April 21, 2002 [online].

10. League of Conservation Voters, "Bush and the Environment: A Citizen's Guide to the First 100 Days," www.lcv.org/images/client/pdfs/100_Day_Report_FINAL01.pdf (accessed November 11, 2009).

11. Sam Hananel, "Environmental Group Grades Bush's Record," *Associated Press*, June 25, 2003, http://forests.org/articles/reader.asp?linkid=23814 (accessed October 22, 2004).

12. National Energy Policy Development Group, "Reliable, Affordable, Environmentally Sound Energy for America's Future," White House, May 2, 2001, http://www.whitehouse.gov/energy/html (accessed November 13, 2002).

13. George W. Bush, "The President's News Conference," May 11, 2001, *Public Papers of the Presidents of the United States: George W. Bush, 2001* (Washington, D.C.: Office of the Federal Register, National Archives and Records Service, U.S. Government Printing Office, 2003), 1:517.

14. Polly Ghazi, "Environmentalists Ready to Battle with Bush," *Guardian Unlimited*, January 23, 2001, http://www.guardian.co.uk/environment/2001/jan/23/usnews.climatechange (accessed November 18, 2009). Ghazi pointed out that the Clinton legacy consisted of the creation of nineteen new national monuments, protecting 5.6 million acres of wilderness from development; the introduction of strict emission standards for polluting diesel vehicles; and the banning of new roads and commercial logging in a third of all government-owned national forests.

15. "Undermining Environmental Law" (editorial), *New York Times*, September 30, 2002, http://www.nytimes.com/2002/09/30/opinion/30MON1.html?pagewan (accessed September 30, 2002).

16. Christopher Marquis, "Bush Administration Rolls Back Clinton Rules for Wetlands," *New York Times*, January 15, 2002, 16A; Marvin Olav Sabo, "Using Patriotism to See Extremism," TomPaine.com, March 23, 2003, http://www.tompaine.com/feature.cfm/ID/7504/view/print (accessed March 28, 2003).

17. Douglas Jehl, "On Rules for Environment, Bush Sees a Balance, Critics a Threat," *New York Times*, February 23, 2003, http://www.nytimes.com/2003/02/23/science/23ENVI.html?pagewanted=print&position=top (accessed February 26, 2003).

18. Barry G. Rabe, "Power to the States: The Power and Pitfalls of Decentralization," in Vig and Kraft, *Environmental Policy: New Directions for the Twenty-First Century*, 6th ed., 48–49.

19. "UVM Analysis of States' Greenhouse Gas Efforts Appears in '*Nature*,'" University of Vermont, http://www.uvm.edu/

news/print/?action=Print&storyID=7032 (accessed December 7, 2005).

20. Eli Sanders, "Rebuffing Bush, 132 Mayors Embrace Kyoto Rules," *New York Times*, May 14, 2005, http://www.nytimes.com/2005/05/14/national/14kyoto.html?ek=5070&en=8e11a5303f34b. (accessed May 18, 2005).

21. 549 U.S. 497 (2007). See also J. R. Pegg, "U.S. EPA Chills Progress towards Regulating Greenhouse Gases," July 11, 2008, Environmental News Service, http://www.ens- newswire.com/ens/ju12008/2008–07–11–10.asp (accessed July 15, 2008).

22. Deborah Zabarenko, "Bush Climate Action Now? 'Bogus': Schwarzenegger," July 14, 2008, Environmental News Network, http://www.enn.com/top_stories/article/37637/print (accessed July 15, 2008).

23. Rick Weiss, "Putting Science on Trial," *Washington Post National Weekly*, August 3–September 5, 2004, 10.

24. Eric Pianin, "Moving Target on Policy Battlefield," *Washington Post*, May 2, 2002, A21.

25. Maggie Fox, "Bush Administration 'Distorts Science' Group Says," Democratic Underground, http://www.democraticunderground.com/discuss/duboard.php?az=view_all&address=102x372462 (accessed November 16, 2009).

26. Greenstein, *Presidential Difference*, 206 (see chap. 4, n. 36).

27. Greenstein, *Presidential Difference*, 207.

28. Margot Higgins, "100 Days of Bush: Disaster Zone for the Environment?" April 30, 2001, http://www.enn.com/news/en . . ries/2001/04/04302001/bushover_43213.asp (accessed June 6, 2001).

29. Poll data provided in Michael A. Dimock, "Bush and Public Opinion," in *Considering the Bush Presidency*, ed. Gary L. Gregg II and Mark J. Rozell (New York: Oxford University Press, 2004), 75.

30. Higgins, "100 Days of Bush: Disaster Zone for the Environment?"

31. George C. Edwards III, "Riding High in the Polls," in *The George W. Bush Presidency*, ed. Colin Campbell and Bert Rockman (Washington, D.C.: Congressional Quarterly Press, 2004), 22.

32. Edwards, "Riding High in the Polls," 22.

33. George W. Bush, "Address of the President to the Joint Session of Congress on Administrative Goals," February 27, 2001, *Public Papers of the Presidents: George W. Bush, 2001* (Washington, D.C., 2003), 1:140.

34. George W. Bush, "President Calls for Conservation and Stewardship on Earth Day," April 22, 2002, White House, Office of the Press Secretary, http://georgewbush-whitehouse.archives.gov/news/releases/2002/04/20020422–1.html (accessed November 10, 2009).

35. Dan Balz and Dana Milbank, "On Earth Day, Bush v. Gore," *Washington Post*, April 22, 2001 [online].

36. George W. Bush, "The President's State of the Union Address," January 29, 2002, White House, Office of the Press Secretary, http://georgewbush-whitehouse.archives.gov/news/releases/2003/01/print/20030128–19.html (accessed November 18, 2009).

37. George W. Bush, "President Delivers 'State of the Union,'" White House, http://www.whitehouse.archives.gov/news/releases/2003/01/print/20030128–19.html (accessed November 18, 2009).

38. Byron W. Daynes and Glen Sussman, "There Ain't a Green Bush Among 'Em: An Examination of George H. W. Bush and George W. Bush as 'Environmental

Presidents'" (paper presented at the annual meeting of the American Political Science Association, Philadelphia, August 28–31, 2003).

39. Glen Sussman and Byron W. Daynes, "President George W. Bush and Environmental Policy: A Midterm Assessment" (paper delivered at the conference on "Assessing the Presidency of George W. Bush at Midpoint: Political, Ethical, and Historical Considerations," University of Southern Mississippi, Gulf Coast Campus, November 22–23, 2002).

40. George W. Bush, "Address before a Joint Session of the Congress on the State of the Union, February 2, 2005," American Presidency Project, ed. Woolley and Peters, at http://www.presidency.ucsb.edu/ws/index.php?pid=58746 (accessed May 9, 2009); George W. Bush, "Address before a Joint Session of the Congress on the State of the Union, January 31, 2006," American Presidency Project, ed. Woolley and Peters, http://www.presidency.ucsb.edu/ws/index.php?pid=65090 (accessed May 9, 2009).

41. George W. Bush, "Address before a Joint Session of the Congress on the State of the Union, January 23, 2007," American Presidency Project, ed. Woolley and Peters, http://www.presidency.ucsb.edu/ws/index.php?pid=24446 (accessed May 9, 2009); George W. Bush, "Address before a Joint Session of the Congress on the State of the Union, January 28, 2008," http://www.presidency.ucsb.edu/ws/index.php?pid=76301 (accessed May 9, 2009).

42. "The Republican Party Platform of 2000," American Presidency Project, ed. Woolley and Peters, www.presidency.ucsb/ws/index.php?pid=25849 (accessed November 16, 2009).

43. Brad Knickerbocker, "Environmental 'Magna Carta' Law Under Fire," Christian Science Monitor, November 7, 2002,

http://www.csmonitor.com/2002/1107/p02s02-usgn.htm (accessed November 12, 2002).

44. Knickerbocker, "Environmental 'Magna Carta' Law Under Fire."

45. Christopher Marquis, "Bush Energy Proposal Seeks to 'Clear Skies' by 2018," New York Times, July 30, 2002, 10A.

46. Douglas Jehl, "On Environmental Rules, Bush Sees a Balance, Critics a Threat," New York Times, February 23, 2003, sec. 1, p. 22.

47. Jehl, "On Environmental Rules, Bush Sees a Balance, Critics a Threat."

48. Carl Pope, "The Mighty Sequoia," Sierra Club pamphlet (2002).

49. Juliet Eilperin, "Since '01, Guarding Species is Harder," Washington Post, March 23, 2008, http://www.washingtonpost.com/wp-dyn/content/story/2008/03/23/ST2008032300179.html (accessed November 12, 2009).

50. "Bush Emphasizes Production in National Energy Blueprint," CNN.com, http://archives.cnn.com/2001/ALLPOLITICS/05/17/bush.speech/index.html (accessed November 12, 2009).

51. "Bush Renews Campaign for Arctic Oil," New York Times, http://www.nytimes.com/apon . . onal/AP-Bush-Energy.html?pagewanted=print (accessed February 24, 2002); David E. Rosenbaum and David E. Sanger, "White House Urges Senate to Allow Drilling in Alaska," New York Times, April 10, 2002, http://www.nytimes.com/2002/04/10/national/10CND-ENER.html?pagewanted=print&position=top (accessed April 12, 2002); "Democrats Against Wildlife Drilling," New York Times, http://www.nytimes.com/aponline/AP-Energy-Bill.html?pagewanted=print&position=top (accessed April 12, 2002).

52. Katharine Q. Seelye, "Bush Favors

Dozens of Sites for Exploration," *New York Times*, April 19, 2002, http://www.nytimes.com/2002/04/19/us/bush-favors-dozens-of-sites-for-exploration.html (accessed November 19, 2009).

53. H. Josef Hebert, "Energy Bill Has $23 Billion in Tax Breaks, Mostly for Energy Companies," http://cw.groupstone.net/Scripts/WebObjects-3dll/CMWebRequest.woa/wa/displayContent (accessed November 18, 2003).

54. Miller, *Environmental Politics*, 33 (see chap. 9, n. 16).

55. Glen Sussman and Byron W. Daynes, "An Early Assessment of President George W. Bush and the Environment" in *George W. Bush: Evaluating the President at Midterm*, ed. Bryan Hilliard, Tom Lansford, and Robert P. Watson (Albany: State University of New York Press, 2004), 58.

56. Dana Milbank and Dan Morgan, "Task Force Made Hasty Overture to Opponents," *Washington Post*, April 11, 2002, 8A.

57. Mark J. Rozell, "Executive Privilege in the Bush Administration: The Conflict Between Secrecy and Accountability," in Gregg and Rozell, *Considering the Bush Presidency*, 130.

58. Andy Sullivan, "U.S. Judge Rejects Mid-Case Appeal on Cheney Papers," http://www.enn.com/extras/printer-friendly.asp?storyid=4907 (accessed November 29, 2002).

59. Adam Clymer, "Judge Says Cheney Needn't Give Data on Energy Policy to G.A.O." *New York Times*, December 10, 2002, http://www.nytimes.com/2002/12/10/Politics/10Chen.html?scp=1&sp=judge%20says%20cheney%20neednt%20give%20data%20on%20energy&st=cse (accessed November 18, 2009).

60. "Payoff for Polluters," *Boston Globe*, November 24, 2002, 10D.

61. Rosenbaum, *Environmental Politics and Policy*, 9 (see chap. 8, n. 11).

62. "EPA Sets New Pollution Standards for Two-Wheelers," December 24, 2003, http://www.nea.gov.vn/THONGTINMT/news/.%5Cnoidung%5Cenn_24_12_03.htm (accessed November 19, 2009).

63. Sussman and Daynes, "Early Assessment of George W. Bush and the Environment," 59.

64. "Bush Environmental Slate is Business-Heavy," *San Diego Union Tribune*, May 12, 2001, 12A.

65. Katharine Q. Seelye, "Bush Is Choosing Industry Leaders to Fill Several Environmental Posts," *New York Times*, May 12, 2001, 10A.

66. Brian J. Gerber and David B. Cohen, "Killing Me Softly: George W. Bush, the Environment and the Administrative Presidency" (paper presented at the annual meeting of the American Political Science Association, Philadelphia, August 28–31, 2003), 10.

67. Amy Goldstein and Sarah Cohen, "The Rules that Apply," *Washington Post National Weekly*, August 23–29, 2004, 6.

68. Karen Hult, "The Bush White House in Comparative Perspective," in *The George W. Bush Presidency: An Early Assessment*, ed. Fred I. Greenstein (Baltimore: Johns Hopkins University Press, 2003), 68–69.

69. John Solomon and Juliet Eilperin, "Bush's EPA Is Pursuing Fewer Polluters," *Washington Post*, September 30, 2007, A1.

70. Michael E. Kraft, *Environmental Policy and Politics*, 3rd ed. (New York: Pearson/Longman, 2004), 127.

71. Chris Baltimore, "Bush Administration Is Said to Be Backing Off Pollution Cases," November 6, 2003, http://list.audubon.org/wa.exe?A2=ind0311&L=audubon-pa&p=786 (accessed November 17, 2009).

72. Linda Greenhouse, "Justices Say EPA Has Power to Act on Harmful Gases," *New*

York Times, April 2, 2007, http://www
.nytimes.com/2007/04/03/washington/
03scotus.html (accessed November 10,
2009).

73. Michael Grunwald, "Warnings on
Drilling Reversed," *Washington Post*, April
7, 2002, http://www.washingtonpost.com/
ac2/wp-dyn/A7474–2002Apr6?language
=printer (accessed November 10, 2009).

74. Joby Warrick and Juliet Elperin, "Big
Energy in the Wild West," *Washington Post
National Weekly*, October 4–10, 2004, 6.

75. Joby Warrick, "Flattening Appala-
chia's Mountains," *Washington Post National
Weekly*, September 6–12, 2004, 11.

76. Erik Stetson, "Former Republican
EPA Head Criticizes Bush," July 19, 2004
, Democratic Underground, www.demo-
craticunderground.com/discuss/duboard
.php?az=view.all&address=102x696001
(accessed November 18, 2009).

77. Ross Gelbspan, "Beyond Kyoto Lite,"
American Prospect, February 25, 2002, 26.

78. Alister Doyle, "Greenhouse Gas
Jump Spurs Global Warming Fears," http://
www.enn.com/top_stories/article/157 (accessed November 10, 2009).

79. Eric Pianin, "A Second Opinion on
Global Warming," *Washington Post National
Weekly*, June 11–17, 2001, 31.

80. Juliet Eilperin, "Censorship is
Alleged at NOAA," at http://www
.washingtonpost.com/wp-dyn/content/ar-
ticle/2006/02/10/AR2006021001766.html
(accessed November 10, 2009); Peter Spotts,
"EPA Staffers Go to the Hill over Global
Warming," http://www.csmonitor
.com/2006/1201/p02s01-uspo.html (accessed November 18, 2009).

81. Peter Spotts, "Has the White House
Interfered on Global Warming Reports?"
Christian Science Monitor, January 31, 2007,
http://www.csmonitor.com/2007/0131/
p01s04-uspo.htm (accessed February 2,
2007).

82. Margaret Kriz, "Pre-Emptive Exemptions," *National Journal*, April 26, 2003,
www.nationaljournal.com/about/
njweekly/stories/pdfs/nj042603Kriz.pdf
(accessed November 19, 2009); John Heilprin, "Bush Administration Wants Military
Exemptions to Environmental Laws,"
http://www.cpeo.org/lists/military/2003/
msg00320.html (accessed November 18,
2009).

83. Eric Pianin, "War Effort Pushes
'Green' Issues Aside; Environmental
Groups Rethink Agenda as Nation Focuses
on Anti-Terror Fight," *Washington Post*,
October 21, 2001, ProQuest [online].

84. Marc Kaufman, "Navy Cleared
to Use a Sonar Despite Fears of Injuring
Whales," *Washington Post*, July 16, 2002, 3A.

85. Kaufman, "Navy Cleared to Use a
Sonar."

86. Kenneth R. Weiss, "The State; Judge
Bars Use of Experimental Sonar in Track-
ing Gray Whales; Ruling Ends Test Plans,
Faulting Scientists for Lack of a Full Study
of Effects on the Marine Mammals that
'Finder' Was Designed to Help," *Los Angeles
Times*, January 25, 2003, B8.

87. David E. Sanger and Christopher
Marquis, "U.S. Said to Plan Halt to Exer-
cises on Vieques Island," *New York Times*,
June 14, 2001, ProQuest [online].

88. George W. Bush, "Remarks Announcing Support for the Stockholm
Convention on Persistent Organic Pollutants," April 19, 2001, American Presidency
Project, ed. Woolley and Peters, http://
www.presidency.ucsb.edu/ws/index
.php?pid=45626 (accessed November 19,
2009).

89. Eric Pianin, "White Move on Toxic-
Chemicals Pact Assailed," *Washington Post*,
April 12, 2002, 13A.

90. See Andrew Revkin, "Bush Plans
Vast Protected Sea Area in Hawaii,"
June 15, 2006, http://www.nytimes

.com/2006/06/15/science/earth/15hawaii
.html?ei=5070&en=207e4dacf (accessed
June 15, 2006); Mercury News, "Bush Protects Unique Area across the Pacific," January 7, 2009, Environmental News Network,
http://www.enn.com/ecosystems/article/
39026/print (accessed January 7, 2009).

91. Daynes and Sussman, "There Ain't a
Green Bush Among 'Em."

92. David Morgan, "Bush Hails His
Environmental Record on Earth Day,"
http://cw.groupstone.net/Scripts/Web-
Objects-3.dll/CMWebRequest.woa/wa/
displayContent? (accessed April 25, 2004).

93. Peter N. Spotts, "Has the White
House Interfered on Global Warming Reports?" January 31, 2007, Christian Science
Monitor, http://www.csmonitor
.com/2007/0131/p01s04-uspo.html (accessed November 9, 2007).

94. Walter Cronkite, "Make Global
Warming an Issue," Philadelphia Inquirer,
March 15, 2004, http://www.truthout.
org/article/walter-cronkite-make-global-
warming-issue (accessed November 9,
2004).

95. Mike Peacock, "Blair to Press on
Climate Change, Challenge Bush," Septem-
ber 14, 2004, http://cw.groupstone
.net/Scripts/WebObjects-3.dll/CMWeb-
Request.woa/wa/displayContent (accessed
September 15, 2004).

96. Byron W. Daynes and Glen Sussman, "President George W. Bush: 'Pale
Green' Responses to the Environment?"
American Review of Politics 29 (Winter
2008–9): 382.

97. Daynes and Sussman, "President
George W. Bush: 'Pale Green' Responses to
the Environment?" 382.

Conclusion
The epigraph quote is taken from
James Gustave Speth, Red Sky at Morning:
America and the Crisis of the Global Environ-

ment (New Haven, Conn.: Yale University
Press, 2005), 77.

1. Glen Sussman and Mark Kelso, "Environmental Priorities and the President as
Legislative Leader," in Soden, Environmental Presidency, 135.

2. A. L. Riesch Owen, "Conservation
under Franklin D. Roosevelt," 183 (see
chap. 1, n. 1).

3. Kennedy, "Letter to the President of
the Senate," March 29, 1961, 240 (see
chap. 2, n. 15).

4. Lyndon B. Johnson, "Report on
Natural Beauty in America," October 2,
1965, Public Papers of the Presidents,:
Lyndon B. Johnson, 1965 (Washington, D.C.,
1966), 1036.

5. Stanley I. Kutler, The Wars of Watergate: The Last Crisis of Richard Nixon (New
York: Alfred A. Knopf, 1990), 78.

6. Richard Nixon, "Annual Message to
the Congress on the State of the Union,"
January 22, 1970, Public Papers of the Presidents,: Richard Nixon, 1970 (Washington,
D.C., 1971), 1:13.

7. Kernell, Going Public, 1 (see chap. 6,
n. 31).

8. Hunter and Noonan, "Energy, Environment, and the Presidential Agenda,"
317 (see intro., n. 14).

9. Hunter and Noonan, "Energy, Environment, and the Presidential Agenda,"
313–14.

10. Riesch Owen, "Collaborators in the
Conservation Movement," in Conservation
under FDR, 54 (see chap. 1, n. 3).

11. Franklin D. Roosevelt, "A Suggestion for Legislation to Create the Tennessee Valley Authority," April 10, 1933, The
Public Papers and Addresses of Franklin D.
Roosevelt: The Year of Crisis, comp. Samuel I.
Rosenman (New York: Random House,
1938), 2:129.

12. Riesch Owen, Conservation under
FDR, 105–6.

13. Kennedy, "Special Message to the Congress," March 1, 1962, 177 (see chap. 2, n. 7).

14. Kennedy, "State of the Union Message," January 14, 1963, 1:14 (see chap. 2, n. 23).

15. Lyndon B. Johnson, "Remarks upon Signing the Air Quality Act of 1967," November 21, 1967, *Public Papers of the Presidents: Lyndon B. Johnson, 1967* (Washington, D.C., 1969), 992.

16. Glen Sussman and Mark Kelso, "Environmental Priorities and the President as Legislative Leader," in Soden, *Environmental Presidency*, 135.

17. Jimmy Carter, "The State of the Union: Annual Message to the Congress," January 19, 1978, *Public Papers of the Presidents: Jimmy Carter, 1978* (Washington, D.C., 1979), 1:91.

18. "Grading Clinton," *Defenders*, Winter 1993–94, 33–36; Dowie, "Friends of Earth—or Bill?" (see chap. 5, n. 8).

19. Shanley, *Presidential Influence and Environmental Policy*, 15–16 (see intro., n. 22).

20. Harry Truman, "Annual Budget Message to the Congress: Fiscal Year 1954," January 9, 1953, *Public Papers of the Presidents,: Harry S. Truman, 1953* (Washington, D.C., 1966), 1:1143, 1145–50.

21. Johnson, "President's News Conference," February 26, 1966, 218 (see chap. 2, n. 79).

22. Landy, Roberts, and Thomas, *Environmental Protection Agency*, 33 (see chap. 3, n. 30).

23. Landy, Roberts, and Thomas, *Environmental Protection Agency*, 41.

24. Dowie, "Friends of Earth—or Bill?" 514.

25. Daynes, "Two Democrats, One Environment," 116 (see intro., n. 38).

26. Riesch Owen, *Conservation under FDR*, 18–19.

27. Daynes, "Two Democrats, One Environment," 117.

28. Franklin D. Roosevelt, "Proposal Conservation Conference," no. 1172, April 17, 1945, in E. B. Nixon, *Franklin D. Roosevelt and Conservation, 1911–1945*, 2:646–47 (see chap. 1, n. 29).

29. Long, Cabral, and Vandivort, "Chief Environmental Diplomat," 196 (see chap. 1, n. 63).

30. Northwest Atlantic Fisheries Organization (NAFO), http://www.nafo.int/about/frames/about.html (accessed November 9, 2009); Blair, "Truman Predicts World of Plenty" (see chap. 1, n. 66); George Barret, "Truman Again Bid to U.N. Dedication," *New York Times*, June 11, 1949, 5.

31. Truman, "Special Message to the Congress," January 19, 1953, 1:1208 (see chap. 1, n. 42).

32. Kennedy, "Address before the 18th General Assembly," September 20, 1963, 2:696 (see chap. 2, n. 45).

33. Soden and Steel, "Evaluating the Environmental Presidency," 328 (see chap. 2, n. 48).

34. John F. Kennedy, "Address by the President of the United States John F. Kennedy at the Dedication of Ceremonies of the New Facilities of the School of Aerospace Medicine of the Aerospace Medical Division," November 21, 1963, *Public Papers of the Presidents: John F. Kennedy, 1963* (Washington, D.C., 1964), 882.

35. Johnson, "Statement by the President Announcing the Reaching of an Agreement," December 8, 1966, 2:1441 (see chap. 2, n. 84).

36. Carter, "Global 2000 Study," July 24, 1980, 1415 (see chap. 4, n. 66).

37. James Brooke, "U.S. and 33 Hemispheric Nations Agree to Create Free-Trade Zone," *New York Times*, December 11, 1994, 1, 4.

38. Ford, "Remarks at Anchorage, Alaska," November 17, 1974 (see chap. 7, n. 23).

39. John G. Geer, "Campaigns, Party Competition, and Political Advertising," in *Politicians and Party Politics*, ed. John G. Geer (Baltimore: Johns Hopkins University Press, 1998), 188.

40. Eisenhower quoted in James L. Sundquist, *Politics and Policy: The Eisenhower, Kennedy, and Johnson Years* (Washington, D.C.: Brookings Institution Press, 1968), 323.

41. Sundquist, *Politics and Policy*, 331.

42. Ford, "Message to the Congress Proposing Establishment of New National Wilderness Areas," December 4, 1974, 704 (see chap. 7, n. 31).

43. Ford, "Message to the Congress Transmitting Annual Report," December 12, 1974, 740 (see chap. 7, n. 1).

44. See Kline, *First Along the River*, 72 (see chap. 10, no. 5); Nester, *War for America's Natural Resources*, 91 (see chap. 6, n. 50).

45. Senate Committee, *Hearing ... on the Nomination of Hon. Rogers C. B. Morton*, 11 (see chap. 3, n. 76).

46. Senate Committee, *Hearing ... on the Nomination of Russell W. Peterson*, 87 (see chap. 3, n. 79).

47. Marjorie Hunter, "President Asks $46 Billion Cut in Spending Now," *Special to the New York Times*, November 27, 1974, 77.

48. Elizabeth A. Palmer, "White House War on Red Tape: Success Hard to Gauge," *Congressional Quarterly Weekly Report* 50, no. 18 (May 2, 1992): 1155.

49. John H. Cushman Jr. "Quayle, in Last Push for Landowners, Seeks to Relax Wetland Protections," *New York Times*, November 12, 1992, A8.

50. Department of State, *United States Treaties and Other International Agreements* (Washington, D.C.: U.S. Government Printing Office, 1977), vol. 27, pt. 4 (1976): 3918–32.

51. Department of State, *United States Treaties*, vol. 29, pt. 1 (1976–77): 441–491; and vol. 29, pt. 4 (1976–77): 4647–87.

52. Daynes and Sussman, "George W. Bush: 'Pale Green' Responses" (see chap. 10, n. 96).

53. Daynes and Sussman, "President George W. Bush: 'Pale Green' Responses," 380–81.

54. Vig, "Presidential Leadership and the Environment from Reagan and Bush to Clinton," 76 (see chap. 9, n. 32).

55. Michael E. Kraft and Norman J. Vig, "Environmental Policy from the 1970s to 2000: An Overview," in Vig and Kraft, *Environmental Policy: New Directions for the Twenty-first Century*, 14 (see chap. 5, no. 61).

56. Kraft and Vig, "Environmental Policy from the 1970s to 2000," 14.

57. Friends of the Earth, *Ronald Reagan and the American Environment* (see chap. 9, n. 47).

58. George C. Eads and Michael Fix, *Relief or Reform? Reagan's Regulatory Dilemma* (Washington, D.C.: Urban Institute Press, 1984), 17.

59. Chester A. Newland, "The Reagan Presidency: Limited Government and Political Administration," *Public Administration Review* 43 (January–February 1983): 1–21; Michael E. Kraft and Norman J. Vig, "Environmental Presidency in the Reagan Presidency," *Political Science Quarterly* 99 (Fall 1984): 414–39.

60. James Gustave Speth, "Perspectives on he Johannesburg Summit," *Environment* 45 (January–February 2003): 24.

61. James Glanz, "At the Center of the Storm Over Bush and Science," March 30,

2004, NYTimes.com, http://www.nytimes
.com/2004/03/30/science/30ADVI.html?
pagewanted=print (accessed April 3, 2009).

62. Robert Roy Britt, "Scientists Say
Bush Stifles Science and Lets Global Leadership Slip," January 30, 2008, http://www.
livescience.com/technology/080130-bush-
legacy.html (accessed April 3, 2009).

63. Quoted in Britt, "Scientists Say Bush
Stifles Science and Lets Global Leadership
Slip."

64. See U.S. State Department, "Environmental Diplomacy: The Environment
and U.S. Foreign Policy," http://www.state
.gov/www/global/oes/earth.html (accessed
June 10, 1999).

65. Switzer, *Environmental Politics*, 66
(see chap. 8, n. 13).

66. Lammers and Genovese, *Presidency
and Domestic Policy*, 356 (see intro., n. 24).

67. Roger Schlickeisen quoted in
"Obama Victory Signals Rebirth of U.S.
Environmental Policy" at http://www.enn
.com/pollution/article/38581 (accessed
November 9, 2009).

68. See "President Obama Announces
Launch of the Major Economies Forum on
Energy and Climate," http://www.white-
house.gov/the_press_office/President-
Obama-Announces-Launch-of-the-Major-
Economies-Forum-On-Energy-and-Climate
(accessed November 20, 2009); "Obama
Signs Wilderness Protection Bill," http://
www.cbsnews.com/stories/2009/03/30/
tech/main4904524.shtml (accessed No-
vember 9, 2009); Jesse Lee, "Protecting That
Which Fuels Our Spirit," March 30, 2009,
http://www.whitehouse.gov/blog/09/03/30/
Protecting-That-Which-Fuels-Our-Spirit/
(accessed May 17, 2009); "Executive
Order: Chesapeake Bay Protection and
Restoration," http://www.whitehouse
.gov/the_press_office/Executive-Order-
Chesapeake-Bay-Protection-and-Restora-

tion/ (accessed November 20, 2009); Bryan
Walsh, "Obama to Tighten Fuel-Economy
Standards," May 19, 2009, Environmental
News Network, http://www.enn.com/
pollution/article/39931/print (accessed
May 19, 2009).

69. Paula Newton, "Obama: Leaders
Will Work Together on Climate," CNN,
http://www.cnn.com/2009/WORLD/
europe/07/09/g8.summit/index.html (accessed November 6, 2009).

70. See White House, "Press Background Briefing on White House Announcement on Auto Emissions and Efficiency Standards by Senior Administration
Official," May 18, 2009, http://www
.whitehouse.gov/the_press_office/Back-
ground-Briefing-on-Auto-Emissions-and-
Efficiency-Standards (accessed November
20, 2009); White House, "President Obama
Announces National Fuel Efficiency Policy," May 19, 2009, http://www.whitehouse
.gov/the_press_office/President-Obama-
Announces-National-Fuel-Efficiency-Policy
(accessed November 20, 2009).

71. See Scott Horsley and Robert Siegel,
"In Canada, Obama Pledges Stronger Ties,"
February 19, 2009, National Public Radio,
http://www.npr.org/templates/story/story
.php?storyId=100885544&ft=1&f=100
3 (accessed May 17, 2009); "U.S.-Mexico
Announce Bilateral Framework On Clean
Energy and Climate Change," http://www
.whitehouse.gov/the_press_office/US-
Mexico-Announce-Bilateral-Framework-
on-Clean-Energy-and-Climate-Change
(accessed November 20, 2009); Michele
Kelemen, "Secretary Clinton: 'We Want
China To Grow,'" February 21, 2009,
National Public Radio, http://www.npr
.org/templates/story/story.php?storyId=
100969586 (accessed May 17, 2009).

72. Juliet Eilperin, "Salazar's Wolf Decision Upsets Administration Allies," *The*

Washington Post, March 14, 2009, www .washingtonpost.com/wp-dyn/content/ article/2009/03/13/AR2009031303211 _pf.html (accessed December 7, 2009); Brent Lang, "Salazar Approves Removing Gray Wolves from Endangered Species List," *CBS News*, March 6, 2009, www.

cbsnews.com/blogs/2009/03/06/politics/ politicalhotsheet/entry4849589.shtml (accessed December 7, 2009); "Bush-Era Ruling on Gray Wolves is Upheld," *MSNBC*, March 6, 2009, www.msnbc.msn.com/ id/29550694/print/1/displaymode/1098/ (accessed December 7, 2009).

Other Books in the Joseph V. Hughes Jr. and Holly O. Hughes Series
on the Presidency and Leadership